ADMINISTRATIVE JUSTICE

AND THE

SUPREMACY OF LAW

IN THE UNITED STATES

BY

JOHN DICKINSON

THE LAWBOOK EXCHANGE, LTD.
Clark, New Jersey

ISBN 978-1-58477-273-6

Lawbook Exchange edition 2003, 2018

THE LAWBOOK EXCHANGE, LTD.
33 Terminal Avenue
Clark, New Jersey 07066-1321

Please see our website for a selection of our other publications and fine facsimile reprints of classic works of legal history:
www.lawbookexchange.com

Library of Congress Cataloging-in-Publication Data

Dickinson, John, 1894-1952.
Admimstrative justice and the supremacy of law in the United States / by John Dickinson.
p. cm.
Originally published: Cambridge: Harvard University Press, 1927, in series: Harvard studies in administrative law; v. 2.
Includes bibliographical references and index.
ISBN 1-58477-273-5 (cloth: alk. paper)
1. Judicial review of administrative acts—United States. 2. Administrative procedure—United States. 3. Rule of law—United States. I. Title.

KF4575 .D5 2002
342.73'066—dc21 2002025947

Printed in the United States of America on acid-free paper

ADMINISTRATIVE JUSTICE
AND THE
SUPREMACY OF LAW
IN THE UNITED STATES

BY

JOHN DICKINSON

CAMBRIDGE
HARVARD UNIVERSITY PRESS
1927

PRINTED AT THE HARVARD UNIVERSITY PRESS
CAMBRIDGE, MASS., U. S. A.

TO

ROSCOE POUND

AND

FELIX FRANKFURTER

PATHFINDERS OF THE LAW

PREFACE

At recurrent intervals during the last twenty years the attention of lawyers has been directed to the relation between administrative tribunals and the courts by some noteworthy extension of administrative jurisdiction such as was effected, for example, by the Hepburn amendments to the Interstate Commerce Act in 1906, and by the establishment of the Federal Trade Commission in 1914. The controversies centering about these measures produced a plentiful harvest of addresses and articles; and many excellent monographic studies of particular administrative tribunals, especially those functioning under the Federal government, have appeared. So far, however, there has been singularly little effort to study the development as a whole, or to examine from any central point of view the boundary between the province of administrative adjudication and the courts.

Indeed, the time is somewhat more than ripe for a comprehensive treatise on judicial review of administrative determinations, distributed systematically under the different fields of administrative action and the different forms of procedure available for review. Such a treatise would be of direct aid to the practising lawyer in a department of law not yet worn smooth by precedent, and where opportunity is still left to urge general principles on the attention of the courts; and it would at the same time be of deep interest to students of legal science as showing development in actual process at one of the growing points of the law.

It seems unnecessary to say that this essay makes no pretension to fill the place of such a treatise; it will perform its task if it emphasizes the need for one. No effort has been made to attain mechanical completeness in the cases cited, or to arrange them into such an index of all the possible situations as a reference book is properly expected to furnish. I have tried, however, to include and discuss all the fundamental cases, and the treatment is comprehensive in the sense that the problem of review is dealt with as a whole, rather than in connection with some particular field of administrative action. Most of the difficult points in the law of judicial review center about the question of how far the review shall extend. These difficulties can be properly considered only in the light of an examination of the reasons underlying the practice of review, and of the purposes which it is expected to serve. To such an examination the greater part of this book is devoted. It is addressed to the queries of the student of principles, rather than to the eleventh-hour needs of the brief-maker.

The discussion will be found to focus ultimately upon the distinction which the courts draw between "questions of law" and "questions of fact." Here is the crux of the most difficult issues. It is a meridian line which cuts a boundary far beyond the immediate vicinage of this study; and the attempt to follow it to the point where it will yield up its meaning has resulted in some rather far-flung notes on other topics of the law, and on the underlying technique of legal reasoning. There is always a danger that cross-fertilization between widely separated branches of the law may produce a barren hybrid; but in a new field it seems an almost unavoidable maxim of profitable tillage. I have accordingly been guided by the conviction that if the law has its compartments, they are separated by lines of convenience and not by water-tight bulkheads. Also I have not hesitated to draw freely from sources of a non-legal character, such as works on economics, philosophy, and general history, wherever these have seemed to me to offer helpful light on a legal problem. It has been well said that "the growth of the law is from without"; and he who seeks to understand the present no less than the past of the law must search not only the law, but much else besides.

A word may be desirable as to the relegation of so much of the material to footnotes. This has been due primarily to a desire not to interrupt the continuity of the text, while at the same time elaborating with a decent measure of thoroughness conclusions which are admittedly controversial. I long debated whether to group some of these notes, closely related in subject-matter, into appendices, but in the end concluded that they would serve their most useful purpose if retained in direct local connection with the portion of the text which they were introduced to support. The whole matter of the arrangement of the book has presented difficulties growing out of the fact that it has been put together at intervals during a period of several years, and for the most part in odd moments borrowed from active practice.

My obligations are so many that I cannot hope to enumerate them specifically. I am, however, very greatly in debt to Dean Pound and Professor Frankfurter, whose teaching is no doubt mainly answerable for whatever of value this study may contain. I also owe much to the suggestive writings of Professor Thomas Reed Powell and Professor Ernst Freund, and to the fundamental work of President Goodnow of Johns Hopkins University. I am under special obligations to my friend Professor Edward S. Corwin of Princeton University, who kindly read a part of the proofs and offered a number of telling suggestions, and to the instruction of others of my former teachers, particularly Professor Westel W. Willoughby of Johns Hopkins University, Professor William F. Willoughby, now Director of the Institute for Government Research, and Professors Eugene Wambaugh and Joseph Warren, of the Harvard Law School; and I owe a debt of gratitude to my friends, Professor Lindsay Rogers of Columbia University and Mr. David R. Hawkins of the New York Bar, for their patience in submitting to hear and criticize many of the ideas here put forward while they were in process of taking form. I wish also to thank Professor Henry A. Yeomans, of Harvard University, for placing at my disposal material which has saved me valuable time and many steps. If I have avoided, as I have tried to do, the sin of treating law too abstractly, it is largely due to the example of the experienced lawyers under whom I have had the privilege of serving an apprenticeship — the late John C. Hammond, of Northampton, Massachusetts, formerly President of the Massachusetts

Bar Association, George S. Franklin, Esq., of New York, and Hon. William Gibbs McAdoo; and to the counsel and advice, always freely given, of my uncle, Hon. John A. Aiken, of Greenfield, formerly Chief Justice of the Superior Court of Massachusetts.

JOHN DICKINSON

BRIER HILL, ASHFIELD, MASSACHUSETTS
September, 1926

CONTENTS

ADMINISTRATIVE JUSTICE AND THE SUPREMACY OF LAW IN THE UNITED STATES

"*Government, to define it* de jure, *or according to ancient prudence, is an art whereby a civil society of men is instituted and preserved upon the foundation of common right or interest; or, to follow Aristotle and Livy, it is the empire of laws and not of men.*"

JAMES HARRINGTON, *Oceana*, in *Works*, ed. 1737, p. 37.

"δεῖ γὰρ τὸν μὲν νόμον ἄρχειν πάντων" (*The law ought to be supreme over all*).

ARISTOTLE, *Politics*, IV (VI), iv, 31.

" ἀλλὰ μὴν κἀκεῖνον δεῖ ὑπάρχειν τὸν λόγον τὸν καθόλου τοῖς ἄρχουσιν. κρεῖττον δὲ ᾧ μὴ πρόεστι τὸ παθητικὸν ὅλως ἢ ᾧ συμφυές. τῷ μὲν οὖν νόμῳ τοῦτο οὐχ ὑπάρχει, ψυχὴν δ' ἀνθρωπίνην ἀνάγκη τοῦτ' ἔχειν πᾶσαν" (*Truly rulers ought to be governed by principles of rational generality; and he is a better ruler who is free from passion than he who is governed by his impulses. Whereas the law is passionless, passion is destined always to rule the heart of man*).

ARISTOTLE, *Politics*, III, xv, 5.

" ὅσα γε μὴ δοκεῖ δύνασθαι διορίζειν ὁ νόμος . . . ὁ νόμος ἐφίστησι τὰ λοιπὰ τῇ δικαιοτάτῃ γνώμῃ κρίνειν καὶ διοικεῖν τοὺς ἄρχοντας . . ὁ μὲν οὖν τὸν νόμον κελεύων ἄρχειν δοκεῖ κελεύειν ἄρχειν τὸν θεὸν καὶ τὸν νοῦν μόνους, ὁ δ' ἄνθρωπον κελεύων προστίθησι καὶ θηρίον. ἥ τε γὰρ ἐπιθυμία τοιοῦτον, καὶ ὁ θυμὸς ἄρχοντας καὶ τοὺς ἀρίστους ἄνδρας διαφθείρει. διόπερ ἄνευ ὀρέξεως νοῦς ὁ νόμος ἐστίν" (*As to cases which the law seems unable to determine . . . the law appoints officers and leaves such matters to them to determine to the best of their judgment. . . . He who bids the law rule, bids God and reason rule, but he who bids man rule adds an element of the beast; for desire is a beast, and passion perverts rulers, even though they be the best of men. Therefore the law is reason free from desire*).

ARISTOTLE, *Politics*, III, xvi, 4, 5.

" δεῖ τοὺς νόμους εἶναι κυρίους . . . τὸν ἄρχοντα δέ, ἄν τε εἷς ἄν τε πλείους ὦσι, περὶ τούτων εἶναι κυρίους περὶ ὅσων ἐξαδυνατοῦσιν οἱ νόμοι λέγειν ἀκριβῶς διὰ τὸ μὴ ῥᾴδιον εἶναι καθόλου διορίσαι περὶ πάντων" (*The laws should be the rulers, and the mag-*

istrate or magistrates, whether there be one or more, should be supreme only over those matters concerning which it is impossible for the laws to speak with precision because of the difficulty of a general principle embracing all particulars).

ARISTOTLE, *Politics*, III, xi, 19.

"ὁ μὲν νόμος καθόλου πᾶς, περὶ ἐνίων δ' οὐχ οἷόν τε ὀρθῶς εἰπεῖν καθόλου . . . τοῦτο γὰρ αἴτιον καὶ τοῦ μὴ πάντα κατὰ νόμον εἶναι, ὅτι περὶ ἐνίων ἀδύνατον θέσθαι νόμον ὥστε ψηφίσματος δεῖ. τοῦ γὰρ ἀορίστου ἀόριστος καὶ ὁ κανών ἐστιν" (*Law is in all cases universal, but in some cases it is not possible to speak universally with correctness . . . This is the reason why not all things are according to law, because on some subjects it is impossible to make a law and there must be a special determination from case to case; for the rule of what is indeterminate must itself be indeterminate also*).

ARISTOTLE, *Nicomachean Ethics*, V, x, 4, 6.

"αἱ γὰρ ἀνομαιότητες τῶν τε ἀνθρώπων καὶ τῶν πράξεων καὶ τὸ μηδέποτε μηδέν, ὡς ἔπος εἰπεῖν, ἡσυχίαν ἄγειν τῶν ἀνθρωπίνων οὐδὲν ἐῶσιν ἁπλοῦν ἐν οὐδενὶ περὶ ἁπάντων καὶ ἐπὶ πάντα τὸν χρόνον ἀποφαίνεσθαι τέχνην οὐδ' ἡντινοῦν" (*The differences of men and their actions, and the fact that in human affairs nothing ever stands still, do not permit a general and universal rule in anything. No art can lay down a rule which will last forever*).

PLATO, *Statesman*, 294 B.

CHAPTER I

REGULATION BY GOVERNMENT VERSUS REGULATION BY LAW

THE multiplication in recent years of bodies like public-service commissions and industrial-accident boards, accompanied by the vesting of ampler powers in health officers, building inspectors, and the like, has raised anew for our law, after three centuries, the problem of executive justice. That government officials should assume the traditional function of courts of law, and be permitted to determine the rights of individuals, is a development so out of line with the supposed path of our legal growth as to challenge renewed attention to certain underlying principles of our jurisprudence.[1] What is the meaning and occasion of the current development? What is its bearing on the doctrine of the "supremacy of law" which has so long been regarded as central to our legal tradition? What can be said of the present validity of that doctrine? And what considerations are proper to be applied in delimiting a boundary-line between the respective provinces of administrative agencies and the courts?

In the age of Coke such questions as these arose in connection with what has since been called "executive justice." To-day the term "executive" seems fitted to a narrower need,[2] and "administrative justice" suggests itself as a better name for the broader current development. This procedure, under which the rights of individuals are coming to be determined by agencies of the executive arm of government, is but a more advanced phase of a process which occurs whenever an executive agency, before taking action, finds it necessary

[1] See Hon. Geo. Sutherland, President's Address, American Bar Association, *Reports Amer. Bar Ass'n* (1917), xlii, 204 ff.; Hon. Wm. D. Guthrie, President's Address, New York State Bar Association, *Reports N. Y. State Bar Ass'n* (1923), xlvi, 175 ff.

[2] See below, p. 27.

to investigate and decide the issues on which the nature of the action to be taken depends. There is hardly any executive or administrative act which does not involve as a preliminary some such determination. Even a policeman who arrests a man for drunkenness must decide by a rough investigation the existence of the fact of drunkenness. The term "adjudication" may properly be applied to the more elaborate process by which the Commissioner of Patents determines the facts on which to base the granting or refusing of an application,[3] because, while the policeman's act in making the arrest leads only to subsequent proceedings in the courts before the rights of the person arrested are determined, the decision of the Commissioner of Patents will, unless brought to the test of judicial review, fix the rights of the parties definitively.[4]

[3] In the language of Mr. Chief Justice Fuller, "the investigation of every claim [for a patent] involves the adjudication of disputed questions of fact . . . and is therefore essentially judicial in its character," United States *v.* Duell, 172 U. S. 576. "That it was intended that the Commissioner of Patents, in issuing or withholding patents, in re-issues, interferences, and extensions, should exercise quasi-judicial functions, is apparent from the nature of the examinations and decisions he is required to make," Butterworth *v.* Hoe, 112 U. S. 50, at p. 67.

[4] The question of what kinds of determinations are "judicial" is, it will be seen below, a vexed one which the courts have frequently attempted to meet, but upon which their utterances are far from clarifying. It has sometimes been suggested that the test of "judicial" action is whether it is taken to settle a controversy between two or more parties. Rice *v.* Parkman, 16 Mass. 326. See below, note 13, this chapter. An illustration would be a case where, application having been made for a patent, a third party intervenes with an interference, and it becomes the duty of the patent authorities, before issuing the patent, to determine which party has the better right. Such cases were United States *v.* Duell and Butterworth *v.* Hoe, from which the quotations in note 3, above, are taken. On the other hand, in cases of money claims against the government, where the investigation is merely into the rights of a single party, the claimant, the court generally refuses to regard it as an "adjudication," In re Sanborn, 148 U. S. 222. But see the language of Nelson, J., in United States *v.* Commissioner, 5 Wall. 563, and of Miller, J., in Johnson *v.* Towsley, 13 Wall. 72, to the effect that the action of the Commissioner of the Land Office, in determining whether or not to issue a land patent to a single applicant, is "judicial." The utterances of the courts are in fact hopelessly at odds: *e. g.*, it is said that the functions of the land officials are "judicial," St. Louis Smelting & Refining Co. *v.* Kemp, 104 U. S. 636 at p. 640, Noble *v.* Union River Logging Co., 147 U. S. 165; that they are not "judicial," Craig *v.* Leitensdorfer, 123 U. S.

I

Administrative adjudication, wrote an observer twenty years ago, "is new in countries where the common law system prevails. Indeed, so new is this function of the administration that no discussion of it is to be found in our law writers. It is still the doctrine that all controversies must be decided in the judicial courts; it must be so, it is said, because the theory of the law of the land involves the supremacy of the ordinary tribunals. In the face of such theories, the jurisdiction of the administration to determine its own controversies has been established to an extent not often appreciated." [5]

189. In Hagar *v.* Reclamation District, 111 U. S. 701, the Supreme Court said that tax officials "in estimating the value of property act judicially." Industrial accident boards, administering workmen's compensation acts, have been said to act "judicially," Western Metal Supply Co. *v.* Pillsbury, 172 Cal. 407, or as a "court," Pigeon *v.* Employers' Liability Assurance Corp., 216 Mass. 51; and not "judicially," Borgnis *v.* Falk, 147 Wis. 327; Mackin *v.* Detroit Timkin Axle Co., 187 Mich. 8. The courts often cut the Gordian knot by using the phrase "quasi-judicial."

[5] Bruce Wyman, *Principles of Administrative Law*, etc. (St. Paul, 1903), p. 112. See also Dean Pound, "Executive Justice," *American Law Register* (1907), lv, 137, and "Justice according to Law," *Col. Law Rev.*, xiv, 13 ff. In recent years we have sometimes seemed in danger of regarding administrative adjudication as a much more modern growth than it really is. With the introduction of excise taxes into England in 1643, jurisdiction to enforce the law and punish violations by penalties and seizures was vested in "commissioners," "to the total exclusion of trial by jury, and disregard of the common law," Blackstone, *Commentaries*, ed. Christian, i, 318. This was the gist of Dr. Johnson's famous diatribe in his *Dictionary*: "excise,—a hateful tax adjudged not by the common judges of property, but by wretches hired by those to whom excise is paid." By statute, 23 Henry VIII, c. 5 (3 Statutes of the Realm, 368), commissioners of sewers were given jurisdiction to "take order" for the conservation of sewers within their jurisdiction, and to fine and imprison for contempts, Blackstone, *op. cit.*, i, ii, 73. By another act of Henry VIII, physicians practising in London were required to be licensed by a "college of physicians" which had authority to punish unskilful practitioners: see Dr. Bonham's case, 8 Coke Rep. 118; Groenvelt *v.* Burwell, 1 Ld. Raymond, 454. All these administrative bodies were recognized as "tribunals of a special or limited jurisdiction": Lord Hale in Terry *v.* Huntingdon, Hardres, 480; Blackstone, *op. cit.*, iii, 73; Lord Holt in Groenvelt *v.* Burwell, *supra*. By statute, 1 James I, c. 31 (4 Statutes of the Realm, pt. ii, p. 1061), mayors of towns were authorized to confine persons infected with the plague to their own houses, and set a guard over them. By statute, 3 William & Mary, c. 12, sec. 23 (6 Statutes of the Realm, 319), justices of the peace were required annually to fix the rates to be charged by common

This language applies especially to adjudication by bodies like public-service commissions, industrial-accident boards, licensing boards, and health boards, which have been growing up in step with an expanding police power. These are the instances where administrative adjudication strikes the Anglo-American lawyer as such a novel and challenging thing. On the other hand, adjudication of the right to a pension or a patent or a land-grant by an administrative agency does not seem anomalous in quite the same way. The reason is partly, no doubt, that the rights determined by administrative adjudication in the latter cases have been created by the special favor of the state expressed in legislation,[6] and have not been enjoyed as of so-called "common right." Ever since their creation such rights have perforce been adjudicated by administrative agencies. On the other hand, the rights adjudicated by public-service commissions, industrial-accident boards, and the like, are the traditional rights which have always been protected by the common law administered in the ordinary courts. An institutional change of very great magnitude is involved in submitting such rights to the determination of administrative agencies.

The change is one which registers the penetration of government for purposes of regulation into fields hitherto left to be regulated mainly or wholly by law administered in the courts. A developing police power has resorted to a new way of dealing with old problems which are vexing modern society in novel and acute shapes. For the business of the police

carriers in their parishes. Dealers in wines and liquors were required to be licensed; see Bassett *v.* Godschall, 3 Wilson, 121 (1770). Other instances could no doubt be discovered, but those already cited cover practically all the main fields in which administrative adjudication has ramified in modern times. Of course not all these regulations were reproduced in colonial America, as not adapted to pioneer conditions; but instances of administrative adjudication began to increase in the United States at the beginning of the nineteenth century and met with no unfavorable reception at the hands of the courts: see Seaman *v.* Patten, 2 Caines (N. Y.), 312 (1805); Cary *v.* Curtis, 3 How. 236 (1845); Downer *v.* Lent, 6 Cal. 94 (1856). Hostility began to appear after the middle of the century with the strong resurgence of the doctrine of vested rights. See below, Chapter III, note 20, p. 44 at pp. 46, 47.

[6] See Chafee, *Freedom of Speech*, p. 233.

power has been not so much to generate new rights as to provide new methods of enforcing interests which in a rough way have always been safeguarded by the common law.[7] Thus, a man has always had an action in a law court for a nuisance; to-day he is more adequately protected by the authority of a health board or building inspector, who may of their own motion order the nuisance to be abolished.[8] An unskilful physician has always been liable in an action on the case *sur assumpsit* by the injured party;[9] to-day the public is protected by the requirement that candidates for the practice of medicine shall apply for a license and be examined. The fixing of railroad rates by a commission steps into the place of the old action by the injured shipper to recover the excess charges in general assumpsit.[10] The human interests and legal rights protected remain the same; but the old legal procedure has been superseded by direct governmental action on the plea of prevention, or greater speed and effectiveness of the remedy.

The distinctive feature of the older system, which is here designated for convenience of contrast as a system of "regu-

[7] Freund, *Police Power*, §8.

[8] The scope of the action of nuisance was restricted by the fact that it was available only to owners whose property was injured by the existence of the nuisance, and could not be brought by one whose only interest was that his comfort and health were impaired thereby. Kavanagh *v.* Barber, 131 N. Y. 211.

[9] For early cases see James Barr Ames, *Lectures on Legal History*, p. 130; G. F. Deiser in *Harv. Law Rev.*, xxv, 428, at p. 431; Slater *v.* Baker, 2 Wilson 359; Sears *v.* Prentice, 8 East, 348. In the modern practice, the plaintiff has an election between suing either in assumpsit or case. Kuhn *v.* Bromfield, 34 W. Va. 252 (1890).

[10] Heiserman *v.* Burlington, Cedar Rapids & Northern R. Co., 63 Ia. 732. In most of the cases where recovery of excess charges against a railway was allowed in an action at law, the railway's common-law duty to carry for reasonable rates had been reënforced by a specific statutory obligation: Parker *v.* Gt. Western R. Co., 7 Manning & Granger, 253 (1844); Gt. Western R. Co. *v.* Sutton, L. R., 4 Eng. & Ir. Ap. 226 (1869); McGregor *v.* Erie R. Co., 35 N. J. L. 89 (1871); Peters *v.* Scioto & Hocking Valley R. R. Co., 42 Ohio St. 275 (1884). The right of recovery is explained as a quasi-contractual right to recover money extorted by the railway through taking an unfair advantage of the shipper's necessities, and has been based upon Lord Mansfield's language in Moses *v.* Macferlan, 2 Burr. 1005. See F. C. Woodward, *The Law of Quasi-Contracts*, § 220.

lation by law," is to postpone the action of the executive branch of government to the last stage in the settlement of a private controversy between individuals. Under such a system the action of government is conditioned upon the existence of a controversy between individuals in the first place. A has a legal right. He thinks B has violated that right. He brings an action against B in a law court, and if a violation is found to have occurred, judgment is given that A recover compensation. The function of the executive begins only at this point, and is simply to step in, in the person of the sheriff, and enforce the judgment against B.[11] Government is thus limited to the rôle of arbitrating differences between individuals through the courts after the difference has arisen, and then enforcing the court's award through the executive.[12] The only regulating force operating on individuals prior to action by them is their own knowledge, or presumed knowledge, of the law applying to their contemplated act.[13] Two

[11] In theory the sheriff does not even act to "enforce" the judgment of the court. The theory is more individualistic. The judgment is merely a declaration of the plaintiff's right and an authority to the plaintiff to enforce it. The sheriff, in levying execution, acts as the plaintiff's agent or representative in exercising this authority. Pound, *Class Lectures on Equity*, Harvard Law School (MS.). For the application of the analogy of master and servant to the relation see Welsh *v.* Cochran, 63 N. Y. 181; Clark *v.* Woodruff, 83 N. Y. 518.

[12] An extreme theory of pure regulation by law is advanced in Hume's essay "Of the Origin of Government": "Man . . . is engaged to establish political society in order to administer justice, without which there can be no peace among them, nor safety, nor mutual intercourse. We are therefore to look upon all the vast apparatus of our government as having ultimately no other object or purpose but the distribution of justice, or, in other words, the support of the Twelve Judges. Kings and parliaments, fleets and armies, officers of the court and revenue, ambassadors, ministers and privy councillors are all subordinate in their end to this part of administration," *Essays, Moral, Political and Literary* (ed. Green and Grose), i, 113, 114. Cf. also Lord Brougham: "All we see about us, kings, lords, commons, the whole machinery of the state, all the apparatus of the system and its varied workings, end in simply bringing twelve good men into a box," "Speech on the Present State of the Law, Feb. 7, 1828," *Hansard*, New Series, xviii, 131; *Speeches* (in two volumes, Phila., 1841), i, 519.

[13] "The essential feature of litigation is [that] the court is moved to action only by the claim of a definite person or group of persons in the same interest, a claim which cannot be satisfied without dealing with other claims also; nor does the court . . . profess to assist those who do not assert their rights," Pollock,

defects in this system have been partially supplied in our law by the departures from it embodied in equity jurisdiction and in the criminal law. Equity makes it possible in certain cases for an individual to secure protection for his right before it has been actually violated. The criminal law recognizes that, in addition to the interests of individuals, there is a social interest which should be protected. But the preventive jurisdiction of equity is artificially restricted, and does not reach to criminal acts as such; the courts have generally held that it exists for the protection only of private, and not of public, rights.[14] On the other hand, the need for regulation in the public interest is not limited to acts which can justly be treated as criminal.

Of course, no system of pure "regulation by law" could exist, or has ever existed. Government has always acted on its own motion, and for other purposes than to enforce the judgments of a court. But in English-speaking countries such independent executive action has in modern times been mainly in the field of what may be called the more exclusively

Essays in the Law, p. 276. Regulation by the adjudication of private controversies is the earliest form of state interference with private activities in the interest of social order. It was the entering wedge of a system of more forceful control by society over its members than could be exerted by the power of religion or *mores*. See Vinogradoff, *Historical Jurisprudence*, i, 310, 346 ff. "The fact that the procedure of justice originated as methods of supplying impartial umpires for conflicts waged between individuals has had serious consequences. It has had, indeed, the desirable consequence of quickening men to the perception of their rights and to their obligations as social members to maintain them intact. But it has also had the undesirable result of limiting the function of the public interest to the somewhat negative one of securing fair play between contentious individuals. The battle is not now fought out with fists or spears or oaths or ordeals; but it is largely a battle of wits and of technical resources between opposite parties and their lawyers, with the state acting the part of a benevolently neutral umpire." Dewey and Tufts, *Ethics*, p. 404. This passage represents the dissatisfaction with a system of regulation by legal adjudication which is promoting the substitution of regulation by governmental action.

[14] Atty. Gen. *v.* Utica Ins. Co., 2 Johns. Ch. (N. Y.) 371. But equity will enjoin in the interest of individuals many acts which also happen to be criminal; and recently by statutes the injunction has been made an instrument for enforcing certain parts of the criminal law. The outstanding instance is in the case of anti-trust legislation. See also E. S. Mack, "The Revival of Criminal Equity," *Harv. Law Rev.*, xvi, 389 ff.

political activities of government, — in making war and peace, raising armies and collecting taxes, — and not in the field of so-called police regulation. At least after the Industrial Revolution, regulation by "law" and not by "government" became in England, and *a fortiori* in America, the settled order in the latter field;[15] a field which includes such matters as sanitation, fire protection, accident prevention, and the regulation of common callings, the very matters which are of most intimate concern to the average citizen.

The congested conditions of modern life make efficient police regulation a thing of foremost consequence if the threads of human intercourse are to be saved from costly tangles, and if room is to be kept clear for healthy individual and social growth. An illustration of the inadequacy of regulation by law alone is afforded by the relatively simple matter of traffic on city streets. So long as towns remained small, collisions were well enough prevented by the reasonable care which drivers were induced to take by the knowledge that if they drove carelessly they would be subject to an action for damages by the injured party. Regulation by law was sufficient. But such a preventive no longer works. Something more is needed than mere absence of negligence. A police officer is accordingly stationed in the street to prevent accidents by orders given to drivers in advance. The officer, having a complete view of the traffic situation as a whole, and able to control each part of it with reference to the others, is in a better position to avert collisions than is any individual driver, however careful, with his imperfect knowledge of what is around the corner and his lack of means to control the conduct of other drivers.

[15] In the Middle Ages, and indeed down to the Industrial Revolution, there were, of course, many instances of direct governmental control and regulation of such matters as wages and prices. See Freund, *Police Power*, §§ 374, 375. In some instances this regulation was statutory, but in others it was administrative. An example of administrative regulation is the statute of William and Mary which provided that justices of the peace should annually fix the rates to be charged by common carriers in their parishes. (3 William & Mary, c. 12, sec. 23; 6 Statutes of the Realm, 319.) And see Beard, *The Office of Justice of the Peace in England* (*Columbia University Studies in History, Economics and Public Law*, vol. xx), pp. 58–70, *passim*.

The distinctive feature of the system of regulation represented by the traffic policeman, as contrasted with a system of pure regulation by law, is that under the former the executive arm of government interferes with individuals of its own motion, prior to and apart from the existence of any controversy between them. And further, under a thoroughgoing system of regulation by government, the executive carries through its action upon the individual from first to last without the intervention of a law court. This is not true of the traffic officer. If his orders are disobeyed, all he can do is to bring the offender into court to be tried, and punished if found guilty. But a health officer can proceed at once to the destruction of unwholesome provisions [16] or diseased animals,[17] a building inspector can condemn a dangerous structure,[18] and in some jurisdictions the award of an industrial-accident board is entitled to have judgment entered on it, as a matter of course, in a court of record.[19] In these cases the rights of individuals are not merely investigated, but determined and concluded, without the intervention of a law court. This represents the pure form of administrative adjudication toward which regulation by government is tending, through an intermediate stage in which the executive officer or body is required to resort to a law court to compel obedience to its orders. Many public-utility commissions occupy, or have occupied, this intermediate position.[20] Here the tendency toward pure executive regulation takes the form of an effort to require the courts to treat the order or decision of the executive body as final and enforce it without looking behind it to the merits. Should this effort succeed, the action of the courts would become in such cases merely an automatic stage in the executive process, and they would be reduced to formally registering, and directing the enforcement of, executive decrees.

[16] Fath *v.* Koeppel, 72 Wis. 289.

[17] Miller *v.* Horton, 152 Mass. 540.

[18] Klinger *v.* Bickel, 117 Pa. St. 326.

[19] Act No. 10, Public Acts of Michigan, 1912.

[20] *E.g.*, see the W. Va. Public Utilities Act, Public Acts of 1913, ch. 9, secs. 5 and 23. But *cf.* sec. 27 thereof, added by Acts of 1915, ch. 8.

The impelling need for regulation by direct governmental action springs in great measure from the fact that in so many cases it has come to be beyond the knowledge and power of the private individual, however careful, to avoid injuring others. To allow the injury to occur, and then adjust the damage through the medium of a law-suit to determine the resulting controversy, is a clumsy and wasteful way of repairing what admits of prevention.[21] And if prevention is to be effective, it cannot be left to depend on the act of an interested individual in making application to a court for relief against expected injury, for the threefold reason that in all likelihood no such application will ever be made,[22] that the preventive relief which a court can give is artificially limited, and, finally, because of the delay incidental to the procedure

[21] "It is obvious that the law of nuisance is inadequate as a substitute for modern police regulation; it takes cognizance of practices only when danger passes into actual mischief." Freund, *Standards of American Legislation*, p. 67.

[22] The Cullom Committee of 1885 considered the question whether an administrative commission was essential to effective railway regulation, or whether it would be sufficient to pass a statute defining the duties of the carriers more narrowly, and leaving action under the statute to be taken by aggrieved individuals in the courts. During the examination of Mr. Simon Sterne the following colloquy occurred:

THE CHAIRMAN: "Now suppose we pass a law . . . for the control of railroads without any commission at all — what would be the result of that?"

MR. STERNE: "That would be a bull against the moon. . . . The ordinary courts are open theoretically, but they are closed practically, to the individual man who has a grievance, and there are two reasons for that. The first is the expense, and the second, which is a still stronger impediment, is the fact that the individual trader does not want to incur the enmity of an instrumentality which he is compelled to use from day to day. I live, say, at Batavia. I am compelled to use the New York Central Railway Company for the purpose of my transportation. I have a grievance. They have done me, in a freight bill, out of $2.50, or even $25, if you please. I lay the matter before them and they do not choose to redress it. I can go to court, but two reasons restrain me: first the expense, and, in the next place. . . . I am compelled to deal with the road every day, and I must keep on good terms with its officers, as they have power to punish me in controlling the delivery of my freight. The local freight agent will be just to me in relation to freight charges, because the company are afraid of me in that respect; but they will deliver everybody's freight ahead of mine. And so in many ways I am subjected to annoyances which a hundred times over outweigh the redress I get. For small grievances the courts are practically closed." (*Report of the Senate Select Committee on Interstate Commerce*, 49th Congress, 1st Session, p. 63.)

of a body organized, as is a court, primarily to hear and determine controversies. Such, however, are the relations between individuals to-day that, if one person fails to make timely insistence on his rights, the result may often be damaging to many others; as where an immediate neighbor fails to enforce the removal of a disease-breeding nuisance on abutting property. There must be some agency to initiate action on behalf of the public in such cases, based on wider information than private individuals generally have, and the action taken must be more summary in form than a proceeding at law. What is needed is not so much an adjudication of disputed rights as a seasonable order telling someone what to do in time to avoid committing an injury.[23]

The traditional law, within the larger frame of rights and obligations which it marks out, has left to individuals a certain area of private discretion, and it is into this area that it is coming to be necessary to introduce order at an ever increasing number of points by the issue of commands to govern its exercise. Such commands cannot advantageously take the form of legal rules, definitely and rigidly prescribed in advance by the legislature to govern all cases of a like kind, and then left to be learned and followed at their peril by the individuals affected. It would be inefficient government of traffic at a crossing to allot by statute fixed alternating periods for the

[23] "It should be noticed that administrative commissions only in a limited sense *pass upon* property rights. They do not decide that certain property belongs to A or to B. They do say that certain property that belongs to A can be used by him only in a certain way. They tell public-service corporations how they must run their trains, or what rates they may charge in the sale of their gas or electricity, or whether they may establish new rates or not. They tell those who manufacture drugs or food products that they can sell them only if they do not contain certain ingredients. The right to hold a certain office may or may not be regarded as a property right; but even in those states where it is regarded as one, nevertheless all that a civil service commission does is to see to it that the man who holds his office complies with the rules. In other words, a commission merely passes upon the method that a man must adopt in using what belongs to him," H. J. Friedman in *Harv. Law Rev.*, xxv, 711. But if, as is well settled, the right to use property is itself property (Railroad Commission Cases, 116 U. S. 307; Chicago, Milwaukee & St. Paul R. Co. *v.* Minnesota, 134 U. S. 418), a determination affecting the use of property is a determination affecting property.

movement of traffic on each of the cross streets, and then, without supplying a signal, undertake to punish criminally individuals who happen to be found crossing at the wrong time. For the discretion of carriers as to what is a reasonable rate, it is not generally helpful to substitute a flat statutory rate of so much per ton-mile. What is wanted is not a rigid rule at all, but the intelligent and flexible discretion of a responsible directing mind. In short, when discretion is taken from the individuals who act, it must still remain as discretion, but as discretion concentrated in the judgment of a directing official or officials who give orders, and are in a position to weigh items of current public advantage in a manner that a law court, sitting to decide the private rights of individuals, cannot generally do. These considerations apply also to the regulation of banks, insurance companies, and carriers, where control by administrative regulation has been found to work more successfully than strict statutory mandate or prohibition.

The particular advantages which a system of regulation by government thus has over one of regulation by law differ in the different fields of regulation, but the differences are in the matter of emphasis; the respective advantages fall, with greater or less incidence, under one or more of the following heads:

(1) Regulation by government opens a way for action to be taken in the public interest to prevent future harm where there would be no assurance that any action would be taken if the initiative were left wholly to interested individuals.

(2) It provides for action that will be prompt and preventive, rather than merely remedial, and will be based on technical knowledge which would not be available if it were taken through the ordinary courts of law.

(3) It ensures that the action taken will have regard for the interests of the general public in a way not possible if it were only the outcome of a controversy between private parties to a law-suit.

(4) It permits the rules for the prevention of socially hurtful conduct to be flexible rules, based on discretion, and

thus makes possible the introduction of order in fields not advantageously admitting the application of rules of a rigid and permanent character.[24]

II

What may be called administrative adjudication enters necessarily as a central element into this system of governmental regulation through officials. The essence of the system is to expand the functioning area of executive officers backward over the fields which, under a system of regulation by law, are occupied by the law-making body and the courts. Thus the administrative official who is to give orders to avert harmful conduct may find it desirable, before dealing with specific cases, to fix upon rules to govern the exercise of his discretion, and then proceed to apply these rules to fit the facts of each special case. These two steps may be taken separately or they may be combined. Either an administrative regulation [25] may be framed beforehand and applied in

[24] "The two rival agencies in government are law and administration. Administration achieves public security by preventive measures. It selects a hierarchy of officials to each of whom definite work is assigned, and it is governed by ends rather than rules. It is personal. Hence it is often arbitrary, and is subject to the abuses incident to personal as contrasted with impersonal or law-regulated action. But well exercised it is extremely efficient; always more efficient than the rival agency can be. Law, on the other hand, operates by redress or punishment rather than by prevention. It formulates general rules of action and visits infractions of these rules with penalties. It does not supervise action. It leaves individuals free to act, but imposes pains on those who do not act in accordance with the rules prescribed. It is impersonal, and safeguards against ignorance, caprice, or corruption of magistrates. But it is not quick enough, or automatic enough, to meet the requirements of a complex social organization." Dean Pound in *Proc. Amer. Pol. Sci. Assoc.* (1907), iv, 232, 233.

[25] The subject of administrative regulations lies outside the scope of this book. The formulation of such regulations, which lay down general rules and leave them to be applied in a later proceeding to the facts of particular cases, although said to be "judicial" in Foster *v.* Farrar, 8 Allen (Mass.), 325 (1864), is not an instance of administrative adjudication as the term is here used. It is rather what one would expect to be called a "quasi-legislative" function (Wyman, *Administrative Law*, § 96), although the courts have avoided this term, probably because of the constitutional rule against "delegation" of "legislative" powers (Cooley, *Constitutional Limitations*, 7th ed., pp. 163 ff.). See N. G. Dubach, "Quasi-Legislative Powers of State Boards of Health," in *Amer. Pol.*

a separate proceeding to each case as it arises; or the executive may, in one and the same proceeding, make and apply a rule, or, what is substantially the same process, apply a "standard," to the case before it.[26] In either instance, however, the second of the two steps is, for all practical purposes, adjudication. The health commissioner who in the exercise of his authority orders the destruction of a man's property is in effect adjudicating that man's property rights in as full a sense as a court when it orders the abatement of a nuisance.

The place of administrative adjudication in the process of police regulation by government tends, however, to be obscured by a number of causes.[27] First of all, the language and

Sci. Rev., x, 80 ff.; J. A. Fairlie, "Administrative Legislation," in *Michigan Law Rev.*, xviii, 1 ff. (1920). See the distinction taken in Salem *v.* Eastern Railroad Co., 98 Mass. 431 (1868), between the action of a local board of health in making general regulations respecting articles capable of conveying infection, and the board's authority to examine into any specific case of nuisance and order its removal. The present study is confined to the exercise of the latter sort of functions by administrative agencies. For a discussion of administrative regulations and review of them by the courts, see T. R. Powell in *Pol. Sci. Quarterly*, xxvii, 215, at p. 225, and xxviii, 34, at p. 36, and in *Harv. Law Rev.*, xxiv, 268 ff.

[26] Where a standard, such as reasonableness, wholesomeness, or professional fitness is prescribed by law and its application entrusted to an administrative body, it is in many cases not possible for the administrative body to translate the standard into greater definiteness in the form of regulations before applying it judicially to concrete cases. In such a situation the administrative agency is doing substantially what the courts do in negligence cases, for instance, where they apply directly the standard of "due care" to the facts of the case before them. It is never supposed that the courts are exercising a delegated "legislative" power because they must fill out the idea of due care with the details necessary to apply it to the facts of a particular case of negligence. Where this process, however, is entrusted to an administrative agency, it has been frequently urged by the parties affected that "legislative power" has been unconstitutionally delegated: Intermountain Rate Cases, 234 U. S. 476; Mutual Film Corporation *v.* Ohio Industrial Commission, 236 U. S. 230; First National Bank *v.* Fellows, 244 U. S. 416. The courts have not sustained this contention, but its influence is seen in such a decision as Burcher *v.* People, 41 Colo. 495, happily exceptional, where it was held that to leave to the courts the decision whether a steam laundry was an industrial establishment falling within the legislative definition of industries subject to the eight-hour law for women, was an unconstitutional delegation of legislative power to the courts.

[27] For a very thorough-going and ingenious attempt to differentiate between "legislative," "administrative" and "judicial" powers, see Green, "Separation of Governmental Powers," *Yale Law Journal*, xxix, 371. In Eng-

analysis contained in many judicial decisions serve to obscure it. Our constitutional distinction between "legislative," "executive" and "judicial" powers draws the courts frequently into discussions in which the "legislative" or "executive" aspect of an administrative act is generally emphasized at the expense of the "judicial."[28] Thus, for example, the act of a public-utilities commission in fixing a rate has been held to be "legislative" for constitutional purposes.[29]

land, where there is no troublesome constitutional difficulty about the "separation of powers," there is a much greater readiness to admit that administrative agencies can act judicially. See F. H. C. Wiltshire, "The Appellate Jurisdiction of Central Government Departments," in *Journal of Public Administration*, ii, 370 ff.

[28] Dean Pound in *Col. Law Rev.*, xiv, 15 ff., gives an extended list of instances where powers formerly held "judicial" are no longer treated as being so when entrusted to administrative agencies.

[29] Interstate Commerce Commission *v.* Cincinnati, New Orleans & Texas Pacific R. Co., 167 U. S. 479; Prentis et al. *v.* Atlantic Coast Line Co., 211 U. S. 210. One reason why our courts have held rate-fixing by a commission to be "legislative" would seem to be because it is a function which legislative bodies have been in the habit of exercising. See the language of the Supreme Court in Louisville & Nashville R. Co. *v.* Garrett, 231 U. S. 298, at p. 305: "It has been frequently pointed out that prescribing rates for the future is an act legislative and not judicial in kind, — it pertains, broadly speaking, to the legislative power. The legislative may act directly, or in the absence of constitutional restriction, it may commit the authority to fix rates to a subordinate body." See also Honolulu Rebate & Transit Co., 211 U. S. 282, where the power to regulate carriers was said to be "legislative," "and may be exercised directly by the legislature. But the legislature may delegate to an administrative body the execution in detail of the legislative power of regulation." Yet, in spite of the well-settled principle that notice and hearing are not a prerequisite of so-called "legislative" action (Bi-metallic Investment Co. *v.* State Board of Equalization, 239 U. S. 441), a statute will be held unconstitutional which entrusts the rate-fixing power to an administrative agency without requiring that the carriers affected shall be given notice and an opportunity to be heard, Chicago, Milwaukee & St. Paul R. Co. *v.* Minnesota, 134 U. S. 418. In this case it was said that the determination of reasonable rates is a "judicial question"; and in Interstate Commerce Commission *v.* Louisville & Nashville R. Co., 227 U. S. 88, it was said that an order of the Interstate Commerce Commission setting aside a rate as unreasonable is "quasi-judicial" in character. In New York, rate-fixing orders of the Public Service Commission have been held to be "quasi-judicial" in such sense as to be subject to review by certiorari, People ex rel. Joline *v.* Willcox, 129 App. Div. (N. Y.) 267; 194 N. Y. 383. It has been pointed out that a serious difficulty about holding administrative rate-making orders to be "legislative" in character is that it to all intents and purposes renders nugatory the well-entrenched constitutional dogma that

From one aspect of juristic analysis, legislative it no doubt is —that is, from the aspect of its future operation and its applicability to a whole class of cases. But the writ of mandamus is future in its operation, and yet is not for that reason regarded as legislative; and if we examine rate-fixing from the standpoint of the general applicability of the resulting rate to an indefinite number of future cases as a class, we observe the significant peculiarity that, while the rate applies indifferently, indeed, as against all future shippers, it applies only to the particular carrier or carriers who were parties to the hearing and other proceedings before the commission, and for whom, as the outcome of those proceedings, the rate is prescribed.[30] From the standpoint of shippers, therefore, the rate may no doubt be regarded as legislation, but from the standpoint of the carriers it seems quite as truly adjudication.[31] Even with respect to the shippers, however, it may be

"legislative" power cannot be delegated, E. A. Harriman in *Proc. Amer. Pol. Sci. Ass'n* (1909), vi, 33 ff. Richard Olney, starting from the doctrine that administrative rate-making is "legislative," argued that it is therefore unconstitutional as involving a "delegation of legislative power": "To make rates is to lay down the rule by which conduct shall be governed, and does not merely fix the time, or ascertain the circumstances in which such rule shall apply," *North Amer. Rev.* (Oct., 1905), clxxxi, 481 ff.

[30] See Interstate Commerce Act, secs. 13 and 15.

[31] The point may be illustrated by two contrasted situations. A rate fixed by statute under the practice prevailing before the establishment of utility commissions was a flat rate of so much per mile or so much per ton, applying to all carriers throughout the jurisdiction. Such a statute was the Iowa act of 1874, summarized in *Report of the Senate Select Committee on Interstate Commerce* (Cullom Committee), 49th Congress, 1st Session, p. 99; see Chicago, Burlington & Quincy R. Co. *v.* Iowa, 94 U. S. 155. This is, after all, legislation in a different sense from a rate prescribed by a commission after a hearing for a particular carrier and a given commodity over a given portion of its line. Such a determination would seem to be legislative only in the sense of the divorce and inheritance bills which mark the period of so-called legislative justice in our legal history, Calder *v.* Bull, 3 Dallas, 356; Corwin, *Doctrine of Judicial Review*, p. 69. The doctrine of classification (Barbier *v.* Connolly, 113 U. S. 27; Hayes *v.* Missouri, 120 U. S. 68) may be invoked to show that there can be legislation applying to only a single legal person, Walker *v.* Potter, 18 Ohio St. 85, State *v.* Pugh, 43 Ohio St. 98, at p. 112; but there comes a point where the doctrine of classification cannot conceal the presence of a judicial element in the regulation promulgated, State ex rel. Kinseley *v.* Jones, 66 Ohio St. 453. The administrative act of rate-making may be further contrasted with the action of a board of

likened to the procedure whereby an injunction is obtained against a group of persons designated by a class-description and not named personally in the bill. If the latter procedure is judicial, there is certainly an element of adjudication in administrative rate-fixing; and that is all I wish to insist on here.[32] There is no intention to deny that rate-fixing involves as one of its elements the exercise of a function which may as well as not be called "legislative." The whole discussion should go to demonstrate the futility of trying to classify a particular exercise of administrative power as either wholly

tax equalization in raising the rate of assessment throughout a given area, such action having likewise been held to be legislative, Bi-metallic Investment Co. *v.* State Board of Equalization, 239 U. S. 441. In the latter case the only parties affected are the tax-payers within the designated area, and they are affected as members of a class and not as individuals. They stand in the same position as the shippers in the rate case, but there is no opposite party, no single individual, corresponding to the carrier, whose rights are determined by the assessment adopted. The state, as the party to receive the taxes assessed, may seem to stand in some such position; but the position of the state in its public political capacity before its own tribunals cannot be compared to that of a private party to a record; and it has accordingly been decided that such action by an equalization board, unlike the act of a public service commission in fixing a rate, may be taken without any hearing. As to the judicial nature of rate-fixing, see E. V. Abbot, *Justice and the Modern Law*, pp. 101 ff.

[32] See the reasoning in People ex rel. Joline *v.* Willcox, 194 N. Y. 383, discussing the Prentis case and holding the acts of a utility commission "judicial." The court denied that the acts of the commission were "non-judicial" because prescribing a rule of conduct for the future, and pointed out that a judicial decision often determines in advance what future action will be a discharge of existing liabilities or obligations — *e. g.*, a decree of specific performance operates *in futuro.* See also Laurence Curtis 2d, in *Harv. Law Rev.*, xxxiv, 862 ff. Of course I do not mean to deny that an "administrative" adjudication, like rate-fixing, differs in important respects from a "judicial" adjudication; and notably in the fact that the decision is determined largely on the basis of direct considerations of governmental policy rather than by an impartial delimitation of the rights of the parties; see below, p. 23. But this does not make it "legislative"; or if it does so in the case of rate-fixing orders, it should have the like effect in the case of all other "administrative" adjudications, *e. g.*, in the case of orders of health boards, for here too the decisions are grounded on policy; but such orders, however they are classified, are practically never called "legislative." I know of no case which in this respect follows Commonwealth *v.* Sisson, 189 Mass. 247, criticized below. On the other hand, considerations of policy hardly enter into decisions of industrial accident boards, yet these, too, the courts are reluctant to pronounce "judicial," Mackin *v.* Detroit Timkin Axle Co., 187 Mich. 8.

legislative or wholly judicial.[33] The tendency of the administrative procedure is to foreshorten both functions into a continuous governmental act.

A plainer instance of administrative adjudication occurs where an administrative agency at one and the same time makes a rule and applies it to a concrete situation. Such a case was Commonwealth *v.* Sisson.[34] A sawmill was discharging sawdust into a fresh-water pond. The state board of fish and game commissioners concluded that the sawdust was harmful to the fish in the pond and ordered the mill to make another disposition of it. The order having been made without giving the mill-owners an opportunity to be heard, it became important to determine whether it was legislative or judicial in character. The court, probably to save the validity of the order, held it to be legislative because applying to the future.[35] If such an order is legislative, it is hard to see why an ordinary injunction is not. The essential difference between legislation and adjudication is not that one looks to the future and the other to the past — there is nothing inherent in the judicial process which requires that it should look wholly backward. Nor may the term adjudication properly be limited to cases of controversy between private individuals with an agency of government intervening as arbi-

[33] All adjudication involves in some degree the exercise of legislative and administrative functions also. See Pound, *Introduction to the Philosophy of Law*, pp. 105 ff.

[34] 189 Mass. 247 (1905). For a criticism of the case and a review of previous decisions in the same jurisdiction, see E. N. Parker in *Harv. Law Rev.*, xx, 116 ff.

[35] Judge Loring, writing the opinion for the court, also argues that where a statute empowers an administrative agency to apply and enforce the statute in particular cases, the action of the administrative body amounts to no more than completing the details of the statute and hence is legislative in character. If this is so, it is hard to see why a law court in every ordinary case when it applies a statute to a concrete case is not acting "legislatively." This is substantially the doctrine of Burcher *v.* People, 41 Colo. 495, cited above in note 26. Furthermore, if action taken by a legislative body to apply rules to particular cases remains properly legislative action, there would seem to be no ground for objection to divorce and inheritance bills, or to the performance of other apparently judicial functions by legislatures. For strained attempts to reconcile the passing of such "legislation" with the doctrine of the "separation of powers" see the cases reviewed in Cooley, *Constitutional Limitations*, 7th ed., pp. 140–157.

trator — such a definition would deprive every criminal trial of judicial character. What distinguishes legislation from adjudication is that the former affects the rights of individuals in the abstract and must be applied in a further proceeding before the legal position of any particular individual will be definitely touched by it; while adjudication operates concretely upon individuals in their individual capacity.[36] On such an analysis, the order of the fish and game commissioners which was at issue in Commonwealth *v.* Sisson would seem to be an instance of adjudication in quite the same sense as an order of a board of medical examiners granting or refusing to an applicant a license to practise medicine. What we have in both cases, as in a criminal trial, is the balancing of the rights of a particular individual against the rights of the public, with a resulting restriction on that particular individual's conduct. In a criminal trial the conduct under investigation is past conduct; that is the only substantial difference.

The clearest instance of administrative adjudication is where an administrative agency is entrusted with the task of hearing and determining controversies between parties. The most familiar illustration is that of the industrial-accident boards which are generally made the agency for determining

[36] See language of Field, J., dissenting, in Sinking Fund Cases, 99 U. S. 700, at p. 761: "The distinction between a judicial and a legislative act is well defined. The one determines what the law is, and what the rights of parties are, with reference to transactions already had; the other prescribes what the law shall be in future cases arising under it." See also Bates *v.* Kimball, 2 Chip. (Vt.) 77; Merrill *v.* Sherburne, 1 N. H. 199, at p. 203; Cooley, *Constitutional Limitations*, 7th ed., pp. 131 ff. The test of "future operation" as the distinguishing mark of "legislative" action no doubt goes back to Blackstone's statement that "all laws should be made to commence *in futuro*, and be notified before their commencement" (*Commentaries*, ed. Christian, i, 46); and to the doctrine that on the other hand it is the function of the judiciary *jus dicere et non jus dare*, "not to pronounce a new law, but to maintain and expound the old one," Broom's *Legal Maxims*, first Amer. ed. (Phila., 1845), p. 64. Confusion seems to have crept into most of the attempts of the courts to define legislative and judicial power from a failure to keep separate two different distinctions: (1) the distinction between present and future operation; and (2) the distinction between the announcement of a general rule without reference to any particular case, and the application or elaboration of a rule to fit a specific case.

the claims of employees against employers under workmen's compensation acts. Even this power has been held not to be "judicial" where the order of the board could not be enforced until judgment had been entered on it in a court of record,[37] although the order was entitled to such entry of judgment as a matter of course.[38] The decision was necessary to save the constitutionality of the statute under a state constitution which forbade the combination of "judicial" and "executive" functions in the same body; but it serves as a warning against understanding the term "adjudication," as here used, in the limited sense of a function which our courts have pronounced to be "judicial" for constitutional purposes.[39] We are concerned with issues broader than those of our

[37] Mackin *v.* Detroit Timkin Axle Co., 187 Mich. 8 (1915). The court said: "No action which is merely preparatory to an order or judgment to be rendered by some different body can properly be termed judicial" (p. 19). The Michigan court in this case was following a line of thought suggested earlier in Indiana Bridge Co. *v.* Louisville & Nashville R. Co., 37 Fed. 567 (1889), where it was held that the powers of the Interstate Commerce Commission were not "judicial" because the orders of the commission had to be enforced in a court action. But the cases are not on all fours, because of the provision of the Michigan law that the orders of the Industrial Board should be entitled to have judgment entered on them as a matter of course. In such a case, as Prof. Powell says, "the fact that the enforcement of the order must be entrusted to a marshal or sheriff rather than to an agent of the administration seems of slight importance" in determining whether or not the action of the administration is judicial (*Pol. Sci. Quarterly*, xxvii, 236). But in Sears-Roebuck & Co. *v.* Federal Trade Commission, 258 Fed. 307, at p. 312, the court said: "Though the action of the Commission [in making an order against a particular company] may be counted quasi-judicial on account of its form, with respect to power it is not judicial because a judicial determination is only that which is embodied in a judgment or decree of a court, and enforceable by execution or other writ of the court." The result almost seems to justify the statement of a political scientist: "Every act which proceeds from the legislature is classed as legislative; every act performed by the executive department is classed as executive; and so on, regardless of its real nature," J. W. Garner, *Introduction to Political Science*, p. 423. Professor Garner should have added a qualifying clause: "except when the courts choose to hold otherwise."

[38] Act No. 10, Public Acts of Michigan, 1912.

[39] Thus in speaking of an industrial accident board, the courts have said: "It is an administrative body or arm of the government, which in the course of its administration of the law is empowered to ascertain some questions of fact and apply existing law thereto, and in so doing acts quasi-judicially; *but it is not thereby vested with judicial power in the constitutional sense,*" Borgnis *v.* Falk, 147 Wis. 327, at p. 358. (Italics mine.)

own constitutional law; and for this reason it is necessary to look below forms, as fixed by constitutional interpretation, to the actual substance and meaning of the processes themselves.

A second cause which operates to conceal the essentially judicial character of much administrative action is that administrative adjudication, unlike adjudication by a court, is not usually a separate and distinct process, — that is to say, it is not singled out by being the isolated function of an independent agency existing and acting solely to perform it, — but is a mere moment, an integral part, in a larger process, which is nothing less than the carrying on of the business of government. The element of adjudication which is present is inevitably to some extent obscured by being performed primarily in aid of that business. In theory its purpose is to inform administrative officers what to do, rather than to determine the individual rights which will be affected by their resulting action or failure to act.[40] The two things are in

[40] "What is the distinction between judicial officers and administrative officers? The former are in the main entrusted with the administration of justice, the latter are in the main entrusted with the administration of government. If we analyze the work done by officers engaged in the application or execution of the law, we find that a part of this work may be differentiated from the rest by the fact that it consists in the decision of controversies between individuals, or between individuals and government officers, as to the applicability in the cases in question of a particular rule of law. The other branch of the work done by government officers may be distinguished by the fact that the action taken by such officers is not necessarily, or even often, the result of any controversy, and is not merely dependent on the solution of the question, What is the law? but is made also as a result of considerations of expediency. Thus, in the first kind of work, all the officer has to do is to determine what is the law applicable to the facts brought before him; in the second, he must determine, of course, what is the law, in order to determine whether he is competent to act; but furthermore he must decide whether, in case he is competent to act, it is wise for him to act. In the first case, for example, the officer is to determine whether under the law a given piece of property belongs to A or to B; in the second case, he is to determine, for example, whether, conceding he has the power, it is wise for him to grant A a license to sell liquor, or to lay out a highway over A's property. In these last cases, it is true, the law may provide that before he grants A his license he must hear the objections which A's neighbors may have to the granting of the license, or A's objections and the objections of other interested persons to the laying out of the highway as proposed. But it is not a controversy as to the applicability of the law so

the nature of the case inseparable, but there is a difference of emphasis which is precisely the distinguishing factor between administrative adjudication and adjudication by a court. In the case of an adjudication by a court, the subsequent action of the sheriff in enforcing the judgment is indispensable, it is true, to the effectiveness of the procedure, but it is not the goal kept in view throughout the proceedings; the attention of the tribunal is focused rather on the rights of the parties before it than on the governmental action which will follow its decision.[41] Enforcement ensues incidentally and as a wholly separate element in the process. On the other hand, an administrative tribunal, while it is simultaneously an adjudicating and enforcing agency, is primarily the latter; it adjudicates for the direct purpose of informing itself how best to perform its functions of enforcement.

Every officer of government must be continually making investigations and determinations to enlighten him as to how to transact the ordinary business of his office. The policeman who is about to make an arrest must satisfy himself as to the identity and guilt of the person upon whom he intends to lay hands. The postmaster who is about to accept a parcel for the mail must determine its weight and the amount of postage due upon it. Determinations of this kind are usually of such minor consequence, and at the same time so necessary a part of administrative routine, that to give them the separate identity implied in the term "adjudication" would be misleading. But further along the scale stands the case where the Postmaster-General is called upon to determine whether a given publication is entitled to second or third class mailing privileges. At first glance the situation seems identical with

much as to the expediency of the action which it is proposed to take." Goodnow, *Principles of the Administrative Law of the United States*, p. 9.

[41] In theory the judgment of the court has only an indirect connection with the action of the sheriff. The judgment is an authority to the plaintiff. The sheriff in levying execution acts as the plaintiff's representative. The operation of equity procedure is different and discloses the essentially "administrative" character of equity jurisdiction. Pound, *Class Lectures on Equity*, Harvard Law School (MS.). See also Langdell, *Brief Survey of Equity Jurisdiction*, Art. II, in *Harv. Law Rev.*, i, at pp. 116, 117.

that of a local postmaster determining the amount of postage due on a letter; and we may therefore say that the Postmaster-General makes his decision merely to enlighten himself in transacting the routine duties of his office; but it is obvious that his decision will substantially affect individual property rights, and may even cause the success or ruin of a private business venture. Yet in such cases the courts often speak of the determination as a mere part of carrying on the business of an executive department.[42] So it has been said that the action of the Commissioner of the General Land Office in passing on the validity of land claims "necessarily involves the exercise of judgment and may properly be called a quasi-judicial proceeding; but it is none the less a proceeding taken in the discharge of an executive duty of the Commissioner. . . . They are none the less executive duties because they require in their performance the examination of evidence and the exercise of judgment thereon." [43]

III

Just as certain things thus tend to obscure the fact that administrative adjudications are adjudications at all, so because the administrative process belongs as a whole to the so-called "executive" branch of government, it is not always clearly recognized that it permeates a number of essentially different governmental operations, in each of which it has a different significance and character. First of all, the executive department performs a group of tasks which have always belonged to it, and are of a primarily "political" nature — for example, the making of treaties and war and peace, the command of the army and navy, and the control of foreign rela-

[42] See Public Clearing House *v.* Coyne, 194 U. S. 497, language cited below at pp. 57, 58. The important bearing which an administrative determination of the Post-Office Department, *e.g.*, a decision to issue a fraud order, may have on private rights is clearly pointed out in the dissenting opinion of Mr. Justice Holmes in Leach *v.* Carlile, 258 U. S. 138. See below, p. 57, note 60.

[43] The passage quoted is from a ruling of Mr. Justice Lamar, while Secretary of the Interior, in 5 Land Decisions, 483; but the courts have often held the same language: see, *e. g.*, Matthews, J., in Craig *v.* Leitensdorfer, 123 U. S. 189, at p. 211, cited below at p. 279.

tions. In order properly to perform these tasks, which go directly to the safety and existence of the state, determinations of law and fact have to be made which sometimes affect the rights of individuals; and these determinations must be made by the executive itself if it is to discharge its duties efficiently in a field where so much depends on promptness and undivided responsibility. Thus, for example, it is for the executive to determine whether the need exists to call out the militia; [44] whether a state of war exists; [45] and whether or not a given individual is a diplomatic representative of a foreign power.[46] Such determinations for the most part affect private rights only in the more or less exceptional instances where the latter lie athwart the larger lines of governmental policies; and to adjudications of this character there will not be much occasion for reference hereafter.[47]

[44] Martin *v.* Mott, 12 Wheat. 19; Hartranft's Appeal, 85 Pa. St. 433.

[45] Prize Cases, 2 Black, 665.

[46] In re Baiz, 135 U. S. 403.

[47] Act of State.—This class of matters for exclusive executive determination covers, and in the main coincides with, what is called "matter of state": see W. Harrison Moore, *Act of State in English Law*, London and New York, 1906. The courts refuse to adjudicate such matters, or to look behind the determinations reached as to them by the executive, because of their essentially "political" nature. Other questions of this sort besides those mentioned in the text are whether territory belongs to one sovereign or another (Foster *v.* Neilson, 2 Peters, 253; Williams *v.* Suffolk Insurance Co., 13 Peters, 415; in re Cooper, 143 U. S. 474); whether given territory is or is not hostile (Blackburn *v.* Thompson, 3 Campbell, 61); whether a foreign government is duly recognized (United States *v.* Palmer, 3 Wheaton, 610). When in a case coming before a court the defendant establishes that the question at issue is properly a "matter of state," the court will give judgment in his favor without going into the merits (Buron *v.* Denman, 2 Exchequer, 167; *cf.* Mitchell *v.* Clark, 110 U. S. 633). Whether the courts will look behind the determination of the executive as to the existence of a state of war is a question on which there is some confusion. It would seem that they will not (Prize Cases, 2 Black, 665); but they will examine the question whether or not a state of actual war exists in a given territory at a given time (Ex parte Milligan, 4 Wall. 1; Ex parte Marais, [1902] A. C. 109; Moore, *op. cit.*, p. 39). Immigration cases, or, at any rate, exclusion cases as distinguished from expulsion cases, seem *prima facie* to belong in this category of acts of state; see Musgrove *v.* Chung Teeong Toy, [1891] A. C. 272, and Moore, *op. cit.*, p. 95. Thus the United States Supreme Court in the Chinese Exclusion Cases (130 U. S. 581) derived the power of Congress to pass the exclusion acts from its power to make war and take other defensive measures against encroachment from abroad; and in Tiaco *v.* Forbes,

These "political" tasks, forming as they do the traditional backbone of the activities of the executive branch of government, may be arbitrarily designated as "executive" to distinguish them from the heavier weight of other tasks which have been laid on that department in recent years. These other functions may be called more aptly "administrative," and may be treated as falling into two groups: (1) the public-service functions of government, and (2) its functions of police regulation.

Governments have been more and more becoming agencies for the direct supply of public services to their constituents.[48] The oldest instance is the post-office. Other examples in the case of our Federal government are the Bureau of War Risk Insurance, the Shipping Board, and the Irrigation Service. Municipalities frequently engage in the supply of water and light to their inhabitants. Closely analogous to the administration of such business or quasi-business projects is the task of administering the distribution of a fund, as in the case of pensions, or of a domain, such as the public lands. In all these instances the government stands on one side of an essentially business relationship, and the individual, as customer or beneficiary, on the other. In this field, accordingly, it is not unfair to regard administrative adjudication as primarily a step in carrying on the business of government; it adjudicates what may be called for the sake of con-

228 U. S. 549, the expulsion of aliens by the Governor-General of the Philippines without express Congressional authorization was upheld by the Supreme Court in part on the doctrine of "act of state." For an out-and-out denial of the doctrine of "act of state" except as against aliens, see Stephen, *History of the Criminal Law*, ii, 65. Revenue or tax cases have never been treated on the doctrine of "act of state," but much the same freedom and finality of governmental action has been allowed. See the language of Miller, J., in Cheatham *v.* U. S. (1875), 92 U. S. 85: "The revenue measures of every sovereign government constitute a system which provides for its enforcement by officers commissioned for that purpose. In this country this system provides safeguards of its own against mistake, injustice or oppression without resort to the courts." See also language of the Court in Passavant *v.* United States, 148 U. S. 214, at p. 220. An excellent view of the extreme lengths to which the courts go in refusing to disturb the determinations of tax officials can be had from the review of New York tax cases in E. V. Abbot's *Justice and the Modern Law*, pp. 205 ff.

[48] Duguit, *Law and the Modern State*, tr. Laski, *passim*.

venience the statutory "privileges" of individuals rather than their more fundamental "rights."

Finally comes the executive's function of police, or law enforcement — that is, of compelling individuals to respect the interests of others and the claims of the social security.[49] This, unlike the class of matters just considered, is a very old function of the executive, but its character has been deeply affected by the recent developments. It is here that the substitution of regulation by government for regulation by law has gone on, resulting in increased work of an altered kind for the executive. No longer does it have merely to step in through sheriff or marshal to enforce the ready-made judg-

[49] Freund, *Police Power*, § 3. Professor Freund's classification differs from that here adopted in that he groups the functions of government into (1) those pertaining to the maintenance of the national existence; (2) those having to do with the maintenance of right and justice; and (3) those concerning the public welfare (*op. cit.*, § 4). His first group thus corresponds exactly with what have been spoken of above as political or "executive" functions, including the exercise of the taxing power. On the other hand, he does not recognize as a separate group the functions pertaining to the supply of public services, but includes these in his third group (§ 8). In this third group he also includes the exercise of the police power as he defines the term. In the classification which I suggest, the police function would cover not only a part of Professor Freund's third group, but also much that he includes in his second group, for the distinction that he draws between his second and third groups seems largely to follow the procedural line between matters left to be regulated between individuals by the courts and those where the state thrusts itself in, either by administrative regulation or criminal punishment, as an interested party. Procedurally such a line can be drawn, coinciding, except as to criminal action, with the distinction taken above between regulation by law alone and regulation by government. This seems to be the distinction Professor Freund has in mind when he says that "no community confines its care of the public welfare solely to the enforcement of the principles of the common law" (§ 8). But functions which are in substance the same will in the course of time pass from one side to the other of the procedural line as the substitution takes place which we are here studying. Every matter of private law may, and generally does, invólve some issue of public policy. There is merely a difference of remoteness. In considering Professor Freund's classification it must therefore be kept in mind that in many fields of regulation public welfare or policy first makes its appearance in common-law adjudications of differences between individuals. This policy in the course of time may come to be enforced directly by an administrative agency or by criminal proceedings. But it would seem that the function of government performed is in both instances the same, namely, "that of promoting the public welfare by restraining and regulating the use of liberty and property" (*ibid.*, pref. p. iii).

ment of a law court, but it is armed with machinery for making and enforcing orders of its own, aimed more accurately at some of the same objects as the law administered in the courts. The fact that in this field, as elsewhere, administrative adjudication is only preparatory to a governmental act creates a specious resemblance, and often produces a misleading confusion, between administrative adjudication in the exercise of the police power and in the field of administering the business of government.

In both, government adjudicates in order to act; but it should not be overlooked that the purpose of the act ahead bears a decidedly different emphasis. In the one instance it is primarily the getting of a piece of business done; in the other it is the safeguarding of rights and interests. In the latter situation the element of adjudication is accordingly more vital than in the former. It may properly be objected that rights and interests ought to be no less attended to by government when it is getting its business done than when it is administering police regulation; and the case of the Postmaster-General determining the classification to accord to a given piece of printed matter enforces the criticism. At the same time it is clear that the administrative method of enforcement, when applied in the field of police regulation, has a strong tendency to cause considerations of policy to become controlling even in that field to almost the same degree that they control the conduct of the business or political functions of government.

The widened area thus opened to the influence of considerations of policy and expediency is the critical issue involved in a substitution of police regulation by governmental action for regulation by law alone. To entrust an administrative agency with the determination of individual rights and interests, as in connection with the rates to be charged by a public carrier or the freedom to practise a profession, cannot but make those rights more flexible, and more responsive to uncertain factors of discretion, than when they are left to be defined by the more rigid processes of a court applying supposedly permanent rules of law. Under the old system of adjudication by courts of law alone, the process of adjudication went on within a separate cell or compartment, as it were, tightly closed off from the sphere of governmental action. There was thus made possible a single-minded attention to the individual rights of the parties immediately before the court, with only an accidental regard for the interests of the public at large, and with a disregard for the exigencies of social policy which has been congenial to the naïve individualism embedded in the philosophy of our law.[50] The introduction of administrative justice, on the other hand, with the resulting opportunity for policy and discretion to affect the determination of individual rights, is one of the ways in which the newer philosophy of social solidarity has been making its influence felt. It marks a recognition of the fact that in the determination of the rights of individuals, as well as in the conduct of governmental enterprises, the interests of the community as a whole ought to be consulted. But there is still a truth embodied in the older system which is not obsolete. While it must be admitted that the shifting complex of human relations calls for an ever-changing course of conduct on the part of governments as well as of individuals, and for that intelligent manipulation of these changes which is what we mean by discretion or policy, it is equally true that the more intricate and mobile a field of human relationships is, the more it needs to be reduced to order if healthy individual and social growth is to have room to go on; and order demands

[50] For the extent to which consideration of social policy worked themselves into the system of the common law, see Freund, *Standards of American Legislation*, ch. ii. "Most of the common law has developed in that atmosphere of indifferent neutrality which has enabled courts to be impartial, but also keeps them out of touch with vital needs. When interests are litigated in particular cases, they not only appear as scattered and isolated interests, but their social incidence is obscured by the adventitious personal factors which color every controversy. If policy means the conscious favoring of social above particular interests, the common law must be charged with having too little policy," *ibid.*, p. 48. An example of the characteristic refusal of the courts to look beyond the particular litigants to the social issues of the controversy was exhibited on the trial of Michaels Stern & Co. *v.* The Amalgamated Clothing Workers of America, at Rochester, N. Y., in 1920. See *The New Republic*, May 19, 1920, p. 372.

the maintenance of some fixed points of permanence and stability. This is the enduring kernel embedded in our traditional system of adjudication by courts applying a body of supposedly definite and permanent law, uninfluenced by changing considerations of political expediency. To use Bagehot's expression, society needs a "cake of custom" as well as the capacity to break through it; but, what Bagehot did not so much emphasize, it seems always to need both at the same time.[51] Thus arises an apparent antinomy between administrative justice on the one hand and the "supremacy of law" on the other.

[51] See Pound, *Introduction to the Philosophy of Law*, p. 19; also *Interpretations of Legal History*, p. 1: "Law must be stable and yet it cannot stand still. Hence all thinking about law has struggled to reconcile the conflicting demands of the need of stability and the need of change."

CHAPTER II

THE SUPREMACY OF LAW AND THE REVIEW OF ADMINISTRATIVE DETERMINATIONS BY THE COURTS

THE introduction of administrative justice has encountered in our constitutional doctrine of the "separation of powers" a barrier which has been evaded only by the invention of a new set of glaring legal fictions embodied in such words as "quasi-legislative," "quasi-judicial," and the like.[1] To review the development of these fictions would supply an instructive commentary on an important branch of American constitutional law, but it would not shed helpful light on the more fundamental problems presented by the substitution of administrative justice for adjudication by courts of law. These problems reach below the special limitations of American constitutional law and turn up for inspection some of the deepest principles of the Anglo-American legal system.

I

In Anglo-American jurisprudence, government and law have always in a sense stood opposed to one another; the law has been rather something to give the citizen a check on the government than an instrument to give the government control over the citizen.[2] There is a famous passage, which was long attributed to Bracton, to the effect that "the King has a superior, to wit, the law; and if he be without a bridle, a bridle ought to be put on him, namely, the law."[3] This "rule of law," as Dicey calls it, or "supremacy of law," in Lieber's phrase, has been uniformly treated as the central and most characteristic feature of our Anglo-American juris-

[1] Maitland said that "*quasi* is one of the few Latin words that English lawyers really love." H. A. L. Fisher, *F. W. Maitland*, p. 161.

[2] See Sir J. F. Stephen, *History of the Criminal Law*, ii, 65.

[3] Bracton, fol. 34; see McIlwain, *High Court of Parliament*, p. 101; Maitland, *Bracton's Note Book*, i, 29–34.

tic habit; and nothing has been held more fundamental to the supremacy of law than the right of every citizen to bring the action of government officials to trial in the ordinary courts of the common law. That government officials, on the contrary, should themselves assume to perform the functions of a law court and determine the rights of individuals, as is the case under a system of administrative justice, has been traditionally felt to be inconsistent with the supremacy of law. It was the ground of attack on the Court of Star Chamber, and on equity jurisdiction in the days when the Chancellor was still mainly an administrative officer of the King.[4] Lieber mentions freedom from "government by commissions," and from the jurisdiction of executive courts, as one of the elements of Anglo-American liberty.[5]

[4] G. M. Trevelyan, *England under the Stuarts*, p. 164; A. V. Dicey, *Law of the Constitution*, 8th ed., p. 375; A. Lawrence Lowell, *The Government of England*, ii, 474 ff. James I in deciding in favor of Lord Chancellor Ellesmere in his famous controversy with Coke based his decision on the significant ground that "it appertained only to his princely office to judge over all his judges . . . as he in his princely wisdom should find to stand most with his honour," Blackstone's *Commentaries*, ed. Christian, iii, 55.

[5] *Civil Liberty and Self-Government*, 2d ed. (1859), p. 109. *Cf.* also the following from the "Essex Result" of 1778: "Should the executive and judicial powers be united, the subject would then have no permanent security of his person and property. The executive power would interpret the laws and bend them to his will; and, as he is the judge, he may leap over them by artful constructions, and gratify, with impunity, the most rapacious passions. Perhaps no cause in any state has contributed more to promote internal convulsions, and to stain the scaffold with its best blood, than this unhappy union. And it is a union which the executive power in all states, hath attempted to form; if that could not be compassed, to make the judicial power dependent upon it." Theophilus Parsons, *Memoir of Theophilus Parsons* (Boston, 1859), at p. 374. This is almost pure Montesquieu (*Esprit des Lois*, xi, 6); but it serves to show that what our ancestors had in mind in their hostility to "executive" courts was mainly the ever present fear that the great political officers of government, — *i. e.*, the king and his ministers, or, under a republican form of government, the chief executive, — might come to control the machinery of justice, rather than any theoretical objection to the union of administrative and judicial *functions* in the hands of *minor* officials. As a matter of fact, at least the more southern colonies early borrowed the English system of local administration which embodied a wide combination of executive and judicial duties in the hands of justices of the peace and county courts. Thus in Maryland the county courts levied taxes (Acts of 1704, *Archives of Maryland*, xxvi, 292), fixed the boundaries of parishes (Acts of 1713, *ibid.*, xxix, 338), and appointed road supervisors (Acts of 1704, *ibid.*, xxvi, 250) and other administrative officials. In

What do we mean when we speak of the supremacy of law, and why do we so insist on it? What is the bearing on it of the widening area of administrative jurisdiction? And wherein is administrative jurisdiction opposed to it?

The orthodox doctrine of the supremacy of law has been stated by Dicey as including two principles: "It means in the first place that no man can lawfully be made to suffer in body or goods except for a distinct breach of law established in the ordinary courts of the land."[6] It means in the second place "that no man is above the law, but that every man, whatever his rank or condition, is subject to the ordinary law of the realm, and amenable to the jurisdiction of the ordinary tribunals. . . . With us, every official, from the Prime Minister down to a constable or collector of taxes, is under the same responsibility for every act done without legal justification as any other citizen."[7]

Virginia they supervised the schools, levied taxes, voted expenditures, and appointed the sheriffs (Philip Alexander Bruce, *Institutional History of Virginia*, i, 337; ii, 558). In New York they had similar duties (G. E. Howard, *Introduction to Local Constitutional History*, p. 363). Thomas Jefferson wrote in 1816 of the Virginia county courts: "I acknowledge the value of this institution; it is in truth our principal executive and judiciary," letter to John Taylor, July 16, 1816 (*Complete Works*, ed. H. A. Washington, vii, 18). In Kentucky and Tennessee the county courts still combine judicial and administrative functions (Beard, *American Government and Politics*, ed. 1925, p. 770; Fairlie, *Local Government in Counties, Towns, and Villages*, p. 98). On the other hand, the kind of combination of judicial and executive functions to which our fathers objected is illustrated by the case of Magdalen College, *State Trials*, xii, 1–114. There James II sought to deprive the Fellows of their rights, and Dr. Hough, the President of the College, of his office, by the decree of an executive commission, acting ostensibly in a judicial manner, but really in entire subserviency to the King's arbitrary personal policy. This drew from Dr. Hough his famous protest: "I am possessed of a freehold according to the laws of England . . . and therefore I cannot submit to this sentence because I think I cannot be deprived of my freehold but by course of law in Westminster Hall" (*State Trials*, xii, 31). "I do protest against your proceedings as illegal, unjust, and null; and do appeal to our sovereign lord the King in his courts of justice" (Smith's Narrative, in *ibid.*, xii, 62). The objection was not so much to a combination of "executive" and "judicial" *functions*, as to the subordination of the machinery of justice to the central political arm of the government, — *i. e.*, the "executive."

[6] *Law of the Constitution*, 8th ed., p. 183.

[7] *Ibid.*, p. 189. An interesting suggestion has been made as to the origin in the English legal system of this principle which is so peculiar to it and found

In short, every citizen is entitled, first, to have his rights adjudicated in a regular common-law court, and, secondly, to call into question in such a court the legality of any act done by an administrative official.

The first of these principles is overridden by a procedure under which a man may have his property destroyed by a health officer, or a railroad be ordered to decrease its rates by a utilities commission, or an employer be compelled to pay compensation to an injured employee by an industrial-accident board. For these bodies are not "ordinary courts" in Dicey's sense. "Judicial" as their functions clearly seem to be, they are not "courts" in the common-law meaning of the term. And they differ from common-law courts in precisely the particulars which furnish the reasons for the common law's insistence that every individual shall be entitled to have his rights tried in a law court. The crucial qualities of a common-law court which are absent from the administrative tribunals are at least three, two of them being procedural and one substantive. Administrative tribunals are not bound by the procedural safeguards which mould the outcome of an action at law; more specifically, they are, in the first place, not bound by the common-law rules of evidence,[8] and in the second place, parties to proceedings before them do not have the benefit of a jury trial. The substantive difference between the administrative procedure and the procedure at law is that the administrative tribunals decide controversies

nowhere else: "Since the courts [in England] were royal courts, since the law was royal law, since no justice was known but the King's and its conduct lay wholly in the hands of his trained servants, there was no reason for the King to look with jealousy on the authority exercised by the law over any of his officers or servants. It may possibly be due to this fact that, in England alone of all countries in the world, the police, the civil servants, the soldiers, are tried in the same courts and by the same code as any private citizen." Mrs. John Richard Green, *Henry II*, p. 124.

[8] See Perry *v.* Industrial Accident Commission, 180 Cal. 497; Reck *v.* Whittlesberger, 181 Mich. 463; In re Feldman, *Justice of the Peace*, lxxi, 269; John H. Wigmore, "Administrative Boards and Commissions: Are the Jury Trial Rules of Evidence in Force for their Inquiries?" *Illinois Law Rev.*, xvii, 262 ff.; F. A. Ross, "Rules of Evidence before Commissions," *Harv. Law Rev.*, xxxvi, 263 ff.

coming before them, not by fixed rules of law, but by the application of governmental discretion or policy.[9]

It is this last point of difference that is of capital interest here. The competition between administrative and legal justice is in one of its aspects a phase of the age-old struggle between discretion and fixed rule, between νόμος and ἐπιείκεια, between equity and the strict law.[10] But it has other aspects also. Administrative tribunals do not have that independence from government which is one of the traditionally prized guaranties of the justice administered by our common-law courts. Their adjudications, taking place as very part and parcel of the process of government, are exposed to the influence of all the political forces which act upon government.[11] But the independence of the courts is closely associated with the fact that their procedure centers on a controversy between individuals, which can be adjudicated more or less in a vacuum by the application of abstract rules. So that their valued independence is important among other reasons as but a further way of bringing about the subordination of policy to fixed and general rules.

II

In so far as administrative adjudication is coming in certain fields to take the place of adjudication by law courts, the

[9] In a sense the difference between administrative tribunals and law courts in the matter of admitting evidence, the one following the more or less rigid common-law rules, the other not, is an added illustration of the contrast between rule and discretion.

[10] "The chief problem to which legal thinkers have addressed themselves has been how to reconcile the idea of a fixed body of law, affording no scope for individual wilfulness, with the idea of change and growth. . . . Put more concretely, the problem of compromise between the need of stability and the need of change becomes in one aspect a problem of adjustment between rule and discretion, between administering justice according to settled rule, or at most by rigid deduction from narrowly fixed premises, and administration of justice according to the more or less trained intuition of experienced magistrates. In one way or another almost all of the vexed questions of the science of law prove to be phases of this same problem." Pound, *Interpretations of Legal History*, p. 1.

[11] *E.g.*, in connection with the granting or denial of mailing privileges: *cf.* United States ex rel. Milwaukee Social Democratic Pub. Co. *v.* Burleson, 255

supremacy of law as formulated in Dicey's first proposition is overridden. But a possible way of escaping this result is left open by his second proposition. An administrative determination is an act of a governmental officer or officers; and if it be true that all the acts of such officers are subject to be questioned in the courts, it is then possible to have the issue of any questionable administrative adjudication raised and decided anew in a law court, with the special advantages and guaranties of the procedure at law. We here see the reason why the question of court review of administrative determinations has come to be of such central importance and has been the focus of so much discussion since the rise of the administrative procedure. For just in so far as administrative determinations are subject to court review, a means exists for maintaining the supremacy of law, though at one remove and as a sort of secondary line of defence. The special advantages of the administrative procedure may be substantially retained, while at the same time, in a given case, the result can be brought to the test of the procedure at law.[12] Administrative

U. S. 406 (the "Milwaukee Leader" case), and dissenting opinions of Holmes and Brandeis, JJ.

[12] There seems to be a growing doubt in England as to the validity of Dicey's sweeping generalization. Thus in a very recent book it is said: "Professor Dicey has laid great emphasis on what he calls the 'Rule of Law' as distinguishing the liability of public servants in this country to answer for their acts in the same way and to the same extent as any private person who infringes the legal rights of another. . . . How far is this true? Now it may be said at once that even at Common Law many public servants, using that term in its widest sense, enjoy a special immunity from the consequences of their acts which does not apply to private persons — immunities which are entirely ignored by Professor Dicey in the elaboration of his attractive thesis. The immunity of judges is an obvious case. It is no doubt a rule of law made in the public interest, but it none the less puts a large class of public servants, including even Justices of the Peace, who are many, in a special position. So, too, with officers of police whose protection at Common Law, when they act 'wrongfully' but in the execution of a warrant regular on the face of it, has been extended by statute. Customs and Excise officers also enjoy a considerable measure of statutory protection. . . . These are all cases of that 'protection given to servants of the State in the *bona fide* attempt to discharge public duties' which Professor Dicey would regard as something invidious and peculiar to foreign countries." Professor J. H. Morgan, in *Public Authorities and Legal Liability*, by Gleeson E. Robinson, London, 1925, pp. xlix–li.

justice exists in defiance of the supremacy of law only in so far as administrative adjudications are final or conclusive, and not subject to correction by a law court. To some undefined extent, however, they are final, and there seems to be a tendency at work to make them increasingly so. The purpose of the following chapter will be to inspect this tendency as it is exhibited in the cases.

CHAPTER III

THE CONCLUSIVENESS OF ADMINISTRATIVE DETERMINATIONS[1]

I

FOLLOWING its usual process of growth by analogy, our law has begun with the fact that administrative tribunals are composed of public officers, and has applied to them the rules governing court control of the acts of such officers. Long before administrative boards and commissions grew up under the police power, a fairly complete judicial control was exercised over public officers in three ways: first, by civil suits or criminal prosecutions against such officers in their private capacity for alleged illegal acts committed in the discharge of their official duties; second, by the opportunity of the courts to pass on the validity of the acts of public officers where the latter were obliged to resort to the courts for aid in enforcing their orders; and, lastly, by the power of the courts to issue certain extraordinary writs to restrain or compel administrative action.

An early example of the first method is the case of the Marshalsea.[2] This was an action in the King's Bench against the Marshal of the King's Household for falsely imprisoning the plaintiff under a *capias* issued out of the Court of the Marshalsea of the Household in an action of assumpsit, neither of the parties to the latter action having been members of the Household. Whether or not the Court of the Marshalsea had jurisdiction of such an action was a disputed point of law. The King's Bench held that the Court of the Marshalsea was without jurisdiction, and that there-

[1] It is not the purpose of this chapter to attempt to present a complete summary of what is one of the largest and most confused topics of the modern law. All that is intended is to open up by way of the cases some of the vexed issues which are treated in greater detail in subsequent chapters.

[2] 10 Coke Rep., 68b.

fore, although the defendant had acted on the precept of his lawful superior, he was liable in damages for false imprisonment. "When the court has jurisdiction of the cause and proceeds erroneously, there no action lies against the officer or minister who executes the precept of the court. But when the court has not jurisdiction of the cause, there the whole proceeding is *coram non judice*, and actions will lie against them without regard to the precept or process, for it is not of necessity to obey him who is not a judge of the cause." And in Simpson's case, where a pursuivant was sent by the High Commission to arrest X, and X, in resisting arrest, killed the pursuivant, it was held to be no murder, for the High Commission had no jurisdiction to order the arrest.[3]

An example of the second method of judicial control over public officers occurs in connection with the collection of taxes. Here it has been held that tax officials may not, in the absence of statutory authority, resort to summary methods of collection, but must proceed against the delinquent taxpayer by an action at law.[4] But the courts have generally, on grounds of policy, limited their control over tax officials by accepting as final, and refusing to review, the valuation of property made by assessors "in the proper exercise of their discretion," and will give judgment against the officials only where the latter are shown to have "exceeded their authority," or applied rules clearly contrary to law.[5]

Finally, judicial control over the acts of public officers has been exercised by means of the extraordinary writs of mandamus, certiorari, habeas corpus and injunction.[6] The purpose of these writs is to protect individual rights where administrative decisions may be directly enforced without the aid of the courts, or where, because of the nature of the administrative action in question, a subsequent suit against the

[3] 12 Coke Rep., 49. [4] Bergen *v.* Clarkson, 1 Halsted (N. J. L.) 352.

[5] Taylor *v.* Louisville, etc. R. R. Co., 88 Fed. 350; Spencer & Gardner *v.* People, 68 Ill. 510; and cases cited in Freund, *Cases on Administrative Law*, p. 579, note.

[6] With the writs of *quo warranto*, used to try title to public offices, and of prohibition, used to control the action of inferior courts, we are not here concerned.

officer would not afford an adequate remedy.[7] Thus an injunction will issue to prevent the taking of property by government officials under the power of eminent domain where no provision has been made for the assessment of compensation.[8] Mandamus has lain to a jailer, to compel the delivery to an executor of a body to be buried;[9] it has lain to a court of common pleas, to compel them to restore to office an attorney whom they had improperly disbarred;[10] and to the Postmaster-General of the United States to compel him to credit the petitioners with sums found due them under an award.[11]

In the exercise of their control of public officers, the courts have, however, set limits to their jurisdiction in a variety of ways, involving very nice distinctions. In the first place, the extent of court review is limited by the theory on which it is usually placed. This is, that the courts are mulcting public officers in damages, or refusing to aid them, or restraining them by injunction, because the action which they have taken, or propose to take, is not authorized by law. More narrowly, on this theory, what the courts are concerned with is only whether the officer is, or is not, acting "within his jurisdiction." The theory is that every public officer has marked out for him by law a certain area of "jurisdiction." Within the boundaries of this area he can act freely according to his own discretion, and the courts will respect his action as final and not inquire into its rightfulness. But if he oversteps those bounds, then the courts will intervene. In this form, the law of court review of the acts of public officers becomes simply a branch of the law of *ultra vires*. The only question before the court is one of jurisdiction, and the court has no control over the officer's exercise of discretion within that jurisdiction.[12]

[7] Goodnow, *Principles of the Administrative Law of the United States*, p. 419.

[8] Gardner *v.* Village of Newburgh, 2 Johns. Ch. 162, 2 Kent Com. (4th ed.) 339, note *f*.

[9] Queen *v.* Fox, 2 Q. B. 246.

[10] People *v.* Judges of Delaware, 1 Johns. Cases, 181.

[11] Kendall *v.* United States in re Stokes, 12 Peters, 524; see also Garfield *v.* Goldsby, 211 U. S. 249.

[12] For an exposition of this theory see Wyman's *Administrative Law*, ch. 1. See also W. S. Holdsworth, in *Journal of Society of Public Teachers of Law* (1924), pp. 17 ff., and French *v.* Edwards, 13 Wallace, 506; Mygatt *v.* Washburn, 15 N. Y. 316.

The difficult point to determine is what particular issues go to jurisdiction, and what go to the exercise of discretion. It is sometimes said or assumed that public officers have no jurisdiction to determine questions of law and that therefore, as to these, their action is not final, but is subject to court review. But not even this can be laid down safely as a general rule,[13] and nice distinctions have been taken. It was an old rule that, where suit was brought against an officer for action taken under the precept of a court, judgment would be given against the defendant only where the court was shown to have been without jurisdiction and not where there had been mere error in its exercise of jurisdiction, though it were error of law. Thus it was said that "if the Court of Common Pleas in a plea of debt awards a *capias* against a duke or earl, which by the law does not lie against them and that appears in the writ itself; and if the sheriff arrests them by force of the *capias*, although the writ be against law, notwithstanding, inasmuch as the Court has jurisdiction of the cause, the sheriff is excused." [14]

[13] The courts have often used language clearly stating that administrative officers may have a final power of interpreting the law; *e.g.*, Mr. Justice Shepard in Seymour *v.* United States, 2 Ap. D. C. 240: "The executive department is charged with perfectly independent duties which require the ascertainment of facts, involve the interpretation of laws, and in many respects call for the exercise of judgment and discretion; and this independence is so complete that no matter how gross an error may be committed in the exercise of these duties, the courts are nevertheless powerless to interfere." *Cf.* also language of Mr. Justice Bradley in Dunlap *v.* Black, 128 U. S. 40: "The courts will not interfere by mandamus with the executive officers of the government in the exercise of their ordinary official duties, even where those duties require an interpretation of law." So in Riverside Oil Co. *v.* Hitchcock, 190 U.S. 316, at p. 364, the Court said: "Whether the Secretary of the Interior decided rightly or wrongly is not the question. Having jurisdiction to decide at all, it was his duty to decide as he thought the law was." It is to be noted that all these were cases of application for mandamus. This procedural fact no doubt led the courts into broader language than they would otherwise have used. See below, p. 63. The fact that the courts will not issue a writ of mandamus in a given situation hardly means that they would not review the executive action taken if the question could be got before them in some other way.

[14] Case of the Marshalsea, 10 Coke Rep. 76; Countess of Rutland's Case, 6 Coke Rep. 54.

Again, the rules governing the issue of the extraordinary writs have, with the accretion of precedent, become extremely rigid and technical. One writ must be used in one kind of case and another in another; and a writ which will issue for a given purpose in one state may not be available for the same purpose elsewhere. Thus in some states decisions of particular administrative authorities must be reviewed by certiorari;[15] in others, certiorari will lie only to review the action of a "judicial" body.[16] The tendency has

[15] Certiorari is used for three different purposes: (1) to bring up for review the judgment of an inferior court where review is not a matter of right, but of discretion on the part of the upper court; (2) to review convictions in an inferior court of criminal jurisdiction (Rex *v.* Hale, Cowper, 728; Jackson *v.* People, 9 Mich., 111); (3) to review "quasi-judicial" determinations by administrative officials. We are concerned only with the third use of the writ. See Goodnow in *Pol. Sci. Quart.*, vi, 493 ff.

[16] In some states it is held that certiorari will lie to review proceedings not "judicial" in nature: Treasurer *v.* Mulford, 26 N. J. L. 49 (municipal ordinance); Christie *v.* Bayonne, 64 N. J. L. 191 (municipal ordinance); State *v.* Clark, 21 N. D. 517 (resolution of city council); State *v.* Hughes County, 1 S. D. 292 (regulation made by county commissioners). But in most jurisdictions the courts say that the writ will issue only to review acts "partaking of a judicial nature." This raises the whole question of what acts are judicial. This is the same question that is presented by the constitutional doctrine of the separation of powers, but the decisions when the question is raised as to whether certiorari will lie do not square at all with those reached when the question is as to the separation of powers. Thus, for purposes of certiorari it has been held in state courts that the determinations of public service commissions are judicial (People ex rel. Joline *v.* Willcox, 194 N. Y. 383; People ex rel. Brooklyn Heights R. R. Co. *v.* Public Service Commission, 157 App. Div. N. Y. 698; Gulf and Ship Island R. R. Co. *v.* Adams, 85 Miss., 772), though the same kind of determinations are held "administrative" or "legislative" for the purpose of the doctrine of separation of powers. See also Imperial Water Co. *v.* Imperial County, 162 Cal. 14, and cases cited in 11 *Corpus Juris*, art. "Certiorari," 369. In New York the scope of certiorari is unusually broad: it has been allowed for the review of determinations of tax-officials, appointing officers, and other administrative agencies (People ex rel. Manhattan R. Co. *v.* Barker, 152 N. Y. 417; People ex rel. Cook *v.* Board of Police, 39 N. Y. 506). But it was said that certiorari would not lie to review the determination of a health board on a question of nuisance, People ex rel. Copcutt *v.* Board of Health, 140 N. Y. 1, at p. 10, because the board could act without a hearing. The scope of certiorari is especially limited in the procedure of the Federal Courts. It has been held (Degge *v.* Hitchcock, 229 U. S. 162) that certiorari will not lie to review the issuance of a fraud order by the Postmaster-General. The court said: "It is true that the Postmaster-General gave notice and a hearing to the persons specially to be affected by the order, and that in making his

been in effect to restrict each remedy arbitrarily to the particular situations enumerated in prior decisions within the jurisdiction.

II

To the boards and commissions which have sprung up in recent years the courts have applied the same methods of control which had been worked out in the decisions dealing with the older types of public officers.[17] Thus in Miller *v.* Horton, where a horse was killed by order of a board of animal inspectors, the owner was allowed to recover damages in trespass on a finding by a jury that the animal was not in fact diseased and that hence the officers acted "without jurisdiction." [18] So in Pearson *v.* Zehr, the court sustained a judgment against members of a board of live-stock commissioners for killing horses which the jury found did not have the glanders, saying that unless the fact of glanders existed, the killing was "in excess of jurisdiction" and without authority of law.[19] Fath *v.* Koeppel,[20] an action against a meat

ruling he may be said to have acted in a quasi-judicial capacity. But the statute was passed primarily for the benefit of the public at large, and the order was for them and their protection. That fact gave an administrative quality to the hearing and to the order, and was sufficient to prevent it from being subject to review by writ of certiorari." Is not the sentence of a law-court in a criminal trial "primarily for the benefit of the public at large," and does that render the action of the court "administrative"?

[17] Certain kinds of administrative determinations may also be opened up for review by collateral attack. Thus, where the United States Land Office has patented land to one claimant, a usual method of seeking court review is for the other claimant to bring an action in ejectment or a proceeding to quiet title, and when the patentee sets up his title by patent, to attack its validity. Johnson *v.* Towsley, 13 Wall. 72. Review by such collateral attack is, however, exceptional. As a general rule, it is held that a so-called "quasi-judicial" administrative determination is, like a judgment, not subject to collateral attack: Kennedy *v.* Gibson, 8 Wall. 488 (order of controller of currency); Providence Rubber Co. *v.* Goodyear, 9 Wall. 788 (patent for invention); Casey *v.* Galli, 94 U. S. 673 (order of controller of currency); United States *v.* McDowell, 21 Fed. 563 (appraisement by customs appraiser). Of course review in the form of a damage suit against the official is properly "collateral" attack and is for this reason occasionally disallowed. United States Trust Co. *v.* Mayor, 144 N. Y. 488.

[18] 152 Mass. 540.

[19] 138 Ill. 48.

[20] 72 Wis. 289 (1888). The same doctrine was applied in Ela *v.* Smith, 5 Gray (Mass.), 121 (1855) to the act of the mayor of a city in calling out the

inspector for the destruction of fish which the plaintiff claimed were not in fact unwholesome, was dismissed on an interesting ground. The court said that the meat inspector was performing a judicial function: "The officer exercising such a power is within the protection of the principle that a ju-

militia. The court said, per Bigelow, J. (at p. 136): "Whenever the law vests in an officer a right of judgment and gives him a discretion to determine the facts on which such judgment is to be based, he necessarily exercises, within the limits of his jurisdiction, a judicial authority. So long as he was within the fair scope of this authority he is clothed with all the rights and immunities which appertain to judicial tribunals.... Of these none is better settled than the wise and salutary rule of law by which all magistrates and officers, even when exercising a special and limited jurisdiction, are exempted from liability for their judgments." So in Downer *v.* Lent (1856), 6 Cal. 94, an action against pilot commissioners for wrongfully revoking a license, the court said: "It is beyond controversy that the power of the board of pilot commissioners is quasi-judicial, and they are not civilly answerable. They are public officers to whom the law has entrusted certain duties the performance of which requires the exercise of judgment. They are unlike a ministerial officer, whose duties are well-defined, and who must fail to exercise them properly at his own peril. Whenever, from the necessity of the case, the law is obliged to trust to the sound judgment and discretion of an officer, public policy demands that he should be protected from any consequences of an erroneous judgment." This tendency to hold that administrative determinations were judicial in character, and that the officers making them were protected by judicial immunity, at least when acting in good faith and from pure motives, is conspicuous in the cases from about 1770 to about 1870. Thus Lord Mansfield said, "No justice of the peace ought to suffer for ignorance where the heart is right," King *v.* Cozens (1780), Douglas, 426; and in a suit against tax-officials for selling the plaintiff's property under a discriminatory assessment, it was said by the New York Supreme Court: "Though they may err in point of law or in judgment, they should not be either civilly or criminally answerable, if their motives are pure. This is the rule applicable to public officers, bound to exercise their deliberative judgments in the discharge of their official duties, and is applicable to all inferior magistrates and others called to the performance of functions in their nature and character judicial," Easton *v.* Calendar (1823), 1 Wendell, 90. These cases rest upon an emphasis of the old distinction between "ministerial" and "judicial" duties of officers (Blackstone, *Commentaries*, ed. Christian, i. 343, 348; Cooley on Torts, 2d ed., pp. 443–445), and represent a willingness to regard administrative decisions as "judicial." It was settled in the time of Coke that a judge was immune from private suit for acts done in his judicial capacity, Floyd *v.* Barker, 12 Coke Rep., 23 at p. 25. "If an action be brought against a judge of record for an action done by him in his judicial capacity, he may plead that he did it as judge of record, and that will be a complete justification," Lord Mansfield in Mostyn *v.* Fabrigas (1774), Cowper 161, at p. 172. But a clear distinction was originally taken between tribunals of "general" and "limited" jurisdiction, — *i. e.* between law-courts on the one hand, and jus-

dicial officer is not responsible in an action for damages to any one for any judgment he may render, however erroneously, negligently, ignorantly, corruptly, or maliciously he may act in rendering it, if the act was within his jurisdiction." Such a ground of decision is hard to square with the doctrine

tices of the peace and administrative tribunals on the other. Thus in Terry *v.* Huntingdon, Hardres, 480, an action of trover for goods levied by warrant of the commissioners of excise, the question was whether an action lay against the officers if they adjudged "low wines" to be "strong waters." Hale, Chief Baron, said: "The commissioners have only a stinted limited jurisdiction, and if they exceed it, that does not take away the jurisdiction of this court. Special jurisdictions are circumscribed (1) with respect to place, as a leet or corporation; (2) with respect to persons; (3) with respect to the subject-matter of their jurisdiction; and the statute limits their jurisdiction in all these three respects, and therefore if they give judgment in a cause arising in another place, or betwixt private persons, or in other matters, all is void and *coram non judice*, as if they should adjudge rose water to be strong water." This is the doctrine of Miller *v.* Horton and Warne *v.* Varley (1795), 6 Durnford & East, 443, holding that where searchers were authorized to seize undried leather, they were liable in an action for seizing leather which was shown in the action to have been not in fact undried. This doctrine permits a reëxamination in the action at law of the administrative determination of facts held to be "jurisdictional." Whether the court review for which room is thus made will be broad or narrow depends upon whether a broad or narrow view is taken as to what facts are "jurisdictional." In Groenvelt *v.* Burwell, 1 Ld. Raymond, 454, where a college of physicians had by their charter authority to punish for malpractice, and had found the plaintiff guilty thereof and punished him, it was held by Lord Holt that their jurisdiction extended not merely over physicians who were in fact unskilful, but over the question of the unskilful administration of physic, and the court therefore regarded their decision as to the plaintiff's skill as conclusive because within their jurisdiction. "A man convict by the defendants in pursuance of their judicial authority cannot traverse the fact of which he is convict," *ibid.*, at p. 467. The whole doctrine of review of findings on "jurisdictional facts" was brushed aside in Seaman *v.* Patten (1805), 2 Caines (N. Y.) 312, nominally on a point of statutory construction, and it was held that where the defendant officer was authorized to remove beef in danger of spoiling, his jurisdiction extended to all beef which in his judgment he regarded as in danger of spoiling. In suits against licensing officials, the courts refused to examine whether there was any proper ground for the refusal of the license, saying that no right of the plaintiff had been violated since "the plaintiff has no right to have a license unless the justices think proper to grant it. The matter is wholly in the discretion of the justices," Basset *v.* Godschall (1770), 3 Wilson 121 at p. 124. These instances of narrowing the scope of review went hand in hand with the extension of the principle of judicial immunity from suit to a large number of administrative officers exercising quasi-judicial functions (Cooley on Torts, 2d ed., p. 479) with only the limitation that they must act in good faith (*ibid.*, pp. 480–482). But with the extension of administrative interference with individual property rights after the middle of the

of separation of powers, and the case has been subsequently overruled.[21]

The second opportunity for judicial review occurs where boards and commissions are required to seek the aid of the courts in enforcing their orders. Thus, under the original Interstate Commerce Act, orders of the Interstate Commerce Commission could be enforced only through proceedings brought by the Commission in a United States Circuit Court;[22] and in such a proceeding the court had of course to pass on the validity of the order. The same opportunity for court review occurs where enforcement of an order takes the form of an action at law to recover a penalty.[23]

Again, the extraordinary writs above enumerated lie to administrative boards and commissions, Thus, mandamus has lain to a board of dental examiners to compel them to

nineteenth century, and with the greater theoretical importance attached at the same time to such rights, a change becomes noticeable in the current of the decisions. Thus in McCord *v.* High (1868), 24 Ia. 336, an action against a road supervisor for disposing of water in a manner injurious to the plaintiff's land, the court said, per Dillon, C. J.: "That the road supervisor is exempt from liability for certain mistakes of judgment, honestly made in the performance of his official duties, I have no question. If his acts be not strictly judicial, they are in certain cases (as, for example, the kind of bridge he will build, or the requisite capacity of a culvert) in the nature of judicial acts, and rest to some extent upon the same principle. . . . The principle which upon the whole I believe to be sound in this: that where a public officer, other than a judicial one, does an act invasive of the private rights of others, and there is otherwise no remedy for the injury, such officer is personally liable, without proof of malice and an intent to injure." This doctrine was crystallized in Mechem on Public Officers, § 642: "Inasmuch as the law quite universally protects private property . . . the judgment or discretion of the quasi-judicial officer, though exercised honestly and in good faith, does not protect him where by virtue of it, he undertakes to invade the private property rights of others, to whom no other redress is given than an action against the officer." The question remains open as to when the quasi-judicial act of an official constitutes an "invasion of the private property rights of others." It is interesting to note that Mechem cites only two cases for his proposition, McCord *v.* High, *supra*, and Cubit *v.* O'Dett, 51 Mich. 347, where the opinion was written by Judge Cooley.

[21] Lowe *v.* Conroy, 120 Wis. 151 (1904).

[22] By the Hepburn Act of 1906 the Commission's orders became effective automatically, subject only to be restrained by injunction.

[23] Village of Carthage *v.* Colligan, 216 N. Y. 217; Oceanic Steam Navigation Co. *v.* Stranahan, 214 U. S. 320; Wadley Southern R. Co. *v.* Georgia, 137 Ga. 497.

grant a license improperly refused;[24] and to the Interstate Commerce Commission to compel it to take jurisdiction of rate questions in Alaska.[25] An injunction will lie to restrain enforcement of an order of a rate commission establishing a rate so low as to be confiscatory;[26] to restrain collection of a confiscatory tax;[27] and to restrain the enforcement of a fraud order issued by the Post-Office Department on legally insufficient grounds.[28] Habeas corpus will be granted to a person improperly detained by immigration officials.[29]

A fourth opening for judicial review is offered when statutes establishing administrative bodies expressly provide that an "appeal" from their orders may be taken to a court.[30]

Finally, a fifth way of getting such review is where the administrative body is allowed by statute to sue for the expense of executing an order after its non-observance by the person to whom it is directed. In such a suit the latter may raise the question of the validity of the order.[31]

[24] Dental Examiners *v.* People ex rel. Cooper, 123 Ill. 227.

[25] Interstate Commerce Commission *v.* United States ex rel. Humboldt Steamship Co., 224 U. S. 472.

[26] See Interstate Commerce Act, 38 U. S. Statutes at Large, p. 219.

[27] Johnson *v.* Wells Fargo Co., 239 U. S. 234.

[28] American School of Magnetic Healing *v.* McAnnulty, 187 U. S. 94.

[29] Chin Yow *v.* United States, 208 U. S. 8; Gegiow *v.* Uhl, 239 U. S. 3; Kwock Jan Fat *v.* White, 253 U. S. 454.

[30] See, *e. g.*, the West Virginia Public Utilities Law, Acts of West Virginia, 1912, ch. 9, sec. 16. The doctrine of the separation of powers stands squarely in the way of the constitutionality of a statute permitting an appeal to a court from the decision of an agency of the executive branch of government, United States *v.* Ferriera (1851), 13 Howard, 40. A way around the difficulty has been found by providing in the statute that the appeal to the court shall be taken under such circumstances — *e. g.*, with permission to introduce new evidence, etc., — that it can be held to be an original proceeding. This was the case in United States *v.* Ritchie (1854), 17 Howard, 525. The same reasoning was used to uphold the constitutionality of the West Virginia statute mentioned above: United Fuel Gas Co. *v.* Public Service Commission, 73 W. Va. 571; City of Bluefield *v.* Water Works, 81 W. Va. 201, at p. 204. But the federal courts have directly consented, without any such subterfuge, to hear appeals from the Board of General Customs Appraisers (United States *v.* Liis, 170 U. S. 628); and from the Commissioner of Patents (United States *v.* Duell, 172 U. S. 576). See, however, Keller *v.* Potomac Electric Power Co., 261 U. S. 428 (1923).

[31] Hutton *v.* City of Camden, 39 N. J. L. 122.

It is therefore clear that, apart from statutory restrictions, full power resides in the courts to control the actions of the new boards and commissions, if they care to exercise it. But here, as with the older types of public officers, the courts have of their own motion narrowed the use of their power in subtle ways. If any question is raised as to the dangers inherent in administrative adjudication uncontrolled by judicial review, it is a question, not as to the power of the courts, but as to their policy in placing limits on their power. As Professor Powell has put it: "Judicial review of administrative action is always possible, if we mean that the courts may always inquire as to its validity. But the courts have themselves established as a rule of law that in many instances where the power of the administrative to act is lawfully vested, they will assume without examination of the evidence the correctness of the administrative determination." [32] And again: "The limitations upon the reviewing power of the courts are and must be, in the last analysis, self-imposed ones." [33] Our question is as to the bearing of this self-denying policy on the maintenance of the "supremacy of law." To what extent ought the courts to go in supervising and controlling the action of administrative tribunals? How far is it wise for them to limit their control? First of all comes the question how far they tend to limit it in actual practice.[34]

III

Statutes sometimes expressly make the findings of particular administrative bodies final as to "questions of fact," and not subject to judicial review; other statutes provide that such findings shall be taken to be *prima facie* correct.[35]

[32] *Pol. Sci. Quarterly*, xxviii, 47.

[33] *Amer. Pol. Sci. Rev.*, i, 592.

[34] Throughout the following sections I am indebted to articles by Professor T. R. Powell, in *Amer. Pol. Sci. Rev.*, i, 583 ff., and *Harv. Law Rev.*, xxiv, 333 ff. and 441 ff.

[35] For typical provisions, see the summary of statutory provisions of various states in O. L. Pond, "Methods of Judicial Review in Relation to the Effectiveness of Commission Control" in *Annals of American Academy of Political and Social Science* (May, 1914), liii, 54–65.

Apart from such enactments the cases show the widest divergency. It is quite generally and properly held that where a complainant has failed to use all his opportunities under the administrative procedure to question the rightfulness of the proposed administrative action, he will not be heard to question it in court; the time of the courts is too valuable to be taken before the possibilities of administrative relief are exhausted.[36] Where the courts will consent to review, the general rule is sometimes stated that they will inquire into two things: first, whether the administrative body had "jurisdiction"; and if so, then, whether it acted "arbitrarily," as for instance on the basis of evidence insufficient to support its findings. What is substantially the same rule is elsewhere stated in the form that the courts will review for error of law, but not findings of fact, at least where, on the evidence, the findings are within the bounds of reason.[37]

The statutes and cases are full of this distinction between "law" and "fact," which is taken for granted, and has formed the basis of decision in so many instances [38] that it becomes

[36] United States *v.* Sing Tuck, 194 U. S. 161; Texas & Pacific R. Co. *v.* Abilene Oil Co., 204 U. S. 426; Wisconsin-Minnesota Light & Power Co. *v.* Railroad Commission, 267 Fed. 711.

[37] The typical formulae for expressing the scope of court review are hopelessly confused because of a persistent confusion between at least three different theories of review: (1) the distinction between "ministerial" and "judicial" duties, resulting in the doctrine that the exercise of "judicial discretion" is not reviewable even for errors of law, except perhaps where "impure motive" or some other abuse is present. This theory survives most strongly in the mandamus cases. (2) The "jurisdictional" theory of review, resulting in the doctrine that even determinations of fact, where "jurisdictional," are reviewable. (3) The doctrine that errors of law, but not of fact, are reviewable. All three theories represent developments in different directions of the nebulous fundamental doctrine that the exercise of discretion within the limits of jurisdiction is not reviewable. At times under the guise of determining whether a duty is "ministerial" or "discretionary," the courts really review an administrative determination for an erroneous construction of law, Winsor *v.* Hunt (Ariz.) 243 Pac. 407. The cases reveal the impossibility of so defining the terms "ministerial" and "jurisdiction" as to make them an adequate basis for the law of judicial review. See Goodnow, *Principles of the Administrative Law of the United States*, pp. 405–407.

[38] See, *e. g.*, American School of Magnetic Healing *v.* McAnnulty, 187 U. S. 94; Illinois Central R. R. *v.* Interstate Commerce Commission, 206 U. S. 441. This formula for expressing the boundaries of review is most explicit in cases

important to see what there is in it.[39] Take first a case like United States *v.* Ju Toy.[40] There a statute authorized the immigration authorities to exclude alien immigrants of Chinese nationality. The officials found that Ju Toy had been born in China and was therefore an alien within the scope of the statute. He claimed to have been born in the United States. The Supreme Court held that the determination of the officials as to his place of birth was conclusive, and that he was not entitled to have the question examined in a court of law. Here the administrative finding was as to a pure "question of fact" — where Ju Toy was born. So far the case conforms to the rule as usually stated. But it is to be noted that on the result of that finding turned the question whether or not the officials had any "jurisdiction" to deal with the case at all; and in allowing their finding to be conclusive, the Supreme Court practically allowed them to be the judges of the extent of their own jurisdiction.[41] The same result was reached in the cases under the Selective Draft Act of 1917 which held that the finding of a draft board was conclusive as to whether or not a conscripted person was a non-declarant alien, and so subject or not to the jurisdiction of the board.[42]

involving review of workmen's compensation orders and orders of public utility commissions; also in postal and immigration cases.

[39] In Reetz *v.* Michigan the United States Supreme Court said that no provision in the Federal Constitution prevents a state from granting to a tribunal, whether a court or a board, the final determination of a legal question. 188 U. S. 505.

[40] 198 U. S. 253.

[41] This view was urged in argument and rejected in a dictum in United States *v.* Sing Tuck, 194 U. S. 161. The case went off on another ground. In Borgnis *v.* Falk, 147 Wis. 327 at 359, a case considering the constitutionality of a workmen's compensation act which provided that determinations of "fact" made by the industrial accident board should be conclusive, the court said: "The decision of such a board may be made conclusive where the board is acting within its jurisdiction, not otherwise. Hence the question of its jurisdiction is one always open to the courts for review; it cannot itself conclusively settle that question, and thus endow itself with power. . . . Clear violations of law in reaching the result reached by the board, such as acting without evidence, or making a decision contrary to all the evidence, constitute jurisdictional error and will justify reversal of the board's action." For a further consideration of the doctrine of "jurisdictional fact" see below, note 79, this chapter, p. 62; also Chapter IX, notes 13 and 17, pp. 257, 260, and Chapter XI, pp. 309 ff.

[42] Angelus *v.* Sullivan, 246 Fed. 56, 62.

To allow an executive body thus to determine conclusively the limits of its own "jurisdiction" looks suspiciously like allowing it to determine a "matter of law." And this seems to have been one of the grounds why a contrary result was reached in Miller *v.* Horton, and Pearson *v.* Zehr. The court held in the latter cases that the intention of the legislature was that the statute should apply only to a certain class of animals, namely diseased animals, and that whether the animal in question fell within the limits of that class was therefore a question going to the jurisdiction of the administrative officer, and so one which the owner was entitled to have tried in a court of law. So in Hutton *v.* City of Camden,[43] where the statute gave a board authority to abate nuisances, it was held that the owner of the property affected must have an opportunity to show in a court of law that it did not in fact constitute a nuisance and so come within the authority of the board.[44]

Such questions as whether a thing is a nuisance, or whether an act or condition or rate is reasonable, are called in the books "mixed questions of law and fact." A finding involves not merely that certain "facts" are true, but also that they sum up into a conclusion of law.[45] Questions of this kind originally gave trouble in connection with the power of juries. The earliest tendency was to hold that as between court and jury a

[43] 39 N. J. L. 122.

[44] *Cf.* Polk's Lessee *v.* Wendell, 9 Cranch, 87, per Marshall, C. J.; also Warne *v.* Varley, 6 Durnford & East, 443 (1795), where Lord Kenyon said: "This statute, after directing that searchers shall be appointed, authorizes them to seize leather of a certain description. . . . It seems reasonable that if these searchers exercise their authority bona fide, and only seize such leather . . . as in their judgment ought to be examined, they should be protected . . . . But the act of Parliament affords them no such protection. It only allows them to seize leather which is not dried;" also Ashurst, J.: "The act of Parliament only authorizes the searchers to seize goods of a certain denomination; the goods in question are not of that description; therefore the seizure is illegal and the defendants are trespassers." For a discussion, see above, note 20, this chapter.

[45] "Negligence, like ownership, is a complex conception. Just as the latter imports the existence of certain facts and the consequence . . . which the law attaches to those facts, so the former imports the existence of certain facts . . . and also the consequence which the law attaches to those facts." Holmes, *Common Law*, p. 115.

question of "reasonableness" was one of "law" for the court. "Reasonableness in these cases," says Coke, "belongeth to the knowledge of the law and therefore to be decided by the justices." [46] This rule has survived in regard to reasonable and probable cause in actions for malicious prosecution and false imprisonment.[47] But formerly it was carried much further. Thus in Tindal *v.* Brown, a negotiable instrument case, Lord Mansfield said that reasonableness of time, when the facts were once ascertained, was a question of law for the court.[48] Ten years later Lord Kenyon ruled to the contrary with regard to due diligence, and the law to-day, with a few exceptions, is that such a question is properly for the jury. It has even been said that it is not a question of law at all, but one of pure fact,[49] a view which had the approval of Mr. Thayer.[50] Where a question of this kind is the subject

[46] Co. Lit. 56 b.

[47] Johnstone *v.* Sutton (1786), by Lord Mansfield, 1 T. R. 493, 545. The leading case is Panton *v.* Williams, 2 Q. B. 169 (1841), at p. 193. See also Stone *v.* Crocker, 24 Pick. (Mass.), 81, at p. 84, and J. B. Thayer, *Preliminary Treatise on Evidence*, pp. 221 ff. *Cf.* also the rule that what constitutes "necessaries" for an infant is still to some extent a question of law for the court. See Mackarell *v.* Bachelor, Cro. Eliz. 583, and compare Peters *v.* Fleming, 6 M. & W. 42 with Ryder *v.* Wombwell, L. R. 4 Exch., 32. The rule at present appears to be that it is the province of the court to determine whether the articles sued for are within the class of necessaries; and, if so, it is then the province of the jury to pass on the questions of quantity, quality, and their adaptation to the conditions and wants of the infant. McKanna *v.* Merry, 61 Ill. 177. See Thayer, *Prelim. Treat. on Evidence*, p. 211.

[48] 1 T. R. 167. It has continued to be said that what is "reasonable time" for the presentment of a negotiable instrument *for payment* is a "question of law" for the court (Byles on Bills & Notes, 8th Amer. ed. by H. G. Wood, N. Y., 1891, p. 211), and this doctrine was repeated in a recent case under the Uniform Negotiable Instruments Law, Commercial National Bank *v.* Zimmerman, 185 N. Y. 210, with a limitation, however, to cases where the evidence was not conflicting. On the other hand, the doctrine has been questioned in Citizens' Bank *v.* First Nat'l Bank, 135 Ia. 605; and it seems always to have been held that what constitutes a "reasonable time" for the presentment of a bill of exchange *for acceptance* is a "mixed question of law and fact" for the jury, Fry *v.* Hill, 7 Taunt. 395; Byles, *op. cit.*, p. 182. Such distinctions appear accidental and purely arbitrary.

[49] Interstate Commerce Commission *v.* Alabama Midland R. Co., 168 U. S. 144 (1897), at p. 170.

[50] Thayer, *Prelim. Treat. on Evidence*, pp. 249–253. For a very suggestive contrary view, see Holmes, *Collected Legal Papers*, pp. 232–238. "When we

of an administrative determination, the courts are divided as to how far they will review. Thus in a bill to enjoin the destruction of property declared to be a nuisance, Mr. Justice Miller said: "It is a doctrine not to be tolerated in this country that a municipal corporation, without any general laws either of the city or of the state within which a given structure can be shown to be a nuisance, can, by its mere declaration that it is one, subject it to removal by any person supposed to be aggrieved, or even by the city itself. This would place every house, every business and all the property in the city at the uncontrolled will of temporary local authorities."[51] So in the Trinity Church case the court said that no decision of a board of health will be allowed to conclude the owner upon a question of nuisance.[52] But there is much authority the other way.[53] And the United States Supreme Court has said, in a case involving an order of the Post-Office Department, that, on a "mixed question of law and fact" the finding of an administrative body ought not to be disturbed.[54]

rule on evidence of negligence, we are ruling on a standard of conduct, which in theory is always the same upon the same facts. . . . It is obvious that a standard of conduct does not cease to be law because the facts to which that standard applies are not likely often to be repeated," *ibid.*, pp. 235, 236. See also Holmes, *Common Law*, pp. 122–129.

[51] Yates *v.* Milwaukee, 10 Wall. 497 (1870). See accord, Hutton *v.* Camden, 39 N. J. L. 122; People ex rel. Copcutt *v.* Board of Health, 140 N. Y. 1.

[52] 145 N. Y. 32; accord Hutton *v.* Camden, 39 N. J. L. 122; People ex rel. Copcutt *v.* Board of Health, 140 N. Y. 1.

[53] Kennedy *v.* Board of Health, 2 Pa. St. 366; Green *v.* Mayor, 6 Ga. 1; City of St. Louis *v.* Stern, 3 Mo. Ap. 48; Metropolitan Board *v.* Heister, 37 N. Y. 661; Van Wormser *v.* Mayor, 15 Wendell, 262. It is significant that all these were early cases decided during the period when the courts showed no reluctance to allow to administrative determinations a "judicial" finality. See above, note 20, this chapter. In Green *v.* Mayor (1849), *supra*, the court said: "The Statute conferred on the Mayor and Aldermen the authority to pass such laws and ordinances as they might consider fit and proper, to remove such nuisances, or causes of disease, which might affect the citizens of the City of Savannah, or in any wise injure their health. The Mayor and Aldermen have already *adjudged* [italics mine] that the cultivation of rice, within the corporate limits of the City, was injurious to the health of the City. . . . Whenever a Statute gives a discretionary power to any person, to be exercised by him upon his own opinion of certain facts, it is a sound rule of construction, that the Statute constitutes him the sole and exclusive judge of the existence of those facts" (at p. 11).

[54] Bates and Guild Co. *v.* Payne, 194 U. S. 106.

In truth, the distinction between "questions of law" and "questions of fact" really gives little help in determining how far the courts will review; and for the good reason that there is no fixed distinction. They are not two mutually exclusive *kinds* of questions, based upon a difference of subject-matter. Matters of law grow downward into roots of fact, and matters of fact reach upward, without a break, into matters of law. The knife of policy alone effects an artificial cleavage at the point where the court chooses to draw the line between public interest and private right. It would seem that when the courts are unwilling to review, they are tempted to explain by the easy device of calling the question one of "fact"; and when otherwise disposed, they say that it is a question of "law." Thus, while the reasonableness of a rate is said to be a matter of fact and not reviewable, yet when the rate-fixing body has omitted to take into consideration some element or factor which the court thinks ought to have been included, error of law is promptly held to have been committed and the power to review is exercised. How hopeless it is to separate "law" and "fact" stands out in relief from such a case as Smith *v.* Hitchcock, 226 U. S. 53 (1912). There the question was whether the complainant's publication was to be classified as a book or a magazine within the terms of a statute. Whether a particular bundle of printed pages is a book or whether it is a magazine in the ordinary use of language is doubtless a question of fact; but which of the two words as used in a statute applies to just that unit of printed matter is with equal truth a question of statutory construction. The court held the question to be one of law and consented to review. If this is a question of law, it is hard to see why the same should not be true of any question of reasonableness, as Coke said it was.[55]

[55] See Thayer, *Prelim. Treat. on Evidence*, pp. 213 ff. In a criminal case in Massachusetts involving the question whether a certain game was a lottery within the meaning of a statute, the court said, per Holmes, J.: "Whether or not a definitely described game falls within the prohibition of the statute is a question of law," Commonwealth *v.* Sullivan, 146 Mass. 142, at p. 145. This view is what might be expected in the light of the position taken by Mr. Justice Holmes in *Collected Legal Papers*, pp. 232–238; *Common Law*, pp. 122–129. In Heath *v.* Wallace, 138 U. S. 573, it was said that the question whether lands

IV

A more pragmatic test than the distinction between "law" and "fact" for predicting the willingness of courts to review would seem to be the distinction between the different fields of governmental action in which the contested determination may arise. In the Federal jurisdiction there are cases involving determinations of the Public Land Office; of the Commissioner of Patents; of the Pension Office; of customs officials; of immigration officials; of the Interstate Commerce Commission; of the Federal Trade Commission; of the Pure Food and Drug Board, etc. It has been the subject of comment how seldom the courts in a case arising in one of these fields reason from cases coming from the others. There are exceptions; the leading immigration case of United States *v.* Ju Toy was decided on the authority of Murray's Lessee *v.* Hoboken Land Co.,[56] a revenue case, and Public Clearing House *v.* Coyne,[57] a postal case, among others; land cases were relied on in the postal case of School of Magnetic Healing *v.* McAnnulty; [58] but broadly the generalization stands, and it will be seen to have significance. It is possible to make a loose classification of the various fields of federal administration according as the courts seem more or less willing to review determinations arising in them.

First of all may be put cases where the complainant has sought some gratuity or benefit from government. Here it may be argued plausibly that he should abide by what procedure the government chooses to apply. Common-law rights are not at stake. The typical case is the distribution of public lands. The courts have shown great reluctance to review decisions of the Land Office, and have even gone so far as to refuse to review the interpretation placed by the land officials on a statute. "Whether he [that is, the Secretary of the Interior] decided rightly or wrongly is not the question," it is said in one case. "Having jurisdiction to decide at all,

were "swamp and overflowed" within the meaning of the Swamp Land Act was a question of "fact." See below, chapter XI, notes 20 and 21, pp. 313 ff.

[56] 18 How. 272. [57] 194 U. S. 497. [58] 187 U. S. 94.

it was his duty to decide as he thought the law was, and the courts have no power whatever to review his determination by mandamus or injunction."[59] Such a decision shows once more the slight value of the distinction between "law" and "fact" as a test. Secondly, the courts are reluctant to reverse determinations of the Post-Office Department resulting in the issue of fraud orders. The Supreme Court has said that the postal service is no necessary function of civil government, like the protection of life, liberty, and property, but an extraneous service assumed voluntarily by the government for the convenience of the public; and that therefore Congress may attach to its use such conditions as it deems proper.[60] The Court put in significant language a conception of policy which reaches far beyond the post-office, when it said: "If all

[59] Riverside Oil Co. *v.* Hitchcock, 190 U. S. 316, at p. 324. It should be noted that this was a mandamus case. See below, p. 63. In American Casualty Ins. Co. *v.* Fyler, 60 Conn. 448, at p. 462, it was said: "The construction of a statute is not a ministerial act; it is the exercise of judgment. If it is the duty of the defendant to admit or not to admit the plaintiff to do business in this state, according to the interpretation to be put on the insurance statutes, then the admitting or refusing to admit involves the exercise of discretion and judgment. . . . It is not a purely ministerial act and a mandamus ought not to issue." But at times the courts will hold that in order to determine whether a duty is or is not ministerial, they must review the administrative construction of law, Winsor *v.* Hunt (Ariz.), 243 Pac. 407. In Silver *v.* Ladd, 7 Wall. 219; Johnson *v.* Towsley, 13 Wall. 72; and Burfenning *v.* Chicago, St. Paul, etc. R. Co., 163 U. S. 321, the Supreme Court reviewed determinations of the Land Office on a "question of law."

[60] But a decision of the Post-Office Department to issue a fraud-order may have a fatal effect on the business affected, in view of the statutory prohibition against the transmission of letters by any other general means than the post-office (U. S. Criminal Code, secs. 183–185). This was pointed out by Mr. Justice Holmes, dissenting, in Leach *v.* Carlile, 258 U. S. 138: "The statute under which fraud orders are issued by the Postmaster General has been decided or said to be valid so many times that it may be too late to expect a contrary decision. But there are considerations against it that seem to me never to have been fully weighed. . . . The decisions thus far have gone largely if not wholly on the ground that if the Government chose to offer a means of transportation which it was not bound to offer, it could choose what it would transport; which is well enough when neither law nor the habit that the Government's action has generated has made that means the only one. But when habit and law combine to exclude every other, it seems to me that the First Amendment in terms forbids such control of the post as was exercised here." Mr. Justice Brandeis concurred in this dissenting opinion. See also Chafee, *Freedom of Speech*, pp. 233, 234.

the ordinary daily transactions of the departments which involve an interference with private rights were required to be submitted to the courts before action was finally taken, the result would entail practically a suspension of some of the important functions of the government." [61] But the opinion left open a wide door to discretionary review through the ambiguous statement that "error of law" is reviewable.

In no cases has there been greater willingness to give finality to administrative decisions than in connection with collecting the public revenue. Revenue cases involve the vital power of government to provide means for its own existence.[62] Cary *v.* Curtis, an early case, ruled that a statute was constitutional which not only deprived the person aggrieved of all remedy in the courts against a collector of customs to whom an excessive duty had been paid, but made the Secretary of the Treasury the final tribunal for the determination of the proper rate of duty without recourse to the courts at all.[63] The statute was promptly amended so as to restore to the importer his common-law right; but the Supreme Court weakened the force of the amendment by denying review of an appraisement of value, though in its own opinion the method used by the appraisers to reach their determination was unreliable and inadequate.[64] In a later case the complainant offered to show the true value of the goods imported and the carelessness and want of experience of the appraisers; but the Court held the evidence immaterial since it did not tend to indicate that they were assuming powers in excess of their authority, but only that they were careless or irregular in the discharge of their duties.[65]

[61] Public Clearing House *v.* Coyne, 194 U. S. 497. See also Degge *v.* Hitchcock, 229 U. S. 162.

[62] In proceedings for the collection of public revenue it has been held that summary remedies may be used which could not be applied in cases of a "judicial" character: King *v.* Mullins, 171 U. S. 404, at p. 429; Bells Gap R. R. *v.* Pa., 134 U. S., at p. 239. For very broad language see Miller, J., in Cheatham *v.* United States, 92 U. S. 85, at p. 88.

[63] 3 How. 236 (1845).

[64] Bartlett *v.* Kane, 16 How. 263 (1853).

[65] Hilton *v.* Merritt, 110 U. S. 97 (1884); to same effect Passavant *v.* United States, 148 U. S. 214.

In the immigration cases (at least the exclusion as distinguished from the expulsion cases) the government, as in land and postal cases, seems to be conceived as extending a privilege to persons not entitled to it as of common right; and, perhaps for that reason, the courts have tended to leave to the officials a very free hand.[66] The leading case is that of Ju Toy.[67] But these cases involve interference with a new sort of interest; while only property rights were in issue in the other cases (reputation is also involved in postal fraud orders), the immigration cases turn on an interference with liberty. Hence it is open to argument that a stricter protection ought in justice to be extended to the individual. Recognition of this consideration is perhaps shown in the recent case of Kwock Jan Fat *v.* White, where an administrative finding was reversed.[68]

The different classes of cases dealt with up to this point have all been in the nature of direct controversies between the individual and government — cases, that is, in which the government can be said to have been involved as a direct party in interest. Such cases may be summed up in three groups:

1. Those where individuals seek to take advantage of a privilege extended by government — land cases and immigration cases. To this class belong also pension and patent cases.

2. Those where government offers to perform a business service to individuals on favorable terms — postal cases.

3. Those involving a necessary function of government — revenue cases. Here also belong draft cases, civil-service cases, and cases involving military and naval regulations.[69] These shade off into so-called "matter of state."[70]

[66] It may be argued that refusal to admit an alien, as a matter bearing on international policy, comes within the doctrine of "act of state" as applied in Buron *v.* Denman (2 Exchequer 167 above, p. 26), and that therefore the courts should treat the action of the executive as final. That is the ground of the English case of Musgrove *v.* Toy [1891], A. C. 272.

[67] 198 U. S. 253.

[68] 253 U. S. 454.

[69] Gratiot *v.* United States, 4 How. 80; Ex parte Reed, 100 U. S. 13.

[70] See above, Chapter I, note 47, p. 26.

In all these situations it seems inevitable and not unreasonable to allow wider latitude to governmental discretion than where the question is as to the restriction of individual freedom in the interest of other individuals or of society at large — that is to say, cases arising under the police power and the power to regulate common callings. In these it may be laid down, roughly, that the courts tend to apply a firmer control to administrative action. But there is, if possible, an even greater variety and uncertainty in the decisions. Most of the cases under the police power naturally arise in the states, as the police power of the Federal government is attenuated to the interstices of the expressly granted powers. Some of the state decisions have already been incidentally noted, holding that aggrieved persons have a right to court review of administrative findings on such questions as whether or not a nuisance is being committed. That is perhaps the weight of the more recent authority on the question of nuisance.[71]

On the other side stand a large number of decisions where the courts have refused to review administrative findings on so-called "mixed questions of law and fact" in the absence of an express charge that the administrative officials have arbitrarily abused their discretion. This is especially true of cases dealing with the issue of licenses. A typical example is Granville *v.* Gregory.[72] A state board of medical examiners had refused a license to an applicant on the ground that the institution from which he had been graduated was not a medical college in good standing. The applicant applied to the courts to compel the board by mandamus to issue the license. The writ was refused. The court said that should it assume revisory powers in this case, "it would be palpably usurping functions conferred exclusively by law upon others";

[71] This is Professor Powell's opinion, *Harv. Law Rev.*, xxiv, 339.

[72] 83 Mo. 123. One reason for the reluctance of the courts to review the issue of licenses has been the old theory, announced in Basset *v.* Godschall, 3 Wilson 121, that an applicant has no right to a license unless the authorities grant him one, and that he is therefore deprived of no right by their refusal. This theory is becoming less tenable as more and more occupations are brought under licensing regulations, and the possibilities of making a living in unlicensed occupations are becoming proportionately narrower.

and that a serious objection to the exercise of court review in a case of this kind was the character of the investigation the court would be compelled to make: "it would find itself wandering amid the mazes of therapeutics or boggling at the mysteries of the pharmacopoeia." Here we meet for the first time a convincing and familiar argument against a broad exercise of court review — namely, the specialized and technical character of the subject-matter of many administrative determinations.

But even where this argument does not apply, there are cases going further than the Granville case. A good example is Commonwealth *v.* Sisson,[73] already discussed. Fish and game commissioners, without a hearing, directed an order to the defendants, who operated a saw-mill, to cease discharging sawdust into a stream and to erect a blower to dispose of the sawdust. They were prosecuted by the commissioners for failure to comply with the order. The defence was that the act of the commissioners in directing an order to a particular individual was a judicial act, and could therefore be performed only after a hearing on the questions at issue. The court held that the order, although addressed to but one individual, was legislative in character, and therefore no hearing was necessary. This strained interpretation struck down at one blow not merely the right to judicial review of the administrative finding, but the very possibility of review; for in the absence of a hearing there cannot well be any finding, properly so called. The decision cannot be defended on a ground sometimes available in other cases reaching a like result — the need for haste and summary action by officials to protect the public in the face of imminent peril. This argument is effective where health boards act to avert a threatened epidemic. Their promptness and zeal must not be paralyzed by fear of personal liability for every chance mistake. In Raymond *v.* Fish,[74] an owner having failed to remove brush as ordered by a board of health, it was destroyed by the board. In an action for damages by the owner, judgment was given in

[73] 189 Mass. 246 (1905). *Cf.* Train *v.* Boston Disinfecting Co., 144 Mass. 523.

[74] 51 Conn. 80 (1883).

favor of the board, although the trial court had found expressly that the property destroyed was not a producing cause of disease. It has been held that officers who quarantined persons erroneously suspected of having a contagious disease were not personally liable in damages.[75] In another case it is said, with reference to the action of a health officer in removing to a hospital a person suspected of having smallpox: "If there was any cause for his judgment, or any fact or appearance from which an inference of smallpox might arise, his determination was final as to the legality or propriety of the removal." [76] So, in Oceanic Steam Navigation Co. *v.* Stranahan, the decision of a health officer was held conclusive as to whether an immigrant was afflicted with disease.[77] In some of these cases it was said that the party aggrieved might have had an injunction if he had applied for one before the administrative action had been taken, but that damages would not be awarded afterwards because of their possibly deterrent effect on the zeal of the officials. On the other hand, damages were awarded in such cases as Miller *v.* Horton and Pearson *v.* Zehr. The deterrent effect of awarding damages has in some instances been guarded against by statutes placing the burden of payment on the public treasury.[78]

V

Besides the nature of the field in which the administrative action takes place, a further factor which influences the courts in limiting or extending the scope of their review is the form of the proceeding in which review is sought.[79] Thus

[75] Beeks *v.* Dickinson County, 131 Ia. 244; Valentine *v.* Englewood, 76 N. J. L. 509.

[76] Brown *v.* Purdy, 8 N. Y. St. Reporter, 143 (dictum).

[77] 214 U. S. 320 (1909).

[78] A federal statute extending such protection to certain public officers was the Act of Congress of Mar. 3, 1863 (12 U. S. Statutes at Large, 761), considered in United States *v.* Sherman, 98 U. S. 565 (1878). See also N. Y. Agricultural Law (1901) § 70a; New York City Charter (N. Y. Laws, 1901, c. 466), § 1196.

[79] SCOPE OF REVIEW ON CERTIORARI. There has been much confusion and diversity of decision as to the scope of review upon certiorari. The writ was originally used to bring up the record of a proceeding in an inferior jurisdiction before an authority of superior jurisdiction for any purpose, particularly in

they are particularly cautious about interfering with administrative action by the writ of mandamus. There seems a double reason for this caution. On the one hand, where the law allows a field of discretion to the administrative body, there may be a number of ways in which that discretion can legally be exercised, and the effect of mandamus would often

cases where the inferior jurisdiction was not competent to grant full relief. "If a man do recover debt or damages before justices of *oyer* and *terminer*, and hath not execution, he may remove the record and the process into the King's Bench and there sue execution, and have a *scire facias* upon the record, etc.," Fitzherbert, *Natura Brevium*, 246 b (7th ed. with Hale's commentary, London, 1730, p. 556). Thus where a presentment could not be traversed at a court-leet, Lord Mansfield, in the King's Bench, held that "the proper method is to grant a certiorari that it may be traversed here," Rex *v.* Roupell, Cowper, 458. The writ came to be extensively used to remove orders of justices of the peace and quarter-sessions into the King's Bench to be either quashed or confirmed, Blackstone, *Commentaries*, ed. Christian, iv, 272. Upon such review, the order would be quashed if based upon "insufficient evidence," Rex *v.* Hale, Cowper, 728. Meanwhile Lord Holt had laid down that certiorari would issue out of the King's Bench to all inferior jurisdictions erected by Parliament to "see that they keep themselves within their jurisdiction; and if they exceed it, to restrain them," Rex *v.* Inhabitants of Glamorganshire, 1 Lord Raymond, 580. With the extension of "quasi-judicial" administrative activity, the question arose as to whether certiorari brought up for review anything more than the "jurisdiction" of the administrative tribunal. In many states it has been settled that it does not. "The inferior tribunal, when the record is brought before the court by certiorari, may have erred in its rulings on questions of law during the progress of the trial, or it may have erred in the application of the law to the facts in reaching its final judgment, and yet those errors cannot be reviewed and corrected in a proceeding of this character. On a return to a writ bringing the record before the court, the only proper inquiry is whether the inferior tribunal had jurisdiction and proceeded legally — *i. e.*, followed the form of proceedings legally applicable in such cases," People ex rel. Maloney *v.* Lindbloom, 182 Ill. 241. But in New York it was early established that the writ extended to the correction of all "errors of law" made by the inferior tribunal, Morewood *v.* Hollister, 6 N. Y. 309. Furthermore, the theory that certiorari brings up for review only the question of "jurisdiction" has been broadened to permit a more extended review of "questions of fact" by the doctrine that the writ raises the question for the reviewing court of whether the "jurisdictional" facts have been sufficiently proved. "Inferior magistrates, when required by writ of certiorari to return their proceedings, must show affirmatively that they had authority to act; and when their authority and jurisdiction depend upon a fact to be proved before themselves, and such fact is disputed, the magistrate must certify the proofs in relation to it for the purpose of enabling the higher court to determine whether the fact be established . . . The reviewing court must necessarily re-examine, if required, the decision of the magistrate on all questions on which his jurisdiction depends, whether

be to compel its exercise in one particular way. To issue the writ in such a case would therefore amount to an assumption by the courts of the task of dictating the policy and directing the discretion of an executive body, a task for which they are not equipped. Or, again, a result reached by an administrative body on a ground alleged to be improper might perhaps

of law or of fact," People ex rel. Bodine *v.* Goodwin, 5 N. Y. 568. This is apparently the most widely accepted rule: People ex rel. Whitney *v.* San Francisco Fire Dept., 14 Cal. 479; State ex rel. Milwaukee Medical College *v.* Chittenden, 127 Wis. 468. But even where the courts on certiorari will undertake to examine the existence of the "jurisdictional" fact upon which the competence of the administrative body to act depended, they will look no farther than to see whether that body had before it evidence upon which reasonable men might have found the existence of the fact in question: Milwaukee Fuel Co. *v.* Industrial Commission, 159 Wis. 635, Western Indemnity Co. *v.* Pillsbury, 170 Cal. 686. And in some states the courts will not examine the evidence at all, but only the record, to determine whether the administrative tribunal had jurisdiction: Dolan's Appeal, 108 Pa. St. 564; Chicago & Rock Island R. Co. *v.* Whipple, 22 Ill. 105, at p. 108. Finally the limitation of review by certiorari to questions of "jurisdiction" has been frankly abandoned in some states. Thus it was said in Jackson *v.* People, 9 Mich. 111: "It is an unavoidable conclusion that the usual office of the common-law writ is to inquire into something more than jurisdiction. . . . When the evidence set out is not sufficient to justify a conviction, or other judicial act complained of, it will be quashed on certiorari. . . . The office of a certiorari is not, however, to review questions of fact, but questions of law. And in examining into the evidence, the appellate court does so, not to determine whether the probabilities preponderate one way or the other, but simply to determine whether the evidence is such that it will justify the finding as a legitimate inference from the facts proved, whether that inference would or would not have been drawn by the appellate tribunal." And in People ex rel. Cook *v.* Board of Police, 39 N. Y. 506: "May the court on a common-law certiorari go beyond the inquiry whether the inferior tribunal had jurisdiction? . . . To hold that conclusions of fact upon conflicting evidence and matters of mere detail . . . and matters which are clearly submitted to the judgment or discretion of the inferior tribunal, when the evidence presents a case for its exercise, can be reviewed would . . . produce great inconvenience and embarrassment. It may be desirable not to multiply cases in which the appellate courts can be called upon to interfere in matters of small importance, but that furnishes no reason for denying the power to see that the rules of law are not violated. . . . I conclude, therefore, that . . . this court have power to examine the case upon the whole of the evidence to see whether as a matter of law there was any proof which could warrant a conviction of the relator. . . . If there was no evidence of neglect of duty — if the case was such at the close of the trial that it would have been erroneous to submit the question to the jury, were the like question before a jury in an ordinary action, — then the error is an error in law, and the conviction is illegal." See below, Chapter IX, note 13, p. 257, and note 17, p. 260.

equally well have been reached on a proper ground.[80] In such a case the courts cannot assume that the administrative acted on the improper ground. This difficulty arises, for example, where an administrative board is given a wide discretion to issue or refuse licenses, and a person whose application has been denied seeks to compel the license to issue by mandamus. In such a case the writ would be refused although the relator, if he assumed the risk of acting without a license and were criminally prosecuted, might be found to have a good defence to the criminal action in the unjust discrimination practised against him.[81]

The courts sometimes, erroneously it would seem, speak as if the principles governing review by injunction were the same as those governing review by mandamus.[82] This is true

[80] "Where there is no reasonable ground to justify a decision by an officer or board other than one way, and there is a failure to act accordingly, the function of a mandamus proceeding is broad enough to remedy the mischief by compelling the making of such decision, in perfect harmony with the rule that the office thereof is not to control discretionary authority, but to compel the exercise thereof," State ex rel. Coffee *v.* Chittenden, 112 Wis. 569, at p. 574 (dictum). Where it appeared affirmatively that the grounds on which a certificate was refused were improper, the writ was granted, MacFarland *v.* Miller, 18 D. C. App. 554.

[81] See T. R. Powell in *Harv. Law Rev.*, xxiv, 284. For a note on "Control of Executive Officers by Mandamus," with a discussion of the distinction between "ministerial" and "discretionary" duties, see *Harv. Law Rev.*, xxxiii, 462 ff.

[82] *E. g.*, Miller, J., in Gaines *v.* Thompson, 7 Wall. 347, at p. 352, and in Litchfield *v.* Register and Receiver, 9 Wall. 575. This language is partly a survival of the old doctrine applied in damage suits against officers, that error of "discretion" was not reviewable, and partly a legacy from cases like Decatur *v.* Paulding, 14 Peters, 497 (see below, p. 287), embodying the Jeffersonian doctrine that the principle of separation of powers forbids judicial interference with the duties of the other departments by means of mandamus. See Jefferson, Letter to Jarvis, Sept. 28, 1820 (*Complete Works*, ed. Washington, vii, 178). I surmise that the attitude of the courts toward these two writs has been largely governed by a feeling that, since they are anticipatory in their operation, to grant them would amount to a judicial attempt to "supervise" administrative discretion in a sense not true of a subsequent damage suit against an officer for a discretionary act after the act had been performed. The slant of the judicial mind is to favor remedial rather than preventive action. The talk about an injunction being a judicial interference with administrative discretion is conspicuously absent from cases involving orders of railroad and public utility commissions, where injunctions are freely granted; and it has even been said in effect by the United States Supreme Court that the right to such an injunction, apart from statute, at least to test constitutional issues, is a necessary element of due

where by indirection an injunction is sought for the same purpose as mandamus, that is, to compel administrative action.[83] But where the injunction is sought to check improper administrative interference rather than to compel administrative permission, — in some situations it is hard to draw the line, — different principles should apply. Thus, while it has been held that the courts will not enjoin the revocation of a liquor license, a board has been restrained from improperly closing the plaintiff's place of business for the alleged violation of a liquor ordinance.[84] The true considerations governing the issuance or refusal of an injunction lie in a balancing of the irreparable injury threatened to the plaintiff against the need of summary action to protect the public. Thus an injunction has been granted against the imprisonment of a leper in a pest-house where it appeared that less stringent measures would adequately protect the public;[85] but an injunction has been refused to prevent the summary destruction of food unfit for human use.[86]

Where the summary nature of the action demanded by the public safety requires the refusal of an injunction, it does not follow that the rights of the person affected should not be subsequently examined in an action for damages;[87] while if the case was a proper one for injunctive relief, but no such relief was asked, the injured party ought to be precluded from later insisting on damages.[88] The cases only point to this distinction, but do not make it articulate.[89] Finally, the freest

process. Louisville & Nashville R. Co. *v.* Garrett, 231 U. S. 298. Injunction proceedings are also the normal method of securing review of the issue of fraud orders by the Postmaster-General. See below, p. 299.

[83] Moneywright Scale Co. *v.* McBryde, 199 Mass. 503 (to enjoin a sealer of weights from disapproving a certain type of scales); Wolf *v.* Medical Examiners, 109 Minn. 360 (to enjoin the revocation of a license). But *cf.* Nelson *v.* State Board, 108 Ky. 769.

[84] City *v.* Manning, 43 Col. 144; *cf.* Manning *v.* City, 45 Col. 571.

[85] Kirk *v.* Board of Health, 83 S. C. 372; dictum that the members of the board could not be held personally liable in damages.

[86] North American Cold Storage Co. *v.* Chicago, 211 U. S. 306.

[87] Miller *v.* Horton, 152 Mass. 540.

[88] Van Wormser *v.* Mayor, 15 Wend. (N. Y.) 262.

[89] This distinction has been drawn by Professor Powell. See *Harv. Law Rev.*, xxiv, 442–459.

exercise of judicial review occurs naturally enough where the administrative tribunal is required to bring court proceedings to enforce its orders. But here, as elsewhere, the nature of the field to which the administrative action belongs has great weight, and in revenue cases, where tax officials are required to collect taxes through an action at law, the courts will not go far in reviewing their determinations as to the value of the property taxed.

VI

Returning to this distinction between the different fields of administrative action, the last class of cases to be considered includes those arising under the power to regulate common callings. Here the largest property interests are involved, and the general statement may be hazarded that the readiness of the courts to review tends to vary strongly with the size of the property interests at stake.[90] But in this field it is possibly even harder than elsewhere to draw from the cases guiding principles as to the extent to which the courts will review. A simple way to bring out the issues will be to glance at some decisions of the United States Supreme Court, and chiefly those which review orders of the Interstate Commerce Commission.[91]

The Interstate Commerce Act in its original form practically necessitated court review by providing that orders of the Commission could be enforced only by a proceeding brought by the Commission in a United States Circuit Court. Although this provision was subsequently repealed, ample opportunity for court review has been preserved in the statute. But the question of how far the review shall reach has been left largely with the Supreme Court, and is being pricked out by the decisions in a zigzag line which sometimes seems to defy plotting. Occasionally the Court has thought fit to

[90] Observe language of Brewer, J., in Chicago, Milwaukee & St. Paul R. Co. *v.* Tompkins, 176 U. S. 167, at p. 172.

[91] For a full discussion of Supreme Court cases reviewing orders of the Interstate Commerce Commission and of state regulating commissions, with an attempt to harmonize the decisions, see below, chapter VI.

formulate principles which it says it will follow in exercising its reviewing power. Thus, in Interstate Commerce Commission *v.* Illinois Central R. R. Co.,[92] it was said: "In determining whether an order of the Commission shall be suspended or set aside, the Supreme Court must consider (*a*) all relevant questions of constitutional power or right; (*b*) all pertinent questions as to whether the administrative order is within the scope of the delegated authority under which it purports to have been made; (*c*) whether, even although the order be in form within the delegated power, nevertheless it must be treated as embraced therein because its authority has been manifested in such an unreasonable manner as to cause it to be within the elementary rule that the substance and not the shadow determines the validity of the exercise of the power; but (*d*) the Supreme Court may not, under the guise of exerting judicial power, usurp merely administrative functions by setting aside a lawful order upon its conception as to whether the administrative discretion has been wisely exercised."

These principles are further elaborated in Interstate Commerce Commission *v.* Union Pacific R. Co.[93] There the Court said: "In cases thus far decided it has been settled that orders of the Commission are final unless (1) beyond the power which it could constitutionally exercise; (2) beyond its statutory power; (3) based upon mistake of law. But questions of fact may be involved in the determination of questions of law, so that an order, regular on its face, may be set aside if it appears: (4) that the rate is so low as to be confiscatory and in violation of the constitutional prohibition against taking property without due process of law; or (5) if the Commission acted so arbitrarily and unjustly as to fix rates contrary to evidence, or without evidence to support it; or (6) if the authority involved has been exercised in such an unreasonable manner as to be within the elementary rule that the substance and not the shadow determines the validity of the exercise of the power."

How wide a door these principles open to court review of

[92] 215 U. S. 452.

[93] 222 U. S. 541, at 547.

so-called "questions of fact" is obvious; yet the Court has not given any clue as to what kinds of questions it will consider "questions of fact"; nor do the precedents afford much help. They contain frequent statements that a finding will be reversed if no account was taken "of facts and circumstances that ought to have been included." [94] But what kinds of "facts or circumstances" ought to have been included, seems to remain purely within the discretion of the Court in each given case. Thus, in Interstate Commerce Commission *v.* Alabama Midland Railroad [95] a finding of the Commission was reversed on the ground that the Commission had not taken competition into account as a "circumstance" in determining whether a rate violated the provisions of the long-haul and short-haul clause. But in the Illinois Central case, where the Court was asked to reverse a finding of the unreasonableness of a rate on the ground that the Commission had refused to treat expenditures for improvement and equipment as an element of operating expenses, the Court refused to interfere.[96] In United States *v.* Baltimore and Ohio Railroad Co.[97] the Commission found that certain allowances paid by the carrier to a shipper for the use of terminal facilities amounted to a concealed rebate and ordered its discontinuance. The Supreme Court apparently drew its own inferences from the evidence, determined that in fact the shipper was renting the facilities to the carrier for the latter's use, and reversed the order. In Interstate Commerce Commission *v.* Chicago, Rock Island and Pacific R. Co.[98] the Commission ordered a reduction of rates from the Atlantic seaboard to Missouri River cities. The carriers claimed that the Commission had based its findings on the competitive disadvantage existing between the Missouri River cities and cities like St. Paul and Minneapolis, and that it had no power to make such economic considerations a main test of reasonableness. The Supreme Court sustained the Commission's order,

[94] Illinois Central R. R. Co. *v.* Interstate Commerce Commission, 206 U. S. 441.

[95] 168 U. S. 144.

[96] 206 U. S. 441.

[97] 231 U. S. 274.

[98] 218 U. S. 88.

three justices dissenting. But in Southern Pacific Railroad *v.* Interstate Commerce Commission,[99] decided the next year, the Court held that the Commission had no power to find rates unreasonable because their economic effect would be to shut out the Willamette Valley lumber industry from the market.

Although the Court has said that orders of the Commission will be reversed when omitting to take into account factors which ought to have been included, or when based on considerations which ought not to have been included, it has given no general test to determine what factors it will regard as falling on either side of the line. It has attempted this more concretely in connection with rates fixed by state commissions. Here obviously the only question is whether or not the rate is confiscatory in such a sense as to deny due process of law. But what test is to determine whether or not a rate is confiscatory? The court has laid down the general standard that the rate must yield a fair return on the fair value of the property.[100] This simply raises the further question of what considerations are to be taken into account in determining the elements of fair value. Mr. Henderson's papers show the uncertainties and inconsistencies of the decisions on this point.[101] They seem to hold that, while going value may be included,[102] it is improper to include good will,[103] but offer no certain test as to where to draw the line. Does fair value mean exchange value, or original cost, or reproduction cost? Mr. Henderson concludes that as to some factors of total value the court means one of these and as to

[99] 219 U. S. 433.

[100] Smyth *v.* Ames, 169 U. S. 466.

[101] *Harv. Law Rev.*, xxxiii, 907 ff. and 1031 ff.

[102] Des Moines Gas Co. *v.* Des Moines, 238 U. S. 153 (1915); Denver *v.* Denver Water Co., 246 U. S. 178 (1918). See Chas. A. Prouty, in *Rep. Amer. Bar Assoc.* (1919), xliv, 438, for an attempt to explain these cases on the ground that the going value so included is an allowance for losses during the early history of the company. But in Galveston Electric Co. *v.* Galveston, 258 U. S. 388 (1921) the court held that going value as represented by past deficits in operation must not be included. (See p. 393 of opinion.) In Houston *v.* Southwestern Bell Telephone Co., another case decided at the October term, 1921 (259 U. S. 318, at p. 325), the court says: "Whether going-concern value should be considered and allowed at all in determining the base for rate-making, depends upon the financial history of the company."

[103] Willcox *v.* Consolidated Gas Co., 212 U. S. 19 (1909).

other factors another; but it appears doubtful whether the decisions admit of even this generalization. It is not a conclusion of pessimism or fatigue to say that, at least upon the surface of the cases, the field luxuriates in riotous uncertainty.[104]

In short, taking the fields of administrative adjudication as a whole, it seems *prima facie* fair to conclude:

1. That there are no iron-clad rules applicable to the cases in general, to forecast with certainty how far a court will review in a given case.

2. A wide latitude is given to the administrative officers and boards to determine conclusively the matters brought before them.

VII

The policy in favor of vesting administrative determinations with finality has been forcefully stated as follows, with special reference to public utilities commissions: "The effectiveness of the orders of the commission . . . is largely determined by the conclusiveness of its findings. For the commission to be most efficient and of the greatest practical value, its orders and regulations, issued after due investigation, must become and remain effective with the final disposition of the commission. The necessary delays attending review by the courts and their lack of time and opportunity for investigating situations at first hand and as a current operating concern, constitute at once the occasion and the chief reason for commission control."[105] Further, it is said that expert commissions

[104] As to court review of determinations of the Federal Trade Commission, the Supreme Court has said (Federal Trade Commission *v.* Beechnut Packing Co., 257 U. S. 446, at p. 453): "The commission in the first instance subject to the judicial review provided, has the determination of practices which come within the scope of the act. As was said in Federal Trade Commission *v.* Gratz, 253 U. S. 421, 'The words *unfair methods of competition* are not defined by the statute and their exact meaning is in dispute. It is for the courts, not the commission, ultimately to determine as matter of law, what they include.'" This language seems to foreshadow a broad exercise of judicial review; indeed, the statute has been said to confer a broader power of review than the Interstate Commerce Act. See Federal Trade Commission *v.* Curtis Publishing Co., 260 U. S. 568; and for a full discussion, see below, Chapter VIII.

[105] O. L. Pond in *Annals Amer. Acad.*, May, 1914; also in Orth, *Readings on the Relations of Government to Property*, p. 399. See also H. J. Friedman in

are better qualified than the courts, not merely to find the facts in the technical provinces where they do their work, but also to draw the proper conclusions. This view is often expressed in the cases. One judge has said: "How is a judge who is not supposed to have any of this special learning or experience, and could not take judicial notice of it if he had it, to review the decision of commissions who should have it, and should act upon it? It seems to us that a judge is not fit to act in such matter. It is not a case of the blind leading the blind, but of one who has always been deaf and blind in these matters insisting that he can see and hear better than one who has always had his eyesight and hearing and has always used

Harv. Law Rev., xxv, 715. It was the experience of the Interstate Commerce Commission from its establishment in 1887 down to the extension of its powers by the Hepburn Act of 1906 which served especially to emphasize the inconveniences of extended court control over the orders of an administrative body. The Commission's orders were not self-executing, but could only be enforced in a proceeding brought by the Commission in a United States Circuit Court. In the court proceeding the Commission's findings had only the effect of *prima facie* evidence. "There was intolerable delay in the redress of grievances. . . . Intolerable delay in procedure was the constant complaint. Years elapsed before final judgments were rendered. The average duration of cases appealed was not less than four years. Sometimes they extended over twice that period. . . . The Georgia Railroad Commission cases were not settled for nine years. Nor did the tedious process end here. After the judicial review, the entire question had to be remanded to the Commission for a new order in conformity with the findings of the court. After nine years of litigation in the Chattanooga case, back it went to the Commission to be retried. First decided in 1892, it was reopened in 1904. Is it any wonder that the number of formal proceedings instituted by shippers steadily dwindled year by year? In 1901 only nineteen petitions were filed. Business of this sort was almost at a standstill. A second unsatisfactory feature of the relations of the Commission to the courts lay in the refusal of the latter to accept the evidence taken before the Commission in the original proceedings as final. . . . The court treated [the proceeding before it] as an original proceeding even as to questions of fact, and proceeded to consider it *de novo*. This of course involved a duplication of all expenses; which, in cases sufficiently important to appeal, were very heavy. . . . Both shipper and railroad therefore commonly came to regard the proceedings before the Commission as merely a necessary formality to be observed prior to the conclusive adjudication of the matter by the courts. This placed the Commission in a most awkward predicament. It was compelled to render a decision upon an entirely imperfect presentation of facts. And this decision was thereafter liable to be reviewed upon the basis of entirely new testimony." (W. Z. Ripley, *Railroads, Rates and Regulation*, 2d ed., pp. 460–462.)

them to the utmost advantage in ascertaining the truth in regard to the matter in question." [106]

On the other hand, the tendency toward allowing administrative bodies, for whatever reasons, to settle private rights conclusively has had to breast a combined current of business opposition and legal tradition. A spokesman for the business point of view has expressed it thus: "The main principle on which the government of the United States rests is that it should be a government of laws and not of men; that no one should have his life, liberty, or property taken without the right to appeal to the courts to determine if the taking is just. The doctrine that regulating commissions or other administrative bodies should be given an arbitrary power over public utilities is simply the doctrine that the property rights of the owners of public utilities should not be given the same protection as the property rights of other persons." [107]

The legal argument was brought to greatest clarity in the debate in the United States Senate during the winter of 1905–1906, when the proposed Hepburn amendments to the Interstate Commerce Act were under consideration.[108] It was then proposed specifically to limit court review of the orders of the Interstate Commerce Commission to the question whether the orders had been regularly made and were within the Commission's "jurisdiction." Senators Spooner and Foraker opposed the proposal, and insisted on the right of shipper and carrier alike to have the benefit of the independent opinion of a court as to whether or not the Commission's conclusions were correct on the facts. The argument was put on its broadest grounds by Senator Foraker in a speech delivered February 28, 1906. He admitted that even under the proposed amendment the Commission's orders could still be set aside by the courts as unconstitutional if the rates they pre-

[106] Canty, J., in Steenerson *v.* Gt. Northern R. Co., 69 Minn. 353, at p. 377.

[107] Samuel O. Dunn, "Regulation by Commission," in *North Amer. Rev.*, Feb., 1914, reprinted in Orth, *Readings on the Relation of Government to Property*, p. 332, at p. 343.

[108] See Theodore Roosevelt, *Autobiography*, pp. 450 ff.

scribed were so high as to be extortionate, or so low as to be confiscatory. But he demanded a larger power for the courts: "Between extortion on the one hand and confiscation on the other, there is in most cases a considerable latitude within which the action of the Commission without review by the courts would be final and conclusive. Why should this jurisdiction be withheld from the courts? Who distrusts them? Only violators of the law have ever had occasion to fear the justice they administer. They have been from the beginning of the common law the sure bulwark of the liberties and rights of the Anglo-Saxon race. Unmoved by passion, prejudice, or public clamor, they have ever been the steadying, reassuring factor in the American government. Why should the advocates of this measure, affecting as it does the highest interests of the American people, seek to exclude them from their appropriate participation in the determination of the great questions that such legislation is sure to precipitate? That there is this unwillingness to allow the courts an *unrestricted*[109] review is enough, not only to excite distrust of this remedy, but to condemn it." [110]

More recently the same view has been stated from the standpoint of a professor in an important law school. In the judicial application to particular cases of rules and regulations made by the same administrative body which applies them, he sees a danger of recurrence to the days when St. Louis and his Frankish predecessors sat under the oak-tree of Vincennes and dealt out a rude and arbitrary executive justice.[111]

And so we are brought again to the initial issue. We have made a wide circuit of the cases and taken a rough survey of the latitude allowed to executive bodies acting in a judicial

[109] Italics mine.

[110] *Cong. Rec.*, 59th Cong., 1st Sess., pp. 3117, 3118. For further particulars as to this controversy, see Chas. A. Prouty in *Amer. Rev. of Revs.*, xxxiii, 594, and J. Wallace Bryan in *Amer. Law Rev.*, xli, 809 ff. For other general discussion see Hon. George Sutherland in *Rep. Amer. Bar. Assoc.* (1917), xlii, 204 ff.; William D. Guthrie, in "The League of Nations and Other Essays," Presidential Address, N. Y. State Bar Assoc., Jan. 19, 1923.

[111] Green, "Separation of Governmental Powers," *Yale Law Jour.*, xxix, 371, especially at pp. 387, 388.

capacity; what bearing does this latitude have on the supposed right of individuals under our legal system to be ruled by law, and by law alone? In the United States the question is complicated by special constitutional doctrines as to the separation and delegability of powers, as to "due process," and as to the position of the courts as the ultimate interpreters of a written constitution. All these constitutional safeguards, however, are but the outworks of an elaborate structure devised to buttress from different sides the central doctrine of the supremacy of law;[112] and discussion can be simplified by striking down to this essential issue. What is involved in the demand that the determination of rights should in the last analysis be a matter for the courts alone?

[112] See J. F. Dillon, *The Laws and Jurisprudence of England and America* (Boston, 1894), pp. 225 ff.

CHAPTER IV

HISTORICAL DOCTRINE OF THE SUPREMACY OF LAW

WHAT essential difference is there under current American conditions between the law courts on one hand and administrative tribunals on the other which should cause the ones to be feared and the others favored?[1] The judges of our law courts are in some jurisdictions appointed by the state governor; industrial boards, health boards, and utilities commissions are often selected by the same method. In most of the states the judges are elected by the people; so are the members of many administrative boards. Judges generally hold office not for life but for a definite term of years, like administrative officials. They are often elected on party tickets; frequently there is some provision to secure bi-partisan, if not non-partisan, membership of administrative bodies. In the light of the theory of sovereignty which has come to be practically axiomatic within the last hundred years, we act everywhere on the assumption that judges and officials alike are government officers engaged in substantially the same work of carrying into execution the will of the state, as expressed in law. For law is primarily conceived to-day as the will of the state,[2] applied to the conduct of individuals through

[1] See language of Thompson, J., in State Public Utilities Commission *v.* Springfield Gas & Electric Co., 291 Ill. 209, at p. 216: "It is clear from the salary fixed for the commissioners and the great power vested in the commission that the legislature intended to create an office of dignity and great responsibility. . . . The commission sits to administer justice . . . . The notion that commissions of this kind should be closely restrained by the courts, and that justice in our day can only be had in courts is not conducive to the best results. There is no reason why the members of the Public Utilities Commission . . . should not develop and establish a system of rules and precedents as wise and beneficial within their sphere of action, as those established by the early common-law judges."

[2] Among Anglo-American legal writers this view goes back at least to Blackstone: "Municipal law is a rule of civil conduct prescribed by the su-

various appropriate contacts. This necessitates adjudication; what gives rise, then, to the feeling that the process of adjudication should function through the medium of a body of officers called by one name rather than another, though similarly chosen and holding their authority by substantially the same tenure?

There are a number of answers. The first is that we here touch into life an obscure nerve of slumbering tradition — a nerve running back into a remote period strangely out of keeping with the railroads and electric-power companies and modern sanitary arrangements which its dead hand still so powerfully affects. The reference just made to judges as government officials, and the statement that their function, like that of other officers, is to execute law as the will of the state, should direct attention to a paradox already noted but not emphasized. The paradox consists in setting law and government over against each other as opposites. Such an antithesis is wholly foreign to current assumptions which can let pass without objection an assertion that judges are governmental officers of the state. Yet a mode of thought wherein the opposition was not a paradox but a self-evident commonplace rules us from the grave when, like Senator Foraker, we appeal from the decisions of administrative bodies to our right to be judged in a court of law. To make the point clear requires a descent into the sub-cellars of our legal history.

I

Few governments have ever more completely violated our American dogma of the separation of powers than the mediaeval government of England.[3] Its central organ, the *Curia Regis*, was at once Parliament, Privy Council, and courts of law in one. Differentiation took place slowly, and separate bodies ultimately emerged from the common germinal cell. But before this process had ended, feudalism had given place

preme power in a state," *Commentaries*, ed. Christian i, 46. See also T. E. Holland, *Elements of Jurisprudence*, 10th ed., pp. 53, 54; W. W. Willoughby, *The Nature of the State*, p. 163.

[3] G. B. Adams, *Origins of the English Constitution*, pp. 194, 195.

to the strong despotism of the Tudors. Parliament, the Privy Council, and the law courts, although by this time separate organs,[4] were all alike more or less completely subservient to the will of a personal sovereign. What might have happened to the law courts in England is illustrated by two centuries of the history of the Parliament of Paris.[5] Maitland has summed up their position under the Tudors by saying that "the judges of the courts of common law were very distinctly the king's servants. It is needless to accuse them as a class of any disgraceful subserviency, but some of them were disgracefully subservient — past history had made their position difficult. The king was the fountain of all justice; they were but his deputies — this was the old theory." [6] A hundred years later all this had changed. The judges had become independent of the crown. They no longer held office *durante bene placito*. By the Act of Settlement their commissions were to be made out *quamdiu se bene gesserint*, their salaries were to be permanently fixed, and they were not to be removable except on the address of both Houses of Parliament.[7] In the history of those hundred years, and

[4] Maitland, *Constitutional History of England*, p. 253.

[5] See G. Hanotaux, *La France en 1614*, pp. 177–180.

[6] Maitland, *op. cit.*, p. 267. For the part that the common-law judges played in exalting the royal prerogative in the reign of Henry VIII, see H. A. L. Fisher, *Political History of England from 1485 to 1547*, pp. 214, 215: "It was a dictum ascribed to Fyneux, the lord chief-justice, that 'the prince's prerogative and the subjects' privileges are social felicities together, but empty notions asunder.'" Lord Herbert of Cherbury observed in his *Life and Reign of Henry VIII* that "that king was noted not to admit reason of law everywhere for reason of state; therefore he used to take the advice of the judges obliquely, and no otherwise than to discover how safe his own designs were, and so with less danger to vary from them. Which deviations yet he would so regulate as his actions had still, if not their ground, at least their pretext, from the common law" (ed. 1649, pp. 3, 4). *Cf.* also the well-known passage from Lord Bacon's "Essay of Judicature": "Let judges be lions, but yet lions under the throne, being circumspect that they do not check or oppose any points of sovereignty"; also Bacon's "Speech to Sir John Denham, when he was called to be one of the Barons of the Exchequer" (1617): "The king's prerogative and the law are not two things; but the king's prerogative is law, and the principal part of the law, the first born or 'pars prima' of the law; and therefore in conserving or maintaining that, you conserve and maintain the law" (James Spedding, *The Letters and the Life of Francis Bacon*, vi, 203).

[7] Maitland, *op. cit.*, p. 312.

the signal change which it embodied, the view and habit had crystallized which concern us here — and largely as a result of forces represented, and in great measure shaped, by a single man, Chief Justice Coke. The origin of these forces requires still another descent into legal origins.

Feudalism has been described as organized anarchy. More definitely, it was an unstable equilibrium of multitudinous political forces pulling in different directions. The only stabilizing force was the power of the king, stronger in England for various reasons than elsewhere; and hence against the king's power were everywhere pointed the weapons of every feudal class in turn. The motives of Gregory at Canossa, and of the barons and Stephen Langton at Runnymede, were not dominantly unselfish, and their object was the same — to put a bridle on the power of a king. The growth of trade, the visitations of the plague, the temptations of wool-growing, the invention of gunpowder, and the increase in the quantity of money worked in England, as some of the same and other causes worked in France, in the king's favor, and proved too strong for the forces of opposition. The result was the sudden emergence on the map of Europe, near the time of the discovery of America, of a brood of centralized monarchies, governed by dynasts steeped in the feudal view that public office was private property and that kingdoms and provinces were estates to be farmed in the interest of a sovereign person.[8] What had before been the selfish interest of separate classes now became perforce the cause of a whole nation; and seventeenth-century advocates of public liberty against the patrimonial theory of sovereignty resorted to the argumentative weapons which had been forged by feudal and ecclesiastical polemic in older struggles against the royal power. Of these none was more congenial than the idea of "sovereign law."

[8] "The King is above all a functionary with the full control of all public power . . . and above all a lord with full ownership of public power. . . . Also for long the kings of France have had sovereign power by prescriptive right of property," Loyseau, *Traité des Offices*, quoted in Duguit, *Law in the Modern State*, trans. Laski, p. 7.

II

Dilettante speculation under the Roman Empire conventionalized the notion that men had invented laws to control their rulers. Both Seneca and Tacitus, different as were their general points of view, adopted it.[9] It was congenial also to Church fathers, who appealed to it as an argument in their clashes with refractory emperors.[10] By way of reaction, imperialists emphasized the Byzantine doctrine that the emperor was *legibus solutus;*[11] and the issue thus joined resounded throughout the Middle Ages until it touched our own problem in the historic controversy between James I and Coke.

Controversial phrases have a habit of deepening into philosophical absolutes, especially when they respond to some vague and widely felt necessity; and so it was soon said, not that the king is bound by laws, but that the king is under "the law."[12] This was in part due, no doubt, to the Germanic view of law, to which we shall have to turn in a moment; perhaps it was also in part a reversion to Aristotle's theory of the "sovereignty of law."[13] At all events, an abstract entity, so congenial to the mental habit of the Middle Ages, had been conceived, which was thought of as a protective power existing above the king, and placing a limit upon his sovereignty. "We will not condemn or dishonor or oppress anyone contrary to the law and to justice," announced the grandsons of Charlemagne at Mersen; in Magna Charta, John acknowledged the supremacy of "the law of the land."

The idea was carried forward in English legal thought by

[9] Seneca, *Epistolae*, xiv, 2, 6 (ep. 90); Tacitus, *Annals*, iii, 26.

[10] R. W. and A. J. Carlyle, *History of Mediaeval Political Theory in the West*, i, 163, 164.

[11] *Ibid.*, p. 171.

[12] *Ibid.*, p. 230.

[13] *Politics*, III, xvi, 5: *ὁ μὲν οὖν τὸν νόμον κελεύων ἄρχειν δοκεῖ κελεύειν ἄρχειν τὸν θέον καὶ τὸν νοῦν μόνους, ὁ δ'ἄνθρωπον κελεύων προστίθησι καὶ θηρίον* ("He who bids the law rule may be deemed to bid God and reason rule, but he who bids man rule adds an element of the beast"); *ibid.*, IV, iv, 31: *δεῖ γὰρ τὸν μὲν νόμον ἄρχειν πάντων, τῶν δὲ καθ' ἕκαστα τὰς ἀρχάς καὶ ταύτην πολιτείαν κρίνειν* ("The law ought to be supreme over all, and the magistracies and the government should judge only of particulars").

Bracton; and through the old cases runs a red thread of "fundamental law" which neither the king nor his Parliament can touch.[14] With the reaction against the abuse of royal power by the Stuarts, this "fundamental law" rises into central prominence,[15] dominates the pamphlets of the times, and stores up its energy for the future in Harrington's famous phrase which, at one remove, sways our American courts still, when they announce that government should be by laws, and not by men.[16]

Throughout this development, law is thought of as something separate from and independent of government. We ought to note also that government, as we speak of it to-day, was not spoken of in the Middle Ages, for no such thing existed: in its place stood the power, or *imperium*, or "sovereignty," as it later came to be called, of the ruler. The phrases of a period must be read in the light of its problems, and of the facts which lie behind them; and the pertinent fact in the later Middle Ages was that the functions which we to-day call government were in effect conceived as the private property of a sovereign person, expressed in terms of land law. The king owned his supreme lordship with its incidents of power, as his knights owned the lordship of their several fiefs.[17] There was no public law, in our sense, for there was as yet no real "commonwealth." The commonwealth, or nation, first emerged as a clear fact in Europe in the sixteenth century, the product of the multiple social and economic and military changes of a period of change.[18]

[14] See Pound, *Spirit of the Common Law*, pp. 64 ff.

[15] McIlwain, *High Court of Parliament*, pp. 81–92. Even an innovator like Cromwell was driven by the logic of his position to insist upon an immutable "fundamental" law, supreme over government: "Some things are Fundamentals! . . . In every government there must be somewhat Fundamental, somewhat like a Magna Charta, which should be standing, be unalterable . . . Of what assurance is a Law . . . if it lie in the Legislature to *un*law it again? . . . It will be a rope of sand; it will give no security; for the same men may unbuild what they have built," Speech of Sept. 12, 1654, in Carlyle's *Cromwell.*

[16] Harrington, "Oceana," *Works*, ed. Toland, 3d ed., 1737, p. 37.

[17] Loyseau, quoted in Duguit, *Law in the Modern State*, trans. Laski, p. 7. See also Bodin, *Six Livres de la République* (Paris, ed. 1577), p. 89.

[18] For the growth and emergence of a nation or "commonwealth" in France and the various forces that contributed to it, see Gabriel Hanotaux,

When it emerged, it had no political organs of its own — no organs, that is, responsive and responsible to it.[19] On one side of a gulf stood the people, at last welded into a more or less organic unity, and on the other, wholly divorced from them, their rulers, claiming authority by a transcendental title, and subject to no popular check or control. Government, in short, was not an organ of an organized people, but an alien force imposing itself from above and claiming to rule by an inherent and not a derived authority.[20] The history of

La France en 1614, pp. 105–131. Bodin's *Republic* represented the coming of this development to self-consciousness.

[19] At the outset, "commonwealth" was a crude personification identified with the person of the monarch. The king was the "bearer of the public person" of the *universitas*, or community, subject to him; the *universitas* acts through him, John of Salisbury, *Policraticus*, iv, 2; v, 4. This is the conception which still lies at the heart of Hobbes's political theory. "*Sola patria*, which is the prince, doth challenge to herself all duties," wrote a member of Parliament during Mary Tudor's reign, Hatfield MSS, i, 530, 531, quoted in Pollard, *Political History of England from 1547 to 1603*, p. 132. This identification no doubt goes back to the mediaeval inability to conceive the possibility of a *universitas*, *e.g.*, a kingdom, taking corporate action except through its "head," *i. e.*, the king. See my article on "The Mediaeval Conception of Kingship as Developed in the *Policraticus* of John of Salisbury" in *Speculum* (July, 1926), i, 308 at pp. 332, 333. As late as the time of Coke, the view was urged in argument at the bar that a corporation could not exist without a head, any more than could a "body natural," and several cases from the Year Books cited in support of it, Case of Sutton's Hospital, 10 Coke Rep. 30b. Its natural consequence was the dictum of Bartolus, "*imperator est ipsum imperium*," *Com. in Cod.*, x, rubr. 1, nr. 13. It probably lies at the basis of the common-law doctrine that "the king is a body politic": "and oftentimes in the reports of our book-cases, and in acts of Parliament also, the crown or kingdom is taken for the king himself," Calvin's Case, 7 Coke Rep. 12a. But in the same case the position of the king was further aggrandized by the holding that allegiance is due to him in his natural personal capacity, "and it is not due to the politic capacity only, that is, to his crown or kingdom distinct from his natural capacity," *ibid.*, 10a. This was the outgrowth, no doubt, of the feudal conception of "homage," J. Flach, *Les Origines de l'Ancienne France*, ii, 429, *ibid.*, iii, 388; Funck-Brentano, *I e Roi*, p. 9, pp. 21 ff.; Seignobos, *The Feudal Régime*, tr. Dow, pp. 38–39; also my article above referred to, *Speculum*, i, pp. 322–325. The result was to buttress personal absolutism from two entirely inconsistent directions.

[20] See Filmer, *Patriarcha*, ch. ii. The doctrine was even advanced that all the goods of the subject belonged to the sovereign, who might at his good pleasure resume the whole or any part. In a debate in the House of Commons, Sergeant Heale said: "I marvel much, Mr. Speaker, that the House should hesitate about a subsidy asked by the Queen, when all we have is her Majesty's, and she may lawfully at her pleasure take it from us; yea, she hath as much right to all our lands and goods as to any revenue of her crown," *Parl. Hist.*,

subsequent centuries is full of popular effort, first to place checks on this alien force, as is best seen in seventeenth-century England, and afterwards to demolish it altogether and substitute in its place a power frankly delegated by the people.

This second step was not fully taken until our own and the French revolutions; even Burke could still regard as a shocking novelty the doctrine that sovereign rulers should be required to derive their titles from the ruled.[21] During the formative period of the ideas which guided our so-called "founding fathers," government as men knew it was largely, in fact as in thought, a power existing independently of the people; an autocratic power in the full etymological sense, belonging of right to an individual, and around which the people were seeking under difficulties to weave a web of effective control. This effort took the form in England of developing a representative Parliament as a responsible agency of the people, with power sufficient to check and balance the independent power of the king. The meaning of this struggle is embalmed for us to-day in the doctrine that legislative power must be kept separate from executive.[22]

i, 920, quoted in Campbell's *Lives of the Lord Chancellors*, ii, 204. This was but a logical extension to chattels of the basic principle of feudal land-law; but was not the good sergeant committing the unpardonable sin of his calling in reasoning from land to chattels?

21. See his strictures in the first part of *Reflections on the Revolution in France* against Price and Priestly for maintaining the doctrine. Grattan told Samuel Rogers that "Burke could not sleep quietly on his pillow at night unless he thought that the king had a right to take it from under him." *Recollections of the Table-Talk of Samuel Rogers* (N. Y., 1856), p. 173.

22 For the connection see Locke, *Second Essay of Civil Government*, cc. xii, xiii; see also Rapin, *Dissertation sur les Whigs et les Tories*, and the writings of Bolingbroke, *passim*, especially *Remarks on the History of England*, Letter vii, and *Dissertation on Parties*, Letters xi, xii, xiii. The theory was a compromise with the idea of a monarch ruling by original rather than by derived right; Parliament existed as a check. An effective survival in practice is the independent ordinance-making power of the British crown; see Willoughby and Rogers, *Introduction to Government*, p. 205. For the influence of Rapin, with his theory of separation of powers, on American thought, note that Jefferson preferred Rapin's *History of England* to all other histories of that country, letter to anonymous correspondent, Oct. 25, 1825 (*Complete Works*, ed. Washington, vii, 412); and that John Dickinson used Rapin's *History* in his *Farmer's Letters*, 1767, no. xi (*Political Writings*, Wilmington, 1801, i, 262).

But the effort in England to check royal independence by building up against it a concrete organ of government responsible to the nation was mainly the work of the second half of the seventeenth century; the early part of the century sought to apply a check of a different sort. The Middle Ages were still near enough at hand for the transcendental to preserve its glamour and its force — transcendental authority was still the most respectable authority: and therefore, if the king claimed independent supremacy by a transcendental title, the most effective check on that supremacy would be to erect over him a power more transcendental still. Such a power was "sovereign law." In this conception, foreign as it is to our current ways of thought, we are face to face with the meaning of that separation between law on the one hand and government on the other which is somehow so congenial to us still, but yet so puzzling when we come to set it side by side with some of our other everyday working assumptions. To the Middle Ages and the men who were heirs of the Middle Ages, law was not the will of the state expressed through the government, for what government there was, was not properly an organ of the state, as we conceive it, at all; law was a transcendental force, "the breath of God, the harmony of the world," [23] clothed with an inherent and independent authority, and ruling the sovereign from above and without, as the sovereign in his own turn ruled from above and from without the individuals and groups who were his subjects. This was the idea which had been used as a weapon against kings in the Middle Ages; one of the counts in the indictment against Richard II was that he had enforced enactments which were erroneous and repugnant to law and to reason.[24] And this was the idea for which Coke did battle against James.

What was the nature and content of this law, which was

[23] Hooker, *Ecclesiastical Polity*, Book I, ch. xvi; or, as Mr. Justice Holmes has phrased it, "a brooding omnipresence in the sky," Southern Pacific Co. *v.* Jensen, 244 U. S. 205 at p. 222.

[24] McIlwain, *High Court of Parliament*, p. 69. "The conflict between law and prerogative constitutes a large part of English constitutional history," G. B. Adams, *Constitutional History of England*, p. 79.

not the creature of government but was above government? The idea, as a practical force, appears to have had a Teutonic and not a Roman origin. The Romans made much, of course, of natural law; but at the time of the invasions they had come to recognize positive law as deriving its authority from the will of the emperor — that is, as we should say, from the government. The Germanic conception of positive law, on the other hand, was the product of less sophisticated institutions. The law that they knew was custom — the immemorial usages which had crystallized within the tribe and were pronounced from time to time in the solemn dooms of the elders. "It was part of the national or tribe life; it had grown with the tribe, changing, no doubt, but the people or the tribe were hardly conscious of the changes."[25] "To them the law was not something made or created at all . . . legislative acts were not expressions of will, but records or promulgations of that which was recognized as already binding upon men."[26] Law was thus naturally conceived as a permanent thing, something always existing and to be found by the elders in council, announced by them but not made.[27]

[25] Carlyle, *History of Mediaeval Political Theory in the West*, i, 235; see also McIlwain, *op. cit.*, p. 46.

[26] Carlyle, *op. cit.*, iii, 41. "It is difficult to appreciate that among all peoples in their earlier periods of political development the state was regarded as almost exclusively an organ for the execution of the law, not for its creation," W. W. Willoughby, *Political Theories of the Ancient World*, p. 64.

[27] Discovery Theory of Law. This notion of law as something not made, but existing and to be found, was common to European peoples so long as their institutions remained comparatively primitive. Thus it forms a part of the well-known definition of law attributed to Demosthenes: "Every law is a discovery, a gift from the Gods, a precept of wise men, a righting of intentional and unintentional wrongs, a compact between all the members of the state, in accordance with which all who are within the state should live," First Speech against Aristogeiton, 774. For a very early expression of the view that law is a "discovery," coupled oddly with an anticipation of the doctrine of legislative sovereignty, see Herodotus, III, 31: "Εἰρομένου τοῦ Καμβύσεω, ὑπεκρίνοντο αὐτῷ [οἱ βασιλήϊοι δικασταὶ]. . . φόμενοι ἐξευρηκέναι νόμον τῷ βασιλεύοντι Περσέων ἐξεῖναι ποιέειν τὸ ἂν βούληται." For a very late view, see Calvin Coolidge, *Have Faith in Massachusetts*, p. 4: "Men do not make laws. They do but discover them . . . . That state is most fortunate in its form of government which has the aptest instruments for the discovery of laws." For an intermediate view, which dominated the thought of the middle ages, and which identified the "immutable law" with the "law of God," see St. Augustine, *De Vera Religione*, c. 31:

In fact, almost the greatest possible violation of law was to change it. Hence the clamor against progressive kings raised throughout the Middle Ages by the people, demanding back their "good old laws"; every reform had to be disguised under the appearance of a restoration of long-lost legal rights.[28] Gradually from Roman sources filtered in the idea of a law of nature, in England spoken of as simply a law of reason,[29] which becomes confused in no clearly understood way with the customary law of the land; so that "to discern the law of reason from the law positive is very hard," as we read in "Doctor and Student." [30] Fortescue, whom Coke follows in the main on this point, says that the laws of England are natural, customary, and statute; "the two former,

"Conditor legum temporalium . . . illam ipsam consulit aeternam de qua nulli animae judicare datum est; ut secundam ejus incommutabiles regulas quid sit pro tempore jubendum vetandumque discernat. *Aeternam igitur legem mundis animis fas est cognoscere, judicare non fas est* [italics mine]. Hoc autum interest, quod ad cognoscendum satis est ut videamus ita esse aliquid vel non ita; ad judicandum vero addimus aliquid quo significemus posse esse et aliter." (Migne, *Pat. Lat.*, xxxiv, 147.)

[28] McIlwain, *op. cit.*, p. 66; this was observed and commented on in the *Eikon Basilike* (16mo ed., 1649), pp. 124 ff.

[29] "The work done elsewhere by the 'law of nature' was done in England by 'reason,'" Holdsworth, *History of English Law*, 1st ed., ii, 512 ff. *Doctor and Student* speaks of "the law of nature, which is also called the law of reason" (Dialogue I, ch. ii); "when anything is grounded upon the law of nature, they say [in England] that reason will that such a thing be done" (*ibid.*, ch. v). See also Pollock, *Essays in the Law* (London, 1922), pp. 55–59; *The Expansion of the Common Law* (Boston, 1904), pp. 107–139.

[30] Dialogue I, ch. ix. In Calvin's Case (7 Coke Rep. 1a, at p. 4b, and 12b), Coke said that the law of nature was part of the law of England. In his argument in the same case, Sir Francis Bacon said: "Our law is grounded upon the law of nature. . . . For as the common law is more worthy than the statute law, so the law of nature is more worthy than them both. . . . It was civil and national laws that brought in these words and differences of 'civis' and 'externus,' alien and native. And therefore because they tend to abridge the law of nature, the law favoureth not them, but takes them strictly; even as our law hath an excellent rule, that customs of towns and boroughs shall be taken and construed strictly and precisely, because they do abridge and derogate from the law of the land. So by the same reason, all national laws are to be taken strictly and hardly in any point wherein they abridge and derogate from the law of nature." *Works*, ed. Spedding, Ellis and Heath (Boston, 1861), xv, 202, 226. This exaltation of the "law of nature" above the common law seems unique, and was no doubt for a political reason; ordinarily they were identified; the "reason" of the common law, and the law of nature, were taken to be the same.

when they are reduced into writing and made public by a sufficient authority of the prince and commanded to be observed, they then pass into the nature of statutes."[31] In short, a statute does not make new law; it promulgates, and gives greater emphasis and clarity to, what had always been law before.[32] It is the peculiar relation which subsisted in England between "natural law," or the "law of reason," on the one hand, and the customary law of the land on the other, that lends to the English common law its distinctive flavor. Common law was essentially custom, but it was also something more: it consisted of customs which were regarded as reasonable, or at least not unreasonable. The common law was thus conceived as fused of two elements and presenting two aspects: (1) it was the law of the land, that is, a body of traditional custom; (2) it was the "perfection of reason." So artificial was the manner in which these two elements united to form it, that it was a science and "mystery" in the mediaeval sense, to be known only after hard discipline and study.[33] On the other hand, such was the intrinsic and independent authority of the elements themselves,

[31] *De Laudibus Legum Angliae*, ch. xv. Cf. Oliver St. John, in his argument against Strafford (1641): "If any question arise concerning either a Custom or an Act of Parliament, the Common Law of England, the First, the Primitive, and the General Law, that's the Rule and Expositor of them, and of their several extents." (Rushworth, *Strafford's Trial*, p. 695.)

[32] For the resulting tendency, still at work, in the Anglo-American legal system to treat statutes as of relatively minor authority in comparison with the common law, see Pound, "Common Law and Legislation," in *Harv. Law Rev.*, xxi, pp. 283 ff., and *Interpretations of Legal History*, p. 65. For a particular attempt by the courts to whittle away the effect of a statute by engrafting common-law doctrines into its construction, see Seaboard Air Line R. Co. *v.* Horton (1914), 233 U. S. 492, and Edward P. Buford, "Assumption of Risk under the Federal Employers' Liability Act," *Harv. Iaw Rev.*, xxviii, 163 ff.

[33] *Doctor and Student* (Dialogue I, ch. iv) enumerates six principal sources of the law of England: (1) the law of reason; (2) the revealed law of God; (3) general customs of the realm; (4) principles called maxims; (5) particular customs; (6) statutes. Of the conception of law in this period Professor Sidgwick has said: "Law was to an important extent conceived by both governors and governed as a subject of science, capable of being learnt by special study, but not capable of being altered by the mere arbitrary will of the government any more than the principles of mathematics," *Elements of Politics*, 2d ed., pp. 652, 653. *Cf.* the attitude of Mr. Justice Field in his dissenting opinion in Munn *v.* Illinois, 94 U. S. 117.

natural reason and immemorial tradition, that the common law, so intimately compounded of both, was well qualified from the standpoint of the times to occupy in men's minds a position more venerable than even the sovereign power of a monarch. The place which common law, so conceived, held in the thought of Englishmen at the beginning of the Tudor period has been vividly described by Father Figgis:

"The Common Law, though containing much that may originally have been directly enacted, yet possessed that mysterious sanctity of prescription which no legislator can bestow. The Common Law is pictured invested with a halo of dignity peculiar to the embodiment of the deepest principles and to the highest expression of human reason and of the law of nature implanted by God in the heart of man. As yet men are not clear that an Act of Parliament can do more than declare the Common Law. It is the Common Law which men set up as the object of worship. They regard it as the symbol of ordered life and disciplined activities, which are to replace the license and violence of the evil times now passed away.... Instead of the caprice of the moment or the changing principles of competing dynastic policies, or the pleasure of some great noble, or the cunning of a usurper, there shall rule in England a system, older than Kings and Parliaments, of immemorial majesty and almost Divine authority. . . . The Common Law is the perfect ideal of law; for it is natural reason, developed and expounded by the collective wisdom of many generations. By it kings reign and princes decree judgment. By it are fixed the relations of the estates of the realm and the fundamental laws of the constitution. Based on long usage and almost supernatural wisdom, its authority is above, rather than below, that of Acts of Parliament or Royal ordinances, which owe their fleeting existence to the caprice of the King or the pleasure of councillors, which have a merely material sanction and may be repealed at any moment." [34]

Such an entity was well fitted to fill that position of tran-

[34] *Divine Right of Kings*, 1st ed., pp. 226–228.

scendent and inherent authority which Coke was to give to it in his controversy with James.[35]

III

The policy of James was part of a constitutional process which was at the same time at work all over Europe. Life having gone out of the old struggle between the mediaeval classes in the new-found unity of the nation, the checks and balances which that old struggle had created were silently breaking down, leaving room for the expansion of royal prerogative to fill up the vacuum. James, like the Tudors before him, used his opportunity. He undertook to promulgate his personal will as law in the forms of ordinances which had never secured the consent of Parliament.[36] He established executive courts, which were not bound by the common law and were subject only to his own will, for the trial of cases over which there was already jurisdiction in the common-law courts.[37] He claimed the right to judge in his own person whatever causes he pleased.[38] These pretensions, if realized, would have reduced England in fact, as in theory, into a private estate of the king, just as France was in process of being reduced.[39]

But in the way of these pretensions Coke set as a barrier the supremacy of the common law. The struggle which ensued raised issues which, so far as mere form is concerned, were strikingly like many of those raised to-day in connection with the powers of administrative boards and commissions, and which have by force of precedent carried over to affect our modern attitude toward the latter. Thus, the question whether or not the king can issue ordinances parallels our

[35] The identification of the "common" law with the "fundamental" law which was supreme over the king, goes back at least to 1607, when James referred to it in a speech to Parliament. McIlwain, *op. cit.*, p. 82; *The Political Works of James I*, p. 300. It was made by Philip Hunton in his *Treatise of Monarchy* (1643), and answered by Filmer: see his *Freeholder's Grand Inquest, etc.*, ed. 1680, p. 266.

[36] 12 Coke Rep. 74.

[37] 12 Coke Rep. 40, 50, 58, 82.

[38] 12 Coke Rep. 63.

[39] For an excellent summary, see J. A. R. Marriott, *Falkland*, ch. ii.

modern question as to whether or not an executive body or officer can establish regulations; and the arguments used *pro* and *con* have followed much the same lines. Coke lays it down that the king may not alter the law of the land, and therefore cannot by proclamation make a thing unlawful which was lawful before. "Proclamations which are against law and reason for that are void." [40] But who was to decide the question of lawfulness or reasonableness? Coke's answer was, the common-law judges; and he went farther and held it was their right "for the weal public" to be the final interpreters of statutes, and acts of Parliament as well.[41] Chancey's Case has a significant resemblance to modern cases in administrative law.[42] A statute of Elizabeth conferred certain jurisdiction on the High Commission, an executive court consisting largely of men who were not lawyers. Under this statute the Commissioners took jurisdiction of a petition brought against one Chancey by his wife, charging adultery and non-support. They ordered the defendant to allow the petitioner suitable maintenance, and, on his failure to obey the order, committed him to jail for contempt. Coke issued a writ of habeas corpus out of the Common Pleas for his release. The question turned entirely on the interpretation of the statute of Elizabeth. Coke claimed that it was the right of the judges to interpret it, and in so doing held that it was merely declaratory of previous law and conferred no new jurisdiction on the Commissioners,[43] and hence that they had acted without jurisdiction in their proceedings against Chancey.

Driven forward by the logic of his position, Coke finally claimed for the judges the power, not merely to interpret, but in effect to set aside a statute. This was in the well-known case of Dr. Bonham, a case which also belongs in the family tree of modern administrative law cases. A charter of Henry VIII had forbidden any person to practice physic in London who had not been examined and licensed by the College of Physicians of that city. This charter was confirmed

[40] 12 Coke Rep. 75.

[41] 12 Coke Rep. 85.

[42] 12 Coke Rep. 82, 84.

[43] 12 Coke Rep. 85.

by an act of Parliament which gave to the College power to commit to jail persons who practised in London without its license, and also to impose a fine upon them, one moiety of which was to be paid to the king and the other moiety to the College. Bonham held the degree of doctor of medicine from the University of Cambridge. He took an examination before the London College of Physicians and failed to pass, and thereafter, against the order of the College, continued to practise in London. He was summoned before the College authorities and given a hearing, at which he set up his right as a university graduate to practise without the license of the College. The College punished his defiance by committing him to jail, and he brought an action of trespass for false imprisonment. The case was heard on demurrer, and judgment was given for the plaintiff. The court refused to apply that part of the statute which authorized the College to punish those who practised in London without its license, and held that its power to fine and imprison was strictly limited to cases where actual malpractice was proved. This result was reached only by a palpable misconstruction of the statute, a misconstruction explained by Coke on the ground that the other and obviously sounder interpretation would make the College authorities at once judges and parties in the same cause. Such a result would be contrary to common law; and then follows the famous sentence: "and it appears in our books that in many cases the common law will control acts of Parliament and sometimes adjudge them to be utterly void; for when an act of Parliament is against common right and reason, or repugnant or impossible to be performed, the common law will control it, and adjudge such act to be void." [44]

[44] 8 Rep. 118. Lord Holt approved the doctrine of Dr. Bonham's case in City of London *v.* Wood, 12 Mod. 669, at p. 687. *Cf.* also Coke, *Inst.*, iii, 111: "If any statute be made to the contrary of *Magna Charta*, it shall be holden for none." The doctrine of Dr. Bonham's case was expressed in slightly different form by Lord Chief Justice Hobart a few years later: "An act of Parliament made against natural equity, as to make a man judge in his own cause, is void in itself, for *jura naturae sunt immutabilia*, and they are *leges legum*," Day *v.* Savadge, Hobart, 87 (1623). This is one of the rare cases where our courts have used the term "law of nature." Milton wrote that "all our lawyers admit that if any law or custom be contrary to the law of God, of nature, or of reason, it

The effect of these decisions is that in any dispute of jurisdiction between executive bodies and the law courts, the latter will assume paramount authority to define the jurisdiction of the former. The reason is clear. The executive is the king, — that power in the community which claims

ought to be looked upon as null and void," "Defence of the People of England," c. viii, in *Prose Works*, Bohn ed., i, pp. 168, 169. Locke says that a statute is void if contrary to natural law, *Second Essay of Civil Government*, ch. ii. Blackstone repeats Locke: "The law of nature is superior in obligation to any other . . . no human laws are of any validity if contrary to this," *Commentaries*, ed. Christian, i, 41. But Christian points out in a note the conflict with Blackstone's own doctrine (*ibid.*, p. 91) of legislative sovereignty. Coke's dictum in Dr. Bonham's case may be compared with Selden's language: "The parliament may declare law as well as any inferior court, viz., the King's Bench. In this or that particular case the King's Bench will declare unto you what the law is; but that binds nobody but whom the case concerns: so the highest court, the parliament, may do, but not declare law, that is make law, that was never heard of before," Selden's *Table Talk*, ed. Reynolds, lxxvi, sec. 5. In his *Judicature in Parliament* (*Works*, iii, 1651) Selden maintains that judgments in Parliament had been strictly guided by the "lex terrae," which the Parliament could not alter. But Selden seems to be certainly referring to Parliament when acting in its judicial as opposed to its legislative capacity, for elsewhere he says, "The Parliament of England has no arbitrary power in point of Judicature, but in point of making law," *Table Talk*, cviii, sec. 8. The distinction between Parliament acting in a legislative capacity and Parliament acting in a judicial capacity was, however, as yet imperfectly understood. Oliver St. John seems to have argued that wherever there was a precedent to go by, — *i. e.*, a previously established rule, — the function of Parliament was "judicial"; but that where there was no precedent, and hence no rule, Parliament would have to establish one, and then its action would be "legislative," *Argument of Law concerning the Bill of Attainder of Thomas Earle of Strafford, etc.*, London, printed by G. M. for John Bartlett, 1641, pp. 3, 4, 72, and *passim;* also printed in Rushworth, *op. cit.*, pp. 675 ff. Coke nowhere suggests that the power of "judicature" of the Parliament is to be distinguished from its ordinary power of "proceeding by bill," *Inst.*, iv, 23, 26, 36. This failure to distinguish between "legislative" and "judicial" functions was inevitable so long as human laws in general were conceived as under a necessity of conforming to preëxisting divine or natural laws (Augustine, *De vera Religione*, c. 31, Migne, *Pat. Lat.*, xxxiv, 147), and so long as English statutes were conceived as mere promulgations of preëxisting common law (Fortescue, *De Laudibus Legum Angliae*, c. xv). For the function of human law "making" or statutory enactment could thus have nothing of the creative about it, but consisted entirely in an effort to "discover" and formulate for a present purpose a preëxisting rule, which is essentially a "judicial" function. The conception of law "making" as creative, with the resulting necessity of distinguishing it from the judicial function of law "finding," seems to have been largely a producer of the Civil War. It begins to be emphasized with Hobbes: "Seventhly, is annexed to sovereignty

to be independent of it, — and what the courts are doing is simply choosing the course which will make of the common law an effective practical check on a dangerous and otherwise irresponsible sovereign. They are agencies of the English people in its earliest attempt to find some force which will control a sovereign not ruling by popular right. We must always remember this when we are tempted to reason from these old cases to modern instances. Government has been subsequently tamed — deprived of its transcendental independence, and reduced to a thing which issues out of and returns back to the people. There is no longer the same need as in Coke's time for throwing on the courts so great a power of restraining it, for the courts are no longer the sole or the most effective restraining agency.[45]

The old cases explain historically the circumstances which gave its bent to our law of administrative officers, and which brought the courts to their present position of supremacy. This "law" to which Englishmen turned as their earliest protection from a sovereign claiming to be absolute was an entity powerful only in proportion as it was esoteric. It was not merely the law of reason, it was something more. This something more made all the difference. For reason is a general human endowment; the king himself had it and might plausibly have pleaded that, if he was bound only by the law of reason, it was for his own reason to determine his obligations. But the bonds of the common law were stiffer. It was compounded of such various and special elements that it was capable of being known only by "science" and not by intuition, and must therefore be applied by technical specialists.

the whole power of prescribing the rules whereby every man may know what goods he may enjoy, and what actions he may do. . . . These rules are the civil laws. . . . Eighthly, is annexed to sovereignty the right of judicature, that is to say of hearing and deciding all controversies which may arise concerning law or concerning fact." (*Leviathan*, c. 18, §§7, 8.) So Filmer: "Every power of making laws must be arbitrary; for to make a law according to law is *contradictio in adjecto*," *Anarchy of a Mixed Monarchy*, preface, in *The Freeholder's Grand Inquest*, etc. (ed. 1680). See also Streater's Case, 2 State Trials, 196 ff.

[45] The strength of the tradition is shown by the fact that in the second half of the nineteenth century Sir James Stephen could write: "Courts of law are established for the express purpose of limiting public authority in its conduct toward individuals," *History of the Criminal Law*, ii, 65.

"My Lords," said King James, "I have heard the boast that your English law was founded upon reason. If that be so, why have not I, and others, reason as well as you, the Judges?" "May it please your Majesty," answered Coke, "true it is that God has endowed your Majesty with excellent science as well as great gifts of nature; but your Majesty will allow me to say, with all reverence, that you are not learned in the laws of this your realm of England; and that causes which concern the life or inheritance, or goods or fortunes of your subjects are not to be decided by natural reason, but by the artificial reason and judgment of the law, which law is an art which requires long study and experience before that a man can attain to the cognizance of it."[46] In short, the common law was capable of being an effective check on royal action only in so far as it was beyond the power of the king or his political officials personally to apply it; and its effective operation as such a check depended on its being administered exclusively by an independent judiciary without fear or favor of the crown. It required, therefore, the development, first of a tribunal of technical legal specialists, and, second, of such a tribunal hedged in from royal pressure, and free, by virtue of its isolated position, to pass upon the validity of acts of government.[47] So long as judges were mere officers of the king, law could operate only intermittently as an agency to control the king. Hence the long struggle in England, throughout the century following Coke's death, to secure the independence of the judiciary, and hence the ingrained notion which we have inherited, that it is wrong for judges to be governmental officers.

To summarize: the great political problem of Englishmen in the seventeenth century was to place checks on the power

[46] 12 Coke Rep. 63.

[47] This result, however, involved the consequence of practically transferring supreme authority to the judges. "If the law was to be supreme, and at the same time a mystery open only to the initiated, it is clear that if the claim of the lawyers was to be admitted, the supreme authority would be their exclusive possession," McIlwain, *High Court of Parliament*, pp. 80, 81. Lord Chancellor Ellesmere charged that, "the Lord Coke said the judges of that court [*i. e.*, the Court of King's Bench] were the superintendents of the realm," unpublished MS. printed in Campbell's *Lives of the Lord Chancellors*, ii, 237.

of a government which did not derive its authority from the people. Two such checks of a very different kind were developed — first, a popular organ of government to check the action of the crown by the will of the nation; and second, an independent judiciary to test the crown's acts by the "metwand" of an abstract law.[48] This is the practical evolution of those three powers of government which, soon after they had taken shape, began to be theorized, and which, in the form of a theory, wrote themselves into our own Constitution.

IV

The idea of applying an abstract law as a check on the action of government has had a much wider subsequent development in the United States than in England. The development there has been almost wholly in the direction of the other idea — control by a popular organ of government; and the powers of the House of Commons have expanded until they have absorbed practically all that the monarch once claimed an independent right to exercise. Theoretically, Parliament is bound by the law of the Constitution, as was the king; but only theoretically, for itself, in its capacity of High Court, is in the last instance the supreme judge of that law; and meanwhile the judges of the ordinary law courts exercise no such powers of control as Coke once claimed for them.

On the other hand, in the United States Coke's doctrine has been what we have built upon.[49] A written constitution

[48] See Blackstone's *Commentaries*, ed. Christian, i, 269; Story, *Commentaries on the Constitution*, 4th ed., i, 375 ff. For an illustration of the way in which the functions of the judges were exalted in eighteenth-century English opinion, see the passage from David Hume quoted above in chapter I, note 12, p. 8.

[49] The political life of the colonists branched off from that of England in the seventeenth century, when in England the legal view of politics was strongest — when questions of state were approached from a dominantly legalistic angle. See Lowell, *Government of England*, 2d ed., ii, 472 and 481. For other instances of the way in which American institutions preserve the trend of seventeenth-century England, see Barrett Wendell, *Liberty, Union, Democracy*, ch. i. An added factor tending to give a legalistic turn to American constitutional thinking was undoubtedly the fact that the colonial governments derived their powers from legal instruments, such as charters and deeds, and questions of politics were thus inevitably questions of the law of *ultra vires* as well. See Russell, *The Review of Colonial Legislation by the King in Council;*

is in itself the most effective possible application of the idea of a law sovereign over all laws which emanate merely from government. It carries with it by an almost inexorable logic

Andrews, *British Committees, Commissions, and Councils of Trade and Plantations;* Schlesinger, "Colonial Appeals to the Privy Council," in *Pol. Sci. Quarterly*, xxviii, 279, 433; Hazeltine, "Appeals from the Colonial Courts to the King in Council," *Annual Rep. Amer. Hist. Assoc.* (1894), p. 299. Another feature of the colonial constitutions which tended to enhance the importance of the judiciary is referred to in John Dickinson's *Farmer's Letters*, no. ix (*Political Writings*, Wilmington, 1801, i, 232): "The state of our laws . . . greatly exposes us to the arbitrary decision of . . . judges. The common law of England is generally received, together with such statutes as were enacted before we had a legislature of our own; but our courts exercise a sovereign authority in determining what parts of the common and statute law ought to be extended." Seventy years earlier it had been noted with respect to Virginia that "the fountains of their laws were the laws of England and the acts of their own assembly; but that how far either or both were to apply, was in the judge's breast," Hartwell, Chilton, and Blair, *Present State of Virginia, 1697–98*, quoted in Philip Alexander Bruce, *Institutional History of Virginia*, i, 468. How far English legal thought by the middle of the eighteenth century had departed from its traditional lines in the direction of a theory of creative legislative sovereignty can be seen by comparing the passage from Fortescue, quoted above at p. 86, with the language of Chief Justice Wilmot in Collins *v.* Blantern (1767), 2 Wilson, 341: "The statute law is the will of the legislature in writing; the common law is nothing else but statutes worn out by time, all our law began by consent of the legislature (p. 348). . . . Statute law and common law both originally flowed from the same fountain, the *legislature*," (p. 351). The same eighteenth-century confusion which led Blackstone to combine a theory of legislative sovereignty with an acceptance of the supremacy of the law of nature, stands out in this opinion, where Wilmot practically identified the common law and the moral law: "The bond is void by the common law, civil law, moral law, and all laws whatever; and so held by all writers except in one passage in Grotius where I think he is greatly mistaken, and differs from Puffendorf" (p. 349). Wilmot's doctrine that the common law owes its validity to adoption by the legislature was also the view of Jefferson: "The law being law because it is the will of the nation . . . the common law was not in force when we landed here nor till we . . . had manifested by the organs we constituted that the common law was to be our law. . . . The common law did not become, *ipso facto*, law on the new association; it could only become so by a positive adoption," letter to Edmund Randolph, Aug. 18, 1799 (*Writings*, ed. Ford, vii, 385; *Complete Works*, ed. Washington, iv, 301). So, too, in his letter to Edward Everett, Oct. 15, 1824 (*Complete Works*, ed. Washington, vii, 382) Jefferson indicates his belief that the common law was a survival of lost enactments of the Saxon period: "The authentic text of these enactments has not been preserved; but their substance has been committed to many ancient books and writings, so faithfully as to have been deemed genuine from generation to generation." The other branch of Wilmot's doctrine, viz., that common law was natural justice, was adopted by Alexander Hamilton in his argument

the power of courts to overthrow governmental acts,[50] and it limits in practice the power of governmental agencies to determine for themselves the scope of their lawful powers. Our own Constitution was framed and adopted under the influence of that dread of royal power which had dictated the line of English constitutional development during two preceding centuries. The functions of the king in which the development had left him least fettered — the functions which remained to him after the sphere of Parliament and the courts had been broken off — were those which our Constitution assigned to what we call the executive department; and hence the exercise of those functions and the power of the officials in whom they are vested are with us the most jealously hemmed in by constitutional limitations. During the decade preceding the Federal Convention, American constitution-makers had depended largely on popular legislative bodies vested with almost absolute power to supply the needed check on the executive.[51] After the anarchy of the period

in People *v.* Croswell, 3 Johns. Cas. App. 344: "The common law is natural law and natural reason applied to the state and condition of society." (*Works*, ed. Lodge, viii, 421.)

[50] This was Marshall's argument in Marbury *v.* Madison, 1 Cranch, 137. The idea no doubt is connected with the identification of a constitution with the "fundamental law" which is binding upon legislators, and also upon the courts. The implication was already caught by James Iredell before the Federal Convention; see G. J. McRee, *Life and Correspondence of James Iredell*, ii, 173. The identification of "constitution" with the "natural equity" to which, according to Locke, statutes must conform or be invalid, was a feature of the colonists' argument in their pre-Revolutionary controversy with Great Britain. "The Stamp Act is invalid . . . and therefore it ought to be waived by the judge as against natural equity and the constitution," Argument of John Adams before the Governor and Council of Massachusetts, Dec. 20, 1765, Bancroft, *History of the United States* (10 vol. ed.), v, 376. *Cf.* also Samuel Adams: "There are certain essential rights of the British Constitution of government, which are founded in the law of God and nature and are the common rights of mankind," Resolutions of the Massachusetts House of Representatives, Oct. 29, 1765, *Writings of Samuel Adams* (N. Y., 1904), i, 23. For the identification of "constitutional" rights with "fundamental natural" rights, see below, note 59, this chapter.

[51] "The founders of our republic, wise as they were, under the influence and dread of the royal prerogative which was pressing upon them, never for a moment seem to have turned their eyes from the immediate danger to liberty from that source. They seem never to have recollected the danger from legis-

of the Confederation there came a reaction, and conservative opinion turned to the view that the all-powerful legislatures themselves and the temporary will of the people which they embodied needed to be bridled.[52] American constitutional development has been shaped by the conflict between these two opposing schools of thought.[53] On the one hand have worked those who, like Jefferson,[54] Mr. Chief Justice Waite,[55] and Mr. Justice Holmes, have seen in free legislative action responsive to the will of the people the most effective assurance of good government. On the other side have stood those, like Marshall, Story, and Mr. Chief Justice Taft, who have insisted that popular government itself must be strictly squared to the measure of fundamental law as embodied in the Constitution and interpreted by the judges. The doctrine of the supremacy of law which was evolved to check the usurpations of a king ruling by paramount title has thus been turned into an instrument to control the action of popularly chosen officials and legislators[56]

lative usurpation," Story, *Commentaries on the Constitution*, 4th ed., i, 385. But James Wilson had said in the Federal Convention: "Despotism comes on mankind in different shapes, sometimes in an executive, sometimes in a military one. Is there no danger of a legislative despotism? Theory and practice both proclaim it. If the legislative authority be not restrained, there can be neither liberty nor stability," Speech on June 16th, 1787, Madison's *Debates in the Federal Convention*, in *The Papers of James Madison*, ed. H. D. Gilpin (1841), ii, 874.

[52] Corwin, *The Doctrine of Judicial Review*, p. 37. For a contemporary English example of legislative interference with judicial processes, *cf.* the "Nullum Tempus Bill" and the lawsuit between Sir James Lowther and the Duke of Portland. Trevelyan, *Early History of Charles James Fox*, pp. 395–399.

[53] For the issues involved see W. F. Dodd, "Political Safeguards and Judicial Guaranties" in *Col. Law Rev.*, xv, 293 ff. *Cf.* also A. M. Kales, "New Methods in Due-Process Cases," *Amer. Pol. Sci. Rev.*, xii, 241 ff.

[54] "It is the will of the nation which makes the law obligatory . . . law [is] law because it is the will of the nation," letter to Edmund Randolph, Aug. 18, 1799 (*Writings*, ed. Ford, vii, 385). But see his *Notes on Virginia*, p. 195 (*Writings*, ed. Ford, iii, 223, 224).

[55] "For protection against abuses by the legislature, the people must resort to the polls, not to the courts," Munn *v.* Illinois, 94 U. S. 113.

[56] "In the sixteenth and seventeenth centuries the judiciary stood between the public and the crown. It protected the individual from the state when he required that protection. To-day, when it assumes to stand between the

by the supposedly fixed and absolute standards of an abstract Law.[57]

V

In considering, with due regard for history, the relation between the courts and other executive agencies of government under our constitutional system, it is therefore not quite true, in spite of all similarities in methods of appointment and tenure, to say that both stand upon an equal footing. By virtue of our doctrine that governmental officers are controlled by law, and by virtue of the power of the courts to pronounce the law with finality, the courts occupy higher and more advantageous ground than other officers. Other officers may apply the law in the first instance; but the courts have the last word as to whether or not the application was lawful.

There is accordingly a difference between law as enforced by officials and the law which is applied by the courts. It is true to say of the former that it is the will of the state expressed by the government.[58] But the law which the courts

legislature and the public and thus again protect the individual from the state, it really stands between the public and what the public needs and desires, and protects individuals who need no protection against society which does need it," Pound, in *Harv. Law Rev.*, xxi, at p. 403. Martin Van Buren expressed substantially the same idea: "The theory of independence of the sovereign in the case of the judges in England, which we have copied, entirely fails when applied to us. There they are rendered independent of the crown to secure their fidelity to the public against the influence of the power to which they owe their appointment; here their life-tenure renders them independent of the people for whose service they are appointed. Irresponsible power . . . sooner or later causes, on the part of its possessor, an impatience of popular control, and, in the sequel, a desire to counteract the popular will," *Autobiography*, in *Annual Report Amer. Hist. Soc.*, 1918, ii, pp. 184, 185. For a typical nonprofessional exposition of the view that an independent judiciary with power to pronounce legislative acts unconstitutional is essential to protect individuals against the tyranny of transient majorities, see Henry Cabot Lodge, *The Democracy of the Constitution*, pp. 69–83, 115–121.

[57] "It is the peculiar value of a written constitution that it places in *unchanging form* [italics mine] limitations upon legislative action, and thus gives a permanence and stability to popular government which otherwise would be lacking," Brewer, J., in Muller *v.* Oregon, 208 U. S. 412.

[58] It was the Stuart theory that "the King's will is revealed in his law." Speech of James I in the Star Chamber, June 20, 1616, *The Political Works of James I*, ed. McIlwain, p. 333.

apply cannot be merely a governmental expression, since it is at times a function of this law to limit and control the government. Hence it must in some way be a law superior to and not derived from government. A higher law of this description awakened no inconvenient questionings in the age of Sir Edward Coke; to-day it must at least meet the challenge of more concrete definition. The courts attempt to meet it by saying that the law which regulates the conduct of government is a law emanating from the background of popular sovereignty. The people in their sovereign capacity have established a written constitution which carries in its interstices a great body of traditional or otherwise unwritten law; and it is this law, as declared and applied by the courts, which is superior to all other expressions of the will of the state, whether proceeding from the legislative or executive branch of government. This characteristic American survival of seventeenth-century English doctrine has been beautifully crystallized in language of Mr. Justice Mathews: "When we consider the nature and theory of our institutions of government, the principles upon which they are supposed to rest, and review the history of their development, we are constrained to conclude that they do not mean to leave room for the play and action of arbitrary power. Sovereignty, of course, is not subject to law, for it is the author and source of law; but in our system, while sovereign powers are delegated to the agencies of government, sovereignty itself remains with the people by whom and for whom all government exists and acts. And the law is the definition and limitation of power. It is, indeed, quite true that there must always be lodged somewhere and in some person or body, the authority of final decision; and in many cases of mere administration the responsibility is purely political, no appeal lying except to the ultimate tribunal of the public judgment, exercised either in the pressure of opinion or by means of the suffrage. But the fundamental rights to life, liberty, and the pursuit of happiness considered as individual possessions are secured by those maxims of constitutional law which are the monuments showing the victorious progress of the race in securing to men the blessing of civilization under the reign of just and equal laws so that, in the famous language of the Massachusetts Bill of Rights, the government of the commonwealth may be a government of laws and not of men." [59]

[59] Yick Wo *v.* Hopkins, 118 U. S. 356, at pp. 369, 370. Mr. Justice Matthews' language is a typical example of the orthodox blend of the two essentially different lines of thought which lie at the root of the American doctrine of "judicial review": (1) the doctrine of the supremacy of the supposed will of the people as embodied in a written constitution over the will of their governmental agencies as expressed in statutes of the legislature or acts of the executive department; (2) the doctrine of "fundamental rights" which are the "monuments" of the "progress of the race" toward a reign of "just and equal laws," — *i. e.*, of rights supposed to exist inherently by virtue of a "fundamental law" not depending upon "will" at all for its authority. See Corwin, "The Doctrine of Due Process before the Civil War," *Harv. Law Rev.*, xxiv, 366 ff. and 460 ff. The current theory, which is a product of the fusion of the two, runs to the effect that the people have by certain words, — *e. g.*, "due process," "law of the land," "just compensation," etc., — incorporated into the written constitution a vast body of judicially developed guarantees against legislative and executive action, and have by the same words left open a door for the further judicial development of these guarantees. There was originally a tendency on the part of the courts to feel that they were authorized to enforce these guarantees without having to rely on any express provision of the written constitution for their authority. Thus it was said in one case: "It is clear that statutes passed against plain and obvious principles of common right and common reason are absolutely null and void so far as they are calculated to operate against those principles," Ham *v.* McClaws, 1 E. H. Bay (So. Car.), 93 (1789). And again, per Hosmer J., in Goshen *v.* Stonington, 4 Conn. 209 (1822), at p. 225: "With those judges who assert the omnipotence of the legislature in all cases where the constitution has not interposed an explicit restraint, I cannot agree. Should there exist . . . a case of direct infraction of vested rights too palpable to be questioned, and too unjust to admit of vindication, I could not avoid considering it as a violation of the social compact, and within the control of the judiciary." See also Chancellor Kent in Gardner *v.*Newburgh, 2 Johns, Ch. (N. Y.) 162, and Story, J., in Terret *v.* Taylor, 9 Cranch, 43, at p. 52. This doctrine no doubt goes back to one of the arguments used in the pre-Revolutionary controversy between the Colonies and England, and expressed principally by James Otis: "If the reasons that could be given against an act are such as plainly demonstrated that it is against natural equity, the courts would adjudge such acts void," *Rights of the Colonies*, quoted in Frothingham, *Rise of the Republic of the United States*, p. 299; see also Corwin, *Doctrine of Judicial Review*, p. 30. By way of reaction against this claim of a practically unbounded judicial supremacy, the doctrine came to be settled that "except when the constitution has imposed limits upon the legislative power, it must be considered as practically absolute, whether it operate according to natural justice or not in any particular case. The courts are not the guardians of the rights of the

This language expresses, if it does not explain, the attitude of mind which insists that the rights of citizens should be

people except as those rights are secured by some constitutional provision," Cooley, *Constitutional Limitations*, 7th ed., p. 236. The fusion between the two doctrines was effected in such decisions as Taylor *v.* Porter, 4 Hill (N. Y.) 140, where Bronson, J., "speaking for the majority of the court, annexed the doctrine of natural rights and of limitations inherent to legislative power to the written constitution by casting around that doctrine the phrase 'law of the land,' and the phrase 'due process of law,' which had also since 1821 been a part of the New York constitution," Corwin in *Harv. Law Rev.*, xxiv, at p. 464; see also Corwin in *Univ. of Penna. Law Rev.*, lxxiv, 644, 645. The ideal fusion of a natural fundamental law with the supposed ultimate will of the "people" is effected in the well-known lines of Sir William Jones quoted by Mr. Justice Story in his inaugural address as Dane Professor of Law at Harvard (Story, *Miscellaneous Writings*, Boston, 1835, p. 441):

"Sovereign law, the state's collected will,
O'er thrones and globes elate,
Sits empress, crowning good, repressing ill."

It is significant of the popularity in America of the poem from which these lines are taken that it was included in Charles A. Dana's *Household Book of Poetry* (New York, 1868), p. 391. The identification of a "sovereign" "fundamental" law with a supposed "will of the people" doubtless owes much to the influence of the metaphysical-historical school of jurisprudence, dating back to Herder and Burke, which conceived the "real" will of the people as embodied unconsciously in national institutions rather than focused in a present act of conscious volition. The existing body of law was supposed to be an expression of the nature of the people; according to Savigny, law, like language, stands in an organic connection with national character, "grows as the people grow, develops with the people and declines when the people lose individuality. . . . Throughout, it is the result of inner, silently working forces, not of the arbitrary will of a lawgiver," *Vom Beruf unsrer Zeit für Gesetzgebung und Rechtswissenschaft*, 3d ed., pp. 8–15. Savigny then proceeded to identify this law, which was the unconscious will of the people, with judge-made law: "The law, originally the common property of the collected people, in consequence of the ramifying relations of real life, is so developed in its details that it can no longer be mastered by the people generally. Then a separate class of legal experts is formed which, itself an element of the people, represents the community in this domain of thought. In the special consciousness of this class, the law is only a continuation and peculiar development of the *Volksrecht*," *System des heut. röm. Rechts*, i, § 14. For the influence of Savigny on American law see Pound, *Interpretations of Legal History*, p. 34. For a typical American expression of Savigny's theory, see the address of James C. Carter in *Report of American Bar Association for 1890*, p. 217. Commenting on this address, Judge J. F. Dillon wrote: "Mr. Carter ascribes the unwritten law mainly to custom. I think it is derived, especially in modern times, still more largely from the general sense of justice and right as interpreted and ascertained by the judges" *The Laws and Jurisprudence of England and America*, Boston, 1894, p. 13. Elsewhere Judge Dillon writes: "It is necessary to get rid of the idea that law is whatever the populace

determined in the last analysis not by governmental officers, but by a court of law. It furnishes the background for Senator

of the moment may determine to be their sense of expediency or right, even though enacted by a legislative majority. . . . In this country at any rate, law is 'the beneficence of civil society acting by rule'; it is 'the absolute justice of the state enlightened by the perfect reason and morality of the state,' as ordained, established and declared in the constitutions,' *op. cit.*, pp. 15, 16. *Cf.* W. H. Taft, commenting on Mr. Justice Holmes's statement in Noble State Bank *v.* Haskell, 219 U. S. 104, that "the police power . . . may be put forth in aid of what is held . . . by strong and preponderant opinion to be greatly and immediately necessary to the public welfare": "It is difficult," wrote Mr. Taft, "to state a fact less conclusive of 'a strong and preponderant public opinion' than a single [popular] vote upon such an issue. What was in the mind of the learned justice and of the Court for whom he spoke was a view entertained by most people, and evidenced by expressions of popular will in the press, in the pulpit, in juridical writings, as well as by legislative action and popular elections. All of these evidences should cover a period long enough to leave no doubt about the clarity of the opinion or its deliberate character. Such an opinion is not expressed in election controversy . . . but it is the result of a general and continued acquiescence," *Popular Government*, New Haven, 1913. "In such cases the judges are not removed from the people's influence. . . . It is impossible to prevent the influence of popular opinion from coloring judgments in the long run. Judges are men . . . and in these fields of the law in which the personal equation unavoidably plays a part, there will be found a response to sober popular opinion as it changes to meet the exigency of social, political, and economic changes," *ibid.*, p. 174. This theory that the "will of the people" continues to function in the bosom of the judges provides a loop-hole of escape from Professor Morris Cohen's realistic argument that "it is absurd to maintain that . . . when Reconstructionists forced through . . . the Fourteenth Amendment to the Federal Constitution . . . the 'people' intended that states should not have the right to protect bakers from working more than ten hours per day, but should have the power to prohibit miners from working more than eight hours per day, or that the states should have the power to prohibit women from working more than ten hours a day, but no power to prohibit them from working at night." ("Legal Theories and Social Science," in *Reports of New York State Bar Association* (1915), xxxviii, at p. 190). But if Savigny enables the compromise-theory of judicial review to escape the Scylla of Professor Cohen's realism, it runs upon the Charybdis of Mr. Justice Holmes's historical sense: "The time has gone by when law is only an unconscious embodiment of the common will. It has become a conscious reaction upon itself of organized society knowingly seeking to determine its own destinies.," *Collected Legal Papers*, pp. 129, 130. None the less, the opposite theory of law, in the form of the old idea of "fundamental" rights flowing from a law which does not derive its validity from human will, popular or otherwise, still persists strongly in American thought, and occasionally rises to the surface. It has done so recently as a ground of opposition to the Prohibition Amendment to the Federal Constitution, — see E. V. Abbott, "Inalienable Rights and the Eighteenth Amendment," *Col. Law Rev.*, xx, 183 ff., where the argument is advanced that even a constitutional amendment,

Foraker's position in the debate on the Hepburn bill. The question is how far it represents a position which can to-day be justified.

duly adopted, is ineffectual to take away such rights belonging inherently to individuals. "The protection of inalienable and reserved rights is the inexpugnable law of the land. There is no power resident anywhere in the Union which can overturn it," *Ibid.*, p. 185. "Fundamental" rights are thus frankly divorced from any basis in a supposed "ultimate" will of the people, and the idea of such rights on the one hand, and the sovereignty of the people on the other, are left confronting each other in an unresolved and antagonistic dualism. This dualism was openly accepted by Rufus Choate: "Our political system, while it is purely and intensely republican, aims to accomplish a twofold object, to wit, liberty and security. To accomplish this twofold object we have established a twofold set of institutions and instrumentalities — some of them designed to develop and give utterance to one; some of them designed to provide permanently and constantly for the other; some of them designed to bring out the popular will in its utmost intensity of utterance; some of them designed to secure life, and liberty, and character, and happiness, and property, and equal and exact justice *against all will and against all power* [italics mine]. These institutions and instrumentalities in their immediate mechanism and workings are as distinct and diverse, one from the other, as they are in their offices and their ends. . . . Thus in the law-making department, and in the whole department of elections to office of those who make and those who execute the law, you give the utmost assistance to the expression of liberty. You give the choice to the people. . . . But to the end that one man, that the majority, may not deprive any of life, liberty, property, the opportunity of seeking happiness, there are institutions of security. There is a Constitution to control the Government; there is a separation of departments of Government; there is a judiciary to interpret and administer the laws 'that every man may find his security therein.'" (Address on the Tenure of the Judiciary, in the Massachusetts Constitutional Convention of 1853, *Addresses and Orations of Rufus Choate*, Boston, 1883, pp. 391 ff.)

CHAPTER V

PRACTICAL LIMITS OF THE SUPREMACY OF LAW

THE function of the courts in declaring legislation unconstitutional does not directly concern us here — our business is with their analogous function of reviewing orders of administrative agencies. Both are aspects of what is essentially the same power seen from different sides; and this is true not only when the courts are reviewing the constitutionality of executive action, but when they are reviewing merely its legal competence as well. The one situation applies a doctrine of *ultra vires* to the legislature, and raises the question of the comparative merits of flexible legislation and a theoretically permanent law; in the other, the same doctrine is applied more broadly to the executive and touches the relative advantage to the individual in having his rights in a given case determined by the discretion or "policy" of government officials, or by the more or less fixed rules which a law court is thought to administer.[1] Many of the determining considerations are similar in both cases; but we are here approaching only the second face of the problem.

It will be well to exclude at the outset a number of considerations of much importance in themselves but irrelevant in the present connection. Foremost among these is that court review is essential to preserve certain safeguards in the

[1] See G. Jèze, *Les Principes Généraux du Droit Administratif* (2d ed., 1914), ch. viii, *passim*. M. Jèze maintains the thesis that the individual should be allowed judicial protection against every excess of power by the governing authorities, whether they be legislators or executive officials. See also Page *v.* Hardin, 8 B. Monroe (Ky., 1848), 648, at p. 655: "If, as now conceded by all, a judicial tribunal, acting within its appropriate sphere, may and indeed must, under our system, decide upon the constitutionality of an act of the legislative department, when necessarily involved in the determination of the rights before it for adjudication . . . there can be no reasonable ground for denying to it the power and duty of deciding upon the legal validity or invalidity of any act of the executive department. . . . The executive department and all of its officers are as much bound by the constitution and laws as the legislative."

administrative procedure, for example, the right to notice, the right to a hearing, the right to present competent evidence, and so forth.[2] This consideration establishes the need for review of some kind but not necessarily for retrial of the facts by a law court. Indeed, by a backhanded process of reasoning it has been held in some cases that where review in the form of such a retrial of the facts at law is available, the fundamental safeguards of notice and hearing may be altogether dispensed with in the administrative proceeding.[3]

[2] See Pound, "The Revival of Personal Government," in *Proc. N. H. Bar Assoc.* (1917), p. 13.

[3] NOTICE AND HEARING.—The courts have frequently said that notice and hearing are essential to due process in quasi-judicial proceedings: Hagar *v.* Reclamation District, 111 U. S. 701; Chicago, Milwaukee and St. Paul R. Co. *v.* Minnesota, 134 U. S. 418; Chin Yow *v.* U. S., 208 U. S. 8; Interstate Commerce Commission *v.* Louisville & Nashville R. Co., 227 U. S. 88; but it seems that, provided the notice and hearing are available at some stage in the proceedings, it makes no difference whether it be at the administrative stage or at the stage of court review. Thus it has been held that there need be no notice or hearing in the administrative procedure if such notice and hearing are available on a retrial of the facts at law. In People ex rel. Copcutt *v.* Board of Health, 140 N. Y. 1, where the board had declared a certain mill pond to be a nuisance without a hearing and had ordered its removal, the court refused to review the order by certiorari, on the ground that the owner was entitled to have the question of whether the pond was actually a nuisance tried by a jury in an action at law for damages, and that therefore no hearing before the board was necessary. The same doctrine was announced in Belcher *v.* Farrar, 8 Allen (Mass.) 325. In Salem *v.* Eastern R. Co. (98 Mass. 431) it was held that while health authorities might act summarily to abate nuisances without a hearing, they could not without a hearing throw the expense of abating the nuisance upon the individual charged with having caused it. In North American Cold Storage Co. *v.* Chicago, 211 U. S. 306, the Supreme Court sustained the constitutionality of a municipal ordinance which provided for destruction of provisions unfit for human consumption without a preliminary hearing, on the ground that the owner of the provisions so destroyed "had the right to bring his action at common law against all persons engaged in the abatement of the nuisance and if he should show that the alleged nuisance did not in fact exist, he will recover judgment." The court cited the Copcutt case, *supra;* Miller *v.* Horton, 152 Mass. 540; Lowe *v.* Conroy, 120 Wis. 151; Pearson *v.* Zehr, 138 Ill. 48. Conversely, where the courts deny to the party affected by an administrative determination the right to a retrial of the facts in an action at law, as is the case, for instance, with tax assessments, it has been said that "due process of law requires that at some stage of the proceedings before the tax becomes irrevocably fixed, the tax payer shall have the opportunity to be heard, of which he must have notice either personal, or by publication, or by law, fixing the time and place of the hearing," Londoner *v.* City and County of Denver, 210 U. S. 373. But where

A second consideration is that a retrial in a law court offers certain safeguards which are absent from the administrative procedure, notably trial by jury. Some of the cases seem to have turned on this point, as Miller *v.* Horton and the others which hold that an owner is entitled to have the opinion of an administrative officer overridden by that of a jury on the

the courts say that the administrative action is "legislative" in character, they hold that no notice or hearing is necessary. Thus, it is held that the action of a state board of equalization in increasing the valuation of all taxable property in a particular city without a hearing is "legislative" because affecting a whole class, Bi-metallic Investment Co. *v.* State Board of Equalization, 239 U. S. 441. In that case Mr. Justice Holmes said: "Where a rule of conduct applies to more than a few people it is impracticable that everyone should have a direct voice in its adoption. The constitution does not require all public acts to be done in town meeting or assembly of the whole. General statutes within the state power are passed that affect the person or property of individuals sometimes to the point of ruin, without giving them a chance to be heard." The Londoner case, *supra*, was distinguished on the ground that there a relatively small number of people were affected. In Commonwealth *v.* Sisson, 189 Mass. 247, where a state board of fish and game commissioners without a hearing ordered a sawmill not to discharge sawdust into a certain pond, it was held that no hearing was necessary because the order was "legislative." It seems obvious that on the question of the necessity of notice and hearing, as elsewhere, the distinction between "legislative" and "judicial" powers as generally applied by the courts is more confusing than helpful. Orders of state railroad and utilities commissions and of the Interstate Commerce Commission relating to rates are said to be "legislative" (Prentis *v.* Atlantic Coast Line R. Co. 211 U. S. 210), but can be made only after giving the carriers affected an opportunity to be heard: Chicago, Milwaukee and St. Paul R. Co. *v.* Minnesota, 134 U. S. 418; Interstate Commerce Commission *v.* Louisville & Nashville R. Co., 227 U. S. 88). And in the latter case it was said: "In the comparatively few cases in which such questions have arisen it has been distinctly recognized that administrative orders quasi-judicial in character are void if a hearing was denied," and for this proposition a number of Chinese exclusion cases were cited. As a matter of fact, the utility cases, which require notice and hearing in the administrative procedure and leave no room for a retrial of the facts by a jury in an action at law, but commit to the courts a power to review the fairness of the administrative procedure and the validity of the determination reached, seem much more satisfactory than the cases arising under the police power, like the Copcutt case above referred to, which lay down no requirement of an administrative hearing and seek to provide a substitute by the clumsy and wasteful method of a retrial of the facts on new evidence by a jury. See President Goodnow in *Rep. Amer. Bar Assoc.* (1916), xlvi, 414 ff. Where an administrative hearing is required, there is no general holding as to what hearing will be sufficient. In Hagar *v.* Reclamation District, 111 U. S. 701, the Supreme Court said: "Undoubtedly where life and liberty are involved, due process requires that there be a regular course

question of whether or not his property constitutes a nuisance. The desirability of such a retrial of the facts in a lawsuit, with renewed presentation of evidence after the administrative agency has considered the facts and has acted, may be an open question in nuisance and health cases and certain others arising in the field of police regulation, but in many fields of administrative action the question does not arise at all. No one would insist, for instance, that a finding of the Interstate Commerce Commission, or of a state utility commission, as to what is a reasonable rate, or a finding of the Federal Trade Commission as to what amounts to unfair competition, should be subjected to the verdict of a jury on

of judicial proceedings which imply that the party to be affected shall have notice and an opportunity to be heard. So also where title or possession of property is involved, but where the taking of property is in the enforcement of a tax the proceeding is necessarily less formal." Accordingly in some of the tax cases which do not involve an assessment of property, it is held that the tax or penalty may be levied and enforced without any hearing at all: Murray's Lessee *v.* Hoboken Land Co., 18 How. 272; Oceanic Steam Navigation Co. *v.* Stranahan, 214 U. S. 320. In San Diego Land & Town Co. *v.* National City, 174 U. S. 739, a statute conferred on boards of supervisors the power to fix water rates. The ordinance fixing such rates was to be passed during the month of February of each year, and the water companies were required to file during January a verified statement of the facts upon which such rates could be based. It was claimed that the statute was unconstitutional because it authorized rates to be fixed without notice to the corporation and without a hearing; but the Supreme Court said that, because of the opportunity given to the company to file a statement of the kind specified, "provision was made for a hearing in an appropriate way. The defendants could not have refused to receive the statement referred to in the statute or to have duly considered it and given it proper weight in determining rates." It has been held that officials may act upon personal inspection and without calling witnesses, or hearing sworn testimony: State *v.* Jersey City, 24 N. J. L., 662 (boards of assessment); Dodd *v.* Francisco, 68 N. J. L., 490 (boards of health); United States *v.* Douglass, 19 D. C. 99 (liquor licensing authorities). Even where liberty is involved, as in determinations denying immigrants the right to enter the country, the notice and hearing need only be of the most informal character, Yamataya *v.* Fisher, 189 U. S. 86. The administrative official is not required by constitutional guarantees to take any testimony and may decide on his own inspection and examination the question of the right of the alien to land, Ekiu *v.* U. S., 142 U. S. 651. But the procedure must be "fair." Where testimony is taken, the immigrant must not be prevented from offering relevant testimony, Chin Yow *v.* U. S., 208 U. S. 8; and such testimony must not be suppressed, Kwock Jan Fat *v.* White, 253 U. S. 454. See also note in *Harv. Law Rev.*, xxviii, pp. 198 ff.

the point.[4] Furthermore, a jury trial of the facts is as a rule possible only where review is sought in the form of an action for damages against the officials who made the order complained of, and this form of relief is often wholly impractical, for example in the case of rate-fixing orders, because, aside from the impossibility of estimating damages, it is collateral, and would operate only indirectly on the order, if at all. There is no question of a jury trial in the larger number of instances where the review proceeding takes the form of certiorari, mandamus, injunction, or the special statutory proceedings to which administrative agencies must sometimes resort to enforce observance of their orders.

The crucial issue is therefore not between the finding of an administrative officer and the verdict of a jury, but rather as to the degree of control which judges sitting alone, either *en banc* or as a court of equity, should exercise over administrative determinations. Why is it that in such cases we so insist that a court, rather than an administrative tribunal, should in the last analysis apply the law? We have really begged the question and answered it when we ask it in this form.

On a *prima facie* view, the decree of a court and the order of a public officer are, for practical purposes, not distinguishable, and lead to identical results. Both follow from the application of law to existing facts and embody a command which will be enforced by the organized power of government. If we regard law as simply the will of the state expressed through government, no inherent difference is visible between them.[5] When we do make a distinction, we assert

[4] For procedure under which orders of a state railroad commission were subject to review by a jury see Railroad Connection Case, 137 N. C. 14; 206 U. S. 1. "The owner has a right to be heard, and only a trial by jury satisfies the provision of the Declaration of Rights, that no subject shall be deprived of his property but by the judgment of his peers, or the law of the land," Holmes, J., in Miller *v.* Horton, 152 Mass. 540. The proper field for review in the form of a damage-suit is where the administrative action is non-judicial in character.

[5] This problem presented itself to James Madison, and he found himself on the way to a proper solution of it: "There was an analogy between the executive and judiciary departments in several respects. The latter executed the laws in certain cases as the former did in others. The former expounded and applied them for certain purposes, as the latter did for others. The difference

by implication that the law applicable to given facts is something which by its very nature can somehow be expressed only through a law-court. Is there a sense in which it is true that only a law-court can express and apply law? The question requires for adequate answer a closer analysis of what we mean when we talk of law.

I

The idea of law grew up in history as the opposite of fortuitous occurrence on the one hand, and of arbitrary discretion on the other.[6] In one case the opposition led to the idea of physical laws, and in the other to that of civil laws; but the landmarks of thought show much confusion between the two.[7] Both ideas conceive law as a general rule, an expression

between them seemed to consist chiefly in . . . [the circumstance that] in the administration of the former, much greater latitude is left to opinion and discretion than in the administration of the latter." Speech in the Federal Convention, July 17, 1787, in Madison's *Debates*, in *The Papers of James Madison*, ed. H. D. Gilpin, ii, 1126.

[6] See Barker, *Political Thought of Plato and Aristotle*, pp. 23–26; Bryce, *Studies in History and Jurisprudence*, pp. 556–569, esp. pp. 561, 562. For a theory of the extreme antiquity of the conception of "nature as a series of events occurring in an invariable order," see Frazer, *The Golden Bough* (one vol. ed.), pp. 10 ff. "Law is in its nature contrary to such forces and operations as are violent and casual," Sir Frederick Pollock, *Oxford Lectures and Other Discourses*, London, 1890, p. 100.

[7] See Holland's *Jurisprudence*, 11th ed., pp. 15 ff.; Maine, *Early History of Institutions*, pp. 371 ff. One of the definitions of law attributed to Demosthenes identifies the "scientific laws," which govern the processes of the natural world, with the laws which are binding upon men in their social relations: "*ἐπεὶ καὶ τὸν ὅλον κόσμον, καὶ τὰ θεῖα καὶ τὰς καλουμένας ὥρας νόμος καὶ τάξις, εἰ χρὴ τοῖς ὁρωμένοις πιστεύειν, διοικεῖν φαίνεται*" ("since if we believe what we see, it is evident that law and order govern the whole universe, and the divine processes, and what we call the seasons of heaven"), Second speech against Aristogeiton, 808. Whiston notes a conjecture that this passage may have suggested Hooker's famous description of law, Whiston's *Demosthenes*, ii, 622. See also the passages from Stobaeus quoted by John Dickinson, *Political Writings* (ed. 1801), i, 330. A definition of law by Chrysippus which is incorporated into Justinian's *Digest* (book I, tit. 3, § 2) identifies it with the law which rules "the acts of the Gods." So John of Salisbury (*Policraticus*, iv, 2), "legem tam rerum quam hominum principem et ducem esse." For eighteenth-century expressions of the idea see Montesquieu, *Esprit des Lois*, book I, ch. 1; Blackstone, *Commentaries*, Introd., sec. ii (ed. Christian, i, 38): "Thus we say the 'laws' of motion, of gravitation, of optics, or mechanics, as well as the laws of nature and of nations"; and James Wilson, *Works*, ed. J. D. Andrews (1896), i, 49; also *ibid.*, p. 92: "The great

of the principle that like antecedents have like consequents. Where arbitrary discretion prevails, a given case may be decided in one way and another, of exactly the same kind, in the opposite way. Under a régime of law the same case will necessarily produce the same decision. Laws are general rules which, when applied to the same facts, issue in the same results.[8]

Creator of all things has established general and fixed rules according to which all the phenomena of the material universe are produced and regulated. These rules are usually denominated laws of nature. The science which has those laws for its object is called natural philosophy." For Christian's criticism, see his edition of Blackstone, i, 39, note 1; for Austin's, see W. Jethro Brown, *Austinian Theory of Law*, pp. 84–92. The bridge between the "natural laws" of physical science on the one hand and the "natural laws" prescribing human conduct on the other was effected in the eighteenth century by the doctrine that physical nature functioned teleologically. The laws of physical science were supposed to embody processes which the divine wisdom had selected as the most perfectly adapted to promote human happiness, and they were accordingly regarded as supplying a norm to which human conduct must conform if it was to be good, and from which the laws of such conduct could be deduced. See Thorstein Veblen, "The Preconceptions of Economic Science," in *Quarterly Journal of Economics*, Jan., 1899, reprinted in *The Place of Science in Modern Civilization*, pp. 82 ff. "Seeing it is the only scope of Natural Philosophy to discover the causes of generation, duration, and corruption, and to demonstrate the necessary connection of such effects with their causes, and seeing it is certain that the causes generating and preserving man, for example, by efficacy of which he continues for some time and flourishes with faculties, as well of body as mind, enlarged and determined to their proper functions, are called *good* to him, and that the causes of corruptions, grief and troubles are to him naturally *evil*, it evidently follows that Natural Philosophy explains what things are to him naturally good and evil, and demonstrates that they are *necessarily* such," Richard Cumberland, *Treatise of the Laws of Nature*, made English by John Maxwell, London, 1727, ch. i, § 17, p. 58. "Les lois naturelles sont ou physiques ou morales. On entend ici, par loi physique, le cours réglé de tout évènement physique de l'ordre naturel, évidemment le plus avantageux au genre humain. On entend ici, par loi morale, la règle de toute action humaine de l'ordre morale, conforme à l'ordre physique évidemment le plus avantageux au genre humain. Ces lois forment ensemble ce qu'on appelle la loi naturelle. Tous les hommes et toutes les puissances humaines doivent être soumis à ces lois souveraines, instituées par l'être Suprême; elles sont immuables et irréfragables, et les meilleures lois possibles." Quesnay, *Droit Naturel*, ch. v, ed. E. Daire, *Physiocrates*, pp. 52, 53.

[8] This is the theory which makes possible the conception of "case-law" as an inductive "science." "The common law . . . must be learned, like the laws of the physical world, inductively. The decided cases of the past are so many observations upon the practical workings of these laws, from which the true theory is to be inferred, — precisely as the astronomer infers the true form of

The practical advantages of a régime of law, as opposed to one of arbitrary discretion, have been conceived as twofold. In the first place it introduces certainty into what otherwise would be uncertain; and certainty is a requisite of effective human action. Without it no planning for the future, and hence no incentive for the advancement of civilized living, is possible. A buys a promise from B; if he is not sure whether the promise will be enforceable, he will be unable to outline his future conduct, nor would he have been so ready to buy the promise in the first place. Certainty requires that the uniform rule should apply, not merely horizontally, but vertically; that is, that the same result should be reached in like cases arising at different times.[9]

the planet's orbit from his observation of its position at many different times. The observed facts are authoritative: our inferences from them are theory; but it is the formation of that theory which enables us to carry our observations farther and more intelligently, and thus to arrive gradually at the true understanding of the laws that govern the moral as well as those that govern the material universe. This explanation of the true office of precedents, as data from which we may obtain by induction the jural rule which they prove to exist, is not only the most reasonable in itself, but has been recognized by high judicial authority," W. G. Hammond, in 3d edition of Lieber's *Hermeneutics*, p. 329. *Cf.* Sir F. Pollock, *Essays in Jurisprudence and Ethics*, p. 239: "In order to predict physical results we must suppose that the same thing always happens under the same conditions; and in the same way, in order to predict legal results we must suppose that the same decision is always given on the same facts. . . . In English case-law this object is attained by . . . an understanding that the court shall follow the authority of decisions formerly given on similar facts."

[9] "Certainty is so essential to law that law cannot even be just without it," Francis Bacon, "Treatise of Universal Justice," Aphorism 8, in *De Augmentis*, bk. viii, *Works*, ed. Spedding, Ellis and Heath, ix, p. 314. "The demand for certainty becomes more exacting as men's affairs become more complex. Trade and traffic in their increasing volume, speed and variety of movement, raise new questions at every turn, and men expect not only to get their differences settled for the moment, but to have solutions which will prevent the same difficulties from arising again," Sir F. Pollock, *Harv. Law Rev.*, ix, 301. For a bold criticism of the doctrine of precedent on the ground that it does not even supply the certainty which is its *raison d'être*, see Wigmore, *Problems of Law*, pp. 79, 80: "*Stare decisis* is said to be indispensable for securing certainty in the application of the law. But the sufficient answer is that it has not in fact secured it. Our judicial law is as uncertain as any law could well be. We possess all the detriment of uncertainty which *stare decisis* was supposed to avoid, and also all the detriment of ancient law-lumber which *stare decisis* concededly involves." To the same effect see J. F. Dillon, *The Laws and Jurisprudence of England and*

If certainty were the only end of law, it would be indifferent what system of rules were applied, so long as they were uniform and stable. Law would be purely a matter of convention. A rule that a thief should get good title to all the goods he stole would afford as certain a basis for calculating future conduct as the rule that he gets no title whatever. Kant tried to show that only a system of rules based on justice would fit the requirement of logical certainty; but his argument has not generally been regarded as convincing.[10] So we come upon the need for not merely a system of fixed general rules, but of rules based on justice, or in other words, on a regard for certain demands and capacities of human nature. Otherwise the system would not be workable; offending ingrained proclivities and standards of judgment, it would be continually violated and so fail to yield the certainty which is the excuse for its existence.

So conceived, a law or rule for human action must be fixed at two points: it must be anchored by precedent to the past, so as to produce certainty for the future; and it must be grounded in what men consider justice, so as to be workable in practice. There is a third requirement: all the laws or rules existing together at a given time must be compatible, and fit together into a logical system.[11] Should conflict be found to arise between different rules, the requirement of certainty would again be negatived. So that, summarizing, we can say that a régime of law requires a logically coherent system of general rules based on precedent and accepted principles of justice.

No such abstract formulation of the essentials of legal order was of course made in mediaeval England; but it is evident how closely the mediaeval conception of the Common Law corresponds to the foregoing formulation in essential particulars. It was a law founded on custom, that is to say,

America, pp. 242 ff. Cf. also *Harv. Law Rev.*, xxxiv, 74 ff. James I complained of the uncertainty of precedents in 1607 (*Political Works of James I*, ed., McIlwain, p. 293).

[10] See J. S. Mill, *Utilitarianism*, ch. 1.

[11] "Precedent has a tendency to extend itself along the lines of logical development." Cardozo, *Nature of the Judicial Process*, p. 34.

on precedent; and it was at the same time "the perfection of reason," or, in other words, a more or less consistent logical system of general rules of justice. It followed that no such system could emanate from the occasional commands of a sovereign, or of the governmental officers who were his subordinates. Its function was rather to impose on those commands the check of requiring them to fit into the system at the peril of being otherwise invalid. Indeed, such a system could not be "made" at all; and that was, as we saw, the mediaeval view of law. If a system is anchored to a fixed principle like precedent, or an idea of abstract justice; and if it is governed by the requirement of being logically self-consistent, there can hardly be any room for innovation. If a new case arises, will not the decision be rigorously governed by factors already existing? We seem to have but a simple equation containing one unknown quantity, and all we need do is to write off the solution.[12]

The mediaeval conception of law as transcendental thus had a practical meaning. We can phrase the idea in modern terms by saying that law was regarded as transcendental in the sense that logic and history are transcendental — they are not subject to arbitrary amendment by an individual or by the present generation. In the eighteenth century the emphasis shifted, though less in England than elsewhere, from history to reason, from precedent to fundamental justice. That was the golden century of human "reason," when the miraculous was expected of it. In it was found what the Middle Ages had found in religious faith, and what the nineteenth century was to find in science — a key to unlock all doors, a panacea for all the ills of the world, a mechanical toy that kept men agape for what wonders it was going to work next.[13] And for the type of reason, mathemati-

[12] See the passage from Sidgwick's *Elements of Politics*, 2d ed., p. 652, quoted above, chapter IV, note 33, p. 87.

[13] "How feeble the outset of reason, how diversified its progress, how almost boundless its advancement! From a Tongutsian, scraping his scanty utensils and worshipping fetishes made of shreds, to a Newton, weighing the planets, explaining the principles by which the material universe is sustained, and the motion of its ponderous orbs throughout their vast voyages determined, and

cal reason was chosen—a reason working out with inexorable logic the single correct solution for every problem. Such an idea at work in politics produced the Abbé Sieyès, and in law the era of codes. It was believed that the one and only legal rule for every possible situation could be written off in advance by a proper combination of axiomatic first principles with the same accuracy as the answers to all the problems in the Euclidean geometry.[14] Law ceased to be an instrument for working toward certainty — it became certainty itself.[15]

proving the existence of Deity, from the wonders of his works. Winged by diligence and hope, it springs from earth, awhile surveys its precious objects, then soars to the utmost verge of our system, there sums its powers, aspires into space, bends its course among innumerable suns and worlds, discerns immensity, breathes of eternity, and struck into the deepest humility, prostrates itself before the footstool of His throne to whom they both belong," John Dickinson, *Letters of Fabius*, 1st series, no. xiii (*Political Writings*, ed. 1801, ii, 250). "The skies, shut as it were by immovable obstacles, are unbarred, the motions of worlds and stars, with their laws, are explored, and celestial luminaries are engaged to ascertain the mensurations of the earth. At last the ocean itself with all its winds and waves submits, and obediently bears its adventurous victors, guided by an insensible yet surprisingly empowered conductor, amidst the clouds of day and the darkness of night, through every clime to every shore." (*Ibid.*, ii, 301 ff.)

14 "Napoleon said that he once entertained the idea that all principles of law might be reduced to a few concise forms which ought to be combined according to fixed rules similar to those of mathematics; and that thus simplicity and certainty of law might be established. He soon, however, gave up the idea when he came to discuss the various parts of the French Civil Code with the other members of the committee appointed to draw up that work." Lieber, *Hermeneutics*, 3d ed., p. 30.

15 MATHEMATICAL THEORY OF LAW. — The idea that legal certainty was attainable by the methods of mathematics became commonplace with the great advance of mathematical science in the seventeenth century. It appears to be the assumption of Montesquieu: "Laws in their most general signification are the necessary relations resulting from the nature of things. . . . These rules are a fixed and invariable relation . . . each diversity is uniformity, each change is constancy. Particular intelligent beings may have laws of their own making, but they have some, likewise, which they never made. Before there were intelligent beings, they were possible; and they had therefore possible relations, and consequently possible laws . . . we must therefore acknowledge relations of justice, antecedent to the possible law by which they are established," *Spirit of Laws*, book i, ch. i. D'Aguesseau, writing in praise of Domat's *Traité des Lois*, says: "Personne n'a mieux approfondi que cet auteur le veritable principe des lois, et ne l'a expliqué d'une manière plus digne d'un philosophe. Après avoir remonté jusqu'au premier principe, il descend jusqu'aux dernières conséquences. Il les développe dans un ordre presque géometrique,"

Of course we take no such naïve view of law or reason to-day.[16] We have seen all too clearly how human reason led

Œuvres Choisies, Paris, Didot (1863), p. 225. Leibnitz declared that he knew nothing which approached so near to the method and precision of geometry as the Roman law, Epist. ad Kestner, *Opera* (Geneva, 1768, tom.) iv, pt. 3, p. 254. Leibnitz's own legal writings are permeated by the idea that the method of law should be mathematical. He speaks of it as "my" method (*ibid.*, p. 93), and elsewhere says: "Me vero incuriae humanae admiratio percutit, qui motus corporum ad calculos revocamus, iidem motus animorum nobis intimos nec minus certa lege constantes obiter percurrimus; de horologio aliquo demonstrationes, de salute tot populorum declamationes habemus. Ergo impetum sumsi eo in campo certitudinem humanam periclitandi." Leibnitz gives two elaborate specimens of the mathematical deduction of law, "Specimen Certitudinis seu Demonstrationum in Jure" (*ibid.*, pp. 92 ff.), and "Specimen Demonstrationum Politicarum" (*ibid.*, pp. 522 ff.). See also the fragmentary memorandum, "Ad Stateram Juris," in *Opuscules Inédits de Leibnitz*, par L. Couturat, pp. 211 ff. Spinoza's application of mathematical method to ethics is well known; he sought to apply the same method to the science of civil society (*Tractatus Politicus*, c. i). So also Richard Cumberland (*A Treatise of the Laws of Nature*, made English by John Maxwell, London, 1727, pp. 85, 184 ff.): "The science of morality and politicks both can, and ought to, imitate the analytick art (in which I comprehend not only the extraction of roots but also the whole doctrine of specious arithmetick or algebra) as the noblest pattern of sciences" (*ibid.*, p. 185). So also Samuel Clarke (1675–1729); see Sir James Mackintosh, *Dissertation on the Progress of Ethical Philosophy*, ed. Whewell, Edinburgh, 1837, p. 148: "The adoption of mathematical forms and terms was, in England, a prevalent fashion among writers on moral subjects during a large part of the eighteenth century. The ambition of mathematical certainty, on matters concerning which it is not given to man to reach it, is a frailty from which the disciple of Newton ought in reason to have been withheld, but to which he was naturally tempted by the example of his master." *Cf.* the following expression of the typical eighteenth-century view by an English lawyer: "As to the certainty of our laws, it might suffice to say that most of them are founded on the laws of nature and nations; and so far, they are as certain as any other whatsoever. And as to the rest, they consist either of laws fairly deduced from those principles, or of particular municipal laws and customs peculiarly adapted to the circumstances of the nation, and deductions and

[16] And still this view has by no means as yet disappeared from legal writers. Compare the following passage from a recent book: "There is not nearly so much doubt about our legal questions as we are prone to believe. In the great majority of cases the solution of them is as certain and exact as an answer to a problem in mathematics, and it brings with it precisely the same intellectual satisfaction," E. V. Abbot, *Justice and the Modern Law*, Boston, (1913), p. 236. This book, throughout, is an excellent example of the mathematical or formally logical view of law. "The judicial process in ascertaining or applying the law is essentially similar to the process by which we acquire our knowledge of geometry," *ibid.*, p. 11.

Germans to one conclusion, and Frenchmen to another, to believe there is aught of the inexorable about it. We have

inferences therefrom; and the best laws that are extant have no other composition. But the certainty of law deserves to be a little more particularly considered, both in general, and with particular regard to our own constitution. And as to the nature of law in general, and in regard of the subject matter of it, I can't but think it capable of as great certainty as any science or profession whatsoever (that noble, and perhaps only science, mathematicks, excepted). Nor do I foresee any absurdity in saying that law is capable of the best certainty, even demonstration itself. 'T is hard to say, the ideas of quantity are only capable of demonstration; and that this study, so useful and necessary to mankind, should not be so. The subject of law is moral beings, which are a combination or set of ideas taken from the moral actions of mankind; and from the habitudes, correspondencies and relations which they bear to each other; and consequently exist only in the mind and understanding, being put together there; and have no other being or nature but what the mind gives them. The result of which is, we may exactly know the several ideas that go to make each law-term, and so their real nature and essence may be known, and consequently the congruity or incongruity of the things themselves be perfectly discovered, in which consists real knowledge or demonstration. If every complicated idea of right and wrong were well settled and agreed upon, with distinct names to each of them, forming exact definitions, and those constantly used and kept to; the deductions therefrom would be as true and as certain, and the connection be as distinct and clearly perceived, as mathematical beings themselves. For those beings are formed in the same manner, and exist nowhere but in the understanding; there being no such thing really in nature, and materially existing, exactly according to their definitions, as a square, a triangle, or a circle, but exist only in the mind first, and then are set down in the definitions given of them; nor does that science require that there should be any such beings materially existing in the world. So that in the nature of ideas, legal beings, as I may call them, are as capable of demonstration as mathematical ones; but only in the case of mathematicks, in comparing the equality and excess of any quantity, they do it by numbers or measures, which have every the least difference very clear, and the ideas themselves are more capable of being fixed in the mind by perceptible diagrams, and so more distinctly represented to the senses; whereas the others have only names and words, and such as sometimes are unconstantly used, and so the precise combination of ideas is lost; but when those just collections of ideas are exactly noted down, and tied together as it were in bundles or sorts, with names annexed to them, and exactly kept to throughout the argument; the inference and reasoning therefrom is as strong and true as in mathematical cases." John Fortescue-Aland, of the Inner Temple, preface to his edition of *The Difference between an Absolute and Limited Monarchy*, by Sir John Fortescue (London, 1714), pp. iv ff. Fortescue-Aland, the writer of the foregoing passage, was successively Solicitor-General (1715–1717), a baron of the Exchequer (1717–1718), a *puisne* justice of the King's Bench (1718–1727), and of the Common Pleas (1728–1746). See *Dictionary of National Biography.* His views cannot therefore be regarded as merely academic. The question was one which engaged the attention of practising lawyers and the courts. Sir Matthew Hale had also considered it, and with that peculiar balance which gives so

come to realize that logic is but the tool of premises, and that the premises of social intercourse fluctuate with a human equation which contains at least two variables. Logic will not yield us certainties; in fact nothing will. And yet it is the fate of men to need certainties for their living, and it will do us little good to be rebellious against what the universe demands of us. We are sophisticated children of science who know there are no such things as straight lines; and still we must go on using them every day. We have learned that nowhere can we put our finger on a beginning or an ending; yet we divide the time stream into minutes and years. Over the inseverable phenomenal flux we cast the meshes of our categories; it refuses to be bound by them, but we must be.[17] For imaginary certainties are the artificial dykes which have won the realities of civilization from the chaos of nature; or, to use another figure, they are the bootstraps by which men have pulled themselves up out of the primeval mud.

To say that certainty is never to be attained in fact, relieves us no whit from the necessity of carrying on the endless

modern a cast to his thought, had reached different conclusions: "In matters moral and civil — the common subject of laws — though possibly the general and common notions of them, or whereupon they are founded, are in a great measure common to all men of understanding, yet the applications and particular deductions and conclusions thereof are not so clear, constant, and determinate, as consequences and conclusions in logic or mathematics are; for as the nature of moral actions is in themselves much more indeterminate than the subjects of those arts and sciences, so they most commonly are strangely diversified by infinite circumstances; and therefore men agreeing in the same common notions of justice and morality, oftentimes deduce different conclusions from them, and applications of them, although interest and partiality of mind do not interpose." (Preface to Rolle's Abridgement, 1668.) This argues a wholesome recollection of Aristotle: "Exactness is not to be expected in all subjects in equal degree; . . . goodness and justice, which form the subject-matter of the political sciences, must take account of so many differences and uncertainties as to seem dependent upon arbitrary rule alone, rather than upon the nature of things. . . . We must be content, accordingly, when dealing with such subjects, to make our demonstrations in rough outline, and when dealing with matters of more or less, to draw conclusions of the same character," *Nicomachean Ethics*, i, 3. "The rule of what is indeterminate must itself be indeterminate also," *ibid.*, v, 10. For the same controversy, compare Grotius, *De Jure Belli et Pacis*, ii, c. 23, § 1, and Puffendorf, *Law of Nature and of Nations* (Eng. trans., Oxford, 1703), i, c. 2.

[17] See Bergson, *Creative Evolution, passim;* A. N. Whitehead, *The Concept of Nature.*

search for it in practice; and the failure of the eighteenth-century codifiers is not a convincing argument against a régime of law. It may well be that no general rule is ever strictly possible because the same case never arises twice; but this does not imply that much will not be gained by bringing under an approximately general rule cases more or less alike. So no two men have ever exactly the same idea of justice; but neither does it therefore follow that there are no broad fundamental interests which men insist on with a measure of perseverance from generation to generation. If we have not identities to work upon, we have at least resemblances; and on their basis can be constructed a legal system which, although far from attaining the inexorable and absolute certainty once thought possible, yet introduces a degree of beneficial order into a world that would be much worse off without it.[18] The unbridged interval between identity and resemblance is the slip betwixt cup and lip that lets in upon us all the perplexing problems of the legal order. Those perplexities mean that law is a human instrument, the product of minds whose static categories can snatch at but not grasp the universe that flows across it. But if there were perfection there would be no progress. At the alternative of a price we cannot afford to pay, we must perforce accept the plan of a régime of law worked out by our ancestors, though we conceive it less absolutely and make fewer demands upon it than they. It remains for us as for them, although we more adequately realize its limitations, the one clear condition of all achievements which require time and space for their accomplishment.

But the insistence upon a régime of law entails consequences which are not always well realized. It is quite inconsistent with the Austinian notion that law and the command of a sovereign are synonymous. For from moment to moment the sovereign may issue contrary commands. It may be that

[18] "Exactness is an ideal of thought, and is only realized in experience by the selection of a route of approximation," Whitehead, *op. cit.*, p. 59. See also H. Vaihinger, *The Philosophy of As If* (tr. C. K. Ogden, London, 1924), especially pp. 200–205, "Abstract Concepts as Fictions." But compare Alfred Fouillée, *La Pensée et les Nouvelles Écoles Anti-Intellectualistes* (Paris, Alcan, 1911), pp. 51–56.

these can be harmonized by the aid of some undisclosed higher rule; but, if not, then the certainty and predictability of future happenings are gone which lie at the basis of a legal, as distinguished from an arbitrary, régime. And this is true even where, as on Mr. Justice Matthews's theory, the sovereign is the people itself; for mobs as well as kings can change their minds willfully and ignorantly. Legal order requires that law shall be something more than the mere will of the moment, no matter whose the will; it demands a law which shall grow out of the past and be deeply embedded in human wants and interests that can be prefigured for the future. When law neglects these requirements it becomes nothing but the arbitrary command which for seven centuries English-speaking people have been insisting it shall not be. This view, put in the extreme form which identifies the present with the past, and holds that the same principle must always appear in the same garb down to its very shoe-ties, produces anachronisms like the Lochner case, which shock our modern understanding that history does not re-enact itself on the same plane, and that new situations are ever arising which call for novel responses. But there is no need for taking the theory of legal order in so extreme a form; if we admit that there are no identities, we are not driven to closing our eyes to resemblances; and whether or not we agree with Mr. Bergson, we are all evolutionists enough to acknowledge that the new situations which face us have their roots in the past, and that the wants which we feel are blood-kin to wants which men have always more or less felt, at least as far back as we care to carry our history. We must abandon a mechanical correspondence between past and present; but in the act of doing so we are brought to recognize the organic connection between them.

It is still possible, then, to believe in a régime of law, although we have outgrown the notion of an unchanging code of unvarying rules which will solve automatically every case conceivable. We may still insist that if progress is to be orderly, if men are to be protected against the momentary impulse of an official or a majority, nothing must be held for law which does not fit into a system—not a closed mathematical system of rigid concepts, but a developing organic system of concepts more or less elastic.[19] A law will not be such merely because it emanates from governmental authority. This is the living idea underlying the American doctrine of constitutional law.

II

It follows that, under a régime of law, even the orders of a supreme legislature which we call statutes must be submitted to a test before they can be accepted as fully lawful.[20] The question is how the test is to be applied. In England,

[19] "Law is an artificial system which is always gathering new material. The controverted points of one generation become the settled rules of the next, and fresh work is built up on them in turn. Thus the law is in a constant process of approximation to an ideal certainty which can never be perfectly attained at any given moment," Sir F. Pollock, *Harv. Law Rev.*, ix, 301. "A code is not a herbarium in which we deposit law like dried plants," Lieber, *Hermeneutics*, 3d ed., p. 33. "Legal conceptions are indeed extremely stable; many of them have their roots in the most solid portions of our nature, and those of them with which we are most familiar have been for ages under the protection of irresistible sovereign power. Their great stability is apt to suggest that they are absolutely permanent and indestructible, and this assumption seems to me to be sometimes made, not only by superficial minds, but by strong and clear intellects. I am not sure that even such juridical thinkers as Bentham and Austin are quite free from it. They sometimes write as if they thought that, although obscured by false theory, false logic, and false statement, there is somewhere, behind all the delusions which they expose, a framework of permanent legal conceptions which is discoverable by an eye looking through a dry light, and to which a rational code may always be fitted. What I have stated as to the effects upon law of a mere mechanical improvement in land registration is a very impressive warning that this position is certainly doubtful, and possibly not true. The legal notions which I have described as decaying and dwindling have always been regarded as belonging to what may be called the osseous structure of jurisprudence. The fact that they are nevertheless perishable suggests very forcibly that even jurisprudence itself cannot escape from the great law of evolution," Sir Henry Maine, "Minute on Land Transfer," 1879, in *Life and Speeches of Sir Henry Maine*, by Grant Duff and Whitley Stokes (N. Y., 1892), p. 60.

[20] "Everything which may pass under the form of an enactment is not to be considered the law of the land. If this were so . . . there would be no general permanent law for courts to administer or men to live under. Judges would sit to execute legislative judgments and decrees, not to declare the law or administer justice," Webster, *arguendo* in Dartmouth College *v.* Woodward, *Works*, v, 487. Speaking of "vera lex," Cicero says, "Nec vero aut per senatum aut per populum solvi hac lege possumus," *De Rep.*, iii, 22.

it is supposed to be applied by the legislature itself, in this country by the courts; but there is not, in fact, such a difference as the appearances indicate. For law ends by being what it is made to be by the body which applies it to concrete situations; it takes shape only at the moment when it is fitted to the facts of an actual case.[21] Law is thus moulded in the process of adjudication; and the body which adjudicates has final say as to what is and what is not law.[22] Even

[21] "It is emphatically the province and duty of the judicial department to say what the law is. Those who apply the rule to particular cases must of necessity expound and interpret that rule," Chief-Justice Marshall in Marbury *v.* Madison, 1 Cranch, 137. There is a certain irony in comparing this pronouncement with the statement of Montesquieu, to whom we owe so many of our constitutional difficulties in connection with the "separation of powers" doctrine; "Dans le gouvernement républicain, il est de la nature de la constitution que les juges suivent la lettre de la loi. Il n'y a point de citoyen contre qui on puisse interpréter une loi quand il s'agit de ses biens, de son honneur, ou de sa vie," *Esprit des Lois,* vi, 3.

[22] "It was long a favorite fiction that the judges did not make, but only declared the law. But it is no longer denied, nor can it be, that the judges in the process of the interpretation of statutes, especially where they extend them to cases without their letter but within their supposed reason or equity, as well as in cases which, where the statutes are silent, they decide by rules deduced from previous decisions, or decide by reference to the principles of natural right or universal justice, are actually, though indirectly, engaged in legislating, since they formulate, or at least authenticate, the rules which they apply to the transactions in hand; and these rules constitute the grounds of the judgments they pronounce," John F. Dillon, *The Laws and Jurisprudence of England and America,* p. 267. For a contrary view see W. H. Taft, *Popular Government,* pp. 221 ff. "Whoever hath an absolute authority to interpret any written or spoken laws, it is he who is truly the law-giver to all intents and purposes and not the person who first wrote or spoke them," Bishop Hoadly, *Sermon preached before the King, 1717,* quoted in Gray, *Nature and Sources of the Law* (1st ed.), sec. 229. See also George Buchanan, *De Jure Regni apud Scotos,* cc. xxx, xxxi, xxxii; but *cf.* Cardozo, *Nature of the Judicial Process,* pp. 125 ff. Judge Cardozo draws attention to the important practical qualification that the power of judicial interpretation accomplishes substantial amendment of the law only in exceptional cases. In Mr. Justice Holmes's well-known phrase, the creative activity of the judiciary is "interstitial." But this is of course not true of American constitutional law in so far as the interpretation of phrases like "due process" requires the courts to elaborate rules not in subordination to legislative mandate, but as a mandate to the legislature. Nor, because of the broadness of the words to be interpreted, can the court's activity be regarded as merely interstitial to a popular will embodied in the constitution. "The law of constitutional due process is as much judge-made law as any common law is judge-made law," Thomas Reed Powell, in *Harv. Law Rev.,* xxxvii, 546.

in England the necessity the courts are under of interpreting acts of Parliament in applying them to the litigated cases which come before them gives them a power of shaping the law not unlike, though much inferior in degree, to the power of our own courts; and that this power is a reality is standing out with increasing clearness from cases like Rex *v.* Housing Tribunal [23] and The Chelston.[24] The legislature is after all limited, by the very nature of its function, to making law *in vacuo.*

When we say that the law is thus finally determined by the body which adjudicates cases, we have defined in its essential features the relation which under a régime of law must perforce exist between courts and legislature; there remains the more thorny issue between the courts and administrative tribunals. For these are both adjudicating agencies — both apply the law to concrete situations. We are facing two questions: whether the courts should have power to make their own view prevail over that of the executive; and if so, what should be the extent of that power.

To the first question only one answer seems open after all that has been said. The idea of law is contradicted by the existence, side by side, of two independent law-declaring agencies neither of which is supreme over the other.[25] A régime of law is interrupted by inconsistencies, and Swift *v.*

[23] [1920] 3 K. B. 334. [24] [1920] Prob. Div. 400.

[25] Story (*Commentaries on the Constitution*, 4th ed., ii, 399) quotes with approval the following passage from Paley: "If several courts coördinate to and independent of each other subsist together in the country, it seems necessary that appeals from all of them should meet and terminate in the same judicature in order that one supreme tribunal by whose final sentence all others are bound and concluded, may superintend and preside over the rest. This is necessary for two purposes: to preserve a uniformity in the decisions of inferior courts and to maintain to each the proper limits of its jurisdiction. Without a common superior, different courts might establish contrary rules of adjudications and the contradiction be final and without remedy. A common appellate jurisdiction prevents or puts an end to this confusion. For when the judgments upon appeals are consistent (which may be expected when the same court is at last resorted to), the different courts from which the appeals are brought will be reduced to a like consistency with one another. Moreover, if questions arise between courts independent of each other concerning the extent and boundaries of their jurisdiction, as each will be desirous of enlarging its own, an authority which both acknowledge can alone adjust the controversy."

Tyson[26] and the double-barrelled Supreme Court of Texas are as anomalous as the two sets of legal-tender decisions.[27] Secondly, admitting that within a given jurisdiction there must be a single agency authorized to pronounce the law with finality, the nature of the task points to the courts as the proper agency to perform it. If we are to have a régime of law, the legal rule applied to a given case must be one that shall fit into a whole body of other rules which, taken together, make up a harmonious and consistent system. In Maitland's phrase, the law is a seamless web. The law applicable to a given case can therefore be pronounced only by a body which knows authoritatively, so far as is humanly possible, the whole of the law. In less absolute and more practical language, the law ought to be applied by an agency whose main business is to know the law, rather than to enforce some part of it.

But, admitting that the application of law by administrative bodies ought in some way to be controlled by the courts, how far ought the control to reach? Suppose an attack by a railroad company on an order of a commission fixing a rate. Of course the court will examine whether or not the rate is so unreasonable as to be confiscatory — with us that is a constitutional question; granting, however, that it is decided in the negative, will the court, or should it, examine whether or not in its opinion the rate exceeds the possibilities of reasonable inference from the evidence? Should it go still further and examine whether in its own judgment the rate is a proper one? This is the critical question raised by Senator Foraker.

Abstractly, the issue boils down to how far we desire the "rule of law" to extend. Do we wish it to protect only the large outlines of so-called fundamental rights? Or do we desire it to descend into and define with minuteness all the relations affected by administrative determinations? On an eighteenth-century view of law this alternative would be

[26] 16 Peters, 1.

[27] Hepburn *v.* Griswold, 8 Wall. 603; Legal Tender Cases, 12 Wall. 457; see S. P. Breckenridge, *Legal Tender*, pp. 127–133.

meaningless; we could never make such a cleavage. For from that point of view, carried to its logical consequence, the entire body of rules applicable to human conduct form a closed logical system within which the acceptance of fundamental rules straightway requires the acceptance of a complete set of particular rules following as corollaries by strict logical necessity.[28] It is needless to say that even in the eighteenth century no such theory was ever applied concretely to practice.[29] It puts no obstacle in our way to-day.

[28] See the passage from d'Aguesseau quoted above in note 13 to this chapter. *Cf.* Blackstone, *Commentaries* (ed. Christian), i, 41: "The law of nature . . . is binding over all the globe in all countries, and at all times; no human laws are of any validity if contrary to this; and such of them as are valid derive all their authority, mediately or immediately, from this original. But in order to apply this to the particular exigencies of each individual, it is still necessary to have recourse to reason: whose office is to discover . . . what the law of nature directs in every circumstance of life. . . . And if our reason were always clear and perfect . . . the task would be pleasant and easy; we should need no other guide but this." See also Edmond Wingate, *Maximes of Reason; or the Reason of the Common Law* (London, 1658), pref.

[29] While the main effort of eighteenth-century theory was directed to showing that a system of particular rules could be logically deduced from a small number of "axiomatic" first principles of self-evident justice, a way was left open to provide for the stubborn exceptions which even eighteenth-century rationalism could not blink by drawing a distinction between "immutable" rules on the one hand, and "arbitrary" or "indifferent" rules on the other. This distinction is resorted to by both Domat and Blackstone. Says Domat: "The immutable laws are so-called because they are natural, and so just at all times and in all places, that no authority can either change or abolish them; and the arbitrary laws are those which a lawful authority may enact, change, and abolish, as there is occasion. These immutable or natural laws are such as are necessary consequences of the [first principles] which are so essential . . . to the order of society that it is impossible to alter them without destroying the foundations of the social order . . . and it is the same thing with respect to all the particular rules which are essential to this order. . . . Thus it is a rule essential to the engagement of the person who borrows something belonging to another, that he ought to preserve it; and it is also an immutable law that he ought to be answerable for the faults which he commits contrary to this duty. . . . But the laws concerning matters which are left indifferent by the [first principles of society] . . . are arbitrary laws. Thus, seeing it is indifferent . . . whether there be five, six, or seven witnesses to a testament; whether prescription be acquired in twenty, thirty, or forty years; whether money be of a higher or a lesser value: these are only arbitrary laws, which regulate these sorts of things, and they regulate them differently, according to the times and places," Domat, *The Civil Law in its Natural Order*, translated into English by William Strahan (2d ed., London, 1737), vol. i, p. lix. It is interesting to note that a reprint of this translation of Domat, with American notes by Luther S.

The question before us is simply over how wide a field we desire to cast the net of our legal logic; how inclusive a segment of human relations we wish to congeal into the approximate stability of a régime of law. In other words, how far do we wish to make a legal question of the matters entrusted to administrative tribunals? And within what limits do we feel it safe to commit ourselves, with respect to them, to a régime of discretion or justice without law? In language which Grotius and Coke would never have understood, it is for us to-day simply a question of policy as to what

Cushing, the reporter of the Massachusetts Supreme Court, was published at Boston in 1850 by Little and Brown. *Cf.* also Vattel, *Law of Nations* (ed. Chitty), *Prelim.*, §§ 7–9. Says Blackstone: "Upon the law of nature and the law of revelation ["which is expressly declared to be the law of nature by God himself"] depend all human laws; that is to say, no human laws should be suffered to contradict these. There are, it is true, a great number of indifferent points in which both the divine law and the natural law leave a man at his own liberty; but which are found necessary for the benefit of society to be restrained within certain limits. And herein it is that human laws have their greatest force and efficacy; for with regard to such points as are not indifferent, human laws are only declaratory of, and act in subordination to, the former. To instance in the case of murder: this is expressly forbidden by the divine, and demonstrably by the natural law; and from these prohibitions arises the true unlawfulness of this crime. Those human laws that annex a punishment to it do not . . . superadd any fresh obligation . . . to abstain from its perpetration. . . . But with regard to matters that are themselves indifferent, and are not commanded or forbidden by those superior laws; such, for instance, as exporting of wool into foreign countries; here the inferior legislature has scope and opportunity to interpose, and to make that action unlawful which before was not so," *Commentaries*, ed. Christian, i, 42. The same distinction is drawn by Rutherforth, *Institutes of Natural Law*, Bk. ii, ch. vi, § ix. Blackstone bases on this distinction the doctrine of a difference between *mala prohibita* and *mala in se* which at times has had such importance in certain branches of our law. For Christian's criticism, see his note, *op. cit.*, i, 52. The example given above by Blackstone of an "arbitrary" or "indifferent" law, — namely the prohibition of wool exports — is substantially the same as that of Rutherforth (*loc. cit.*), who instances a prohibition of the importation of foreign manufactures. These examples illustrate the futility of an attempt to establish the two classes of laws as fixed categories; for a conception of fundamental natural law is possible which would regard freedom of trade between nations as a basic axiom, and would thus be directly violated by such prohibitions. This was in fact Vattel's conception: "A nation is obliged to promote and carry on a foreign trade. . . . Whence it follows that it is a duty to sell to each other at a fair price what the possessor himself has no occasion for . . . . Since right springs from obligation, the obligation we have just established gives every man the right of procuring

matters shall be "matters of law." On our opinion as to this question will depend where we draw the line as what is or is not due process of law. Before attempting to find our way into this question of policy, it will be helpful to look at the mechanism of the legal system as a working instrumentality for achieving the results it aims at — certainty in the conduct of affairs and the protection of a number of basic human interests. How does it work, and what work is it consequently fitted to do? What are the conditions which set limits to its effective operation, and where do these limits lie?

the things he wants by purchasing them at a reasonable price from those who have themselves no occasion for them," bk. i, ch. viii, §§ 88, Chitty's ed., p. 38. Similarly Domat derives as a necessary inference from immutable natural law a rule directly at variance with what natural law has at other times been held to require: "It is a natural law that he who buys should not take advantage of the person who sells, and that he should not buy at too low a price," *op. cit.*, vol. i, p. lxi. Everything thus depends on what one chooses to regard as "natural." It is easy, as Mr. Justice Holmes has noted, to forget that what seem to one man "first principles" "are believed by half his fellow-men to be wrong," *Collected Legal Papers*, p. 295; and that "wherever a doubtful case arises, the simple tool of logic does not suffice, and even if it is disguised and unconscious, the judges are called on to exercise the sovereign prerogative of choice," *ibid.*, p. 239. The effort to draw a sharp line between "natural" and "immutable" on the one side, and "arbitrary" and "indifferent" on the other, goes back no doubt to Aristotle's distinction between natural and conventional *justice*, *Eth. Nicom.*, v, 7. It has already become a distinction between "mutable" and "immutable" *rules of law* in Livy, xxxiv, 6. It survived through the Middle Ages, see John of Salisbury, *Policraticus*, iv, 7. But even in the case of "natural laws," the mediaeval writers were forced to develop a distinction between those which were "primary" and "immutable," and those which were "secondary" and subject to change. See Pollock, *Essays in the Law*, p. 51; Gierke, *Political Theories of the Middle Age*, tr. Maitland, p. 175, note 260. This distinction survives in Domat's effort to distinguish between "immutable" laws which admit of exceptions, and "immutable" laws which admit of no exceptions, *op. cit.*, i, p. lxiv. Grotius (*De Jure Belli et Pacis*, I, x) and Burlamaqui (*Principes du Droit Naturel*, Geneva, 1748, pt. ii, ch. v, § x) on the other hand seem to argue that *all* the precepts of the law of nature are immutable. For the influence of Vattel, Burlamaqui and Rutherforth on American practitioners, see Hoffman's statement that "they were placed in students' hands" and were "the sources to which the senior lawyers of the present time are accustomed to resort," *Course of Legal Study*, 2d ed., Balto., 1836, i, 113; and for the influence of the "Naturrecht School" generally, see Marshall's reference to the "wise and learned men whose treatises on the law of nature and nations have guided public opinion," Ogden *v.* Saunders, 12 Wheat. at p. 353.

III

Modern juristic analysis interprets law as operating through four distinct sorts of instruments by the interactions of which it reaches its result of bringing human relations into predictable order — *rules, principles, concepts,* and *standards.*[30] These four elements hold a definite genetic relationship to one another — a principle is the broader idea of policy which stands back of every rule of law and links it with the human demand for justice; the rule of law itself operates directly on situations of fact through the medium of the concepts which enter into its composition, and under which particular states of concrete fact may be subsumed to produce uniformity of result; legal standards are the more or less vague substitutes for rules and concepts in fields not yet ready, or not adapted, for the latter to crystallize.[31] The relation between the four can be illustrated by an example. It is a principle of legal policy that persons engaged in a calling of more than ordinary importance to the public shall not be allowed to take advantage of the public necessity in the same way as those engaged in other lines of enterprise. One formulation of this principle is the legal rule that common carriers must charge no more than a reasonable rate for their services. The application of this rule to any particular state of facts depends on the legal definition of the terms "common carrier" and "reasonable rate." "Common carrier" has crystallized into a legal concept, while "reasonable rate" merely sketches a standard to be applied.

The heart of the legal system is in its concepts. These are the fixed points which introduce an artificial stability into the ebb and flow of human relations — the hard identities which for its own purposes the law impresses upon resemblances, to create certainty through ability to predict the

[30] See Pound, "The Administrative Application of Legal Standards," in *Rep. Amer. Bar Assoc.* (1919), xliv, 445 ff.

[31] This, it is submitted, is the logical relationship. In actual historical development, rules generally precede principles and concepts precede standards. See Pound, *Introduction to the Philosophy of Law*, p. 115.

legal consequences of acts. A delivers to B a wagonload of oats and takes a horse in return; A delivers the oats and B promises to pay twenty dollars in a month's time; A merely promises to deliver the oats in return for B's promise to pay the twenty dollars; all three transactions, different as they are, are in a certain sense "sales," and for certain purposes fall under the same legal rules. A trustee speculates with trust property, meaning to make a fortune for the *cestui* or intending only to make a fortune for himself; in both cases there has been a breach of trust, and it matters not that in one the trustee was a credulous woman and in the other an experienced business man. Because of the presence of some common element, the law pigeonholes differing states of facts in the same category and deliberately disregards the differences. Elsewhere it marks off and recognizes certain particular facts as constituting a valid distinction. A signs a bond of his own free will; he goes through the same act with the gun of B pointed at his head; in the first case he is bound, in the second he is excused, because the law regards the coercion as a pertinent element of difference and attaches a different consequence where it is present. Here, as before, the law isolates particular facts from a great mass of others, binds them together with a conceptual label, and reaches a different result according as this bundle of facts is or is not present, and the label is or is not applicable.[32] In its distinctions as in its inclusions the method of the law is the same — to reach an identical result in all cases where the salient fact or group of facts is present, however different the several situations may be in other particulars. As Sir Frederick Pollock has expressed it: "No two persons or events can be fully alike. What rules of law have to do is to select those conditions which are to have consequences of certain kinds; which being done, it is the business of the courts to attend to

[32] In the language of Mr. Justice Fortescue-Aland, quoted above in note 15, this chapter, legal concepts are "collections of ideas tied together as it were in bundles or sorts with names annexed to them, and exactly kept to throughout the argument." Whether they are "exactly kept to" or not, is often the question.

all those conditions, and, saving judicial discretion where it exists, not to attend to any other." [33]

The process of the law is thus generalization; and, as Mr. Justice Holmes has said, to generalize is essentially to omit.[34] Such omission sometimes leads to results which seem harsh and unjust. Suppose P has made an agreement with V, the owner of land, that on condition of his going into possession and making improvements he is to have an option to buy and pay the purchase price before a certain day. He goes into possession and makes the improvements to double the value required. On his way to pay the price on the day named he is attacked by robbers and the money taken from him. Several days elapse before he can raise the money again, and when he then tenders it, V refuses to go on with the contract. The courts would deny to P a decree of specific performance. The law in its generality omits to regard the specific circumstances which caused P's failure to pay at the date named as falling within any recognized element of difference taking the case out of the general class marked by failure of an essential condition precedent.[35]

The concepts of the law in their rigid inclusiveness can thus be made to yield like results in cases where the presence of differentiating elements which the law ignores seem to laymen to call for a substantial difference in the respective outcomes. This is one objection to a system of legal justice as contrasted with free judicial discretion. Under the latter, the adjudicating officer would be at liberty to attach decisive weight to whatever special circumstances of a case

[33] *Harv. Law Rev.*, ix, 300. See also Wigmore, *Problems of Law*, p. 70: "One of the formal elements of law is uniformity, generality, a rule more or less abstract. And this uniformity consists in selecting one or more circumstances common to numerous situations involving human conduct, and declaring that these few circumstances shall produce a certain result whatever the other variety of circumstances may be."

[34] Donnell *v.* Herring-Hall-Marvin Safe Co., 208 U. S. 267, at p. 273.

[35] Time is always of the essence of an option agreement, though not expressed to be so: Smith *v.* Howard, 32 Ky. Law Rep. 211; 36 Cyc. 711; Standiford *v.* Thompson, 135 Fed. 991; Richardson *v.* Hardwick, 106 U. S. 254; Lord Ranelagh *v.* Melton, 2 Drewry & Smale, 278, at p. 281; Pomeroy, *Equitable Remedies*, § 807.

seemed to him to deserve it in view of all the other circumstances. Under a régime of law he is bound to give deciding weight to certain factors, if present, and to ignore the rest. The difficulty about thus singling out some particular factor from a situation made up of a host of them [36] is first of all the difficulty of determining which factor the law shall select for critical importance. What shall be regarded and what ignored? Take the case of a contract made by a married man; shall the fact of marriage be held to make a difference, or shall the contract of a married man and a single man be treated alike? Shall the contract of a woman be regarded in the same light as the contract of a man, or shall importance be attached to the fact of sex? In reality we know that our law treated the contract of a woman in the same way as that of a man, but that in the case of a woman the law attached critical importance to the fact of marriage, while in the case of a man it was ignored. So in the matter of contracts, the law regarded the fact of infancy, and disregarded it in the case of torts. Such selection is dictated by the general view of public policy which the law embodies. It singles out as decisive the factor or factors which, in view of all the cases considered as likely to arise, must be made decisive as a means of reaching the goal which the contemporary view of public policy dictates to the law as ideal. But the difficulty is that the contemporary view of public policy shifts with successive generations, and what was once the goal of policy ceases in time to be so. That has been the fate, for instance, of the absolute subordination of wife to husband in the marriage relation. Consequently the factor which the law had fixed itself to regard as crucial no longer corresponded with what men felt to be so; and when they saw the law making the

[36] "Among the innumerable facts of actual life, some become accentuated as links in the formation, modification, or assertion of legal rights," P. Vinogradoff, *Common Sense in Law*, p. 101; also, pp. 86–101, *passim*. "We can never be sure in applying a general rule to a particular case that the eliminated elements may not be material; and if, peradventure, they are material, and we apply the general rule without them, we fall into error," Salmond, *First Principles of Jurisprudence*, 1st ed. (1893), p. 92; *cf.* 6th ed. (1920), p. 23. "Equity was originally discretionary interference with the operation of general rules in order to do justice in particular cases," Pound in *Col. Law Rev.*, v, 20.

validity of a woman's contract depend on such a thing as whether or not she was married, they felt that the law was unjust, not only because it was rigid, but because it was unreal and artificial. Again, even where no change has occurred in prevailing views as to the proper goal of policy, the conditions and technique of human action may have so changed that what was once rightly made a decisive factor in the disposition of a case becomes an immaterial one which, if still adhered to, serves to warp the decision to a result felt to be unjust. Examples are the fellow-servant rule in employers' liability cases,[37] and the application to corporate mortgages of an old rule which had been kept alive to protect farmers against the temptation to mortgage their future crops.[38]

These disadvantages of a régime of law result from the rigid outlines of the law's fixed concepts. A second sort of disadvantage results when these concepts, as they sometimes do, get in each other's way. Between most legal concepts of opposite tendency the boundary is at points thin and undefined. Does deceit in making a contract, for instance, give rise to an action for breach of contract, or for tort? [39] Is a given transaction a sale or a bailment? Certain factors, if

[37] It has been suggested that the establishment of this rule was originally due to a temporary consideration of policy — the desire in the early days of railroads to relieve them from a burden of liability which threatened to hamper their growth at a time when the community was vitally interested in their promotion and expansion, Warren, *History of the American Bar*, pp. 485, 486 ff. Substantially the same explanation was given in the House of Commons by Mr. Asquith, 8 *Hansard* (4th series, 1893), p. 1943. For the popular favor with which railroads were regarded at the period of their introduction, see Charles Francis Adams, *Railroads, Their Origin and Problems*, pp. 67, 68. On the other hand Judge Baldwin went so far as to announce that the rule "rested upon general considerations of right and justice, . . . supported by the principle that negligence of a servant . . . does not of itself prove any omission of care on the part of the master in his employment, and only such omission of care can justify holding the master responsible," Hoxie *v.* N. Y., N. H., & H. R. Co., 82 Conn. 352, at p. 360 (1909).

[38] Cf. Zartman *v.* Bank, 189 N. Y. 267, where the Court, in holding a corporate mortgage of after-acquired chattels invalid, followed Rochester Distilling Co. *v.* Rasey, 142 N. Y. 570, which held that a mortgage given by a farmer on crops not yet planted was invalid.

[39] See Pasley *v.* Freeman, 3 T. R. 1. The confusion between the concepts of "tort" and "contract" is illustrated but not clarified in E. V. Abbot, *Justice and the Modern Law*, pp. 41 ff.

present, will make it a sale; others indicate a bailment; but what if, as sometimes happens, some of both sets are present? Suppose shipments are arranged from A to B, on terms whereby A draws against B for the shipment and dictates the price of resale by B; or B guarantees the sale of the shipment by a certain date and agrees to bear the risk of loss of the goods: is B a mere bailee who has made an advance to A or has he bought the goods? [40] Or, take the other case suggested: A, twenty years old and in business, sells goods to B, fraudulently representing their quality to be superior to what it actually is. Is he liable? An infant is liable for his torts, but not for his breaches of contract. A has been guilty of deceit, and deceit is a tort; but here the deceit occurred in connection with a contract, and to allow recovery for the tort would in effect amount to enforcing the contract. Where are we to draw the line, and on which side are we going to let such a case fall?

These examples show the difficulty which the law experiences in so constructing its concepts as to make them mutually exclusive. Slightly different are cases where the facts are such that, regarded from one point of view, they fall within one legal concept, while from another angle they fit equally well into another. Such a case arises where S becomes surety for P, a married woman. At common law P is not bound and hence there is no principal obligation. Is S liable? On the one hand, it may be argued that as there is no principal obligation, there can be no surety obligation, and S is not bound; but it may be urged with equal plausibility that since there could never have been a principal obligation, S's promise could not have been a surety promise in the first instance, but must have been an independent one *ab initio* and that therefore he is bound.[41]

[40] *Cf.* such cases as ex parte Flannagans, Fed. Cases, 4855, and In re Heckathorn, 144 Fed. 499, with Butler Bros. *v.* U. S. Rubber Co., 156 Fed. 1, and Childs *v.* Waterloo Wagon Co., 37 App. Div. (N. Y.) 242. Substantially the same issue arose, and was well discussed by Eyre, C. J., in the old case of Haille *v.* Smith (C. P. 1796), 1 B. & P. 563 ff.

[41] See Kimball *v.* Newell, 7 Hill (N. Y.) 116; Ames, *Cases on Suretyship*, p. 108.

The last case illustrates the ever-present possibility of juggling with legal concepts like hollow shells or counters in a game.[42] There is a temptation attractive to legal thinkers to play this game by combining concepts into a geometrical demonstration [43] which yields results logical in appearance but artificial in fact. A good example is Mr. Lansing's argument on the subject of mandates under the League of Nations. He argued that every point on the world's surface must be subject to sovereignty. Sovereignty means supreme power and can belong only to a territorial state. Territory covered by a mandate is not under the sovereignty of the mandatory nation, because the mandatory is not supreme, being under the control of the League. But the League cannot be sovereign because it is not a territorial state. The scheme of mandates is therefore legally impossible.[44] This conclusion is the result of abstracting a conception of sovereignty from the facts as they exist under one type of legal world-order and then tacitly assuming that it is a mould into which no type of legal world-order can fail to run.

The way of escape from Mr. Lansing's *cul-de-sac* is to take a more realistic view of the nature of legal concepts. They

[42] See Wigmore on Evidence, 2d ed., i., p. xv: "Cases are counters and there are no coins."

[43] The method consists in treating concepts as if they were "things," which preserved their separate identity unaltered in all possible contexts, and could be combined and recombined without waste into successive demonstrations as blocks can be combined and recombined into architectural patterns. This view of the nature of concepts has been described by James and Bergson. "Particular facts decay, and our perceptions of them vary. A concept never varies; and between such unvarying terms the relations must be constant and express eternal verities," William James, *Problems of Philosophy*, p. 53. "Concepts are outside each other, like objects in space; and they have the same stability as such objects, on which they have been modelled. . . . They are not images, but symbols. Our logic is the complete set of rules that must be followed in using symbols. As these symbols are derived from the consideration of solids, our logic triumphs in that science which takes the solidity of bodies for its object, that is, in geometry. Logic and geometry engender each other. . . . Geometry and logic are strictly applicable to matter; in it they are at home, and in it they can proceed quite alone. But, outside this domain, pure reasoning needs to be supervised by common sense, which is an altogether different thing," Bergson, *Creative Evolution*, tr. Arthur Mitchell, pp. 160, 161.

[44] *Rep. Amer. Bar Assoc.* (1919), xliv, p. 246.

are not spatial entities having the independent and inexorable existence of physical objects and excluding each other in all dimensions.[45] Properly regarded, they are seen to be

[45] "The abuse consists in envisaging ideal conceptions, provisional and purely subjective in their nature, as endowed with a permanent objective reality. And this false point of view which, to my thinking, is a vestige of the absolute realism of the Middle Ages, ends in confining the entire system of positive law, *a priori*, within a limited number of logical categories, which are predetermined in essence, immovable in basis, governed by inflexible dogmas and thus incapable of adapting themselves to the ever varied and changing exigencies of life," Gèny, *Méthode d'Interprétation et Sources en droit privé positif*, ed. 1899, sec. 61, p. 115. In actual fact, whenever it comes to defining a legal concept, or stating a legal rule, the difficulty of treating them as clean-cut independent entities at once becomes apparent. Almost every legal concept or principle is found to be but the terminal of a scale which shades at its opposite extremity into another of exactly contrary tendency, and the line between the two oscillates from specific case to case according to the context. Thus the law of nuisance plays between the principle that every person is entitled to use his property for any purpose that he sees fit, and the opposing principle that every man is bound to use his property in such a manner as not to injure the property of his neighbor. As no two cases of nuisance are ever exactly alike, all that can be done in borderline cases between the two principles is to let a jury say where the line shall come. Where the run of the cases involves more uniform issues, it is of course possible to draw a permanent line somewhere by establishing a purely arbitrary rule. This was noted by Domat: "One who is the owner of a thing should continue to have the property of it until he has divested himself of it voluntarily, or until he be divested of it in some legal way; at the same time possessors ought not always to be in danger of being molested in their possession for ever. . . . The contrariety to which these two laws might lead us, requires that it should be regulated by an arbitrary law that they who are not in possession, and who, notwithstanding, claim the right of property, should be bound to assert and prove their right within a certain time . . . and this is what has been done by the arbitrary laws which settle the times of prescriptions," *The Civil Law in its Natural Order*, tr. Strahan, i., p. lx. But even where such an arbitrary line has once been drawn, there is no guarantee that a stable barrier has been erected against the ebb and flow of human uncertainties. These uncertainties persist chiefly for two reasons: (1) alteration in the customs or circumstances in the light of which the arbitrary rule was framed; (2) the uncertainties inherent in the nature of language, to which resort must be had for the statement of an arbitrary fixed rule. A difficulty due to the first cause is illustrated by a point from the law of sales. Here again the purpose of the law is to give effect to two opposing principles: first, the principle that a buyer should keep his eyes open, and, second, the principle that an unfair advantage ought not to be taken of the buyer by the seller. The rule accordingly developed that where the seller is a manufacturer, and goods are ordered without opportunity for adequate inspection by the buyer, the manufacturer warrants their merchantable quality, Laing *v.* Fidgeon, 4 Campbell, 169. But today, with the elaboration of the organization of the market, the consumer, as often as not,

capable of overlapping and intersecting and interpenetrating. For legal concepts, like concepts in general, are nothing more than categories of classification. The variety of possible classifications is as infinite as the infinite number of purposes

orders not from the manufacturer, but from a dealer; does the rule extend its protection, as its reason seems clearly to demand, against a dealer also? See *Harv. Law Rev.*, xxv, 75 and Williston on Sales, 1st ed., §§232, 233. Uncertainties arising from the inherent limitations of language are ubiquitous. Hardly any word useful in the statement of a legal rule or definition is limited, like a mathematical term, to a single meaning. "Necessaries," "domicile," "presence," "ratification," to name but a few, are all capable of application by different minds to different things. Lieber has well said what needs to be said on this point in his *Hermeneutics* (3d ed.): "In no case are words . . . affixed to objects presenting themselves to the mind in a clearly defined state, but on the contrary . . . terms receive a meaning distinct as to some points, but indistinct as to others, or, to use a simile, they may be distinct as to the central point of space they cover, but become less so the farther we remove from that center. . . . This would be a necessary cause of ambiguity, even if the nature of things and ideas were not such that mathematical precision becomes impossible, except in mathematics themselves. Absolute language, by which is meant language which absolutely expresses all that which is to be expressed, neither more nor less, for every mind, is possible in mathematics only" (pp. 14, 15). "It is impossible to word laws in such a manner as to absolutely exclude all doubt, or to allow us to dispense with construction, even if they be worded for the time for which they were made, with absolute (mathematical) distinctness; because things and relations change, and because interests conflict differently with each other at different times. The very object of laws is to establish general rules beforehand. . . . By this inherent generality, however, there is a constant reason for requiring construction in the application of laws, since most cases occurring are of a complex character. It is in vain, therefore, to believe in the possibility of forming a code of laws absolutely distinct, like mathematical theories" (pp. 154, 155). "Interpretation and construction of laws then become necessary on account of the character of human language; . . . on account of their application to complex cases; on account of the change of the circumstances and things to which they must be applied" (p. 157). *Cf.* also Mr. Justice Story: "To a certain extent law must forever be subject to uncertainty and doubt; not from the obscurity and fluctuations of decisions, as the vulgar erroneously suppose, but from the endless complexity and variety of human actions. However certain may be the rules of the statute or common law, they must necessarily be general in their language, and incapable of a minute and perfect application to the *boundless* [italics in the original] circumstances of life, which may modify, limit, or affect them. It is impossible to provide by any code, however extensive, for the infinite variety of distinctions, as to civil justice, arising from the imperfections of human language and foresight, from the conflict of opposing rights, from the effect of real or apparent hardships, and from those minute equities, which are often found in different scales, adding somewhat to the weight of each, but rarely forming an exact equipoise. Until human actions are capable of being limited on every side to a definite range of circumstances, the permu-

for which classifications can be made.[46] Any particular classification made from a single point of view and for a particular purpose will consist of mutually exclusive categories. But the categories of this particular scheme will not necessarily coincide, point for point, with those made from another angle and for some other purpose. A good illustration is the familiar rule that as between a common-law mortgagor and mortgagee the latter has legal title, but that the former has legal title as against third persons.[47] In short, our concept of "legal title" covers different ground when our object is to protect the rights of third persons from what it does when we are concerned with questions between the parties. Similarly, in claims for preference against a bankrupt, transactions are frequently held sales for the protection of unsecured creditors which as between a consignor and a solvent consignee might well be held to be mere bailments.[48] Valuation for taxation is a different thing from valuation for rate-making.[49] For some purposes the corporate fiction may be disregarded.[50] The rules which govern the release of a professional corporate surety from liability are different from those which are applied to an individual surety.[51]

tations and combinations of which may be perfectly ascertained and enumerated; until there shall be an entire separation of right from wrong in all the business of life, and the elements of each shall be immiscible and repulsive; until, in short, we shall become absolutely pure and perfect in our actions, and perfectly conusant of all the operations of the past, the present, and the future; there will remain immeasurable uncertainties in the law," "Review of Hoffman's Course of Legal Study," in *Miscellaneous Writings* (Boston, 1835), pp. 226, 227. See also Plato, *Statesman*, 294b, quoted below, note 62, this chapter.

46 See William James, *Problems of Philosophy*, p. 51.

47 Kent's *Commentaries*, 12th ed., iv, 160; Willington *v.* Gale, 7 Mass. 138; Eaton *v.* Whiting, 3 Pick. 484; Wilkins *v.* French, 20 Me. 111.; *cf.* McCall *v.* Lenox, 9 Serg. & R. 302.

48 See cases cited above, note 40, this chapter.

49 Willcox *v.* Consolidated Gas Co., 212 U. S. 19, at 51; Louisville & Nashville R. Co. *v.* Brown, 123 Fed. 946; Hartman, *Fair Value*, p. 79.

50 See In re Watertown Paper Co., 169 Fed. 256; Westinghouse *v.* Allis-Chalmers Co., 176 Fed. 362; Foard Co. *v.* Maryland, 219 Fed. 827; Hunter *v.* Baker Co., 225 Fed. 1006; Stark Railroad Co. *v.* McGinty Co., 238 Fed. 567.

51 Young *v.* American Bonding Co., 228 Pa. St. 373 at p. 380; United States *v.* U. S. Fidelity & Guaranty Co., 178 Fed. 721; Massachusetts Bonding Co. *v.* Realty Trust Co., 142 Ga. 499. Similar considerations apply in the determination of what are "fixtures." See, *e. g.*, Kent's *Commentaries*, 12th ed., ii, 345.

To a certain type of legal thinker these results are impossible. He regards it as intellectually dishonest to hold that the same man has and has not legal title to the same thing at the same time, or that the same transaction can be, and also not be, a bailment. Such a man thinks in a single dimension. He fails to recognize that there are categories of distinction which apply in one plane and not in another, and that all distinctions are applicable or not solely as the purpose is or is not controlling for which they are decisive.[52] This is not to argue that legal concepts should be arbitrarily applied or disregarded according to the whim of a particular judge in the special case before him, as would be the case under free judicial discretion. It is the reason embodied in the purposes of the law and not the arbitrary discretion of the judge [53] that must determine whether or not a particular legal concept controls a case which from some angles fits within it.[54] A concept ought never to be held in-

[52] "All definitions are relative to the purpose of an inquiry," F. C. S. Schiller, *Formal Logic*, pp. 69, 70. "The purpose of the law is the ever insistent consideration in its interpretation," McKenna, J., in U. S. *v.* AntiKamnia Co., 231 U. S. 654, at p. 667. See Pound, "Mechanical Jurisprudence," *Col. Law Rev.*, viii, 603 ff. In U. S. *v.* Holy Trinity Church the lower court held that the church by calling an alien rector from abroad had violated the provisions of the Federal statute against the importation of "contract" labor (36 Fed. 303). The decision was reversed by the Supreme Court (143 U. S. 457) on an interpretation of the statute based upon its purpose. An illustration of the extension of a rule of law without regard to its purpose is afforded by London & South Western R. Co. *v.* Gomm, 20 Ch. Div. 562, where the rule against perpetuities, which originated to meet problems connected with family settlements, was extended to apply to an option agreement entered into by a corporation. The impossibility of applying satisfactorily the same scheme of classification to situations where the purpose of the classification differs is illustrated by the utter confusion attendant upon the attempts to classify "power" as "administrative" or "judicial," noted in chapter I, above.

[53] This was no doubt the practical idea lying behind the unrealistic terminology of Blackstone's statement that "the judgment, though pronounced or awarded by the judges, is not their determination or sentence, but the determination and sentence of the law." Blackstone's *Commentaries* 396. Filmer had pertinently asked, if the law was to judge, who was to be judge of the law? "Anarchy of a Mixed Monarchy," in *Freeholder's Grand Inquest, etc.*, ed. 1680, pp. 263, 266.

[54] In some classes of cases this purpose may be best furthered by applying the concept rigidly and mechanically at the expense of seeming injustice in the particular case. This will be so wherever certainty in the law is the

applicable to a case to which it seems to apply unless it ought also to be held inapplicable to all similar cases where its application would similarly defeat the purpose of the law. What is needed is not arbitrary discretion, but a rule for making exceptions, — a rule for breaking a rule, — and of such rules the law is of course full. What is essential is that it should go on generating them as need for them is seen to arise. The law often comes to recognize, as it did not before, a circumstance or set of circumstances as constituting a valid element of difference, removing the facts of a case from the pigeonhole in which they would otherwise properly belong. Thus until quite recently fraud in procuring the execution of a sealed instrument made no exception to the legal effect of the instrument.[55] Later it came to be recognized as a reason for reaching a different result where it was present.[56] The law has hardly yet come to realize that a contract for the sale of labor by employee to employer may require in some ways to be distinguished and treated differently from a contract for the sale of goods, though equity has long recognized a difference.[57] The law must and will grow in these ways if it

primary essential and where certainty demands such a rigid application. "There may in some fields be a paramount public policy, one that will prevail over temporary inconvenience or occasional hardship, not lightly to sacrifice certainty and uniformity and order and coherence," Cardozo, *Nature of the Judicial Process*, p. 67. Thus in one case it was said, in following a precedent which the court thought to be unsound: "The writer of this opinion concurs with his brethren that we should adhere to such rulings though he is thoroughly satisfied that such ruling was radically wrong . . . but to overrule it now would not repair the evil it produced, and would unsettle titles," Bowen *v.* Preston, 48 Ind. 368.

[55] Vandervelden *v.* Chicago etc. R. Co. (1894), 61 Fed. 54. Of course, relief could be had in equity by bill to rescind the instrument.

[56] Edelin *v.* Sanders, 8 Md. 118, at p. 131; Partridge *v.* Messer, 14 Gray (Mass.) 180; Stubb *v.* King, 14 Serg. & R. 206. In many states the courts were more conservative and the reform had to be brought about by statute.

[57] In International Harvester Co. *v.* Missouri, 234 U. S. 199, the United States Supreme Court quoted the following language of the Supreme Court of Missouri: "It must be borne in mind that the differentiation between labor and property is so great that they do not belong to the same general classification of rights or things." But it was said in Coppage *v.* Kansas, 236 U. S. 1, at p. 14: "Included in the right of personal property . . . is the right to make contracts for the acquisition of property. Chief among such contracts is that of personal employment."

is based on reason, for rational thinking requires different results wherever facts or purposes alter essentially.[58] The need is for new distinctions [59] based on the purposes of the law, but fixed distinctions, nevertheless; for new concepts of valid difference to secure a juster order and uniformity, rather than for the abandonment of legal definition altogether in favor of justice without rule. It is hardly of much avail to seek middle ground, and talk of substituting for conceptual thinking, legal thinking of some other mode; for a mode of thinking other than the conceptual remains to be discovered which will fit the working processes of the human mind. What is wanted is rather a clear recognition of the nature and limits of conceptual thinking and its application as an instrument with its limitations at all times held steadily in view.[60]

[58] "Unwritten law is really human reason applied by the courts, not capriciously, but in a regular train of decisions to human affairs for the promotion of the ends of justice according to the circumstances of the nation, the necessity of the times, and the general state of things," Chief Justice Marshall in Livingston *v.* Jefferson, 1 Brockenbrough, 203.

[59] See Elihu Root in *Rep. Amer. Bar Assoc.* (1916), xli, 366, 367. If in the following quotation from Professor Max Müller we substitute "legal concept" where he writes "word," and "law" where he writes "reason," the result is an excellent statement of the growth of law: "With every new word there is more reason, and every progress of reason is marked by a new word. The growth of reason and language is coral-like. Each shell is the product of life, but becomes in turn the support of new life. In the same manner, each word is the product of reason, but becomes in turn a new step in the growth of reason," *Contemporary Rev.* (Feb. 1878), xxxi, 488. *Cf.* also the following: "Law and equity are in continual progression; a part of what is now strict law having formerly belonged to equity, while the equitable decisions of this age will be ranked under the strict law of the next," Pound in *Col. Law Rev.*, v, 20.

[60] "La vraie méthode consiste à montrer d'abord les limites de nos concepts, de nos systèmes, leur inadéquation au réel, puis à les dépasser par une doctrine plus large où leurs contradictions apparentes se fondent en harmonies," Alfred Fouillée, *La Pensée et les Nouvelles Écoles Anti-Intellectualistes*, Paris, Alcan, 1911, p. 113. "All intellectualism [need not] be 'vicious,' or blind to its own abstractness. . . . To conceive a thing as *a*, and then assume that it is *only a*, is to be 'viciously' intellectual. But it is evident that provided one recognizes that to be *a* does not prevent a thing's being also *b*, *c*, etc., one may be innocently or even beneficently intellectual," R. B. Perry, *Present Philosophical Tendencies*, p. 234.

IV

The technique of law is thus very far from securing either absolute justice or absolute certainty; it fails frequently in both directions because of the limitations of its logic. But it has three advantages. (1) By its more or less unsuccessful attempt to classify situations into hard and fast categories it makes possible at least a measure of certainty through the gradual accretion of precedent. (2) The same attempt requires continual reference and attention to the fundamental interests which the law protects, and to the purposes which it seeks to express. (3) There is a final advantage in that the technique of the law requires the judges to raise their minds above the facts of the immediate case before them and subordinate their feelings and impressions to a process of intricate abstract reasoning. One danger in the administration of justice is that the necessities of the future and the interest of parties not before the court may be sacrificed in favor of present litigants. The aim of the law is also to prevent controversies from being decided by a mere balancing of forces — to keep a decision from going in favor of the side that happens at the time to be backed by superior prestige or influence. Nothing is so effective to prevent this outcome as that judges should approach the decision of a controversy with minds directed to considerations having no connection with the immediate situation or interest of the parties. Judges are human instruments with prejudices, passions, and weaknesses. As it is, they often decide a new point or a doubtful point, ignore a principle, narrow a rule, or expand a concept under the influence of these human limitations. But this influence is enormously diminished by the necessity of centering their attention on a mass of considerations which lie outside the color of the case at bar; and by the habit of coming at every question from the angle of a dry and abstract logic. As a system of logic, the law may be artificial, inadequate, and harsh; but precisely because it is still a system of abstract logic, it spreads a net of allaying oil over the controversies of the moment and makes necessary an appeal from the claims of particular litigants to the interests of men in general as worked out over a long period into a body of impersonal and artificial rules which command respect. The very generality of the law, which in a given case may produce hardship by requiring the omission of seemingly pertinent considerations, affords a safeguard in most cases because it does not permit the judge to take into account matters which might draw his attention from the merits of the cause to his personal interest in the suitors. A perfectly flexible system of justice without law might afford an instrument for reaching an exactly just result in each case by a free balance of considerations; but under such a system the balance would have to be struck by the private mind of a judge unguarded against his predilections. It is safer to have in the rough logic of the law a balance not so fine but at least more impersonal; a layer of insulation interposed between the man within the judge and his human preferences. The uncharted sea of equity discretion contains dangers of which the coal strike injunction of 1920 affords a pointed warning.

And for this balancing of the peculiar considerations applicable to the case in hand the law within limits leaves ample room. Its concepts are none of them rigid, even when they are supposed to be;[61] many are left frankly open and elastic and without any attempt at hard and fast definition. Such are the concepts of necessaries, nuisance, negligence, due care, and reasonableness of cause, rate, or service, to name but a few. Every concept of this kind requires to be filled out in a particular case by weighing a variety of facts and considerations peculiar to the case. The process falls into two parts: first a complete and accurate examination of the facts; second, a balancing of the facts according to some general

[61] "The common law has often been reproached with the lack of precision and certainty in its definitions, but in truth it is a great advantage of the common law and of the mode of its development by judicial decisions that its definitions are never the matters resolved by the cases; they are never anything but dicta. If at the end of the sixteenth, or seventeenth or even of the eighteenth century, there had been definitions binding by statute on the courts; if the meaning of 'contract' and 'malice' and 'possession' and 'perpetuities' had been fixed, what fetters would have been imposed on the natural development of the law," Gray, *Nature and Sources of the Law*, 1st ed., p. 7.

standard of judgment. Of the standard itself no definition is given except to say that it is the habit, or practice, or opinion which is customary under like circumstances among the class of persons regarded as normal types by the person applying the standard. Absolute objectivity is in the nature of things not possible; some person must apply the standard, and the best we can get is the subjective view of that person as to what the objective normal is. So that in the long run much depends upon who applies the standard. In common-law countries the traditional agency is the trial jury. The court instructs the jury what sort of standard is to be applied, — for example, the care of a reasonable man under like circumstances, — and it is then left for the jury to say not merely what a reasonable man would do under the circumstances, but what sort of man a reasonable man is. We are here looking at the nature of those so-called "mixed questions of law and fact" which have already raised troublesome issues for us.[62] They arise where the concepts of the law itself cannot be fully defined in advance, but take on whatever definition they have from the concrete facts which are filled into them in each specific case. Where the law is thus vague, a wide latitude is allowed, necessarily, to the body which applies it. Where this power is exercised by juries it is subject to limitation in two ways. In the first place the legal standard itself may become hardened in the course of time into a definite rule by instructions given by the judges. This has happened in the crystallization of the vague early rule that notice of the dishonor of a negotiable instrument must be given within a reasonable time into the definite rule that where the parties live at different places, the notice must be sent off on the following day, while if they live in the same town it must be given in time to be received on the following day (Williams *v.* Smith, 2 B. & Ald., 496, 500); and in the hardening of the standard of due care in some states into what is called the "stop, look, and listen" rule. A second check is placed on the discretion of juries by the ever present duty of the courts to

[62] Many of these "mixed" questions, now regarded as questions of "fact," and so for the jury, were once treated as questions of "law" for the court. See above, pp. 52, 53.

set aside a verdict which in the court's opinion is beyond the bounds of rational inference from the evidence. This amounts to controlling the jury's discretion by substituting in its place the discretion of the judges. But it is to be noted that the power is expressed in terms which narrow its exercise to very exceptional cases: the court is not to set aside a verdict which in its own opinion is unreasonable on the facts, but only one which is beyond the bounds of reason.[63] Where is the line to be drawn? The point can be fixed only by the discretion of the judges who do fix it; it is, in other words, in their discretion to say when they will substitute their discretion for the jury's.[64] Finally come cases where mixed questions of law and fact are held to be questions for the court, and not for the jury at all. This is the rule as to the question of reasonable and probable cause in actions for malicious prosecution and false imprisonment,[65] and of material injury by varying the risk of a surety.[66]

[63] See Thayer, *Prelim. Treat. on Evidence*, pp. 208 ff., and cases there cited; and see below, pp. 319 ff.

[64] In Belt *v.* Lawes, a case reported in the London *Times* of March 18, 1884 and quoted in Thayer, *Cases on Evidence*, p. 163, Brett, M. R., after saying that under the rule in such cases the verdict can be impeached only when the court can say that reasonable men could not fairly find as the jury have done, went on to say: "It has been said, indeed, that the difference between the rule, and the question whether the judges would have decided in the same way as the jury, is evanescent, and that the solution of both depends on the opinion of the judges. The last part of the observation is true, but the mode in which the subject is approached makes the greatest difference. To ask 'Should we have found the same verdict?' is surely not the same thing as to ask whether there is room for a reasonable difference of opinion."

[65] That this question is left to the court in cases of false imprisonment has puzzled authorities who are wedded to the distinction between "law" and "fact." Says Pollock: "What is reasonable cause of suspicion to justify arrest may be said, paradoxical as the statement looks, to be neither a question of law nor of fact, at any rate in the common sense of the terms. Not of fact, because it is for the judge and not for the jury; not of law, because 'no definite rule can be laid down for the exercise of the judge's judgment.' It is a matter of judicial discretion such as is familiar enough in the classes of cases which are disposed of by a judge sitting alone; but this sort of discretion does not find a natural place in a system which assigns the decision of facts to the jury and the determination of law to the judge. The anomalous character of the rule has been more than once pointed out and regretted by the highest judicial authority," Pollock on Torts, 9th ed., p. 229.

[66] Holme *v.* Brunskill, 3 Q. B. Div. 495 (1877). Brett, L. J., dissented, say-

Can we say that, where the law operates through such contentless categories as these, it is law which is operating at all? Is it not rather the free discretion of the adjudicating body, involving all the dangers which free discretion always embodies, but compensated perhaps by its greater flexibility? We should ask two questions. First, does the matter admit of reduction to more general rules? Second, does it make any difference what body exercises the discretionary power?

V

Where a subject-matter would advantageously admit of reduction to more definite rules and definitions, and is still left open to the unguided operation of a balancing of interests, I do not see how we can escape saying that *pro tanto* we have not a régime of justice according to law. But there is naturally a wide difference in the relative readiness with which different fields of human relations admit of reduction to rules. Commercial transactions and transfers of property lend themselves to it with peculiar facility, for two reasons. They are in the first place artificial in the sense that the attention of the parties is consciously directed toward producing a legal result. Secondly, the need for orderliness in the "game" of business has normally led the participants, of their own accord, to stereotype certain forms of dealing in much the same manner as the law would do. All that remains is for the law to step in and sharpen these distinctions and accentuate the forms already outlined. The test of whether or not a transaction is adapted to the application of a general rule turns on precisely this point of whether or not a limited number of elements naturally stand out in it as marked with dominant significance. If so, the process of generalization and omission can be applied without doing violence to considerations of fairness. On the other hand, in a field where every case involves a multitude of pertinent elements which vary in importance from case to case, it is practically im-

ing "It is a general rule that we have no right to look at the verdict, but must accept it. . . . It will be most dangerous in this particular case to put ourselves in the place of a jury" (at pp. 508, 509).

possible fairly to select any special factor or factors and apply them as criteria over the whole field.[67] This is true of all ordinary matters of conduct not definitely directed, like business transactions, to the production of a legal result. There can be no concrete definition of negligence, because it may occur in every conceivable human situation — crossing a street, handling a barrel, lighting a lamp, riding a bicycle, or hitching a horse.[68] In these cases it is quite possible for the course of time and the run of the cases to carve grooves of classification and issue ultimately, if not in a single definition, at least in particular definitions to fit particular situations.[69] Thus cases of persons injured in crossing railroad tracks are very numerous. The situation is a relatively simple one and the principal ways of exercising due care are within the scope of everyday experience. Some of the cases have accordingly attempted to crystallize a definite rule that a necessary element of due care in such a situation is to stop, look, and

[67] The inapplicability of legal rules to unique situations was perceived by Plato, Aristotle, and the Roman jurists. See Plato, *Statesman*, 294b: "The differences of men and their actions, and the fact that in human affairs nothing ever stands still, do not permit a general and universal rule in anything. No art can lay down a rule which will last forever." See also Aristotle, *Pol.*, III, xvi, 11: "Some things can, and other things cannot be comprehended under the law; . . . for matters of detail cannot be included in legislation"; *ibid.*, III, xi, 19: "The magistrates must regulate these matters on which the laws are unable to speak with precision owing to the difficulty of any general principle embracing all particulars"; also *Eth. Nicom.*, v, 10: "Law is in all cases universal, but in some cases it is not possible to speak universally with correctness. . . . This is the reason why not all things are according to law, because on some subjects it is impossible to make a law and there must be a special determination from case to case; for the rule of what is indeterminate must itself be indeterminate also." See also Justinian's *Digest*, I, iii, 3–6: "Pomponius — jura constitui oportet, ut dicit Theophrastus, in his quae *ἐπὶ τὸ πλεῖστον* (that is, frequently) accident, non quae *ἐξ παρ αλόγου* (that is, which are unusual); Celsus — ex his quae forte uno aliquo casu accidere possunt, jura non constituuntur; Idem — ad ea potius debet aptari jus quae et frequenter et facile quam quae perrare eveniunt; Paulus — *τὸ γὰρ ἅπαξ ἢ δίς*, ut ait Theophrastus, *παραβαίνουσιν οἱ νομοθέται* (that is, the legislator cannot take into account situations which occur only once or twice)."

[68] "No two cases of negligence have been alike or ever will be alike," Pound, *Introduction to the Philosophy of Law*, p. 142. See also Cooley on Torts, 2d ed., p. 801. "There is nothing unique in a bill of exchange," Pound, *Interpretations of Legal History*, p. 155.

[69] See Wigmore on Evidence, 2d ed., v. 558.

listen.[70] So, conceivably, the rule might crystallize that it would be negligence to hitch a horse with a rope of less than a certain thickness. Such rules are congenial to the formalistic stage in the early history of jurisprudence.[71] But although it is thus not beyond possibility to develop definite rules in even a field like negligence, there is more than a question as to whether they are desirable.[72] The situation

[70] For decisions illustrating the so-called "stop, look, and listen rule," see Cincinnati, Indianapolis, St. Louis & Chicago R. Co. *v.* Howard, 124 Ind. 280; Louisville, New Albany & Chicago R. Co. *v.* Stommel, 126 Ind. 35; North Pennsylvania R. Co. *v.* Heilman, 49 Pa. St. 60; Ety *v.* Pittsburg, Cincinnati, Chicago & St. Louis, R. Co., 158 Pa. St. 233.

[71] For instance, in the stage of primitive jurisprudence represented by the old English laws. The laws of Alfred (sec. 36) provide: "If a man have a spear over his shoulder and any man stake himself upon it, let him pay the *wer* without the *wite* . . . if he be accused of wilfulness in the deed let him clear himself according to the *wite;* and with that let the *wite* abate. And let this be if the point be three fingers higher than the hindmost part of the shaft; if they both be on a level, the point and the hindmost part of the shaft, let that be without danger." The translation is Dr. Holdsworth's, *Hist. of Eng. Law*, 1st ed., ii, 42. So in *Leges Henrici*, 90. 4, "Quod si in sepem animal inpalaverit et ipse sepes mentionalis non fuerit, dominus sepis interfecionis seu debilitatis reus judicatur." Holdsworth, *loc. cit.* So, in the laws of Moses, note the minute particularity of such prescribed rules of conduct as the following: "When thou buildest a new house, then thou shalt make a battlement for thy roof, that thou bring not blood upon thy house if any man fall from thence" (Deut., 22, 8); "Thou shalt not muzzle the ox when he treadeth out the grain" (*ibid.*, 25, 4). Cf. also Deut., 23, 9; Levit., 14, 37–39.

[72] Mr. Justice Holmes in his *Common Law*, written more than forty years ago, took the contrary view and argued that in such a field as negligence the aim of the courts should be progressively to harden the flexible standard of due care into fixed rules such as that cited in the preceding note from the laws of Alfred. "It is obvious that it ought to be possible, sooner or later, to formulate these standards at least to some extent, and that to do so must at last be the business of the court. It is equally clear that the featureless generality that the defendant was bound to use such care as a prudent man would do under the circumstances, ought to be continually giving place to the specific one that he was bound to use this or that precaution under these or those circumstances. . . . If in the whole department of unintentional wrongs the courts arrived at no further utterance than the question of negligence, and left every case, without rudder or compass, to a jury, they would simply confess their inability to state a very large part of the law which they required the defendant to know, and would assert, by implication, that nothing could be learned by experience. But neither courts nor legislatures have ever stopped at that point. From the time of Alfred to the present day, statutes and decisions have busied themselves with defining the precautions to be taken in certain familiar cases; that

differs in essential respects from that of commercial transactions.[73] Tort cases involve matters of unpremeditated conduct where a legal result is not directly intended by the actors, but is imposed by law. There is a real and practical difference behind the theoretical distinction between a so-called legal transaction and other kinds of juristic acts.[74] In the one case it is not advisable to lay down rules and definitions with the same strictness as in the other, because to do so would be to interfere unwisely with that personal freedom to choose between alternatives of conduct which it is good policy for the law to foster. It is mere formalism to require a man to stop before crossing a railroad track in a case where he could see no more if he stopped than if he did not. Or take the rule suggested as to the thickness of rope. Suppose a new material is discovered for making rope with greater tensile strength than any hitherto used. Shall improvement in manufacture be impeded and industry prevented from reaping its advantage by a legal rule hardened out of circumstances which existed prior to its discovery? Fixed rules cannot profitably govern conduct at points where their effect would be to interfere with the introduction of improved methods of human action.

In short, in dealing with matters of general conduct the law in marking out its concepts has to face questions of fundamental physical fact in a more direct and immediate way than in purely commercial transactions. Whether or not a

is, with substituting for the vague test of the care exercised by a prudent man, a precise one of specific acts or omissions. . . . That this should happen is in accordance with the past history of the law," Holmes, *Common Law*, pp. 111–114. *Cf.* Pound, *Interpretations of Legal History*, pp. 154, 155.

[73] Even in the field of commercial law it seems sometimes unwise for the courts to crystallize hard rules for situations where the facts inevitably vary widely from case to case. This is true, for instance, of the law of implied warranty based upon the buyer's justifiable reliance upon the seller. See *Harv. Law Rev.*, xxv, 75: "What will justify the buyer's reliance is essentially a question of fact. In determining this question, all the circumstances of the sale should be considered. But the courts tend to formulate fixed rules to govern given states of fact."

[74] Pound, *Readings in Roman Law*, Pt. I, 2d ed., p. 22; Arndt, *Lehrbuch der Pandekten*, §58, 14th ed. (1889), p. 80.

scroll made with a pen is to have the legal effect of a seal, or whether an exchange of certain words amounts to a contract, raises no issue as to the nature of things; but when the law undertakes to define insanity, the task is of a different kind. In both instances we are dealing with a legal definition, but in the one the definition is of a conventional form rather than descriptive of a fact, and there is no likelihood that the definition adopted will come into conflict with a competing one backed by the authority of subsequent scientific discovery. Actually the law has undertaken to define insanity; and the result is the stock example of the danger of closing a concept which should have been left open for the progress of science to fill in from generation to generation.[75] On the other hand, equally serious danger results in other cases from leaving a concept open to a number of meanings. "We will not affirm," says Judge Smith, "that all difficult questions in labor litigation would be instantly solved if words like malice and intent were used with exactness and in only one signification, but it is safe to say that the difficulties of solution would thus be materially diminished." [76] There are dangers both ways; but it is clear that, however in the course of time rules and concepts may be won for definition out of a field at present left vague, there must and will always remain a large number of legal concepts of an elastic nature, and that some matters can be committed only to the purely relative balance of a standard. Room must be left for life as

[75] See E. R. Keedy in *Harv. Law Rev.*, xxx, 555 ff.

[76] *Harv. Law Rev.*, xx, 255. The possibility of improvement by better definition exists chiefly, of course, where the concepts, like those just enumerated, are artificial legal constructs. James Wilson wrote in 1790: "It may be worth while to note a difference between our own abstract notions and objects of nature. The former are the production of our own minds; we can therefore define and divide them, and distinctly designate their limits. But the latter run so much into one another, and their essences which discriminate them are so subtile and latent, that it is always difficult, often impossible, to define or divide them with the necessary precision. We are in danger of circumscribing nature within the bounds of our own notions, formed frequently on a partial or defective view of the object before us. We govern the course of our inquiries not by the extent or variety of our subject, but by our own preconceived apprehensions concerning it," "Lectures," *Works*, ed. Andrews (1896), i, 52.

well as law to grow in; for growth and adaptability are no less essential than certainty and stability.[77]

VI

Within the field of matters which do not admit of reduction to hard and fast rules, but must be trusted to the discretion of the adjudicating body, can we say that there is a régime of law? Does the answer depend at all upon what body exercises the discretionary power? I believe we must say that it does — that there is a substantial distinction between the discretion of the judges and that of a jury. The mental endowments of judges are, of course, no different from those of the common run of men. But mental equipment consists not merely of natural endowments but of an addition of acquired habits. The accustomed mental processes of the lawyer are generally recognized to have a peculiarity of their own. Sometimes, indeed, this peculiarity is thought by the man in the street to stand in the way of penetrating to the justice of a particular case, and so in certain instances it no doubt does. There is a lawyer's way of looking at things, marked by an attitude of analysis, an attention to detail, a meticulous consideration of more or less remote consequences and a regard for hard abstractions, which to the layman seem generally exaggerated, and sometimes ludicrous. And yet this method embodied in the minds of the members of the profession is the living process of the law. The law is not a mere body of rules but an attitude of mind and outlook which leaves its stamp on the decisions of those who have acquired it. To-day, perhaps more than ever, conditions of life require men to keep a sharp eye on their present position, make quick decisions, and let the past and future shift for themselves. Even the sciences are losing their character of systematic disciplines and becoming a free field for individual experiments. In such a world, a body of thought which comes down unbroken from the Middle Ages, and depends on assumptions of permanence, certainty, and generality, is bound

[77] Gray, *Nature and Sources of the Law*, 1st ed., p. 7; Lieber, *Hermeneutics*, 3d ed., p. 32; Miller, J., in Davidson *v.* New Orleans, 96 U. S. 97, at p. 104.

to stamp those who pursue it sympathetically with an imprint which will distinguish their decisions from those of laymen. Hence we may say that the discretion of judges, as applied to the verdicts of juries, is in no unfair sense an application, if not of law, at least of legal attitude and method, even in cases where no express legal rules exist to guide it.

It would be unfortunate, if it were possible, for men to commit all their decisions to minds which run in legal grooves. The needs of the moment, the circumstances of the particular case, all that we mean and express by the word "policy," have an importance which professional lawyers do not always allow to them.[78] This is true even in the process of adjudication itself; and by a fortunate historical accident the need is met by our institution of the jury.[79] In the first in-

[78] For a criticism of the shortcomings of lawyers as administrators see Sir Alexander W. Lawrence in *The Journal of Public Administration* (London, 1924) ii, pp. 297 ff.

[79] The function of the jury as a "standard-applying" body appears to have resulted from an unconscious evolution of its function of "fact-finding." For limitations on the doctrine that "matters of fact" are for the jury, see Thayer, *Prelim. Treat. on Evidence*, pp. 183 ff., which contain the most profound analysis that I know of the relation between "matters of fact" and "matters of law." It was early recognized that the right of the jury to decide the "facts" in issue carried with it the duty to draw conclusions from those facts; it was said to be the office of jurors "to adjudge upon their evidence concerning matters of fact, and thereupon to give their verdict; and not to leave matters of evidence to the court to adjudge, which does not belong to them," Littleton's Case (1612), cited in 10 Coke Rep. 56b; Thayer, *op. cit.*, p. 189. Mr. Justice Holmes has apparently a strong objection to regarding the application of a standard as primarily and peculiarly the province of the jury. Under the influence of Coke's doctrine that questions of "reasonableness" are questions for the court, he argues that the court is properly the standard-applying body. See his *Common Law*, pp. 122–129, and *Collected Legal Papers*, pp. 232–238. With due deference to great authority, this position seems hard to reconcile with the now well-established doctrine that a court should not overturn a verdict on a question of negligence or reasonableness where there is a mere difference of opinion as to inferences from the facts, but only where the verdict is beyond the bounds of rational inference. See below, pp. 319 ff. The right of the jury not merely to find "facts," as in a special verdict, but to infer legal conclusions such as negligence or fraud or reasonableness from the facts, — *i. e.*, their right to "apply the law to the facts" in the form of a general verdict, subject only to the power of the courts to set aside a conclusion lying beyond the bounds of rationally possible inference — has established itself so solidly in almost all branches of the law that its significance seldom challenges attention except in connection

stance it is the discretion of the "lay gents" which decides; the law stands in reserve and is brought forward only to pre-

with one or two puzzling exceptions. Chief among these is the still surviving rule that in actions for malicious prosecution it is for the court and not the jury to pronounce whether the particular facts in evidence amount to what the law regards as reasonable and probable cause: Johnstone *v.* Sutton, 1 T. R. 493; Panton *v.* Williams, 2 Q. B., 169; Stewart *v.* Sonneborn, 98 U. S. 187. This rule has been criticized by Lord Denman (Rowlands *v.* Samuel, 11 Q. B. 41, *note*); pronounced anomalous by Lords Chelmsford and Westbury (Lister *v.* Perryman, L. R. 4 H. L. 521); and was actually disregarded by Lord Tenterden (Beckwith *v.* Philby, 6 B. & C. 638). On the other hand, so slow was the modern view of the proper functions of the jury in coming into conscious recognition and acceptance, that a writer as late as Forsyth (1852) could select the rule in the malicious prosecution cases not as anomalous but as a typical illustration of the proper distribution of functions between court and jury, *History of Trial by Jury*, 2d (Amer.) ed. (ed. J. A. Morgan, 1875), p. 237. Forsyth's view rests on the theory that the determination of whether or not a mass of facts sum up into a "legal conclusion" like fraud, malice, or negligence, is the determination of a "question of law," and as such must be for the court alone. This idea seems to survive unconsciously at the basis of Mr. Justice Holmes's view, noted above; see also above, Chapter III, note 55, p. 55, and *infra*, Chapter XI, note 20, p. 313. This notion that the power to draw the legal conclusion from the evidence is a power to decide a question of law, and therefore does not belong to the jury, gained great prominence as the central argument on one side of the historic controversy concerning the rights of juries in prosecutions for seditious libel. For political reasons the right of juries to bring in a general verdict declaring whether or not certain words published under certain circumstances summed up into criminal libel was denied in England in a series of famous state-trials during the eighteenth century. In the earliest of these cases, Rex *v.* Francklin, 17 St. Tr. 625 (1731), Lord Chief Justice Raymond charged the jury as follows: "There are here three things to be considered, two of them being for the jury, the third for the Court. 1. Did the defendant publish this *Craftsman* or not? 2. Do the expressions in the letter allude to the King and his ministers according to the innuendoes? These are matters of fact for your consideration, of which you are the proper judges, and if you think in the affirmative on both questions, you will find a verdict of guilty. There is a third question — whether these defamatory expressions amount to a libel or not? This belongs to the office of the Court, for it is a matter of law, of which the Court are the only proper judges. We are not to invade each other's provinces." This doctrine was reaffirmed in Rex *v.* Woodfall, 5 Burr. 2661 (1770), where Lord Mansfield charged the jury that "whether the letter was libelous or innocent was a pure question of law, upon which the opinion of the court might be taken by a demurrer or motion in arrest of judgment," and that therefore all that the jury were entitled to consider was whether the defendant had published the letter, and whether the innuendoes were proved. Lord Campbell has pointed out the defect in Lord Mansfield's argument: "His grand argument for making the question 'libel or not' exclusively one of law, that the defendant may demur or move in arrest of judgment, and so refer it to the court, admits of the easy

vent the jury's verdict from palpably overstepping it.[80] But though the law is thus confined to acting as a check on lay

answer that, although there may be a writing set out in the information as libelous which it could under no circumstances be criminal to publish, yet an information may set out a paper the publication of which may or may not be criminal according to the intention of the defendant and the circumstances under which it is published," *Lives of the Chief Justices* (Amer. ed., Boston, 1873), iii, 383. It might as well be argued that the question of whether the evidence showed negligence was always for the court to decide because the court is always free to determine whether there is any evidence upon which a finding of negligence may rationally be supported. Nevertheless the doctrine that the determination of whether the facts amounted to criminal libel was a determination of a question of law was accepted even by the opponents of the rule that the question was one for the exclusive determination of the court, and they accordingly stated their contention in the form of a claim in no way demanded by their case, and one which has been the cause of much subsequent confusion — the claim, namely, that in criminal cases the jury are properly the judges of the law as well as of the facts. See *e. g.*, Erskine's Speech on Motion for a New Trial in the Dean of St. Asaph's case, *Speeches*, i, 137 ff. In the United States, especially, this doctrine has received an extended development. Thus James Wilson: "The jury must . . . decide the law as well as the fact" (*Works*, ed. Andrews, ii, 220); Chief Justice Jay, charging the jury in Georgia *v.* Brailsford, 3 Dallas, 1 at p. 4, "You have the right to determine the law as well as the fact in controversy"; see Thayer, *Prelim. Treat. on Evidence*, pp. 253 ff. The confusion in which the whole issue thus became beclouded was admirably cleared up by Chief Justice Shaw in two great opinions, Commonwealth *v.* Porter, 10 Met. (Mass., 1846), 253, and Commonwealth *v.* Anthes, 5 Gray (Mass., 1857), 185. A succinct statement is that of Mr. Justice Swayne in Hickman *v.* Jones, 9 Wallace 197, at pp. 201, 202: "The jury should take the law as laid down by the court. But its application to the facts — and the facts themselves — it is for them to determine." In other words, where there is a definite rule of law to be applied to a case, it is the function of the jury, after being informed what the rule is by the court, to apply it to the facts, — *i. e.*, to say whether the facts bring the case within it or not; and when there is no definite rule, but only a standard, it is again for the jury, after being informed of the nature of the standard by the court, to test by it the conduct of the parties. On the other hand it is for the court, in shaping its instructions to the jury, to determine the rules of law by which the case shall be governed; and if the verdict fails to take these into account, or cannot reasonably be squared with them, the court will set it aside. It is not necessary here to go into the peculiarities of criminal procedure which give the jury a power, though not a right, to disregard the law as laid down by the court in its instructions. But in some states the jury are by statute made judges of the law in criminal cases. See Hughes, *Instructions to Juries*, §§ 166–169.

80 "The jury in finding a general verdict do in form return a verdict embracing the matter of law as well as fact; and therefore, as they may mistake the instructions of the court or take the law into their own hands, imagining it to be severe or inequitable, they may return a verdict manifestly against the

discretion, it is law which in the last analysis governs, whether through its own more or less fixed rules or through the discretion of judges, so that over the entire range of questions adjudicated in the courts it is safe to say that a régime of law prevails, though on some points it may at any given moment be thought to be wrong law.

From this vantage point it is possible to approach concretely the question of how far administrative determinations should be subject to control by the courts if a régime of law in the fullest practicable sense is to be maintained. The relation between the courts and administrative tribunals has sometimes been compared to that between court and jury, as another instance of a relation between a body which exercises discretion and a body which limits discretion by rules;[81]

law and truth of the case. To render such a mode of trial safe and tolerable, there must exist a power somewhere to reëxamine verdicts with some freedom, and when it is manifest that juries have been warped from the direct line of their duty from mistake, prejudice, or even by an honest desire to reach the supposed equity contrary to the law of the case, it will be the duty of the court to set the verdict aside. When the evidence is clear, plain, and strong, and the law has been clearly and explicitly stated to the jury, and they decide against the law, it imposes upon the court the duty of interfering." Shaw, C. J., in Cunningham *v.* Magoun, 18 Pick. (Mass.) 13.

[81] Papinaw *v.* Grand Trunk R. Co., 189 Mich. 441, at p. 445. "The findings of the industrial accident board are equivalent to the verdict of a jury or the findings of a judge, and are not to be set aside if there is any evidence to support them," In re Savage (Mass., 1915), 110 N. E. 282. Another analogy suggested in the cases is the relation between the chancellor and a master appointed to take testimony and report his findings of fact and conclusions of law, State of Washington ex rel. Oregon R. R. and Navigation Co. *v.* Fairchild, 224 U. S. 510, at p. 527. It is interesting to note that Judge Learned Hand has conceived the scope of judicial review of the constitutionality of a statute under the due process clause as equivalent to the measure of a court's control of a verdict. "It may well determine those things to be within the range of legislative power against which, sitting as legislators, the justices individually would have voted. The nearest analogy for the function of the court is the function of a court in review of a verdict on the facts. Only in those cases in which it is obvious beyond peradventure that the statute was the result either of passion or of ignorance or folly, can the court say that it was not due process of law," *Harv. Law Rev.*, xxi, 500, citing Henderson *v.* Mayor, 92 U. S. 259, at p. 26; Minnesota *v.* Barber, 136 U. S. 313, at p. 320; Hennington *v.* Georgia, 163 U. S. 299, at p. 304; Booth *v.* Illinois, 184 U. S. 425, at p. 430; Jacobson *v.* Mass., 197 U. S. 31. It is possible to argue that it is misleading to place an administrative or legislative determination and the verdict of a jury on the same footing, because the former is primarily dictated by considerations of

how far does the analogy hold? Should administrative discretion be subject to court review in the same degree as the discretion of a jury or in a greater or less degree? What measure of power in the courts is consistent with the objects which are properly sought from a system of administrative justice?

To the solution of these questions we must carry over the observation that the manner in which law operates, and the extent to which it is capable of operating, vary with the classes of situations to which it is sought to apply it, and with the kinds of facts and issues which they involve. Modern administrative tribunals have jurisdiction over a wide variety of subject-matters; and there is a sound logic in the refusal of the courts to deal with all on an equal footing.

governmental policy, while the latter is in theory at least governed by impartial attention to the rights of contending private parties. This is the view advanced by Professor Freund in *Proc. Amer. Pol. Sci. Ass'n.* (1909), vi. 60: "The administrative finding is treated like the verdict of a jury. This seems not sufficient, for it does not secure to the private interest an independent judgment on the part of an impartial authority." This criticism hardly applies where the administrative agency is required, as for instance is the Interstate Commerce Commission, to act "quasi-judicially." In such a case, in the language of Mr. Justice Brandeis, "the Commission may form its judgment only after a hearing. The provision for a hearing implies both the privilege of introducing evidence and the duty of deciding in accordance with it," Chicago Junction Case, 264 U. S. 258. But even admitting that an administrative decision may be determined by considerations of policy in a sense not true of a jury verdict, it is hard to see how this perfectly obvious difference establishes any need for a difference in the measure of the court review applicable in the two cases. Where the jury have no rule of law to guide them, their determination must be reached on the basis of the same general sense of fitness or propriety as an administrative or legislative determination. With this sense of fitness it is not the business of the courts in either instance to interfere. The only difference in such matters between a jury and a legislative or administrative body is that the latter on grounds of policy is entitled to refuse altogether to act. This right is duly recognized by the courts in their refusal to compel administrative or legislative action in matters of discretion by mandamus, or to review a refusal by an administrative tribunal to act in a certain way: Procter and Gamble Co. *v.* United States, 225 U. S. 282; Lehigh Valley R. R. Co. *v.* United States, 243 U. S. 412. But where the administrative or legislative body has in fact chosen to act, and there is no rule of law which its action contravenes, the element of policy which may properly have governed its determination should receive at least as great, if not greater, respect from the court as a jury's sense of fitness on a "question of fact" or "mixed law and fact." See above, chapter I, note 32, p. 19.

Tentatively we may classify the subjects of administrative adjudication in three groups for separate examination: (1) regulation of public callings and businesses affected with a public interest; (2) regulation under the police power, such as building, health, and license regulations; (3) matters as to which the government is a direct party in interest, *i. e.*, the distribution of pensions or public lands, collection of the revenue, direct governmental performance of public services, and the like.

We must see how far each of these fields includes relations which admit of reduction to fixed rules and definitions. But when this is done, we shall not necessarily have determined the question of how far court control ought to extend. For, as in the case of juries, there may be an advantage in having the discretion of a law-court control even on some matters of discretion. And, on the other hand, it is open to argument that, although a field can be advantageously brought under more or less fixed rules, the proper agency to develop and apply all save the most fundamental of such rules should be a specialized technical body dealing habitually with that field alone. If, however, we thus imply that the main purpose of the technical agency is to adjudicate according to rules, will we not have abandoned the characteristic and special advantage of a system of administrative justice, which consists in a union of legislative, executive, and judicial functions in the same body to secure promptness of action, and the freedom to arrive at decisions based on policy? These are at any rate some of the considerations which will have to be examined in each of the several fields.

CHAPTER VI

COURT REVIEW OF ADMINISTRATIVE DETERMINATIONS IN THE FIELD OF PUBLIC-UTILITY REGULATION: DOCTRINE AND PRACTICE OF THE UNITED STATES SUPREME COURT

In adaptability to the application of general rules, the subject of public callings stands somewhere midway between the field of torts and that of property transactions. Many of the issues which arise within it relate to ordinary matters of conduct not consciously intended to produce legal results. Such are the supply of adequate service, the use of due care, the provision of proper facilities. On the other hand, questions of rates and discrimination involve contractual relations. But the law of public utilities is not concerned, like commercial law, with the formal side of these transactions in order to spell out the legal relation of the parties from the nature of their dealings, but rather with the substance, the concrete terms, of the contracts themselves, going to the amounts charged, the services performed, and the like. Therefore, if we are to have legal concepts and definitions, they must be more than arbitrary and logically clean-cut categories — they must not merely be capable of application to facts, they must themselves grow out of and summarize a body of more fundamental facts. They will have to be definitions not of ideas but of things.[1] The concept of a reasonable rate, for example, must, like the concept of insanity, have verifiable matter of fact in it, corresponding directly to something objective and tangible — distance, grade, density of traffic, capacity of motive-power. And if we are to have rules, they must be something more than the arbitrary rules of a game — they must embody a policy or technique of play, based on

[1] See above, pp. 148, 149.

experience, within the formal rules of the game itself.[2] There is the added difficulty that these substantive definitions and rules, if they are to be formulated at all, must be fitted to a technical and highly specialized field, where changing mechanical inventions and shifting economic methods and conditions enter into the substance of the subject-matter and are forever altering the facts which lie at the basis of the rules. Altogether, the field is one which seems preëminently fitted for the application not of rules but of standards.

There is at the same time in the field of public-utility regulation, or at least in certain corners of it, a greater need for crystallized rules and definitions than, for example, in the general field of torts. For we are here in one of those commercial departments of the law where large interests are at stake, and where a measure of certainty for forecasting the future is therefore desirable, and even almost indispensable, for the smooth play of economic processes. "The commercial world demands rules," says Dean Pound. "No man makes large investments trusting to the uniform exercise of judicial discretion." [3] It is accordingly in matters which touch the stability of investments in public-utility properties that the demand for fixed and certain rules of law is pressed with greatest urgency; and less so where the question is merely as to the adequacy of the service rendered, or the fairness or unfairness of some practice followed by the utility.

These latter questions are substantially like questions of performance in the law of contracts, which are left to be determined by the discretion of a jury. Similarly when such questions arise in the administrative regulation of public utilities, they are commonly left for final determination by the administrative body and will not be reviewed by the

[2] "Even when two persons join socially for the simple purpose of playing a game of tennis or chess, they must conform to certain rules in their contest if they wish to achieve their immediate end. The skill or force displayed constitutes the material or substantive part of the game; the rules as to moves and scoring constitute the formal frame of this kind of intercourse," Vinogradoff, *Common Sense in Law,* p. 15. Public-utility law undertakes to regulate what corresponds to "the skill or force displayed."

[3] *Col. Law Rev.*, v, 20.

courts. The measure of court review is to some extent governed by statutes; but in the absence of special mandate, the courts are apt to hold that what constitutes adequate service or discriminatory practice is a so-called "question of fact" or "mixed question of fact and law," as to which the determination of the administrative body will be accepted as final.[4] Like a jury, it will be allowed a very free hand in the application of a standard. The attitude of the courts may be conveniently studied from the line of cases in which the United States Supreme Court has announced its doctrine as to review of the findings of railroad and utility commissions. The cases will first be considered which deal with orders of the Interstate Commerce Commission.

I

The doctrine that determinations of the Commission on such questions as adequacy of service and discriminatory practices are not subject to court review was clearly stated in Interstate Commerce Commission *v.* Delaware, Lackawanna, & Western R. Co., 220 U. S. 235. The defendant carriers had been denying to forwarding agents the advantages of full-carload rates. The Commission after an investigation found the practice discriminatory and ordered its discontinuance. The Supreme Court held that it was not for the courts to re-examine whether the practice was discriminatory or not. "The Commission affirmatively found that to permit the carrier to exclude the forwarding agent would give rise to preferences and engender discriminations, and this finding embodies a conclusion of fact beyond our competency to re-examine." The case presented the legal issue of whether or not a carrier may make the ownership of goods tendered it for carriage the test by which to measure the charge for carriage, and of that question the court took jurisdiction. But it went on to say: "All the other differences, in so far as they do not rest upon the legal proposition just stated, are

[4] For a criticism of the distinction between "questions of law" and "questions of fact" as a test governing the exercise of the reviewing power, see above, pp. 49–55, and below, pp. 168–170.

based upon conclusions of fact as to which the judgment of the Commission is not susceptible of review by the courts. This at once demonstrates the error of the lower court in basing its decree annulling the order of the Commission upon its approval and adoption of the reasons stated in the opinion of the dissenting members of the Commission. This follows, since the reasons given by the dissenting members, except in so far as they rested upon the legal proposition we have just stated, proceeded upon premises of fact which, however cogent they may have been as a matter of original consideration, were not open to be so considered by the court because they were foreclosed by the opinion of the Commission."

This position was reached by the Court only after a gradual process of evolution. It was the Hepburn Act of 1906 which finally turned the scale. Prior to that time, the Commission's orders could be enforced only in a proceeding brought by the Commission in a United States Circuit Court. The statute provided that in such a proceeding "the findings of fact of said Commission shall be *prima facie* evidence of the matters therein stated," and the Supreme Court necessarily held that under this language the Circuit Court had power to review the findings of the Commission on so-called questions of "fact." Thus it was said in Texas & Pacific R. Co. *v.* Interstate Commerce Commission, 162 U. S. 197, at p. 239: "Nor can it be denied when a petition is filed by the Commission for the purpose of enforcing an order that the [Circuit] Court is authorized to hear and determine the matter as a court of equity, which necessarily implies that the court is not concluded by the findings or conclusions of the Commission." [5] It was held, however, that where the findings of the Circuit Court coincided with those of the Commission, the Supreme Court would not reëxamine the Commission's findings.[6]

[5] Louisville & Nashville R. Co. *v.* Behlmer (1900), 175 U. S. 648, at p. 676; Eastern Tennessee, Virginia, & Georgia R. Co. *v.* Interstate Commerce Commission (1900), 181 U. S. 1, at p. 27; Interstate Commerce Commission *v.* Chicago, Burlington, & Quincy R. Co. (1901), 186 U. S. 320, at p. 341.

[6] Cincinnati, Hamilton, & Dayton R. Co. *v.* Interstate Commerce Commission 206 U. S., at p. 154; Illinois Central R. R. Co. *v.* Interstate Commerce Commission, 206 U. S. 441, at p. 466.

After the passage of the Hepburn Act, which made the orders of the Commission self-executing (subject only to be enjoined by the courts), the Supreme Court ruled that it was no longer open to the courts to review the Commission's conclusions on so-called "mixed questions of law and fact." This position was announced in Interstate Commerce Commission *v.* Illinois Central R. R. Co., 215 U. S. 452. There the Commission had condemned as discriminatory the practice of certain railroads in failing to take "company" fuel cars into account in allocating coal cars to mines. The Court held that the question whether such a practice was discriminatory was wholly for the Commission and that its conclusion was not open to court review. "Judicial powers," said the Court, "may not be curtailed and their discharge may not be by us in a proper case avoided, but it is equally plain that such perennial powers lend no support whatever to the proposition that we may under the guise of exerting judicial power usurp merely administrative functions by setting aside a lawful administrative order upon our conception as to whether the administrative power has been wisely exercised. Power to make the order, and not the mere expediency or wisdom of having made it, is the question." But the Court took jurisdiction of the "legal" questions whether the Commission had any authority over "company" cars, and also whether it was empowered to make orders forbidding discriminations in car supply.

The Court has repeatedly reaffirmed that whether or not a certain state of facts amounts to unfair discrimination is a question for final determination by the Commission. In United States *v.* Louisville & Nashville R. Co., 235 U. S. 314, the issue was whether a certain reshipping privilege allowed by the defendant carriers at Nashville, Tennessee, was discriminatory. The Commission found that it was, and made an order directing the carriers to desist from it. They applied to the Commerce Court for an injunction against enforcement of this order. The Commerce Court, finding that there was no conflicting or disputed evidence as to the nature or character of the privilege in question, concluded that whether such a privilege was an unfair preference was a pure "question of law" upon which it was the Court's duty to reach its own independent conclusion.[7] It did so and granted the injunction. On appeal to the Supreme Court, the decree was reversed, White, C. J., saying: "In view of the doctrine announced in Interstate Commerce Commission *v.* Illinois Central R. R. Co., 215 U. S. 452, Interstate Commerce Commission *v.* Delaware, Lackawanna and Western R. Co., 220 U. S. 235 and Interstate Commerce Commission *v.* Louisville & Nashville R. Co., 227 U. S. 88, it plainly results that the court below in substituting its judgment as to the existence of the preference for that of the Commission, on the ground that where there was no dispute as to the facts it had a right to do so, obviously exerted an authority not conferred on it by the statute. It is not disputable that from the beginning the very purpose for which the Commission was created was to bring into existence a body which from its peculiar character would be most fitted to primarily decide whether from facts disputed or undisputed, in a given case preference or discrimination existed. . . . If the view of the statute upheld below be sustained, the Commission would become but a mere instrument for the purpose of taking testimony to be submitted to the courts for their ultimate action." The same doctrine was again set forth in Pennsylvania Co. *v.* United States, 236 U. S. 351, where the question was as to the fairness of a practice of the defendant in interchanging freight

[7] On the question of the proper functions of court and jury in a case where the facts are admitted, *cf.* language of Bowen, L. J., in Davey *v.* London and Southwestern R. Co., 12 Q. B. D. 70, at p. 76: "It is not because facts are admitted that it is therefore for the judge to say what the decision upon them should be. If the facts which are admitted are capable of two equally possible views which reasonable people may take, and one of them is more consistent with the case for one party than for the other, it is the duty of the judge to let the jury decide between such conflicting views." In certain classes of cases, however, the courts have occasionally said, erroneously it would seem, that where the evidence is not conflicting, the task of drawing the conclusion therefrom is the decision of a "question of law," and in consequence is for the court: Commercial National Bank *v.* Zimmerman, 185 N. Y. 210 (question of reasonableness of time of presentment of a negotiable instrument for payment); Northwestern Iron Co. *v.* Industrial Commission, 154 Wis. 97 at 104 (determination of a question of fact by industrial accident board).

with certain carriers and not with others at Newcastle, Pennsylvania.[8]

The Supreme Court has applied the same doctrine to determinations of the Commission as to rate discriminations. Perhaps the leading case of this kind is Manufacturers' R. Co. *v.* United States, 246 U. S. 457, where a terminal railway in St. Louis owned by the Anheuser-Busch interests complained that the practice of the trunk-lines in refusing to absorb its charges, while absorbing the charges of other terminal railways in the city, was discriminatory. The Commission found that because of special circumstances the practice did not result in an illegal discrimination. The Supreme Court refused to review the finding, saying: "Whether a preference or an advantage or discrimination is undue or unreasonable is one of those questions of fact that have been confided by Congress to the judgment and discretion of the Commission, and upon which its decisions, made the basis of administrative orders operating *in futuro*, are not to be disturbed by the courts except upon a showing that they are unsupported by evidence, were made without a hearing, exceed constitutional limits, or for some other reason amount to an abuse of power. In the present case the negative finding of the Commission upon the question of undue discrimination was based upon a consideration of the different conditions of location, ownership and operation as between the complainant and the other terminal railways. The conclusions were reached after full hearing, are not without support in the evidence, and we are unable to say they show an abuse of discretion. It may be conceded that the evidence would have warranted a different finding; but to annul the Commission's order on this ground would be to substitute the judgment of a court for the judgment of the Commission upon a matter purely administrative, and this cannot be done." [9]

[8] See also Los Angeles Switching Case, 234 U. S. 294; Seaboard Air Line R. Co. *v.* United States, 254 U. S. 57.

[9] 246 U. S. 457, at p. 481. See also Interstate Commerce Commission *v.* Atchison, Topeka and Santa Fe R. Co., 234 U. S. 294; Seaboard Air Line R. Co. *v.* United States, 254 U. S. 57.

Where the administrative determination goes not to the question of the discriminatory character of a practice but of the reasonableness of a rate, there is slightly different emphasis in the Court's language. The leading case is Interstate Commerce Commission *v.* Union Pacific R. Co., 222 U. S. 541. The Commission had ordered a reduction of tariffs which it held unreasonable. The carriers brought a bill to enjoin the order, and the Circuit Court granted the injunction on the ground that certain facts appearing on the face of the order showed that it was unreasonable. The Supreme Court reversed the decree, saying: "In determining these mixed questions of law and fact, the court confines itself to the ultimate question as to whether the Commission acted within its power. It will not consider the expediency or wisdom of the order, or whether on like testimony it would have made a similar ruling. . . . The conclusion of the Commission is of course subject to review, but when supported by evidence is accepted as final; not that its decision, involving as it does so many and such vast public interests can be supported by a mere *scintilla* of proof, but the courts will not examine the facts further than to determine whether there was substantial evidence to sustain the order. . . . It cannot be fairly said that the order here was so arbitrary as to be palpably and gravely unjust and beyond the substance if not the form of the Commission's power. . . . With the sort of evidence before them that was before the Commission, rate experts of acknowledged ability and fairness acting independently of each other may not have reached identically the same conclusion. For there is no possibility of solving the question as though it were a mathematical problem to which there could be only one correct answer. Still there was in the mass of facts that out of which experts could have named a rate. The law makes the Commission's finding on such facts conclusive."

The same doctrine was amplified with greater emphasis upon its limitations in Interstate Commerce Commission *v.* Louisville & Nashville R. Co., 227 U. S. 88. The government had advanced the novel contention that the language of the Hepburn Act made rate-orders of the Commission absolutely conclusive, and that they could not be set aside even if the Commission's finding was wholly without evidence to support it. In overruling this contention the Court said in substance: "The Commission's right to act depends upon the existence of the fact, and if there was no evidence to show that the rates were unreasonable, the Commission had no jurisdiction to order them discontinued. In a case like this the courts will not review the Commission's conclusions of fact (Interstate Commerce Commission *v.* Delaware, Lackawanna & Western R. Co., 220 U. S. 251) by passing upon the credibility of witnesses or conflicts in the testimony. But the legal effect of evidence is a question of law. A finding without evidence is beyond the power of the Commission. An order based thereon is contrary to law. . . . It is therefore necessary to examine the record with a view of determining whether there was substantial evidence to support the order." This statement is not altogether fortunate. If the order must be supported by "substantial" evidence, is not the door thus thrown open to the courts to exercise their independent judgment as to the weight of the evidence? Some attempt seems to have been made to explain the ambiguity in subsequent decisions.

In Florida East Coast R. Co. *v.* United States *et al.*, 234 U. S. 167, the Supreme Court set aside an order of the Commission reducing rates on the ground that it was rendered without any evidence whatever to support it. White, C. J., in delivering the opinion, said (at page 185): "While a finding of fact made by the Commission concerning a matter within the scope of the authority delegated to it is binding and may not be reëxamined in the courts, it is undoubted that where it is contended that an order whose enforcement is resisted was rendered without any evidence whatever to support it, the consideration of such a question involves not an issue of fact but one of law, which it is the duty of the courts to examine and decide." And for this proposition the Louisville and Nashville case, *supra*, was cited.

The carriers took advantage of the Florida East Coast decision to urge in the later case of Louisville and Nashville

R. Co. *v.* United States, 238 U. S. 1, that the Supreme Court would examine the facts to determine whether they "supported" the order of the Commission. The Court yielded so far as to examine the record in detail both as to the facts and as to the method of reasoning which the Commission had used in arriving at its conclusion. This method had been a process of comparison. The question concerned the reasonableness of rates on coal to Nashville, and the Commission had reached its conclusion that these were excessive from a comparison of the Nashville rate with the coal rates to neighboring cities, after making allowance for differences in circumstances. "Giving the widest possible effect," said the Court, "to the fact that mere comparison between rates does not necessarily tend to establish the reasonableness of either, it is still true that where one of many rates is found to be higher than all others, there may arise a presumption that the single rate is too high. . . . The report in this case shows that the rate-making body had before it much and varied evidence on all these matters. After considering it as a whole, the Commission found that the rate was unreasonable. In the light of these findings we cannot say that the facts set out in the report do not sustain the order."

The language of the Court where the order under review involves the reasonableness of a rate thus stresses the necessity of the order's being supported by substantial evidence more emphatically than where it involves only the fairness or unfairness of a practice. But there cannot be doubt that the Court really has intended to treat both classes of cases on the same footing. Cases of one kind are constantly cited in the opinions as authorities governing the other. The Court frequently refers to both in the same breath, and mentions together "the question whether certain charges were reasonable or unreasonable, whether certain discriminations were due or undue." [10] Thus, for instance, it was said in the so-called "Pre-cooling Case": [11] "The administrative body is

[10] East Tennessee, Virginia, & Georgia R. Co. *v.* Interstate Commerce Commission, 181 U. S. 1, at p. 28.

[11] Atchison, Topeka, & Santa Fe R. Co. *v.* United States *et al.*, 232 U. S. 199, at p. 221.

required to fix reasonable rates and establish reasonable practices. The courts have not been vested with any such power. They cannot make rates. They cannot interfere with rates fixed or practices established by the Commission unless it is made plainly to appear that those ordered are void."

An examination of the decisions shows that both types of cases have been dealt with in substantially the same way.

II

Putting together the cases so far considered, the Court has said in effect that it would review the findings of the Commission on so-called "mixed questions of law and fact" only to see whether there was evidence upon which the Commission's conclusion could have been reached by reasonable men, irrespective of whether the Court itself would have reached it.[12] At the same time the Court has always expressed its willingness to examine a finding to see whether there has been failure to apply, or error in applying, some rule or principle of law.[13]

The first limitation means that the courts are not authorized to substitute their discretion, or lump-sum opinion of what ought to be done in the case, for the discretion of the administrative body, because discretion is the very province of the latter; they are merely to prevent such abuse of discretion as would be constituted by a decision which reasonable men could not have made on the same evidence.[14]

[12] Language of Lamar, J., in Interstate Commerce Commission *v.* Union Pacific R. Co., 222 U. S. 541, quoted above at p. 154.

[13] *E. g.*, in Interstate Commerce Commission *v.* Union Pacific R. Co., 222 U. S. 541.

[14] An added reason for the reluctance of the Supreme Court to review administrative discretion, at least in the case of rate-fixing orders, seems to be suggested in recent cases. This is the feeling that any broader power of review in the Courts than the power to reverse for error of law or on the ground of there being no evidence to support the finding, would be unconstitutional as vesting the Court with legislative or administrative power. Thus in the very recent case of Public Utilities Commission *v.* Potomac Electric Power Co., 261 U. S. 428, a Federal statute gave an appeal to the United States Supreme Court from orders of the Public Utilities Commission of the District of Columbia, and provided that the appeal proceedings should "conform to the equity procedure." In refusing to exercise this jurisdiction, the Court, per Taft, C. J., said:

On the other hand, the courts will overrule administrative discretion whenever it reaches a result inconsistent with some general proposition of law applicable to the entire class of similar cases. We here uncover the real distinction which lies behind the attempts to distinguish between so-called "questions of law" and "questions of fact" that have everywhere so confused the language of the opinions. Where the only ground which a court can give for its difference from the administrative body is limited to mere difference of opinion as to some matter or matters peculiar to the case, or some difference in inference from those matters, then the court should not disturb the opinion or inference of the fact-finding body unless the latter is plainly beyond the bounds of reason; for the difference is one of discretion, or "fact." On the other hand, where the ground of difference between court and fact-finding body can be isolated and expressed as a general proposition applicable beyond the particular case to all similar cases, the court, if it holds the proposition one of sound law, must enforce it by overruling the administrative determination.[15] The distinction can be illustrated by an example

"In that procedure an appeal brings up the whole record and the appellate Court is authorized to review the evidence and make such order or decree as the Court of first instance ought to have made, giving proper weight to the findings on disputed issues of fact which should be accorded to a tribunal which heard the witnesses. Such legislative or administrative jurisdiction, it is well settled, cannot be conferred on this Court, either directly or by appeal." The Court thus refused to exercise a "supervisory" power not merely over rate-fixing orders, which are held to be legislative in character, but over purely administrative orders as well, dealing with both on the same footing. Speaking of its power of review over orders of the Interstate Commerce Commission, the Court said: "It is settled that any finding of fact by the Commission, if supported by evidence, is final and conclusive on the courts."

[15] There is a flash of insight into this distinction in Lord Mansfield's language in Tindal *v.* Brown, 1 T. R. 167, at 168: "What is reasonable notice is partly a question of fact, and partly a question of law. It may depend in some measure on facts such as the distance at which the parties live from each other, the course of the post, etc. But *wherever a rule can be laid down* with respect to this reasonableness, that should be decided by the court, and adhered to by every one *for the sake of certainty.*" (Italics mine.) It is clearly stated by William David Evans: "In the common distribution of law and fact, the law is understood to be a general and universal rule, and the fact to be of a limited and particular nature. Whatever therefore is decided respecting the former, becomes properly an authority for succeeding determinations; . . . but the de-

from the law of negligence. Although a court believes from the evidence that the way in which the plaintiff crossed a railroad track was negligent, still if the jury find that it was not, and if that finding is within the bounds of reasonable infer-

cision on matters of fact in one case is not, in its nature, material to the investigation of another," Appendix No. 17 to Pothier, *Law of Obligations*, translated from the French with an Introduction, Appendix, and Notes, by William David Evans, ii, 314 [1806]. I have used the edition printed at Philadelphia, Robert H. Small, 1826. So it was said by Lord Chelmsford in Lister *v.* Perryman, L. R., 4 H. L. 521, at p. 535, that the question of reasonable cause in actions of false imprisonment, though for the decision of the court, is not properly a "question of law" because "*no definite rule can be laid down* [italics mine] for the exercise of the judge's judgment." So Forsyth, *Trial by Jury*, 2d (Amer.) ed. (ed. J. A. Morgan, Jersey City, 1875), p. 223: "A question of law . . . presupposes a definite and general rule to be applied in all similar cases alike." On the other hand, "'It is a question for the jury' merely means that there is no particular rule of law to decide the case in hand, and that men of common sense must decide it by taking all the complicated details into account," W. G. Miller, *Lectures on the Philosophy of Law*, London, 1884, p. 60. The distinction I have sought to draw in the text is close to, but not quite the same as, that drawn by Salmond, *Jurisprudence*, 6th ed., p. 15: "All matters that come for consideration before courts of justice are either matters of law or matters of fact. The former are those falling within the sphere of pre-established and authoritative principle, while the latter are those pertaining to the province of unfettered judicial discretion. In other words every question which requires an answer in a court of justice is either one of law or one of fact. The former is one to be answered in accordance with established principles — one which has already been authoritatively answered, explicitly or implicitly, by the law. A question of fact, on the other hand, is one which has not been thus pre-determined, — one which the court may and must answer and determine with its own individual judgment." Superficially Salmond thus appears to confine rules of law to preëxisting rules, and accordingly leaves room for the inference that the formulation of a new rule, whenever the courts undertake to formulate one, must be the decision of a question of judicial discretion, and so one of fact; for all judge-made law "is necessarily *ex post facto*," Miller, *op. cit.*, p. 69; or, in the language of Austin, "a judicial decision *primae impressionis*, or a judgment by which a new point of law is for the first time decided, is always an *ex post facto* law with respect to the particular case on which the point first arose, and on which the decision was given," *Lectures on Jurisprudence*, 3d ed., 1869, i, 503. But it is precisely for the purpose of thus formulating and announcing what is in substance a new rule of law, that the courts frequently set aside a jury verdict or administrative determination for "error of law." The decision of what is to be the rule of law for the future would seem to be validly a decision of a question of law as truly as the determination of what has been announced to be law in the past. No doubt, however, this would be fully recognized by Salmond, and most probably his method of expression is merely a reflection of the orthodox Blackstonian fiction that judges do not *make* new

ence from the evidence, the court may not substitute its own inference for the jury's unless it can point out as the ground for its different conclusion some general proposition equally applicable to all similar cases of alleged negligence — as, for instance, that the plaintiff neglected to stop, look, and listen. If the court does this, it enunciates a rule of law, — whether of good law or bad law is not here the question, — but in either case a general rule, which requires the setting aside of a verdict or administrative determination inconsistent with the rule so announced. This is the ordinary way in which rules of law originate and develop. As disputes of the same sort become frequent, general principles emerge from the particular facts of successive cases which are seen to be applicable to the whole class; and the courts pick these out as they are observed, and reverse such determinations as run counter to them. The freedom of the courts to carry on this process must not be interfered with if law is to generate new categories and distinctions. It is therefore essential that the whole record of the administrative proceedings should be open to the inspection of the courts, and that they should be free to reverse administrative determinations on the basis of any general principle involved which they feel bound to regard and enunciate as a rule or principle of law.[16]

Two cases where orders of the Interstate Commerce Commission were reversed by the Supreme Court may be selected to illustrate this process. The first is Interstate Commerce Commission *v.* Baltimore and Ohio R. Co., 145 U. S. 263. In that case the railroad had followed a practice of issuing so-called "party tickets" for the transportation of twenty persons at a cheaper rate than the sum of twenty

rules of law, but that all such rules are implicit in previous formulations, from which the judges merely elicit them. The formulation of a new rule would then, on Salmond's theory, be a decision of a question of law because it would be one which "has already been authoritatively answered . . . *implicitly* [italics mine] by the law."

[16] "Of course the consideration and decision of questions of law may involve a consideration of controverted facts to determine what the question of law is," Taft, C. J., in Public Utilities Commission *v.* Potomac Electric Power Co., 261 U. S. 428, at p. 442.

individual fares. The Interstate Commerce Commission applied for an injunction to restrain the practice as discriminatory. The Supreme Court held that the injunction was rightly refused and reached this conclusion by bringing the "party ticket" under the principle of the commutation ticket. In the case of freight shipments, the Court pointed out, the small shipper may be prejudiced to the advantage of his larger competitor by the giving of reduced rates for large shipments. But "the same result does not follow from the sale of a ticket for a number of passengers at a less rate than for a single passenger; it does not operate to the prejudice of the single passenger, who cannot be said to be injured by the fact that another is able in a particular instance to travel at a less rate than he. . . . If these tickets were withdrawn, the single-trip passenger would gain absolutely nothing." This is an example of the development of a rule of law to apply to a new case by the recognition of a valid distinction and the avoidance of a false analogy.

The other case is Southern Railway Co. *v.* St. Louis Hay and Grain Co., 214 U. S. 297. The hay company, with warehouses at St. Louis, was in the business of buying hay in the North and West and selling it in the South. The hay would be sent from the point of origin to St. Louis and there, instead of being shipped directly through to destination in the cars in which it was originally loaded, would be delivered to the company's warehouse, where it would be unloaded, inspected, and reloaded for the Southern market. For the service of delivering the cars to the warehouse and removing the reloaded cars, the Interstate Commerce Commission had held that the carrier was not entitled to charge more than the actual cost of the service. This conclusion was reached on the ground that the competitors of the hay company in East St. Louis, who bought carloads of hay as they came into that terminal but did not reload them into other cars, were not subjected to the additional charge which the hay company had to bear. This the Commission thought resulted in an unfair discrimination against the hay company in favor of its competitors; but because the added service rendered to the company by the carrier was of value to the former, the Commission held that the carrier should be reimbursed to the extent of the actual cost. The Supreme Court pointed out that the position of competitors for whom the carriers did not perform the same service was not pertinent; the issue was whether the carrier might charge more than cost for a service which was admittedly of some benefit to the shipper. "A carrier," said the Court, "may be under no obligations to furnish sleeping or other accommodations to its passengers, but if it does so, it is not limited in its charges to the mere cost, but may rightfully make a reasonable profit out of that which it does furnish. Especially is this true where, as here, the privilege is in no sense a part of transportation, but outside thereof." [17]

These cases illustrate the judicial reversal of administrative orders which run counter to what the Court chooses to enunciate as a general proposition of law; and it is equally necessary for the protection of individual rights that the courts should set aside arbitrary administrative orders having no reasonable foundation in the evidence on which they purport to be based. A leading case of the latter kind was Florida East Coast R. Co. *v.* United States *et al.*, 234 U. S. 167, already cited. A proceeding had been brought before the Interstate Commerce Commission complaining of certain rates on citrus fruits in Florida. Testimony was taken, and the Commission had found the rates reasonable. Later the case was reopened on the ground of changed conditions, and testimony was again taken, on the basis of which the Commission ordered a decrease in the rates on the Florida East Coast as well as on certain other roads. The new testimony, however, had simply tended to show decreased costs of carriage on the Seaboard Air Line and Atlantic Coast Line, while disclosing differences between those roads and the East Coast which negatived the inference of decreased cost to the latter. The Supreme Court therefore set the order aside as to the East

[17] Another instance of reversal of an order of the Commission for violation of what the Court chose to lay down as a rule of law was the Willamette Valley case, Southern Pacific R. Co. *v.* Interstate Commerce Commission, 219 U. S. 433.

Coast, saying: "Whatever may have been the proof as to the Seaboard Air Line and the Atlantic Coast Line, it is beyond controversy that no such proof can be found in the record as to the East Coast Line. . . . The greater magnitude and importance of the two trunk-lines concentrated attention in their direction, and caused the facts concerning the same to eclipse the distinctions between those lines and the East Coast Line — distinctions which if otherwise taken under consideration should have produced a different result."

Sometimes a case which seems to be dealt with by the Court on the ground of absence of evidence to support the finding will be discovered on closer examination to amount to a reversal of the administrative order on a point of law not clearly disentangled from the facts. Such a case was Philadelphia and Reading Co. *v.* United States, 240 U. S. 334. The complainant had a cement factory at Evansville, Pa., a few miles from Allentown. To ship its cement to Jersey City it had to send it over the Reading to Allentown, where it was reshipped on either the Pennsylvania, the Erie, the Lackawanna, or the Jersey Central. The through rate from Evansville to Jersey City *via* Allentown was $1.35 per ton. The four carriers which received this Evansville cement from the Reading at Allentown and participated in the joint rate of $1.35 to Jersey City, also served other cement mills in the vicinity of Evansville either directly or through other connections. The rate to Jersey City from these other mills, none of which was on the Reading, was only 80 cents. The complainant applied to the Interstate Commerce Commission for relief from alleged unlawful discrimination, and the Commission in its opinion said: "It cannot be questioned that complainant is laboring under a prohibitory disadvantage in marketing its product in Jersey City under the present rate in competition with other mills in the same district." An order was accordingly made, which did not pronounce the rate of $1.35 unreasonable or fix any particular rate, but simply directed the carriers to establish rates which would do away with the discrimination. This order the Supreme Court set aside, the opinion, per McReynolds, J., going apparently on the ground that it was unsupported by evidence. The Florida East Coast case was cited, and the Court said: "Undue discrimination against itself or the locality of its plant as alleged by the cement company was not found. . . . As the facts reported afford no foundation for the Commission's findings, enforcement of the order based thereon must be enjoined." In the light of the Commission's express finding of discrimination, this language may be difficult to understand unless we realize that the Court is here inarticulately applying a rule of law as to what is, and what is not, illegal discrimination. This rule, as afterwards expressly stated in Central Railroad of New Jersey *v.* United States, 257 U.S. 247, at p. 259, is to the effect that "connecting carriers can be held responsible for unjust discrimination only if each carrier has participated in some way in that which causes the unjust discrimination. . . . What Congress sought to prevent was not differences between localities in transportation rates but unjust discrimination between them *by the same carrier or carriers.*" In the Evansville cement case the Reading had no part in the 80-cent rate, yet the $1.35 rate was in part due to the Reading's services. Therefore the two rates could not be compared and no question of discrimination arose. Whatever we may think of this rule, it seems the only ground which will satisfactorily explain the decision.[18]

III

In the cases up to this point the question of the constitutionality of an administrative order has not been raised. We have merely examined how far the courts will substitute their own judgment or discretion for the judgment or discretion of the administrative body on questions of reasonableness or unfairness when its statutory authority is called into question. Does a different rule prevail where the administrative order is challenged not as unlawful, but as unconstitutional? Does the raising of the question of constitution-

[18] This doctrine has since been expressly repudiated in United States *v.* Illinois Central R. R. Co., 263 U. S., at p. 515, opinion by Brandeis, J., and an effort made to distinguish the two cases cited in the text.

ality broaden the scope of review? In analyzing the decisions of the Supreme Court on this point, the different situations must be distinguished in which the issue is usually presented to the Court: (1) An order of a federal agency like the Interstate Commerce Commission may be challenged as void under the Fifth Amendment because arbitrary or confiscatory. (2) An order of a state railroad or utility commission may be challenged as void under the Fourteenth Amendment because arbitrary or confiscatory, or under the interstate commerce clause as an undue interference with commerce between the states. (3) An order of a federal or state commission may be attacked under the Fifth or Fourteenth Amendment because made in accordance with a statutory procedure alleged not to provide sufficient opportunity for judicial review. The first two situations permit us to observe how far the Supreme Court in its own practice carries its reviewing power; in the third we get its rulings as to the extent to which judicial review must be available in order to save the constitutionality of the administrative procedure.

The orders of the Interstate Commerce Commission whose constitutionality has been challenged are few, and have dealt with practices rather than rates. They have been upheld on some ground of law which has not necessitated an examination of the facts by the Court.[19] Thus in Kansas City Southern R. Co. *v.* United States, 231 U. S. 423, the accounting system prescribed by the Commission for the railroads was attacked as unconstitutional in so far as it required the cost of certain abandoned property to be charged to operating expenses rather than to surplus or profit and loss. The carriers contended that this requirement, by reducing the funds available for dividends, deprived the holders of non-cumulative preferred stock of their property without due process of law. The Supreme Court overruled this claim by the legal argument that even if the regulation should in fact operate so as to compel these stockholders to forego their customary dividends, this would not amount to an unlawful taking of property, because the funds would go into the upbuilding of

[19] *E. g.*, Pennsylvania Co. *v.* United States, 236 U. S. 351.

the property, thus giving them better assurance of dividends in the future. The Court then went on to consider the reasonableness of the regulation as an exercise of the Commission's statutory power, and in that connection reiterated its refusal to reverse an administrative finding so long as it could have been reached by fair-minded men from the evidence.[20]

Where an opinion on subsidiary questions of reasonableness or value is essential to determine constitutionality, there is no direct expression by the Court as to how far it will accept the conclusions of the Commission on those questions, although one or two dark sayings *obiter* might be construed to show an intention to deal with them more strictly than where they bear merely upon the statutory validity of an order.[21] The attitude of the Court on issues going to constitutionality is much more fully disclosed in the large number of cases where it has had to pass on the constitutionality of orders of state administrative bodies.

IV

Orders made by administrative agencies of the state governments are challenged in the Federal courts occasionally

[20] The Court said: "A statement of the theory is sufficient to show that the regulation is not arbitrary in the sense of being without reasonable basis. And there is evidence to show that the Commission was warranted in adopting it as sustained by expert opinion and proved by experience. . . . But, even did we agree with appellant that the abandonment ought to be charged to surplus expenses, still we should not deem this a sufficient ground to declare that the Commission had abused its power. So long as it acts fairly and reasonably within the grant of power constitutionally conferred by Congress, its orders are not open to judicial review."

[21] In Louisville & Nashville R. Co. *v.* United States, 238 U. S. 1, Lamar, J., said that, "since there is no contention at this time that the rate is confiscatory," the Court would leave it undisturbed as there was evidence to support it. In the course of argument in Interstate Commerce Commission *v.* Louisville & Nashville R. Co., 227 U. S. 88, Assistant Attorney-General Fowler admitted that "the determination whether a rate is reasonable and the determination whether it is unconstitutional are governed by entirely different principles." And in Manufacturers' R. Co. *v.* United States, 246 U. S. 457, at p. 488, the Court, speaking through Pitney, J., said: "So long as the Commission proceeds in accordance with the requirements of the Commerce Act, its administrative orders . . . if made after due hearing and supported by evidence, are not subject to attack in the courts. But the cases recognize that matters of constitutional right are not to be conclusively determined by the Commission."

on the ground that they violate the interstate commerce clause of the Federal Constitution, but more frequently as denying due process of law under the Fourteenth Amendment. There are two ways in which such cases get before the Supreme Court; and the exercise by that Court of its jurisdiction to review depends in part on the way chosen to bring the case up. One way is by a bill for an injunction against enforcement of the order filed in a lower Federal court, from which the case then comes to the Supreme Court on appeal.[22] The other method is to fight enforcement of the order through the various state courts and, if it is finally sustained in the highest court of the state, to sue out a writ of error to the Supreme Court.[23] The two types of cases require separate consideration. Those will first be examined which come up by way of appeal from a lower Federal court, as here review by the Supreme Court is more direct and affords a clearer showing of the extent to which the Court will exercise its power. Indeed, this is substantially the same situation as where the Court sits to review orders of Federal administrative bodies like the Interstate Commerce Commission on constitutional grounds.

The doctrine of the Court in cases of this type was first clearly defined in San Diego Land and Town Co. *v.* National City, 174 U. S. 739. There a board of supervisors in the exercise of their authority under a state statute had made an order fixing water rates. The water company claimed that the supervisors had placed so low a valuation on its properties that the prescribed rates were confiscatory. On this ground the company sought an injunction in the lower Federal court, which was denied. On appeal the Supreme Court affirmed the decision, saying, per Harlan, J.: "Upon a careful scrutiny of the testimony, our conclusion is that no case is made that will authorize a decree declaring that the

[22] Missouri Pacific R. Co. *v.* Kansas ex rel. Taylor, 216 U. S. 262; Portland R. Light & Power Co. *v.* Oregon R. R. Commission, 229 U. S. 397.

[23] Chicago, Milwaukee, and St. Paul R. Co. *v.* Minnesota 134 U. S. 418, at p. 459; St. Louis & San Francisco R. Co. *v.* Gill, 156 U. S. 649, at p. 659; ex parte Young, 209 U. S. 123, at p. 166; Louisville & Nashville R. Co. *v.* Garrett, 231 U. S. 298, at p. 311.

rates fixed by the defendants are such as to amount to a deprivation of property without due process of law. *There is evidence both ways.* But we do not think that we are warranted *in holding that the rules on which the defendant board proceeded*[24] were in disregard of the principles heretofore announced by this court. The case is not one for judicial interference with the action of the local authorities to whom the question of rates was committed by the state."

The same doctrine was expressed more forcefully on substantially the same facts in the later case of San Diego Land and Town Co. *v.* Jasper, 189 U. S. 439, at p. 441, where the Court, per Holmes, J., said: "In a case like this we do not feel bound to reëxamine and weigh all the evidence, although we have done so, or to proceed according to our independent opinion as to what were proper rates. *It is enough if we cannot say that it was impossible for a fair-minded board to come to the result which was reached.*"[25]

The effect of these two decisions is substantially to apply to cases where the constitutional point is raised the same doctrine of review as where the statutory power of the Interstate Commerce Commission is in issue. Even to determine the constitutionality of the administrative body's action, the courts will not go behind the findings of that body on subsidiary questions such as reasonableness or value except where, as Mr. Justice Holmes says, it is impossible for fair-minded men to have reached the same conclusion,[26] or where, in Mr. Justice Harlan's language, the administrative body has proceeded in disregard of what the court announces to be a rule of law.[27] The application of a different measure of review where the constitutional point is raised from that prevailing on the issue of statutory authority would in effect nullify the latter. For if the mere claim of constitutional right were to throw open the door and require the court to

[24] Italics mine.

[25] Italics mine.

[26] Such cases were Rowland *v.* Boyle, 244 U. S. 106; Mississippi Railroad Commission *v.* Mobile & Ohio R. Co., 244 U. S. 388.

[27] For a case which turned on an issue of law see Darnell *v.* Edwards, 244 U. S. 564.

substitute its own conclusions from the facts on subsidiary questions, we may be certain that the issue of statutory power would rarely be raised, but that in every case the constitutional claim would be put forward. By this route the administrative body would again be reduced to a mere power of initial recommendation.

The doctrine of the two San Diego cases has been reaffirmed frequently.[28] In Southern Pacific R. Co. *v.* Campbell et al., 230 U. S. 537, the carrier sought an injunction against the enforcement of freight rates fixed by a state railroad commission. The bill, which set forth facts alleged to show that the rates were arbitrary and confiscatory, was dismissed by the lower court. On appeal the Supreme Court affirmed the decision, saying per Hughes, J.: "The complainants were not entitled to have the court below substitute its judgment for that of the commission, or determine the matters which properly fell within the province of that body. The conditions of traffic, the adjustment of rates with respect to the different commodities transported, and the appropriate basis for classification were subjects for the consideration of the commission, and there was nothing shown which would have warranted the court in overriding the decision of the commission *on the ground that its action was of such arbitrary character as to constitute an abuse of power.*"[29] In Louisville & Nashville R. Co. *v.* Garrett, 231 U. S. 298, an injunction was sought against an order of the Kentucky Railroad Commission fixing rates on certain distillers' supplies. The bill alleged that the rates were confiscatory and therefore a denial of due process of law. The lower court denied the relief prayed, and the Supreme Court affirmed the decree, saying, again per Hughes, J.: "It is the province of the legislature to make the law; and where the legislature or the body acting under its authority established the rate to be thereafter charged by the carrier, it is the duty of the courts to enforce the rule of law so made unless the constitutional limits of the rate-making power have been transgressed. The rate-making power necessarily implies a range of legislative

[28] See cases cited below.

[29] Italics mine.

discretion; and so long as the legislative action is within its proper sphere, *the courts are not entitled to interpose* and upon their own investigation of traffic conditions and transportation problems to *substitute their judgment for that of the legislature or of the railroad commission exercising its delegated power.*[30] The questions of fact . . . which might arise in the consideration preliminary to legislative action would not become, as such, judicial questions to be reëxamined by the courts."[31]

This case illustrates the rule that for the purpose of testing its constitutionality, a rate-fixing order of a state administrative body will be treated by the Federal courts as legislative in character, and dealt with on the same footing as a state statute. This doctrine, now firmly established,[32] attaches to the administrative order the same presumption in favor of its constitutionality which a statute enjoys.[33] The presumption can be rebutted only by showing that on any view of the facts the order must result in confiscation, or, in other words, that it was "impossible for a fair-minded board to come to the result which was reached." The practice of reviewing administrative orders by bill for an injunction against their enforcement carries with it, however, the consequence that in the equity proceeding the court must hear independent testimony,[34] and a situation is thus created somewhat like that which hampered the Interstate Commerce Commission prior to the Hepburn Act. The carriers can hold back their evidence in the proceeding before the administrative body only to release it in the injunction proceeding, with the result that the administrative order may have to be set aside. By adroit use of this opening, prac-

[30] Italics mine.

[31] See also Van Dyke *v.* Geary, 244 U. S. 39.

[32] "The function of rate-making is purely legislative in its character, and this is true whether it is exercised directly by the legislature itself or by some subordinate or administrative body to whom the power of rate-fixing in detail has been delegated," Knoxville *v.* Knoxville Water Co., 212 U. S. 1, at p. 7; Prentis *v.* Atlantic Coast Line Co., 211 U. S. 210. See Commissioner Prouty in *Reports Amer. Bar Ass'n.* (1907), xxxi, 486, at p. 498.

[33] San Diego Land & Town Co. *v.* National City, 174 U. S. 739, at p. 754.

[34] Chicago, Milwaukee, & St. Paul R. Co. *v.* Tompkins, 176 U. S. 167.

tically any order of an administrative body could be defeated. But the Supreme Court closed this door in Knoxville *v.* Knoxville Water Co., 212 U. S. 1, where it held that an injunction should not issue unless from the testimony before the Court a showing of unconstitutionality was made *beyond a reasonable doubt.* In that case the city government of Knoxville in the exercise of statutory authority fixed a water rate which the water company claimed was confiscatory. The city officials had tried without success to obtain from the company a statement of its property, capitalization, and earnings. The company then applied to the Federal court for an injunction and produced its evidence. The injunction was granted. On appeal the Supreme Court reversed the decision, saying per Moody, J.: "Disregarding for the moment all the errors which were committed in the court below, the decision of this cause may be rested upon a broader ground, which is clearly indicated by the previous judgments of this court. The jurisdiction which is invoked here ought to be exercised only in the clearest cases. If a company of this kind chooses to decline to observe an ordinance of this nature, and prefers rather to go into court with the claim that the ordinance is unconstitutional, it must be prepared to show to the satisfaction of the court that the ordinance would *necessarily*[35] be so confiscatory in its effect as to violate the Constitution of the United States. In Ex parte Young, 209 U. S. 123, the last word of caution by this court was said: 'No injunction ought to be granted *unless in a case reasonably free from doubt.*'[35] The same thought was expressed in San Diego Land and Town Co. *v.* National City, 174 U. S. 739, at p. 754: 'Judicial interference should never occur *unless the case presents, clearly and beyond all doubt, such a flagrant attack upon the rights of property*[35] as to . . . deny just compensation for private property taken for public use.' And in San Diego Land and Town Co. *v.* Jasper, 189 U. S. 439, it was said: 'It is enough if we cannot say it was impossible for a fair-minded board to come to the result

[35] Italics mine, here and on next page.

which was reached.' It cannot be doubted that in a clear case of confiscation it is the right and duty of the court to annul the law. . . . But the case before us is not a case of this kind. Upon any aspect of the evidence the company is certain to obtain a substantial net revenue. . . . It is *enough that the whole case leaves us in grave doubt.* The valuation of the property was an estimate and is greatly disputed. The expense account was not agreed upon. . . . The city authorities acted in good faith, and they tried without success to obtain from the company a statement of its property, capitalization, and earnings. . . . The companies will find it to their lasting interest to furnish freely the information upon which a just regulation can be based."

The state administrative orders so far considered have been rate-fixing orders. The remedy by injunction out of the Federal courts has been applied also to orders regulating practices. These cases are few in number and suggest a scope of review so wide as to seem anomalous in comparison with the rate cases. Mississippi Railroad Commission *v.* Illinois Central R. R. Co., 203 U. S. 335, was an early case. There the state commission had made an order requiring certain interstate trains to stop at a specified county seat, and the carrier sought to enjoin the order as an unconstitutional interference with interstate commerce. The commission contended that in making the order its action was judicial, and therefore not subject to be enjoined. The Supreme Court, reversing the trial court, and affirming the decree of the Circuit Court of Appeals, held that the injunction should have been granted. The action of the commission was said to be not "judicial" but merely "administrative," and therefore subject to control by injunction. Whether or not the order amounted to an unconstitutional interference with interstate commerce was held to depend on whether the county seat in question was adequately served without the additional trains, and the Supreme Court drew from the evidence its own conclusion that it was. In the opinion of the Court, Mr. Justice Peckham said: "In reviewing statutes and also orders made by a state railroad commission it frequently becomes necessary *to ex-*

amine the facts upon which they rest and determine from such examination whether there has been an unconstitutional exercise of power. . . . In this case there was no important conflict of evidence.[36] We think that the railroad company has fully performed its duty towards the town in the way of furnishing it proper and adequate accommodation without stopping these interstate trains as ordered, and therefore the order of the commission was improper and illegal. The commission and the Circuit Court indicated that the trains which already stopped at Magnolia were insufficient and that the town should have five trains. . . . *The question is before us upon uncontradicted evidence as to whether there were or were not proper facilities and we hold that there were.*" [37] It may be that this is only another way of saying that the State Commission's order was not supported by evidence,[38] but the language seems plainly to claim a wider power for the Court.[39]

In Grand Trunk R. Co. *v.* Michigan Railroad Commission, 231 U. S. 457, a decree was sustained which refused an injunction against the enforcement of an order of a state commission. The case turned on whether or not delivery of cars

[36] Here the court seems to be applying the doctrine, later condemned in United States *v.* Louisville & Nashville R. Co., 235 U. S. 314, *supra*, that where there is no conflict in the evidence, the conclusion to be drawn from the evidence is a "question of law" for the court.

[37] Italics mine.

[38] *Cf.* the similar case of Atlantic Coast Line Co. *v.* Wharton, 207 U. S. 328. where the order was plainly without the necessary evidence to support it.

[39] It is to be noted that this is a "train-stop" case, and thus one of a series in which the Court has fallen into the practice of exercising a rather broader review than elsewhere, possibly for two reasons: 1st, in the majority of such cases the stop has been ordered by direct legislative fiat rather than by administrative order, with the result that the Court has had no administrative finding of fact below to go upon, — see Illinois Central R. R. Co. *v.* Illinois, 163 U. S. 142; Lake Shore and M. S. R. Co. *v.* Ohio, 173 U. S. 285; C. C. C. & St. L. R. Co. *v.* Illinois 177 U. S. 514; 2d, the claim of unconstitutionality arises under the commerce clause rather than the Fourteenth Amendment, so that the primary issue appears under the guise of a legal definition of interference with interstate commerce rather than in its true character of the "reasonableness" of the order. Further, in such cases the central dispute is where to draw the line between federal and state control, and on such an issue it is obviously impossible to give as much weight to the local determination of reasonableness as where the issue is merely as to due process.

from junction points within the city limits of Detroit to team tracks and industrial sidings was transportation or a mere terminal service. The lower court concluded that because of the special geographical conditions of Detroit the service was transportation; and the Supreme Court sustained this conclusion. The Court in its opinion placed no express reliance on the finding of the commission, but the decision may amount to no more than a holding that it was not beyond the bounds of reason on the evidence. In Mississippi Railroad Commission *v.* Mobile and Ohio Railroad Co., 244 U. S. 388, a decree was affirmed which enjoined an order of a state commission on the ground that it was not supported by the evidence, but again the Court used very broad language. These cases probably should not be regarded as intended to establish any exceptional rule for other than rate-fixing orders, but only as illustrating a certain freedom of treatment in a class of cases where each is bound to differ widely from every other.[40]

V

The other line of decisions reviewing orders of state regulating commissions deals with those which come before the Supreme Court on writ of error from the highest court of a state, to which the question of the validity of the order has first been carried up under the state procedure. The extent to which the Supreme Court will review the evidence on a writ of error to the highest state court has been settled independently in a line of cases having no reference to orders of administrative bodies; and where such orders are involved it is said that no exception is made to the general rule. This rule is that on writ of error to a state court, the United States Supreme Court has no jurisdiction to review determinations by the state courts on pure questions of "fact," but only questions of "law" bearing on the federal right claimed by

[40] In Puget Sound Traction Co. *v.* Reynolds, 244 U. S. 574, another case of this kind, the issue involved was whether as a legal rule an unremunerative service on part of a system could be compelled if the whole system would still earn an adequate return. *Held*, that it could be.

the plaintiff in error.[41] *A fortiori* the Court cannot look behind the facts as found by the state court and review the findings of the administrative body whose order is questioned. The administrative findings, so far as reviewed judicially at all, are therefore left to be reviewed in the state courts, with such scope of review as is fixed by state law. The review so provided must be constitutionally ample under the standards which will hereafter be discussed, but if this requirement is met, the Supreme Court disclaims jurisdiction to go behind the findings of "fact" established in the state proceedings, whether the state law leaves them to be made conclusively by the administrative body, or invokes the independent judgment of a court upon the evidence.

To this rule an important exception was, however, laid down in Kansas City Southern R. Co. *v.* Albers Commission Co., 223 U. S. 573. It was there held that the Supreme Court will examine the entire record, including the evidence if necessary, "to determine whether what purports to be a finding upon a question of fact is so involved with and dependent upon questions of [federal] law as to be in substance and effect a decision of the latter." [42] This rule was applied in Washington ex rel. Oregon Railroad and Navigation Co. *v.* Fairchild, 224 U. S. 510, where the constitutionality of an administrative order was in issue. The state railroad commission of Washington had made an order requiring the complainant carrier to establish track connections at certain points with an interurban electric road. The carrier contested the order under the state procedure, which did not permit the introduction of new evidence in court, alleging that there had been no evidence before the commission tending to show any public necessity for the connections ordered, and that the order would therefore deprive it of property without due process of law. The state Supreme Court upheld the order on the ground that they "were not prepared to

[41] Lewis *v.* Campau, 3 Wall. 106, and numerous subsequent cases.

[42] Kansas City Southern R. Co. *v.* Albers Commission Co., 223 U. S. 573; Washington ex rel. Oregon R. R. and Navigation Co. *v.* Fairchild, 224 U. S. 510; Wood *v.* Chesbrough, 228 U. S. 672.

say" that the finding of the commission as to the public necessity for the track connections "was not justified by the testimony." [43] The United States Supreme Court assumed jurisdiction to examine whether "on the facts proved, the order was so unreasonable as to amount to a taking of property without due process of law." "This necessitates," said the Court, per Lamar, J., "an examination of the evidence, not for the purpose of passing on conflicts in the testimony, or of deciding upon pure questions of fact, but as said in Kansas City Southern R. Co. *v.* Albers Commission Co., 223 U. S. 655, from an inspection of the 'entire record, including the evidence, to determine whether what purports to be a finding upon questions of fact is so involved with and dependent upon questions of law as to be in substance and effect a decision of the latter.' Here the question presented is whether as a matter of law the facts proved show the existence of such a public necessity as authorizes the taking of property." Accordingly, the Court went on to examine the evidence, and reached the conclusion that it was insufficient to sustain the order. It was pointed out that one member of the Railroad commission had dissented, and that in the commission's brief it was admitted that "the testimony introduced before the commission as to the character of the traffic and the nature of the traffic movement in the territory served is not of a very satisfactory or definite character. . . . A careful examination of the record fails to show what, if any, business would be routed over these connections, or what saving would come to the public if they were constructed. There is nothing by which to compare the advantage to the public with the expense to the defendant, and nothing to show that within the meaning of the law there is such public necessity as to justify an order taking property from the company." The judgment was therefore reversed.

The doctrine of the Fairchild case thus amounts in substance to throwing open the door to review of practically the same kind and scope in the Supreme Court when the administrative order comes before it by way of writ of error from a

[43] 52 Wash. 17, 100 Pac. 179.

state court as when it comes up on appeal from a lower Federal court in injunction proceedings. In the one case as in the other, the Court will look to see whether the administrative finding is supported by evidence, and this even though the highest state court has held that it was. Of course in both cases the Court will reverse for disregard of principles of law. A case of reversal for error of law was Great Northern R. Co. *v.* Minnesota, 238 U. S. 340. There the railroad had installed scales in its stock yards at certain stations and not at others. A complaint of illegal discrimination was made to the state railroad commission on behalf of one of the stations not so equipped, and the commission made an order directing scales to be installed there. A judgment of the state court sustaining the order was brought to the Supreme Court on writ of error and reversed on the ground that, as a general rule of law, the railroad was not under any obligation to furnish stock-yard scales at any station. A certain confusion may be created by the language of the opinion in this case, in which the Supreme Court seemed to feel that it was proceeding on the authority of the Fairchild case, and also of the Florida East Coast case (*supra*, p. 163), which depend on essentially different principles.

The Fairchild case contains a suggestion which appears not to have been pressed in later cases, and which, if pressed, would, it is submitted, become unsound. In that case, as already mentioned, the state procedure did not permit the introduction of new evidence in the review proceedings, but required the state court to decide on the same evidence which had been presented before the commission. Certain language in the opinion of the Supreme Court may be interpreted to suggest that where this procedure prevails the ordinary presumption of the validity of the commission's order will not be applied, but the burden will be placed on the commission affirmatively to sustain its order. The Court said: "The company was not permitted to offer additional testimony [in court] for the purpose of establishing its defense, since the statute declared that the validity of the order was to be determined by the court on what had been proved before the commission. The burden was on the commission to establish the allegations in the complaint. . . . The insufficiency of the evidence submitted to the commission could not under this statute be supplied on the judicial review by a presumption arising from the failure of the carrier to disprove what had not been established." The last sentence seems to limit the application of any rule suggested to cases where as a matter of law the presumption of the order's validity would in any event be rebutted by the insufficiency of the evidence to sustain it. If anything broader was intended, it has not been followed up. Thus the state procedure followed in Michigan Central R. Co. *v.* Michigan Railroad Commission, 236 U. S. 615, resembled that in the Fairchild case in that new evidence could not be introduced in the state court by the carrier. The commission had made an order requiring the latter to interchange traffic with an interurban electric railway. The carrier failed to obey, and the commission applied to the state court for a writ of mandamus, which was granted. On writ of error, the Supreme Court affirmed the judgment. Nothing was said of any burden on the commission to sustain its order affirmatively, but the Court followed the usual practice of upholding the order "because no sufficient ground was shown for denouncing the regulation in question as either arbitrary or unreasonable." So in Portland Railway etc. Co. *v.* Railroad Commission, 229 U. S. 397, where again the state procedure did not permit new evidence to be offered in court, the Supreme Court, in reviewing on writ of error the decision of the state court sustaining the order, said that the facts found below were "supported by competent testimony, and this court does not sit to retry issues of fact thus heard and determined by the properly constituted tribunals of the state having jurisdiction on the subject."[44]

How the rule of the Fairchild case serves to equalize the scope of review before the Supreme Court in cases which come up from state courts on writs of error with those com-

[44] See also Atlantic Coast Line Co. *v.* North Carolina Corporation Commission, 206 U. S. 1; Missouri Pacific R. Co. *v.* Kansas ex rel. Taylor, 216 U. S. 262; Chicago, Milwaukee and St. Paul R. Co. *v.* Iowa, 233 U. S. 334.

ing up on appeal from a lower Federal court in injunction proceedings, is illustrated by People ex rel. New York & Queens Gas Co. *v.* McCall, 245 U. S. 345. This was a writ of error to the Appellate Division of the Supreme Court of New York to review a decision sustaining an order of the state Public Service Commission which required a gas company to extend its mains into new territory. The company claimed that the order was void under the Fourteenth Amendment because unreasonable on the facts, and urged that the Supreme Court should reëxamine the facts, citing the Fairchild case. In affirming the decision below, the Court, per Clarke, J., said: "While in such cases as we have here this Court is confined to the federal question involved, and therefore has not the authority to substitute its judgment for that of an administrative commission as to the wisdom or policy of an order complained of, and will not analyze or balance the evidence which was before the commission for the purpose of determining whether it preponderates for or against the conclusion arrived at, yet it will nevertheless enter upon such an examination of the record as may be necessary to determine whether the federal constitutional right claimed has been denied: as whether there was such a want of hearing or such arbitrary or capricious action on the part of the commission as to violate the due process clause of the Constitution. . . . [After reviewing the record] we agree with the Court of Appeals of New York in concluding that the action of the commission complained of was not arbitrary or capricious, but was based on very substantial evidence, and therefore, that, even if the courts differed with the commission as to the expediency or wisdom of the order, they are without authority to substitute for its judgment their views as to what may be reasonable." [45]

[45] In Erie R. R. Co. *v.* Board of Public Utility Commissioners, 254 U. S. 394 (1920) a state commission in the exercise of its discretion under a statute ordered the appellant railroads to abolish certain grade crossings. The order was sustained in the state courts, and the railroads, claiming a violation of their rights under the Fourteenth Amendment, took the case on writ of error to the Supreme Court, which affirmed the decision below, saying per Holmes, J.: "If we could see that the evidence plainly did not warrant a finding that the

VI

The cases so far examined seem to indicate that the scope of review which the United States Supreme Court will apply is essentially the same, whether the question is as to the statutory validity or constitutionality of an order of the Interstate Commerce Commission, or the constitutionality of an order of a state commission, and whether the latter question comes up by way of writ of error from a state court or on appeal from a lower Federal court. Such review is always limited substantially to two questions: first, whether there was evidence before the administrative body upon which reasonable men might fairly have arrived at the conclusions reached; and, second, whether any rule or principle of law was disregarded in reaching them. For the purpose of answering these questions the Court will apply its independent judgment to the evidence; but it will not do so to substitute its own conclusions and inferences from the evidence as to the issues of the case. This being the Supreme Court's own practice, it is interesting to examine the requirements it has laid down as to the scope of judicial review which must be provided for in a statute establishing a system of administrative regulation in order to fulfill constitutional requirements of due process.

The leading case, to which all others go back, is Chicago, Milwaukee & St. Paul R. Co. *v.* Minnesota, 134 U. S. 418. There a state statute required railroads to file their tariffs with a commission, and directed the commission, if it should "find any rate so filed unreasonable," to name a reasonable rate and order the carrier to put it in effect. Complaint was made to the commission of certain rates on milk. The commission transmitted the complaint to the railroad and later heard arguments by attorneys representing the railroad and the complainants. The outcome was that the commission made an order fixing a rate which the railroad refused to

particular crossings were dangerous, there might be room for the argument that the order was so unreasonable as to be void. . . . But if [the commissioners] were reasonably warranted in their conclusion, their judgment must stand. We cannot say that they were not."

adopt, and, following the statutory procedure, the commission thereupon applied to the state supreme court for a writ of mandamus to compel obedience to its order. On the hearing, the railroad applied for a reference to a master to take testimony on the question whether the rate fixed by the commission was reasonable. This application the court refused, construing the statute to make the rate fixed by the commission "not merely *prima facie* reasonable, but final and conclusive as to what are lawful and equal and reasonable charges."[46] Accordingly the state court held that the only issue was whether the commission had in fact made the order, and finding that it had, granted the writ. From this judgment the railroad took the case on writ of error to the United States Supreme Court, contending that in so far as the statute "made the decision of the railroad commission conclusive and not subject to judicial examination," it was in conflict with the Fourteenth Amendment to the Constitution. The Supreme Court held the statute unconstitutional.

The ground of this decision has been frequently said to be that the statute in question made the finding of the commission "a finality" and not subject to judicial review.[47] The opinion of the Court seems to place the result on the narrower ground that the statute did not require the commission to give the carrier a hearing before fixing the rate. Speaking through Mr. Justice Blatchford, the Court said: "All that the commission is required to do is, on the filing with it by the railroad company of copies of schedules of charges, to 'find' that any part thereof is in any respect unequal or unreasonable, and then it is authorized and directed to compel the company to change the same and adopt such charge as the commission 'shall declare to be equal and reasonable. . . .' No hearing is provided for, no summons or notice to the company before the commission has found what it is to find and declared what it is to declare, no opportunity

[46] 38 Minn. 281.

[47] Hon. F. T. Swayze in *Quarterly Journal of Economics*, 1912, pp. 389–424; and see language of Peckham, J., in Ex parte Young, 209 U. S. 123, at p. 147. The statement of the holding of the case in Freund, *Police Power*, §381, is admirable.

provided for the company to introduce witnesses before the commission, in fact nothing which has the semblance of due process of law; and although in the present case, it appears that prior to the decision of the commission, the company appeared before it by its agent, and the commission investigated the rate charged by the company for transporting milk, yet it does not appear what the character of the investigation was, or how the result was arrived at." [48]

The decision in the Minnesota case was certainly understood in this sense when the question next came before the Supreme Court, in San Diego Land and Town Co. *v.* National City, 174 U. S. 739. There a California statute conferred on boards of supervisors the power to fix water rates. The ordinance fixing such rates was to be passed during the month of February of each year, and the water companies were required to file during January a verified statement of the facts on which the rates could be based. The companies claimed that the statute was unconstitutional because it "authorized rates to be established without previous notice to the corporation or person immediately interested in the matter, and without hearing in any form," and contended that the decision in the Minnesota case was controlling. This contention was overruled by the Supreme Court on the ground that the statute, as construed by the state court, satisfied the constitutional requirement as to a hearing. Harlan, J., in delivering the opinion of the Court, said: "What this Court said about the Minnesota statute can have no application to the present case unless it be made to appear that the laws of California invest the municipal authorities with power to fix water rates arbitrarily, without investigation and without permitting the corporations or persons affected thereby to make any showing as to rates to be exacted or to be heard at any time or in any way upon the subject. We are not at liberty so to interpret the instrument."

The state procedure thus held to satisfy the constitutional requirement of due process under the Fourteenth Amendment

[48] 134 U. S. 418 at p. 457.

limited the scope of judicial review to the question of whether, on the evidence before the administrative board, reasonable men could have reached the same conclusion. The state court in construing the law had said: "When [the law] provides for the fixing of rates or compensation, it means reasonable rates and just compensation. To fix such rates and compensation, is the duty and within the jurisdiction of the board. To fix rates not reasonable or compensation not just is a plain violation of its duty. But the courts cannot, after the board has fully and fairly investigated and acted, by fixing what it believes to be reasonable rates, step in and say its action shall be set aside and nullified because the courts, upon a similar investigation, have come to a different conclusion as to the reasonableness of the rates fixed. There must be actual fraud in fixing the rates, or they must be so palpably and grossly unreasonable and unjust as to amount to the same thing."[49] The measure of review thus defined was held by the Supreme Court to satisfy due process. Due process was held not to require a judicial review so broad as to substitute a court's independent conclusions from the evidence as to the correctness of the rates for the conclusions reached by the administrative body, but is sufficiently safe-guarded if the courts are confined to saying whether reasonable men could have reached the administrative body's conclusions on the same evidence. Any other holding would have convicted the Supreme Court itself of a denial of due process in its own practice.

This view of the proper limits of court review has been frequently reaffirmed. "The complainants were not entitled to have the court substitute its judgment for that of the commission," said the Court, per Hughes, J., in Southern Pacific Company *v.* Campbell, 230 U. S. 537, at p. 552. In Louisville & Nashville R. Co. *v.* Garrett, 231 U. S. 298, the state statute was attacked because it contained no express provision for an appeal to the courts from final orders of the state railroad commission or for judicial review of the reason-

[49] Spring Valley Water Works *v.* San Francisco, 82 Cal. 286, quoted by Mr. Justice Harlan in the opinion of the Court.

ableness of the proposed rates. The Supreme Court held that the omission did not make the statute unconstitutional: "If the commission establishes rates that are so unreasonably low as to be confiscatory, an appropriate mode of obtaining relief is by bill in equity to restrain enforcement of the order. Presumably the courts of the state, as well as the Federal courts, would be open to the carrier for this purpose without express statutory provision to that effect." The measure of review, in short, to which the carrier is entitled in the state courts is the same as, and no other than, that which is meted out to it in the Federal courts; and the Supreme Court then went on to define once more what that measure is: "So long as the legislative action is within its proper sphere, the courts are not entitled to interpose and substitute their judgment with respect to the reasonableness of rates for that of the legislature or of the railroad commission exercising its delegated power. It may be assumed that the statute of Kentucky forbade arbitrary action; it required a hearing, the consideration of the relevant statements, evidence, and arguments submitted, and a determination by the commission whether the existing rates were excessive. But on these conditions being fulfilled the questions of fact which might arise as to the reasonableness of the existing rates in the consideration preliminary to legislative action would not become, as such, judicial questions to be reëxamined by the courts." This statement was referred to by the Supreme Court in the later case of Detroit and Mackinac Railway Co. *v.* Michigan Railroad Commission, 235 U. S. 402, as expressing the proper limits of review. In Louisville & Nashville R. Co. *v.* Finn, 235 U. S. 601, the Court went even further, Pitney, J., saying: "In cases arising under the Interstate Commerce Act it has been repeatedly held by this court that an administrative order made indisputably contrary to the evidence, or without any evidence, must be deemed arbitrary and therefore subject to be set aside. It is contended that the due process provision of the Fourteenth Amendment imposes a like rule of procedure upon the states with respect to their exercise of the legislative power of rate-making. *We find it unnecessary to pass upon this question.* . . . There was substantial evidence to support the order."

VII

The effect of the different lines of cases reviewed in this chapter is practically unanimous. The recent case of Ohio Valley Water Co. *v.* Ben Avon Borough, 253 U. S. 287 (1919), has raised the question whether the Supreme Court intended by its decision in that case to overrule the settled precedents and establish a new principle of judicial review.[50]

In the Ben Avon case the Public Service Commission of Pennsylvania, acting on complaint of Ben Avon Borough and others, found, after due notice and hearing, that increased rates adopted by the Ohio Valley Water Co. were unreasonable; and it prescribed a schedule of lower rates which it estimated would yield seven per cent upon its own valuation of the property used and useful in the service. The company, following a procedure established by the statute, appealed to the state Superior Court on the ground that its property had been undervalued and that the prescribed rates were therefore confiscatory and violated its rights under the Fourteenth Amendment. That court, passing on the weight of the evidence introduced before the commission, differed from the commission as to the proper valuation of several items going to make up the property and held that larger amounts should have been allowed. It therefore reversed the order and directed the commission to allow these larger amounts, and upon such revised valuation to fix a schedule of rates that would yield the rate of net return which it had found to be fair. From this decision of the Superior Court the commission appealed to the Supreme Court of the state, contending that the Superior Court in passing on the weight of the evidence before the commission had exceeded its jurisdiction. The state Supreme Court sustained this contention, and holding upon a careful review of the record that there was ample and competent evidence to support the findings of the commission and that they were not unreasonable, reversed

[50] W. D. Guthrie, *The League of Nations and Miscellaneous Addresses* (New York, 1923), p. 372.

the decree of the Superior Court and reinstated the order. In its opinion the state Supreme Court said: "The appeal [to the Superior Court] presented for determination the question whether the order appealed from was reasonable and in conformity with law; and in this inquiry was involved the question of the fair value, for rate-making purposes, of the property of appellant and the amount of revenue which appellant was entitled to collect. In its decision upon the appeal, the Superior Court differed from the commission as to the proper valuation to be placed upon several items going to make up the fair value of the property of the company for rate-making purposes." The Court then went on to consider those items and reached the conclusion that there was competent evidence to sustain the figures fixed by the commission. "A careful examination of the record," said the Court, "has led us to the conclusion that in the items wherein the Superior Court differed from the commission upon the question of values, there was merely the substitution of the former's judgment for that of the commission in determining that the order of the latter was unreasonable." [51]

The case was brought before the United States Supreme Court on writ of error, on the ground that "the interpretation of the Public Service Company law by the Pennsylvania Supreme Court, requiring the Superior Court to sustain the commission's order if there was substantial evidence to support it, deprived the water company of its constitutional right to a judicial review of the commission's action." This contention the United States Supreme Court upheld in a very brief opinion by Mr. Justice McReynolds, which says little more than that, "looking at the entire opinion [of the Pennsylvania Supreme Court] we are compelled to conclude that the state Supreme Court interpreted the statute as withholding from the courts power to determine the question of confiscation according to their own independent judgment. . . . In cases of this kind if the owner claims that confiscation of his property will result, the state must provide a fair opportunity for submitting that issue to a judicial tribunal for deter-

[51] 260 Pa. 289; 103 Atl. 744.

mination upon its own independent judgment as to both law and facts; otherwise the order is void because in conflict with the due process clause, Fourteenth Amendment." [52] The judgment was accordingly reversed. There was a vigorous dissent by Mr. Justice Brandeis, in which Mr. Justice Holmes and Mr. Justice Clarke joined. The gist of the dissenting opinion was that the questions before the state Supreme Court were "first, whether the Superior Court had jurisdiction to weigh the evidence; second, whether in rendering its decision it weighed the evidence; and, third, whether the valuation of the plaintiff's property was so low that a rate based upon it would operate to deprive the plaintiff of due process of law — would confiscate its property. On each of these questions the state Supreme Court found against the contentions of the plaintiff. It held that the Superior Court did not have revisory legislative powers, but only the power to review questions of law, — in the present case whether there was evidence on which the valuation adopted could reasonably have been found; and in so holding it acted upon the established principle applied in reviewing the findings of administrative boards that 'courts will not examine the facts further than to determine whether there was substantial evidence to sustain the order.' Interstate Commerce Commission *v.* Union Pacific R. Co., 222 U. S. 541, 547, 548. It therefore reinstated the order of the commission. . . . It did so because the only question before it was whether there was substantial evidence to support the finding of value; for if the valuation was legally arrived at, the order was confessedly reasonable. San Diego Land and Town Co. *v.* Jasper, 189 U. S. 439, 441, 442. The presumption created (by the statute) by which an order of the commission is made *prima facie* evidence of its reasonableness, is in no sense a limitation upon the scope of review. It is in effect the presumption which this Court has declared to exist in rate cases, independently of statute, in favor of the conclusion of an experienced administrative body reached after a full hearing. Darnell *v.* Edwards, 244 U. S. 564, 569."

It is submitted that the decision of the United States

[52] Opinion, p. 289.

Supreme Court in this case was confused by failure to analyze adequately the meaning of that "independent judgment of the court" to which an appellant is entitled on the question of confiscation or constitutionality. It seems altogether plain, as the majority opinion says, that he is entitled to the "independent judgment of the court" upon the question of whether on both the law and the facts the order or statute complained of is or is not constitutional; [53] but that does not mean that he is entitled to the "independent judgment" of the court on the subsidiary questions which have a bearing on the question of constitutionality. If this were so, a court would be bound to declare every piece of legislation and every administrative order unconstitutional where it would not itself under the same circumstances or on the same evidence have reached the same conclusion as the legislative or administrative body. In other words, every doubt would have to be resolved against the constitutionality of the statute or order. But the rule is exactly contrary. The person asserting a constitutional right is entitled to the "independent judgment of the court" on the ultimate question of constitutionality; but in exercising that judgment the court is bound to give effect to a presumption in favor of the validity of the statute or order,[54] and this can mean only that if there is any construction of the subsidiary facts within the bounds of reason which would make the statute or order constitutional, that construction must be adopted, rather than the construction which the court would "independently" place upon the same facts. The Supreme Court itself has said since the Ben Avon case that "where the constitutional validity of a statute depends upon the existence of facts, the courts must be cautious about reaching a conclusion respecting them contrary to that reached by the legislature; and if the question of what the facts establish be a fairly debatable one, it is not permissible for the judge to set up his opinion in respect to it against

[53] Indeed the case seems to hold him entitled to the opinion of the lower state court, though that of the highest is contrary.

[54] San Diego Land & Town Co. *v.* National City, 174 U. S. 739, at p. 754; Knoxville *v.* Knoxville Water Co., 212 U. S. 1, at p. 7.

the opinion of the law maker." [55] Surely the formal conclusions of fact reached by an administrative tribunal after a hearing and the taking of testimony should be entitled to as much respect as findings of fact supposed to have been made by a legislative body as the implied basis for its enactments. Indeed, judicial review of the rate-fixing orders of utilities commissions proceeds on the theory that such orders are "legislative" in character.[56] If so, they should have the benefit of the language of the Court just quoted as to legislative findings of fact. Applying that language to the situation presented by the Ben Avon case, it follows that if on a certain valuation of property an order would not be confiscatory, and if there is evidence from which reasonable men could have reached that valuation, then the court must uphold the order, and so far from being required, is not even entitled to substitute its own independent opinion of value for that of the legislative or administrative body for the purpose of invalidating the order. This is true in the case of an administrative order whether the question comes before the court on writ of error from a statutory proceeding limiting the scope of review, or by bill for an injunction. In the latter case no more than in the former is the court entitled to substitute its "independent" conclusions as to subsidiary facts for that of the commission.[57] There seems to be a lurking confusion on this point even in the dissenting opinion in the Ben Avon case, where it is apparently assumed that the procedure by bill for an injunction would have entitled the water company to a broader scope of review than that which it received under the statutory procedure in the state courts. Under the Supreme Court decisions which have been here reviewed, the Federal courts themselves in injunction pro-

[55] Radice *v.* New York., 264 U. S. 292, at p. 294. Opinion by Mr. Justice Sutherland.

[56] Prentis et al. *v.* Atlantic Coast Line Co., 211 U. S. 210.

[57] San Diego Land & Town Co. *v.* National City, 174 U. S. 739; San Diego Land & Town Co. *v.* Jasper, 189 U. S. 439; Knoxville *v.* Knoxville Water Co., 212 U. S. 1; Southern Pacific R. Co. *v.* Campbell, 230 U. S. 537, at p. 552; Louisville & Nashville R. Co. *v.* Garrett, 231 U. S. 298; Louisville & Nashville R. Co. *v.* Finn, 235 U. S. 601.

ceedings brought to test constitutionality will go no further than the limits to which the Supreme Court of Pennsylvania restricted review under the statutory procedure in the Ben Avon case.[58]

It is the Ben Avon case which has made necessary the long examination of cases contained in this chapter.[59] It discloses a lingering uncertainty as to the scope and principles of review which makes such an examination pertinent for the purpose of showing the substantially unanimous agreement of the decisions on principles other than those adopted in the

[58] For criticisms of the Ben Avon decision see Ernst Freund in *W. Va. Law Quart.*, xxvii, 207; Laurence Curtis 2d in *Harv. Law Rev.*, xxxiv, 862; T. P. Hardman in *Yale Law Jour.*, xxx, 681.

[59] The disturbing effect of the Ben Avon decision as a precedent may already be observed in such a case as Bluefields Waterworks and Improvement Co. *v.* Public Service Commission of West Virginia, 262 U. S. 679. There the Commission fixed the value of the utility's property for rate-making purposes at $460,000. Its engineer testified that actual investment, less depreciation, amounted to $365,000, and that reproduction cost (at 1915 prices, the valuation being made in 1920), less depreciation, was approximately $398,000. The utility company's engineer on the other hand testified that reproduction cost, less depreciation, at 1920 prices was $1,194,663, and that the proper valuation for rate-making purposes was $900,000. The company brought a petition in the state Supreme Court to set aside the rate order made by the Commission, which was denied, the Court holding that findings of fact by the Commission based on evidence to support them would not be reviewed by the Court. On writ of error to the United States Supreme Court, this decision was reversed. The Court cited the Ben Avon case to the effect that the company was "entitled under the Fourteenth Amendment to the independent judgment of the court as to both law and facts," and then went on to weigh the evidence. The decision of the state court was reversed, and the order held confiscatory, on the ground, among others, that "the court failed to give proper consideration . . . to the testimony of the company's valuation engineer that the property in his opinion was worth $900,000." An additional ground of reversal was the fact that the Commission's reproduction cost figures were based on 1915 rather than on 1920 prices. This fact, together with Mr. Justice Brandeis's concurring opinion, may be taken to place the decision on the ground that the Commission's findings were regarded by the Court as beyond the bounds of reason on the evidence; but from a reading of the opinion it is hard to escape the conclusion that the Court itself weighed the evidence, and drew its "independent conclusions" of value. In Georgia Railway & Power Co. *v.* Railroad Commission, 262 U. S. 625, however, decided the same day, the Court made no reference to the Ben Avon case, but relied on the earlier cases, and refused to disturb the Commission's valuation, saying, "We cannot say that the evidence compelled a conviction that the rate would prove inadequate."

Ben Avon case. It is submitted that that decision, if persisted in, would lead to undesirable results. It amounts to a holding that if the constitutional point is once raised, the courts will be bound to substitute their own judgment for that of the administrative body on all conclusions to be drawn from the evidence which have a bearing on the question of constitutionality — that is, on all subsidiary conclusions of value, adequacy of service, and the like. These are precisely the questions which utility commissions must determine by the application of standards, and as it is always possible to raise the constitutional point, the result would be to make the courts sit to revise the findings of the commissions in practically all utility cases. It is a sound instinct which has led the Supreme Court to say so often that this will not be done. Using the Court's illustration, it would correspond to requiring the courts to revise acts of the legislature. On another analogy it would amount to requiring a court to substitute its conclusions from the evidence for the jury's. There are two good reasons against it. It destroys the effectiveness of administrative regulation by reducing the administrative body to a practical nullity with a barren power of initial recommendation; and it yields no gain in security for the rights of property. Indeed, there is an actual loss in security, because greater confusion and not greater certainty is bound to be the outcome of the practice. For we are not dealing here with the power of a court to select from the mass of facts before the commission certain pertinent ones, and announce as a clear rule of law to govern all future cases that those facts are to be dealt with in a manner different from that in which the commission dealt with them. There can be no doubt that this power must exist in the courts if legal order is to prevail in the field of utility regulation. What is here in issue is the power of the courts to substitute their own inferences and conclusions for the commission's, where there is merely some difference of opinion between them as to matters peculiar to the particular case, or some difference in inference from those matters. Such substitution does nothing to clarify a rule because it relates wholly to something which will be dead and done with after the particular case. It is like permitting the court to substitute its conclusion in place of the jury's as to whether the plaintiff in a negligence action did or did not see an approaching vehicle. If the court's "independent" judgment on such a point is to prevail, there would be little use in having a jury. The argument applies with greater force to the finding of a commission, reached in a separate proceeding at much trouble and expense to both the public and the parties. The double process only reduplicates the uncertainty of any particular case and brings it out at the end of the administrative stage of the proceedings with nothing settled which is not liable to be overruled. After the administrative tribunal has spoken, the whole case would still be as open, and the nature of the ultimate decision as uncertain, as if no proceedings had yet been had. Such a hazard is not one which either the community or the utility companies ought fairly to be called upon to bear. And meanwhile the courts, if left free to revise administrative determinations on no more accurate grounds than their own private opinions as to the facts of particular cases, will inevitably overlook that laborious development of general rules from case to case which is their proper task under a sound division of labor,[60] and one which is essential to the maintenance of the supremacy of law.

[60] *Cf.* the idea underlying the following passage from Francis Bacon: "Some hold that the jurisdiction which decrees according to equity and conscience, and that which proceeds according to strict law, ought to be deputed to the same courts. . . . I am clearly for keeping them separate. For if there be a mixture of jurisdictions, the distinction of cases will not be retained, but discretion will in the end supersede the law. . . . As that is the best law which leaves least to the discretion of the judge [Aristotle, *Rhet.*, i, 1], so he is the best judge who leaves least to himself," Treatise on Universal Justice, Aphorisms 45, 46, in *De Augmentis*, bk. viii, *Works*, ed. Spedding, Ellis and Heath (Boston, 1864), ix, 323, 324.

CHAPTER VII

LEGAL ORDER IN FIELDS OF DISPUTED SOCIAL POLICY

I

JUDICIAL review for so-called error of law is crucial not only as keeping open the necessary opportunity for the courts to compel observance of the law as previously formulated, but also as the channel through which they can carry forward the process of legal development. This is true whether the verdict of a jury or the order of an administrative body is under review. The law is neither static nor complete, and previous expressions of its rules do not exhaust them. New cases call for deductions from old principles to fresh applications, which must be made in the course of court control of the fact-finding body. From the mass of matters which go before a jury the court selects those which it chooses to regard as legally pertinent and instructs the jury to frame their verdict in accordance with their findings on these critical issues. When it wishes to extend the application of an old rule or to apply a novel one, it does so by bringing into the foreground of the case new facts or circumstances to which legal significance has not before been attached, and includes these in its instructions. The process is the same in reviewing administrative orders—when a court observes that an administrative body has failed to deal with a certain fact in a certain way, and when it determines to announce as a rule of law that that fact must be dealt with in that way and no other, it reverses the administrative decision for error of law. It follows that all facts in the record must be open to the courts as potential grounds for reversal if they are to be left free to proceed in this manner with the proper adaptation of the law to new needs.

The history of almost any legal rule illustrates this process of growth. To take a familiar example, it originally produced no effect on the validity of a will that the testator after its execution had married and had issue. In Overbury *v.* Overbury, 2 Shower, 253, the courts for the first time fastened on these special facts as having a bearing on the question of implied revocation of a will of personalty.[1] In the course of time a rule developed that they created a presumption of revocation. A distinction was taken for a while as to wills of land, but it later came to be held that the presumption applied to these also.[2] Finally in Marston *v.* Fox, 8 Adolphus & Ellis, 14, the Court of King's Bench by a frank exercise of judicial legislation converted the presumption into a rule of law, and held that the facts of marriage and subsequent birth of issue produced of themselves the legal effect of revocation.

The classic example of the way in which control of the fact-finding body by the courts gives to the latter an opportunity to develop a body of new law by attaching legal significance to new facts is the development of commercial law in the eighteenth century under the influence of Holt, Hardwicke, and Mansfield. At the time of that development it was scarcely a hundred years since commercial cases had begun to come into the king's courts. The common law had no rules for them, the legislature had done nothing to supply the deficiency, and the judges were, as usual, reluctant to take the step of introducing new rules by judicial decisions. "Hence, when questions necessarily arose respecting the buying and selling of goods, the affreightment of ships, marine insurance and bills of exchange and promissory notes, no one knew how they were to be determined. . . . If an action turning on a mercantile question was brought in a court of law, the judges submitted it to the jury, who determined it according to their own notions of what was fair, and no general rule was laid down which could afterwards be referred to for the purpose of settling similar disputes." [3] Mr. Justice

[1] See Kent's *Commentaries*, 12th ed., iv. 522.

[2] Christopher *v.* Christopher, Dickens, 445. (1771)

[3] Campbell, *Lives of the Chief Justices*, iii, 300.

Buller in a famous passage [4] has described the emergence of modern commercial law: "Within these thirty years the commercial law of this country has been taking a very different turn from what it did before. Lord Hardwicke was proceeding with great caution, not establishing any general principles, but decreeing on all the circumstances of a case put together. Before that period we find that in courts of law all the evidence in mercantile cases used to be thrown together; they were left to a jury, and they produced no general principle. From that time we all know, the great study has been to find some certain general principles which shall be known to all mankind, not only to rule the particular case then under consideration, but to serve for the future." In this way came to be established such specific rules as that the unpaid seller has a right of stoppage in transit,[5] that an assignment of an order bill of lading carries property in the goods,[6] that the second indorser of a bill of exchange can sue his immediate indorser without having previously demanded payment from the drawer,[7] that an insurer must make full disclosure of material risks,[8] and so on. The way in which these rules emerged was generally that the judges in successive cases over a long period of time would instruct the jury to take a particular fact or circumstance into account in reaching their verdict, and would finally tell them to regard it as decisive.[9] The transition can be followed in the case of the rule that the assignment of a bill of lading carries title to the goods, the earlier rule being that the possession of the bill was evidence for the jury, but not conclusive evidence, that title to the goods was in the holder of it.[10]

[4] In his opinion in Lickbarrow *v.* Mason (in the King's Bench), 2 T. R. 63.

[5] Per Ld. Mansfield, Burghall's Assignees *v.* Howard, 1 H. Bl. 366, note.

[6] Per Ld. Mansfield, Wright *v.* Campbell, 4 Burr, 2051.

[7] Per Ld. Mansfield, Heyleyn *v.* Adamson, 2 Burr, 669.

[8] Per Ld. Mansfield, Garter *v.* Boehm, 3 Burr, 1905.

[9] For an example of the way in which in mercantile cases the evidence was originally thrown as a whole before the jury, see the Anonymous case before Holt, J., in Ames, *Cases on Bills and Notes*, i, 146 (Comberbeach, 401). For the emergence of rules of tort law by a similar process, see Holmes, *Common Law*, p. 151.

[10] For a late application of this early rule see Eyre, C. J., in Haille *v.* Smith, 1 B. & P. 570.

II

The process of the law's growth through the courts' exercise of their power to attach legal significance to new kinds of facts is important for the law of public-utility regulation precisely because it is a branch of law still so largely in the making. Here it is through judicial review of the determinations of commissions, and not by court control of juries, that the formative process must go on, and a law of utilities regulation grow up, if it is to grow up at all. In this field, therefore, judicial review is an instrument of the supremacy of law in building out new ground for the operation of general rules and principles. Upon the question of how far the field is adapted to the formulation and application of such rules and principles, — of law rather than of discretion, — a comparison with general commercial law suggests certain significant similarities and differences.

When we read of commercial cases in Lord Hardwicke's time that "all the evidence was thrown together and left to the jury" with instructions to take certain matters into account in reaching a verdict, we observe a significant resemblance to the present state of the law of utility regulation. The utility cases are full of such expressions as that "these questions must be left for the most part to the good judgment of the tribunal which passes upon each particular case." [11] So indeed many of them must be; but so to a considerable extent must still be many of the questions which arise in the field of commercial law. The question is not whether we can arrive at a complete set of formulae which will enable us to write off at one stroke the correct solution of every utility case, but whether it is possible for the courts to develop a number of more or less settled rules or principles to govern in cases of the same general character.

It is especially with reference to matters affecting the financial return from utility properties that the courts are undertaking, in their review of the determinations of regulatory bodies, to establish general rules. The cases disclose

[11] Brunswick & Topsham Water Dist. *v.* Maine Water Co., 99 Me. 371.

propositions of law laid down in many instances to govern matters which in the field of contract or torts would almost certainly be left to the fact-finding body to determine by the application of a standard. Among the rules which have been formulated are those to the effect that in estimating the cost of a particular service or of transporting a particular commodity, a proportionate share of overhead expenses as well as of so-called "out-of-pocket" outlays must be included;[12] that in determining the reasonableness of a rate, its effect on the prosperity of a particular locality or local industry cannot be made controlling;[13] that a rate cannot be fixed on a given commodity below the actual cost of carriage, even though the total return to the carrier from all business would still be profitable;[14] that connecting carriers are guilty of discriminations as to through shipments only if each carrier does something that is discriminatory.[15]

The outstanding instance, however, in which the supposed need of the investor for certainty has led the courts to formulate a rule of law has been in connection with valuation for rate-making purposes. Ordinarily the question of value in the courts is a pure question of fact for the jury, — for example, the value of property alleged to have been converted, or destroyed, or damaged, — and is settled by the fact-finding body by applying to the evidence their judgment as reasonable men.[16] But the value of public-utility property has been erected into a bulwark for investors by the constitutional doctrine that rates must be sufficiently high to yield a reasonable return on the fair value of the property. Obviously "value" when raised into this central position must have a more or less fixed content if it is to prove useful for its purpose, and accordingly the courts have been practically

[12] Northern Pacific R. Co. *v.* North Dakota ex rel. McCue, 236 U. S. 585; Mississippi Railroad Commission *v.* Mobile & Ohio R. Co., 244 U. S. 388.

[13] United States *v.* Southern Pacific R. Co., 219 U. S. 433.

[14] Northern Pacific R. Co. *v.* North Dakota ex rel. McCue, 236 U. S. 585.

[15] Central R. R. of New Jersey *v.* United States, 257 U. S. 247. But this doctrine has since been repudiated in United States *v.* Illinois Central R. R. Co., 263 U. S., at p. 515.

[16] See language of Shaw, C. J., quoted in Head *v.* Hargrave, 105 U. S. 45; Thayer, *Prelim. Treat. on Evidence*, p. 297.

forced to the formulation, if not of a legal definition, at least of rules to be applied to determining the fair value of utility property for rate-making. Through a long series of cases in which determinations of rate-fixing bodies have been reviewed, certain lines of inclusion and exclusion were gradually drawn, culminating finally in the so-called "rule of Smyth *v.* Ames."[17] The result has not been regarded as happy.[18] The rule as crystallized is sufficiently narrow to be frequently overstepped by the practice of the rate-fixing bodies, and on the other hand is so vague as to give them little light or guidance in advance as to how they must proceed.[19] What the Supreme Court did was to lay down a list of a number of more or less inconsistent factors which it has said must govern the ascertainment of value, without indicating the weight to be attributed to them individually, or the way in which they are to be combined.[20] The real ground of the resulting confusion has been the fact that the Court, while in effect laying down a rule, has at the same time been unwilling to admit that it was doing so. It has continued to say that "the ascertainment of value is not controlled by artificial rules. It is not a matter of formulas, but there must be a rea-

[17] 169 U. S. 466.

[18] See Brandeis, J., in Missouri ex rel. Southwestern Bell Telephone Co. *v.* Public Service Commission of Missouri, 262 U. S. 276, at p. 301; G. C. Henderson in *Harv. Law Rev.*, xxxiii, 902 ff., 1031 ff.

[19] It of course does not presume to be an affirmative prescription of a rate-fixing method. It purports to establish limitations to which the method adopted must conform if the resulting rate is to be constitutional.

[20] "We hold that the basis of all calculations as to the reasonableness of rates to be charged by a corporation maintaining a highway under legislative sanction must be the fair value of the property being used by it for the convenience of the public. And in order to ascertain that value, the original cost of construction, the amount expended in permanent improvements, the amount and market value of its bonds and stock, the present as compared with the original cost of construction, the probable earning capacity of the property under particular rates prescribed by statute and the sum required to meet operating expenses, are all matter for consideration, and are to be given such weight as may be just and right in each case. We do not say that there may not be other matters to be regarded in estimating the value of the property." Professor Powell has described this "rule" as a "compound of contradictory considerations concocted by the alchemy of uncontrolled and changeful compromise," *Pol. Sci. Quart.*, xl, 407.

sonable judgment on all relevant facts." [21] Such language appears to have generally concealed from the Court that by its decision in this and other cases [22] it has apparently, if not actually, lent its authority to a particular theory of valuation — the so-called "present value" theory. This theory produces a dilemma between a logical impossibility on the one hand and a practical absurdity on the other. "Present value" seems to mean either exchange value or present cost of reproduction. But exchange value is a logically impossible basis for rate-fixing because it depends on prospective income, and so upon the rates to be fixed. Reproduction cost, on the other hand, involves the absurdity of attributing to land and structures in the absence of the utility the enhanced value which they derive from the utility's presence. The crystallization of this unsatisfactory rule has been the outcome of the Court's reluctance to lay down a rule frankly, a reluctance which no doubt has made the Court less critical of the implications of its decisions, and less thorough and careful in its investigation of the underlying issues.

For this reluctance there is a valid enough explanation. The question is one where large interests are at stake and where public opinion is greatly interested, but because of the comparative newness and complexity of the problem no general agreement has yet been reached either among experts or in the common body of lay thought. A régime of abstract rules like the law works successfully only when its rules correspond generally to the habits, or at least do not too greatly contradict the desires, of the community to which they apply; where opinion is both interested and divided, and no equilibrium of assent has been reached, it is natural that there should be reluctance to formulate and enforce rules on the part of the courts. The modern tendency is to say that the proper resort in such a case is to the legislature; [23] but mean-

[21] Hughes, J., in Minnesota Rate Cases, 230 U. S. 352, at p. 434.

[22] San Diego Land & Town Co. *v.* National City, 174 U. S. 739; San Diego Land & Town Co. *v.* Jasper, 189 U. S. 439; Knoxville *v.* Knoxville Water Co., 212 U. S. 1; Willcox *v.* Consolidated Gas Co., 212 U. S. 19; Minnesota Rate Cases, 230 U. S. 352.

[23] "The constitutional dogma of separation of powers makes the orthodox

while the legislature is no more forward than the courts to take decisive action, and uncertainty breeds confusion. Perhaps we do not enough appreciate to-day that laws are made not so much by popular enactment as by popular acquiescence; and that they almost always originate in the constructive sagacity and courage of some judge or statesman.[24]

Anglo-American lawyer loath to concede that law may be made by anyone or by anything but the legislature, and the dogmatic fiction of the pre-existence of the rule when a court has formulated and applied it in the decision of a cause, makes it harder to think of something which, however real in fact, is in inconvenient contradiction of legal theory. The proposition that legislation may create law encounters no such difficulties. Yet legislation is perhaps the least creative [of the forms of juristic activity]," Pound, *Interpretations of Legal History*, p. 137. "In the past, large additions to our legal rules, notably in equity and commercial law, have been made [by the courts] and further additions must, whenever the necessity arises, continue to be made, and in fact are daily made, from this unexhausted and perennial source. It is a mistake to suppose that this process has ceased. In consequence of modern inventions, aggregations of capital, and changed social conditions, I am inclined to think that at no previous period has this method of legal growth and change been in more constant and active operation than at the present time," J. F. Dillon, *Laws and Jurisprudence of England and America*, p. 5. It must also be noted that when the question becomes with us a question of constitutional law, resort to the legislature is not possible. If there is to be any rule, it must be laid down by the court, apart from the more or less remote possibility of a constitutional amendment. Thus if a law of valuation is to be developed, it is not within the competence of legislative creation. For the "juristic pessimism," which caused the courts to minimize their legislative functions in the latter part of the nineteenth century, see Pound, *Interpretations of Legal History*, pp. 66 ff.

[24] It is significant how frequently the legislature in such cases simply follows slavishly the lead of the courts, if the courts have happened to deal first with the problem. Thus the Railroad Valuation Act of 1913 (37 U. S. Statutes at Large, 701) is little more than a restatement of the "rule" of Smyth *v.* Ames. So the early statutes on the subject of trade unions followed the lines which had been laid down by the courts. *Cf.* P. W. Lowry in *Col. Law Rev.*, xxi, 784: "The *pede claudo* [sic] of the common law is due primarily to the timidity of judges . . . . They would prefer to let the parties fight it out for themselves or leave it to the unscientific legislature to botch a solution. . . . The outstanding figures in the history of the law have been those great judges, unhampered by timidity or incapacity . . . who have understood that the law is of the living; and who were unafraid on occasion to undertake a new application of the maxim, *ubi jus, ibi remedium.*" So also Woodrow Wilson: "There was a time when the thoughtful eye of the judge rested upon the changes of social circumstances and almost palpably saw the law arise out of human life. Have we got to a time when the only way to change law is by statute? The changing of law by statute seems to me like mending a garment with a patch, whereas law should grow by the life that is in it, not by the life that is outside of it," Ad-

III

The history of the valuation experiment discloses significant differences that place difficulties in the way of the development of a law of public-utility regulation which were not encountered in the development of the general law of commercial dealings. Commercial cases are much simpler — each case is generally limited to a transaction between definite private individuals, and does not ramify out to any extent into relations between many other individuals. A public-utility case, on the other hand, involves a whole community. Secondly, the point generally at issue in commercial cases is the effect to be given to words or more or less formal acts. When a rule crystallizes, men can easily take notice of it and adapt their future conduct to it. Utility cases, on the other hand, turn chiefly on things — facts and conditions — which are already established as the inert product of multiple unintentional forces, and which must be the mould rather than the matrix of a rule. Under such conditions any rule adopted is likely to produce widespread dislocations. And, for this reason, finally, utility cases, and particularly rate cases, involve much more openly and clearly so-called questions of debatable public policy than do commercial cases. It may be remarked in this connection, that it is probably not well realized how powerful an influence commercial law itself has had in shaping the broader course of national policy. Each case is in itself so relatively insignificant that the ultimate

dress before American Bar Ass'n., October 20, 1914, in *The Public Papers of Woodrow Wilson: The New Democracy*, ed. Baker and Dodd, ii, 196. And see the opinion of Chief Justice Wilmot in Collins *v.* Blantern (1767), 2 Wilson, 341, at p. 350: "It is for the public good that the common law should give relief. Formerly there was too confined a way of thinking in the judges of the common law courts, and the courts of equity have risen by the judges being too narrowly governed by old cases and maxims." See also Austin, *Lectures on Jurisprudence*, 3d ed. (1869), i, 224: "That part of the law of every country which was made by judges has been far better made than that part which consists of statutes enacted by the legislature. Notwithstanding my great admiration for Mr. Bentham, I cannot but think that, instead of blaming judges for having legislated, he should blame them for the timid, narrow, and piecemeal manner in which they have legislated." For a comparison of statute and judge-made law and an examination of the objections to the latter, see *ibid.*, ii, 641–681.

effect of their combined results is not seen dramatically embodied in them.[25] In the law of utility regulation the contact is immediate and glaring. The decisions of particular cases not merely influence, but are directly visualized as guiding and interfering with currents of economic tendency. Furthermore, for almost the first time since the Middle Ages, the law comes here into direct contact with large groups as its units. In every litigation great corporations are involved on one side and whole communities on the other, and the pressure from both sides is enormous. Law is much less fitted to deal with masses than with individuals. If no two cases between individuals are ever exactly alike, it is clear that there are far fewer elements of valid likeness between cases involving whole groups. The possibility of singling out common elements and basing general rules upon them becomes proportionately more difficult; differences that cannot be neglected overwhelm resemblances, and the latter grow more tenuous and abstract. Each situation is so complex as to be practically unique.

Judges trained in a law whose units are human individuals may well shrink from the task of arbitrating between these contending masses, impelled by the determination which comes from large interests at stake, and animated by the heightened passions which mass interest and mass action always inspire.[26] Is this a proper task for a court? Is it not

[25] Nevertheless, whether or not trade increases, property accumulates and a structure of financial credit is built up, — in short, whether or not a nation becomes a great trading and financial nation, — depends in considerable degree upon whether its commercial transactions are governed by a law favorable to free exchanges and the stability of acquisitions. For better or worse, the adaptation of English law to the needs of trade has affected the course of English history. *Cf.* L. Hennebecq, *Genèse de l'Impérialisme Anglais* (Paris, Alcan, 1913), pp. 144–147.

[26] *E.g.*, the opposition of organized labor to the recent Kansas Industrial Court Act. See Howat *v.* Kansas, 258 U. S. 181. Some students are beginning to believe that rules or principles can be formulated for industrial disputes, and that with their formulation much of the hostility of labor to a judicial settlement of such disputes will disappear. It is contended that in the absence of such rules or principles, the judges have no basis but their prejudices on which to decide such a dispute. For the possibility of a code of rules applicable to industrial disputes, see *The Industrial Code*, by W. J. Lauck and Claude S.

rather a political task for a political body better fitted by its composition and constitution to mediate between competing groups in the community? Should the courts be asked to take sides in what is really a political struggle? [27]

Of course, there are other fields of the law where to a less extent the courts lay down rules which affect the interests of permanent groups in somewhat the same way as in utility decisions. Corporation law is one such field. Every decision

Watts; *The Settlement of Wage Disputes*, by Herbert Feis. For the results of an actual judicial experiment in working out such rules, see Henry B. Higgins, "A New Province for Law and Order," *Harv. Law Rev.*, xxix, 13 ff.; xxxii, 189 ff.; xxxiv, 105 ff.

[27] There is a further difference between the task of developing a law of utilities regulation and a law of commerce, which is perhaps the most critical of all. Not merely are the parties to a commercial case mere individuals, while the parties to a utilities case are groups, but these latter groups find themselves always arrayed on the same side of every case which arises and have not the chance freely to change sides like the individual parties in commercial cases. The significance of this fact will become clearer by illustration. Any rule laid down by the courts to govern a particular aspect either of a commercial transaction or of utility regulation will operate to favor the party who for the time being and in a given case stands on one side or the other of the transaction — will favor either buyer or seller, surety or creditor, the utility or the consumer. Now, in a case of buying and selling, there are no such things as permanent buyers or permanent sellers — a buyer to-day will be a seller to-morrow. Hence, whichever party to the deal is favored by the rule adopted by the courts, a given man of business has as much chance to gain by it in the long run as to lose — for if in one case he happens to stand on the side which loses by the rule, in the next he is quite as likely to be on the side which wins. The rule may therefore arouse the animosity of particular individuals in particular cases, but there is no class or group of persons with a permanent membership whose interests are always affected by the rule in the same way, whether favorably or adversely. The opposite is true of a rule of utility law. The rule may favor utility or public, but whichever side it affects adversely has no opportunity to make up for the loss by standing at some other time on the opposite side of the transaction. A utility is always a utility and to no important extent a consumer, even if street railway companies may to some extent use telephone service. Hence, when a court is called on to lay down a rule of utility law it finds itself faced with the necessity of deciding against one great permanent mobilized class or interest in the state, and to that extent of definitely weakening its position. This consideration has led Judge Taft to argue for a wider scope of discretion for administrative boards: "Many questions that ought to be settled by administrative tribunals with proper authority have been thrust upon the Courts. This . . . involves the Courts in quasi-political and economic controversies which they ought not to be burdened with, and which necessarily expose them to criticism as being prejudiced," *Popular Government*, p. 226.

which limits the discretion or increases the responsibilities of directors or promoters affects adversely an important group-interest. See *v.* Heppenheimer[28] involved issues of policy no less than Willcox *v.* Consolidated Gas Co.[29] So, in an even stronger way, do cases dealing with labor. When the courts decide that under certain circumstances a strike may be enjoined, they enter an arena of political contest where the argument can be made that the task is no proper one for courts of law. It is no proper task for them because such a field of relationships does not admit of being reduced to fixed rules; because order cannot advantageously be introduced without yielding to temporary considerations of policy that the courts do not, or should not, regard; and because, finally, by entering such a field, the courts expose their decisions to charges of partisanship which gravely impair their authority within the area of their proper jurisdiction.

The reasoned argument to support this position is that progress must go forward through the free play of social forces matching their strength against one another and resulting in the final release of the strongest force to reach its goal. Any effort to interfere with this process by applying an abstract law to modify its outcome deflects artificially and to no good purpose the natural and wholesome sequence of events. If society is to thrive, its forces must be free to do their work; policy can recognize and coöperate with them, but the law would not be the law if it did not ignore them. Hence the field is one in which the law has no proper business to interfere.[30]

There is ground for this view in the tendency of some courts to deal unintelligently with issues of this kind. But the view should not claim assent without at least a recognition of its consequences.[31] It would banish law from the fields of human

[28] 69 New Jersey Eq. 36. [29] 212 U. S. 19.

[30] This seems at times to be the view of Mr. Justice Holmes; see his *Collected Legal Papers*, p. 294: "As law embodies beliefs that have triumphed in the battle of ideas and then have translated themselves into action, while there is still doubt, while opposite convictions still keep a battle front against each other, the time for law has not come." See below, note 68, this chapter.

[31] *Cf.* Feis, *The Settlement of Wage Disputes*, pp. 265 ff.

relations which are the areas of social attention, and relegate it to be a sort of village constable watching over interests either more or less secure or else wholly trivial. It would liberate from the control of law the very matters which most threaten to disturb the good order and security that it is the function of law to safeguard. The difficulty of moulding law to apply to a field of social friction and unshaped opinion needs no exposition; but to permit the difficulty to cause the abandonment of the effort is to deny to law the possibility of expansion to meet new needs. Every important legal rule originated in a contest. Let it be admitted that competing social forces are to achieve their results through unchecked collision, and much of the advantage which comes from their friction would be lost in the mutual destruction of extreme by extreme; competition tends to defeat itself when not restrained within rules, as a spring loses its power when released from pressure.

In fact, to make the presence or absence of an issue of contested social policy the test of whether or not a field of human relations admits of the development of a body of law is, it would seem, to set up a mistaken criterion. The question should be approached from a more pragmatic angle. If in any field of human relations situations are of frequent occurrence which, unless adjusted, will lead to disputes and disorder, some standardized way of adjusting them, — that is, some form of adjudication, — must be provided, or anarchy accepted as the alternative. How far legal rules are capable of development to govern such adjudications is not primarily dependent on the question of whether or not an issue of social policy is involved, but on the possibility of isolating facts pertinent to all the cases which may form the basis for a rule. Where this possibility is not present, as, for example, upon the issue of negligence, rules are out of the question, and all that can be done is to entrust a fact-finding body with the application of a standard, and hold that body within the bounds of reason. On the other hand, it is sometimes desirable that the run of the cases should be allowed to evolve from the standards a more definite rule, as the rule that a trustee may not purchase trust property from himself at a profit was evolved from the general standard of fair conduct to which trustees are required to conform. Issues of social policy, many of them debatable, underlie most of the rules of private law. The real reason for the special difficulty of developing legal rules in the fields of economic regulation which happen also to raise issues of debatable policy is that the situations which form the subject-matter of such regulation are generally so complex and unique that the factors which are determining in one case seldom repeat themselves in others. To the extent that this is so, the law must content itself with the vaguer instrument of a standard; but it does not follow either that the courts should altogether refrain from holding the fact-finding body to a reasonable application of the standard, or that they should desist from the formulation and development of rules where such development becomes possible.

A sufficient excuse for distrust of the operation of law in fields of clashing social opinions is afforded by actual experience of the failures of the law in these fields, or what is worse, by its occasional perversion into an instrument of injustice. The trouble, it is submitted, does not go so much to the applicability of law as to the improper manner of its application — on the one hand a rigid artificial and mechanical application of rules and concepts without regard to their intent and meaning, or to the facts to which they are applied; and, on the other, an application of the uninformed personal bias of judges in place of that carefully reasoned development of opposing considerations which the novelty of the cases calls for.

IV

Examples have already been given of the way in which legal concepts can be treated as fixed and empty abstractions existing in and for themselves by their own inherent virtue, and having no other relation to facts than that of being clamped down to govern them.[32] It is application of law in this external spirit which produces an improper and hurtful

[32] See above, Chapter V, pp. 134–140.

interference with the free and healthy operation of social forces. Arbitrary logic is as objectionable as anything else that is arbitrary; perhaps more so, since it is pointed toward nothing real. And yet the rigorous logical discipline which a thorough training in the law involves often tempts lawyers into the belief that a closed circle of logical propositions establishes all the basis needed for a legal rule.[33]

A recent writer has typically stated this attitude. "Every jurist," he writes, "whether he has been some leader of savages at the time of the dawn of civilization, or a modern judge sitting in a court of last resort, has sought for the principles which should determine his judgment in something apart from and above the experience of the race. . . . The judicial process in applying the unwritten law is essentially similar to the learning process by which we acquire our knowledge of geometry. . . . When we teach geometry, we do not appeal to experience." [34] The need for admitting that there is a meaning of "experience" which would make these sentences unobjectionable is eliminated by an argument advanced at a later point in the same book, which seems to indicate that in the passage quoted the word was used in its everyday sense. This argument happens also to be a good example of that method of applying abstract logical propositions as law without any effort to bring them to the touchstone of facts which causes so much of the opposition against subjecting the fields of social conflict to legal order. The argument is to the following effect: The right of the state to regulate and control the conduct of corporations proceeds from the fact that the state is the source of corporate existence, and that corporate existence is therefore a special privilege granted by the state, to which the state can attach such conditions as it chooses. But, in effect, practically all the incidents of corporate existence can now be secured through the form of a partnership. Further, constitutional

[33] To this type of legal reasoning Dean Pound, following Jhering, has applied the name "jurisprudence of conceptions." See his treatment of it in his *Interpretations of Legal History*, pp. 119–124.

[34] E. V. Abbot, *Justice and the Modern Law*, pp. 10, 11.

provisions have established a general freedom of incorporation. Hence, corporate existence is no longer a special privilege, and therefore the state is not entitled to exercise greater control over corporate than over individual action.[35] Conceding, for the sake of argument, the logical conclusiveness of this demonstration, it is submitted that it does not give adequate support to the legal rule which forms its conclusion. Suppose it to be established that a corporation derives nothing more from the state than does an individual; does it therefore follow necessarily that the state may not legally exercise a fuller measure of control over one than over the other? The question can be answered properly only by examining what differences of fact exist between a corporation and an individual, what are the purposes which the law has in view, and what special differences of fact those purposes require to be treated as essential; for legal distinctions are nothing but differences of fact touched into significance in the light of the purpose behind the law. A logical distinction is not necessarily a legal one, and a syllogism does not of its own virtue establish its conclusion as a rule of law.

Legal interference with social forces is hurtful wherever the law pays no regard to the nature and meaning of those forces, but crudely seeks to apply to them rules derived by a mechanical logic from other rules or cases showing formal resemblances which conceal substantial differences.[36] It is partly because law is often so applied that there is so much desire to reserve vital issues for the freer scope of policy. Because many feel that the very nature of law requires it to be so applied, the argument is plausible that a régime of law is not adapted to fields of human relationships which involve significant questions in issue between competing social forces.

[35] Abbot, *op. cit.*, pp. 91–101. For another illustration of the same kind of reasoning see E. Parmalee Prentice, *Federal Power over Carriers and Corporations*, pp. 23–35.

[36] This is particularly true in the field of constitutional law, where unnecessary discredit has been brought upon the law by decisions identifying statutory protection for working men and women with the incapacities imposed upon lunatics and felons, and therefore holding such legislation unconstitutional. State *v.* Haun, 61 Kans., 146.

But this is, after all, an unfruitful conception of law. Its nature sets no such limit. Law, it is true, is less flexible than policy in the ordinary sense, but rightly conceived it is little else than long-range and generalized policy.[37] It omits those makeshifts of opportunism which are designed to secure the temporary advantage of particular individuals or groups, but it strives to embody and treasure up the policy which has been found profitable to the community over an extended period and in a broad variety of questions. Its pigeonholes and concepts do not exhaust its resources, but are only the tools it has fashioned for summarily applying that policy to cases which have become standardized. They are the developed working forms of principles whose scope remains far wider than the special propositions into which they have become narrowed, and which remain free to be fitted to new cases in new ways. Upon a recognition of this operation of the legal process depends whether law will be well or ill applied to novel issues when submitted to it for solution.[38]

An instance of its proper application may be cited from the law of unfair competition. A steamship company, desiring to extend its business, offers particularly favorable terms to shippers who promise to deal with it to the exclusion of its rivals, and cuts its rates at points where it meets competition below those which it charges at other places. A competitor,

[37] *Cf.* Emerson's statement that "law is only a memorandum"; and Lord Bacon's: "Many times the things deduced to judgment may be 'meum' and 'tuum,' when the reason and consequence thereof may trench to point of estate. I call matter of estate not only the parts of sovereignty, but whatsoever introduceth any great alteration, or dangerous precedent, or concerneth manifestly any great portion of people; and let no man weakly conceive that just laws and true policy have any antipathy, for they are like the spirits and sinews, that one moves with the others," *Essay of Judicature.*

[38] The New York *World* of February 6, 1922, contained a report of a speech of Mr. Justice Clarke, from which the following sentences are taken: "The new world we live in brings 'opportunities for pioneer and constructive thinking and action and service equal to, if not greater than that of which the lawyer-framers of the Constitution made so much for us and for all men.' How some lawyers use that chance Justice Clarke tells us as one who on the bench of a high court has been astonished at the trivial cases presented there. Without such experience one can hardly realize the extent to which misapplied ingenuity is converting lawyers into 'casuists rivalling the mediaeval schoolmen in subtlety of distinction and futility of argument.'"

injured by these tactics, was held in the Mogul case to have no redress.[39] There was no showing that the defendants had any preponderant position in the traffic which made it impossible for the plaintiff to retaliate by doing exactly the same things himself. But in Thomsen *v.* Cayser a combination of steamship lines which was proved to have a practical monopoly established a uniform freight rate and offered a rebate to shippers who dealt with it exclusively. The court concluded that this was but a device to maintain and extend the monopoly, and awarded an injured competitor triple damages under the Sherman Act.[40] Both decisions, so interpreted, are consistent. Although practically the same acts seem to have been done in both cases, in the one they were legally justified and in the other not, because of the difference in the economic facts as brought to the attention of the courts.

The example just cited, while illustrating an application of law in a field which may be classed as one of the disputed domains of economic policy, does not display so clearly as some cases of other kinds the situation which arises when the courts are called on to deal *de novo* with an issue involving an unsettled point of social or economic controversy. Such a situation arose when the courts had first to pass on the legality of strikes by workmen. With the disappearance of the old guild system and the emergence of modern industry, employers applied to the courts for relief against strikes. This action of the employers discloses the practical difficulties in the way of holding that questions of this kind are to be left to the legislature, and that the courts should not assume the responsibility of laying the ground-work of law in such a field. Where the legislature has not acted, and where a direct application is made to the courts for relief, any decision, if it be only a refusal to give the relief sought, will have the effect of establishing a precedent, and so a rule of law on the question. Our legal system gives to the courts no alternative. Where thus abruptly confronted, they can only fall back on the nearest analogies which their understanding of the facts

[39] Mogul Steamship Co. *v.* McGregor, Gow & Co., [1892] A. C. 25.
[40] 243 U. S. 66 (1917).

supplies, and which will be happy or misleading as the full meaning of the new situation happens to be well or ill apprehended. In the case of strikes, the courts for historical reasons applied the analogy of conspiracies.[41] In the contemporary understanding of the subject, they could perhaps hardly have done otherwise. But a precedent was thus set which has not proved in keeping with the economic facts as time has developed them,[42] and whatever criticism may attach to the courts must be on the ground that they have not been as prompt to shape the current of decision with the developing trend of the facts as they have been in some other departments of the law.

V

It was a responsibility of this kind which forced upon the courts the formulation of a legal principle of valuation when, in the last quarter of the nineteenth century, public-utility regulation began, and rates came to be fixed by state or federal authorities. In view of the Fifth and Fourteenth Amendments to the United States Constitution, the Federal courts could not well avoid considering whether the rates so fixed were confiscatory.[43] This brought them squarely face to face with the question of valuation. It became increasingly clear with the increasing number of cases that the security of investments required the announcement of at least some more

[41] See Journeymen Tailors' case, 8 Mod. 11 (1721); People *v.* Fisher, 14 Wend., N. Y., 9 (1835). An effort was made to prevail on them to apply the same analogy to the mere existence of a trade union, but this they refused to do, Commonwealth *v.* Hunt, 4 Met. (Mass., 1842), 111.

[42] See criticism by Sir William Harcourt of the attitude of the English courts in 1872; A. G. Gardner, *Life of Sir William Harcourt*, i, 255.

[43] It is true that in the earliest cases, often referred to as the "Granger Cases," — Munn *v.* Illinois, 94 U. S. 113; Peik *v.* Chicago & Northwestern R. Co., 94 U. S. 178; Chicago, Burlington & Quincy R. Co. *v.* Iowa, 94 U. S. 155, — the Supreme Court sought to avoid this question, holding that the legislative body had an absolute control over rates. But in view of the general control of the courts over the legislative body in the matter of constitutionality, it seems clear that this position had to be abandoned. The rule that a rate fixed by governmental authority must not be confiscatory was laid down in Dow *v.* Beidelman, 125 U. S. 680; Reagan *v.* Farmers' Loan and Trust Co., 154 U. S. 362.

or less uniform guiding principles. The courts had commenced by saying that a rate was confiscatory which did not yield a reasonable return on the fair value of the utility property; but what was meant by "value"? At first only two possible meanings appear to have occurred to the judges — original cost, and exchange value. Cost was rejected, partly on the ground that it might be unfair to the public, as in cases of grossly inflated promotions.[44] But "present value," which, so far as it was analyzed at all, was apparently thought of as exchange value, was no doubt adopted for the further reason that the courts seem to have believed that they were dealing with the same question as where a private owner is to be compensated for property condemned for a public use.[45] And they were no doubt influenced also by the feeling that the utility was entitled to a return on any increase which had accrued in the value of its property — that is, was entitled to a return on its full exchange value — "as it stood in the markets of the world." [46] It was only after a time that the economic impossibility of the exchange value theory became apparent, and it was seen to lead into a vicious circle.[47] If, then, the "present value" [48] upon which the courts have said that rates must be based cannot mean exchange value, what can it mean? A possible meaning is "present reproduction cost" — that is, the cost of reproducing the identical property at present prices. The utility companies have pressed this meaning on the courts with unrelenting urgency [49] and with some measure of success, although the Supreme Court has never committed itself to it

[44] Reagan *v.* Farmers' Loan and Trust Co., 154 U. S. 362; Steenerson *v.* Great Northern R. Co., 69 Minn. 353; San Diego Land and Town Co. *v.* National City, 74 Fed. 79; s.c., 174 U. S. 739.

[45] Reagan *v.* Farmers' Loan and Trust Co., 154 U. S. 362; Spring Valley Water Works *v.* San Francisco, 165 Fed. 667; Ames *v.* Union Pacific R. Co., 64 Fed. 165; Smyth *v.* Ames, 169 U. S. 466; Hartmann, *Fair Value*, p. 57.

[46] Brewer, J., in Reagan *v.* Farmers' Loan and Trust Co.; see also language of Peckham, J., in Willcox *v.* Consolidated Gas Co., 212 U. S. 19, at p. 52.

[47] Hartman, *op. cit.*, pp. 80–83; G. C. Henderson, *Harv. Law Rev.*, xxxiii, 902, 1032.

[48] After deducting depreciation, of course.

[49] Hartman, *op. cit.*, p. 104; Vanderblue, *Railroad Valuation*, pp. 96–107.

further than to say that present cost of reproduction is one of the factors to be considered in determining present value.[50] But the reproduction-cost method cannot be consistently applied without producing anomalies and almost insuperable difficulties. Thus, in the case of water or gas companies it leads to the inclusion of an imaginary item of expense for tearing up street pavements where these have been laid subsequently to the laying of the company's mains. It requires the valuation of railroad right of way at its present exchange value, which is greatly enhanced by the presence of the utility as a going concern over any value that it would have in the absence of the utility. It leads to the inclusion of the imaginary expense of acquiring and tearing down valuable buildings which it is boldly assumed would occupy the right of way and terminal sites in urban communities if the railroad were not there. On the other hand, where bridges over a railroad have been built by a municipality, the cost of reproducing them has been included in the estimate of reproduction cost, on the theory that the city was under no legal obligation to build them.[51] In the language of one of the state commissions, "It is an amusing, although regrettable, commentary on the imperfection of regulation to note that the fair-value rule, controlled by the cost-of-reproduction method, is to-day perpetrating the identical evils which its creation was designed to prevent." [52] And, finally, with the fluctuation of

[50] Smyth *v.* Ames, 169 U. S. 466; Knoxville *v.* Knoxville Water Co., 212 U. S. 1, at p. 9. See also Consolidated Gas Co. *v.* New York, 157 Fed. 849, at p. 855; Louisville & Nashville R. Co. *v.* Alabama, 196 Fed. 800, at p. 820.

[51] Minnesota Rate Cases, Report of Charles E. Otis, Master, p. 231.

[52] In re Indianapolis Water Co. (Ind.), *Pub. Util. Rep.*, 1919–A, 448, at p. 465. For a criticism of the "reproduction cost" method of valuation by Judge George W. Anderson, see *Debates in the Massachusetts Constitutional Convention of 1917–18*, i, 521, 522. *Cf.* also Commissioner Prouty: "The Northern Pacific runs through the city of Spokane. When the road was built, that city was of small account, but it has come to be of much account, and in the process of development it has grown up on both sides of this railroad. The Northern Pacific claimed, and it may very well have been true, that the cost of acquiring its right of way through the heart of the city of Spokane at the time of the hearing would be at least five million dollars. The original cost to the railroad was nothing, the right of way having been entirely donated either by the government or by private benefaction. Now to whom belongs this five million

prices from year to year and month to month, the reproduction-cost method necessitates a continual revision, upward and downward, at great trouble and expense, of the rate-base, and subjects the latter to daily change.

Not only has the Supreme Court never held that reproduction cost is the actual measure of "present value," but it has in several instances expressly refused to sanction the consequences of that theory.[53] Meanwhile, the widespread study which has been given to the valuation problem in recent years has borne fruit, and with the approval of the courts many rate-fixing bodies have adopted the practice of basing rates on the reasonable "unimpaired investment" presently represented by the utility property. This method gives to the utility a return on the money fairly put into the business as determined by a competent audit, including all amounts added from time to time in permanent improvements. It thus provides a definite and consistent method based on the underlying postulate of rate regulation, namely that the investor should be protected in a fair return on his investment; and, while not contrary to anything hitherto laid down as law by the Supreme Court, it promises to introduce into the decisions

dollars? Has the Northern Pacific the right to tax the public for a return upon that amount? Whether it has is a thing of great consequence, for nearly one fourth of the entire value of the Northern Pacific Railway, as shown in that proceeding, was the value of its right of way, much of which was due, as in the city of Spokane, to increase in value over its original cost. This question of the unearned increment presents in the valuation of our railways a difficult problem," C. A. Prouty, Address before the Chamber of Commerce of the United States, Feb. 11, 1914, printed in *The Railroad Library*, ed. Slason Thompson, 5th Series, 1913, p. 215, at p. 218.

[53] *E. g.*, in Des Moines Gas Co. *v.* Des Moines, 238 U. S. 153, where the master was sustained in refusing to include the (imaginary) cost of cutting up pavements which had been put down after the gas pipes had been laid. In the Minnesota Rate Cases, 230 U. S. 352, at p. 452, Mr. Justice Hughes pointed disapprovingly to another unacceptable consequence of the reproduction-cost method in connection with the value of land: "The railroad has long been established," he writes for the Court. "Communities have long been dependent upon its service, and their growth and development have been conditioned upon the facilities it has provided. . . . The assumption of its non-existence, and at the same time that the values that rest upon it remain unchanged, is impossible and cannot be entertained." But much of the force of this language was lost by qualifications admitted elsewhere in the opinion.

a certainty and clarity which they at present lack. Accordingly, Mr. Justice Brandeis in his concurring opinion [54] in the recent case of Missouri ex rel. Southwestern Bell Telephone Co. *v.* Public Service Commission of Missouri [55] announced his belief that the time has come for the Court to clarify the law by giving its express sanction to the "present investment" method of valuation, thereby superseding the unsatisfactory "present value" rule of Smyth *v.* Ames.[56]

This opinion should be a landmark as a masterly example of a method of approach which is coming to be more and more necessary as the law expands to the measure of the modern business problems with which it must increasingly deal.[57] It is an essay in legal economics which arrives at its conclusions not merely from a study of the cases, but from a study of the economic facts as well, in quite the same way in which the constructive opinions of our earlier law were based on a study of human conduct and political principles. To-day the law needs to understand the economic facts, because they are no longer so simple that they can be directly apprehended as a result of everyday experience, but have ramified into a tissue of elaborate organization which must be patiently analyzed if its significance is to be correctly grasped. Failure to make such analysis of the complicated problem of valuation is no doubt responsible more than anything else for the present confusion of the law on that subject. For this the courts cannot fairly be censured, as they have only been feeling their way forward until special students of valuation economics developed the different issues which the problem presents, and arrived at conclusions. But a sheaf of such studies is now at hand, and the courts should not hesitate to profit by

54 In which Mr. Justice Holmes concurred.

55 262 U. S. 276, at pp. 289 ff.

56 169 U. S. 466; see above, p. 208, note 20, this chapter. Professor Powell has said of this opinion of Mr. Justice Brandeis that "for the first time a justice of the Supreme Court has ventured upon an explicit consideration of the folly of it all [*i. e.*, the course of valuation law since Smyth *v.* Ames.] . . . Mr. Justice Brandeis's opinion . . . constitutes the most signal judicial contribution to the problem that we have ever had," *Pol. Sci. Quart.*, xl, 407, 410.

57 *Cf.* Felix Frankfurter, "Constitutional Opinions of Mr. Justice Holmes," *Harv. Law Rev.*, xxix, 683 ff.

the light they shed.[58] The "present unimpaired investment" method of valuation has no magic to conjure away all difficulties.[59] But the principles it embodies do not entail a rigid scheme of detail; and if they are in fact the only ones consistent with a theory of rate-regulation in the public interest as now understood, the issue boils down to whether the possibility of some ultimately different understanding should prevent the courts from giving present definiteness to the law in the light of present understanding, in a field where uncertainty and vagueness impair the stability of investments and increase the very disagreements which it is the purpose of the law to allay. In Mr. Justice Brandeis's words, "To give to capital embarked in public utilities the protection guaranteed by the Constitution, and to secure for the public reasonable rates, it is essential that the rate-base be definite, stable, and easily ascertainable." [60] To these requirements the rate-base as defined in Smyth *v.* Ames emphatically does not conform.

[58] See, especially, John Bauer, *Effective Regulation of Public Utilities*, N. Y., 1925.

[59] Vanderblue, *op. cit.*, pp. 136 ff. This is, of course, not the place to enter upon a critique of valuation theory. A consideration of the valuation decisions has been introduced here only for the purpose of disclosing the conditions which surround the attempt to build up a law of public-utility regulation and the primary importance of having regard for the economic facts in the process. It may, however, be suggested that if the "present investment" method of valuation should be thought to work a hardship on investors by failing to give them, equally with investors in property not subject to regulation, protection against the fall in the value of money which is incident to a general rise in the price-level, — the thing which the reproduction-cost method is supposed to do, — this result could be accomplished by first finding the amount necessary to produce a fair return on the investment, and then, in the event that a higher price level should prevail at the time, converting the resulting figure to this higher level by the use of an index number representing the increase. This would do away with the absurdities of the reproduction-cost method and give the investor the same protection more successfully. For certain limitations on the present investment theory of valuation in other than rate-fixing cases, see Nathan Matthews in *Harv. Law Rev.*, xxxvii, 431, especially pp. 457 ff.

[60] Southwestern Bell Telephone Co. *v.* Public Service Commission, 262 U. S. 276, at p. 292. This opinion of Mr. Justice Brandeis seems already to have borne fruit. In the subsequent case of Georgia Railway & Power Co. *v.* Railroad Commission of Georgia, 262 U. S. 625, where the opinion was written by him, the Court said: "The refusal of the commission and of the lower court to hold

VI

The difficulties disclosed in the development of valuation law have been emphasized because they set in relief the problem at present under consideration. This is the outstanding instance in which the courts have used their power to review administrative determinations for the purpose of building up a body of new law, and it illustrates the conditions and difficulties of developing such a body of law in a complex economic field marked by unsettled opinions and by a conflict between mobilized social interests. It shows also the impossibility of the courts' refusing to make the attempt, at least under a constitution which guarantees the protection of property by law. What it markedly emphasizes is that if the courts in making the attempt are not to clarify the practice of valuation by introducing and enforcing certain fairly definite principles, but are merely to take refuge in ambiguities which afford them opportunity to revise at will the discretion of the administrative officials from case to case by substituting their own discretion, then their interference with the determinations of the rate-fixing bodies is not merely not beneficial, but is positively hurtful, in so far as the pyramiding of one purely discretionary power upon another tends simply to duplicate uncertainties for the parties interested. It is hurtful also because, if the courts undertake to intervene in controversies for the purpose of applying not rules or principles of more or less known generality but merely their discretion, they will be in danger of applying, or at least of being thought by the defeated party to apply, their prejudice in favor of one party or the other.

that for rate-making purposes the physical properties of a utility must be valued at the replacement cost, less depreciation, was clearly correct." But at the present moment the law has been more than ever confused by recent decisions. Thus in Bluefield Waterworks & Improvement Co. *v.* Public Service Commission of West Virginia, 262 U. S. 679, the net investment in the property (less depreciation) was fixed by the Commission at $365,000. Reproduction cost new at 1915 prices (less depreciation) was estimated at $398,000. The Commission fixed the value of the property for rate-making purposes at $460,000. This was held unconstitutional because the Supreme Court thought insufficient weight had been given to the great increase in prices which had taken place between 1915 and 1920, the date when the valuation was made.

In fact, one weakness in the operation of law in new fields of disputed policy arises frequently from the attempt of some judges to apply directly, like a clean-cut legal concept, some loose ambiguous generalization such as "freedom of contract," or "freedom of speech," or "inviolability of property."[61] Such a concept, so applied, results in the application of little more than the personal bias or preconceptions or private economic theories of the judge. This gives no proper basis for bringing a charge of wilful "class-consciousness" against the judiciary,[62] but is sufficiently explained by the observation of William James, that "no one sees further into a generalization than his own knowledge of detail extends."[63] Judges see no further into a broad generalization like "freedom of contract" than their own knowledge of the economic organism reaches.[64] When they insist that there is an equal-

[61] "The decisions enforcing so-called inherent limitations [upon the legislative power] are among the most loosely reasoned in our entire case law. There is much talk about inalienable rights on the one side, and about the police power on the other; . . . practically the only criterion that is suggested is that of reasonableness, and to talk of reasonableness, when we are in search of a rule of law, is to offer us when we are asking for bread, I should say not a stone, but a piece of India rubber." Ernst Freund, in *Amer. Pol. Sci. Rev.*, x, at p. 5.

[62] Pound, *Interpretations of Legal History*, p. 63.

[63] *Letters of William James*, i, 65. *Cf.* also Holmes, *Collected Legal Papers*, p. 240: "A generalization is empty so far as it is general. Its value depends on the number of particulars which it calls up to the speaker and the hearer. Hence the futility of arguments on economic questions by any one whose memory is not stored with economic facts." *Ibid.*, p. 184: "In some courts, new principles have been discovered outside the bodies of [constitutions], which may be generalized into acceptance of the economic doctrines which prevailed about fifty years ago, and a wholesale prohibition of what a tribunal of lawyers does not think about right. I cannot but believe that if the training of lawyers led them habitually to consider more definitely and explicitly the social advantage on which the rule they lay down must be justified, they sometimes would hesitate where now they are confident."

[64] These concepts are sometimes elevated into a kind of "absolutes," and invested with a halo, the effect of which Mr. Justice Holmes has evidently sought to reproduce by spelling "Liberty of Contract" with capital initial letters (Adkins *v.* Children's Hospital, 261 U. S. 525, at p. 568). The result is to create an appearance of irreverence in seeking to look behind the veil to the actual facts. An attitude is encouraged which a certain secretary of a Merchants' and Manufacturers' Association is reported to have expressed by saying that "with us the 'open shop' has ceased to be a principle — it has become a religion," Baltimore *Sun*, Aug. 22, 1923, p. 5, col. 1.

ity of bargaining power between employer and employee,[65] it may be either because they are thinking of their own experience in frontier agricultural communities, or because their economic knowledge is petrified into the stereotype of the classical political economy.[66] They are for the moment not attentive to the strict account which the law must always take of actual differences between things, and of the details of concrete reality. And so, no doubt, a good deal of the confusion in the law of valuation may be charged against the fact that many judges as practising lawyers made their original acquaintance with the concept of value in condemnation proceedings, or in actions for conversion or trespass. The lesson which the valuation cases should emphasize is the necessity of dealing with abstract generalizations only in the full light of the facts behind them. To profess that they indicate the inherent unfitness of law to govern in fields where social policy is implicated argues at once disregard of such an opinion as that of Mr. Justice Brandeis in the Southwestern Bell Telephone case, and forgetfulness of other branches of the law as well. For the law could not avoid such questions even were the fields where they most openly arise altogether abdicated to the untrammeled discretion of legislative or administrative bodies. The law of corporations is full of them; and the same touch with economic details which is required to develop a law of valuation is needed also in enforc-

[65] Adkins *v.* Children's Hospital, *supra*, at pp. 546, 547.

[66] Lippman, *Public Opinion*, p. 117. These stereotypes are usually most potent when least articulate; but occasionally they rise to the surface. Thus in the Income Tax Case (Pollock *v.* Farmers' Loan and Trust Co., 157 U. S. 429), Mr. Choate in beginning his argument said: "The act of Congress which we are impugning before you is communistic in its purposes and tendencies, and is defended here upon principles as communistic, socialistic, — what shall I call them?—populistic, as have ever been addressed to any political assembly in the world." It is hard not to believe that it was in response to this invitation that Mr. Justice Field said at the close of his concurring opinion: "The present assault upon capital is but the beginning. It will be but the stepping-stone to others, larger and more sweeping, till our political contests will become a war of the poor against the rich. . . . If the purely arbitrary limitation of $4000 in the present law can be sustained, none having less than that amount of income being taxed, the limitation of future Congresses may be fixed at a much larger sum . . . may be designated at such an amount as a board of 'walking delegates' may deem necessary."

ing that equality of treatment between stockholders which is so troublesome in connection with new stock issues.[67]

In an even stronger degree the same caution must be advanced where the courts are unable or unwilling to lay down specific rules, and where in consequence resort must be had to the application of a standard. In such instances it should not be forgotten that the standard is primarily for the fact-finding body to apply. In tort cases the courts do not undertake to fill out the standard of due care by theories of their own as to what constitutes caution or rashness, or feel in duty bound to overrule a jury whose verdict conflicts with such a theory. It is in the same spirit that they must superintend the application of a standard by an administrative regulating body. The presumption must be in favor of the conclusion reached by that body, and for every reversal the court should be held to give a reason based on a deeper understanding of the facts than some *a priori* theory.

If the courts undertake to carry forward the development of law by constant and careful reference on the one hand to the underlying purposes which the law has in view, and on the other to the changing facts of life and conduct, much of the sound objection to their jurisdiction in fields of social conflict and debate is no longer tenable. It still remains true that the opinions of men and courts will differ, and nowhere more so than in these fields, as to what are the purposes that the law has in view. Such opinions vary from generation to generation and from man to man, and it may well be that in periods of transition the courts will tend to take a view different from that which is in process of acceptance by the public opinion of the community. In such periods it will inevitably be felt by some to be an evil, that they are in a position to affect the decision of such questions at all. The real issue is whether the nature of law inexorably confines it, as Mr. Justice Holmes seems in one place to suppose,[68] to fields where men's

[67] Wilcox *v.* Trenton Potteries Co., 64 N. J. Eq. 173; Hastings *v.* International Paper Co., 187 Ap. Div. (N. Y.) 404; Wilder *v.* Tax Commissioner, 234 Mass. 470.

[68] "It cannot be helped, it is as it should be, that the law is behind the times. . . . As law embodies beliefs that have triumphed in the battle of ideas

opinions are completely settled, or whether it cannot rather be availed of as itself an instrument of change and growth. It depends after all on the idea we have of law, — whether we regard it, like many academic lawyers, as a static system of congealed conceptions, a "herbarium of dried plants," or as a developing body of principles,—whether we look on its province as certainty, or as only the endless but necessary quest after certainty. For even in fields remote from social conflict and debate, the law discloses the same uncertainty and necessity for applying variant views of social policy[69] as in the fields of hottest controversy. We can find no safe haven of certainty by retreating from the law of valuation or of labor to the law of torts,[70] or even of insurance or suretyship.[71] There is a difference in degree, but only in the degree of interest or apathy with which the public regards the decisions—not in the need for weighing imponderables.[72] In fields like labor law and the law of competition, utility law, and constitutional law, there

and then have translated themselves into action, while there still is doubt, while opposite convictions still keep a battle front against each other, the time for law has not come," "Law and the Court," in *Collected Legal Papers*, p. 294. Mr. Justice Holmes no doubt meant only to express a half-truth, the other side of which he had stated fifteen years earlier: "I think that judges have failed adequately to recognize their duty of weighing considerations of social advantage. The duty is inevitable and the result of the often-proclaimed judicial aversion to deal with such considerations is simply to leave the very ground and foundation of judgments inarticulate and often unconscious," "The Path of the Law," *ibid.*, p. 184.

[69] See Mr. Justice Holmes in "The Path of the Law," *Collected Legal Papers*, p. 195. It is interesting that historical scholars have even traced the origin of some of the now technical and arid rules concerning seizin to a definitely political purpose in connection with the power of the feudal barons. F. Joüon des Longrais, *Études de Droit Anglais: La Conception Anglaise de la Saisine du xiie au xive Siècle* (Jouve, 1926).

[70] Rylands *v.* Fletcher, L. R. 3 H. L. 330; Shipley *v.* Associates, 106 Mass. 194; Brown *v.* Collins, 53 N. H. 442; Losee *v.* Buchanan, 51 N. Y. 476; Defiance Water Co. *v.* Olinger, 54 Ohio State, 532; Cahill *v.* Eastman, 18 Minn. 255.

[71] U. S. *v.* U. S. Fidelity & Guaranty Co., 178 Fed. 721; Massachusetts Bonding Co. *v.* Realty Trust Co., 142 Ga. 499, s.c. 241 U. S. 687; Thomas Motor Branch Co. *v.* U. S. Fidelity & Guaranty Co. 153 Ap. Div. (N. Y.) 32, s.c. 211 N. Y. 574.

[72] What is here said does not, of course, apply to property law and some subjects of contract law — but consider a subject like *cy près*, and charitable trusts, or restraints on alienation.

is merely no such intervening scaffolding of technicalities and precedents to conceal the connection between the debatable postulate of policy and the specific case. The law's failures are hence more glaring when it is thought to fail. Yet it is questionable whether, in the long run, more human harm has not been caused, and a greater measure of injustice done, by obscure rules of private law and procedure,[73] backstairs rules of criminal law,[74] rules of evidence,[75] rules of testamentary law,[76] where the courts have gone wrong in some department of their activity not exposed to public scrutiny, than by their spectacular errors in such instances as the Ives[77] and Lochner[78] cases. For a court decision of the latter kind educates public opinion as almost nothing else does. It startles attention, opens up a whole question for examination, and forms a focus around which opinion can crystallize. And here we touch what may be regarded as one of the chief advantages of having issues of social controversy passed upon by courts. It is that there is thereby created an opportunity for a thorough presentation and testing of the issues before an analytical tribunal under safeguards which make for impartiality. A threshing out of the question is made possible such as seldom occurs in a legislative body. The log-rolling, the direct exertion of political pressure, and the resort to a shrewd use of propaganda which honey-comb legislative procedure, are not available. If the actual decision is regarded as unwise, a process of scrutiny has at least been set to work which can seldom fail to fix in a clear light the basic alternatives between which the courts and legislatures of the future must make their choice.

[73] Barnes *v.* Quigley, 59 N. Y. 265; Joseph Dessert Lumber Co. *v.* Wadleigh, 103 Wis. 318; Raymond Syndicate *v.* Guttentag, 177 Mass. 562; Cabanne *v.* Graf, 87 Minn. 510; Flexner *v.* Ferson, 248 U. S. 289.

[74] State *v.* Mainor, 6 Iredell (N. C.) 340; State *v.* Hall, 114 N. C. 909; Spies *v.* People, 122 Ill. 1; State *v.* Lowe, 21 W. Va. 782; People *v.* Hall, 57 How Pr. 342; Lewis *v.* State, 30 Ala. 54.

[75] Emerson *v.* Lowell Gas Co., 3 Allen, 410; Ihinger *v.* State, 53 Ind. 251; State *v.* Glidden, 55 Conn. 46; State *v.* Novak, 109 Ia. 717; State *v.* Storms, 113 Ia. 385; McNish *v.* State, 47 Fla. 69.

[76] Holland *v.* Alcock, 108 N. Y. 312; Tilden *v.* Green, 130 N. Y. 29; and, for the law of trusts, see Sacramento Bank *v.* Alcorn, 121 Cal. 379.

[77] Ives *v.* South Buffalo R. R. Co., 201 N. Y. 271.

[78] 198 U. S. 45.

If, besides, as is sometimes said, the courts are always a generation behind intelligent public opinion as to the aims and methods of the law, it does not follow that this is an unmixed evil. It tends to make progress more solid, consistent, and cautious. A great difficulty in the way of substantial social betterment is that each generation is so impatient of the beginnings made by its predecessors and wants to start afresh from some new angle of its own. The result is little beside a pathetic waste of good beginnings. If stable and consistent gains are to be saved from these scattered efforts, it is necessary that the proposals and reforms of one decade be linked and harmonized with those that went before. This is one effect of submitting the legislation of one generation to the judgment of a tribunal steeped in the ideas of its predecessor. The conflict, if any, which results, is generally no greater than that existing in the body of opinion out of court; and it takes such form as to point toward a synthesis which makes for helpful progress.[79]

VI

If law is to be developed in a field given over to regulation by administrative bodies, the question remains as to whether within certain limits this process should not be carried on by the administrative bodies themselves. They are composed of experts having a much more intimate knowledge than the courts of the technical details which must be so nicely bal-

[79] It is also true to a certain extent and in a sense not objectionable that, as Mr. Dooley said, "th' supreme coort follows th' iliction returns," *Mr. Dooley's Opinions*, N. Y. (1901), p. 26. See also W. H. Taft, *Popular Government*, p. 174, quoted above, p. 103, note 59 to Chapter IV. Professor Thayer's view was contrary: "Great and indeed inestimable as are the advantages in a popular government of this conservative influence, — the power of the judiciary to disregard unconstitutional legislation, — it should be remembered that the exercise of it, even when unavoidable, is always attended with a serious evil, namely, that the correction of legislative mistakes comes from the outside, and the people thus lose the political experience, and the moral education and stimulus that come from fighting the questions out in the ordinary way, and correcting their own errors. . . . The tendency of a common and easy resort to this great function, now lamentably too common, is to dwarf the political capacity of the people, and to deaden its sense of moral responsibility," *John Marshall* (Riverside Biographical Series, Boston, 1901), pp. 106, 107.

anced if the law is not to take a wrong direction. Utility commissions in deciding the cases that come before them pursue practically the same methods as a court. Their written opinions challenge favorable comparison with the opinions of the courts. Are not the commissions, then, rather than the courts, the proper agency to develop and apply a body of law applicable to their special field of action?

The technical equipment which the commissions are supposed to possess, and the limited and specialized nature of their work, in a measure operate to unfit them for the task of developing general rules of law. It is of the essence of legal rules that they should be founded on broader considerations than those which spring from the special class of situations to which any particular rule may apply. They must take into account the habits and attitude of mind of the whole community as gleaned from the sum-total of its transactions. A utility commission, dealing constantly with utility questions and nothing else, comes to see its own problems clearly enough, and drives down to certain fundamental dilemmas which require for their solution a choice between competing hypotheses. The hypotheses of reproduction cost and of present investment in the matter of value-determination are an example. Within its own field these dilemmas are insoluble — to solve them on any other basis than that of arbitrary theory requires an outside view which is more likely to be possessed by a body habitually in touch with a broader variety of questions. The generalizations and precedents which an expert body of specialists develops in the course of its jurisdiction should, of course, form the basis of any rules that are generated. But the narrow angle from which they are formulated, and the fact that they are formulated in such close proximity to purely technical problems and difficulties, strengthens the belief that they should be touched off into greater generality by a tribunal which has under its jurisdiction the whole field of legal relations.[80]

Furthermore, among the rules of law to be developed and applied are those delimiting the scope and nature of the ad-

[80] *Cf.* Vinogradoff, *Common Sense in Law*, p. 133.

ministrative body's activities. These, of course, cannot be left for that body to determine for itself. But one of the ways in which administrative bodies frequently overstep their authority is by building up and enforcing in the exercise of their discretion rules which exceed the scope of their commission.[81] Hence it is necessary that the courts should at least in the last analysis pass on the rules formulated by the administrative agencies.

Closely connected with this consideration is one which grows out of the essential difference between the task of adjudication and the task of governmental administration. The function of an administrative body is to get something done, not to adjudicate controversies nor to mark out and delimit rights. Both these results may follow from its acts, but its action is not primarily pointed toward them. It acts to clear up a situation. Its activity is thus positive, and not what may be called restrictive. It exercises the discretion which the law has taken from the persons regulated, and acts, as it were, in their place. But the development of legal rules can properly result only from a conscious process of adjudicating and delimiting boundaries of action. It belongs, therefore, in the hands of a body which does not keep its own action before it as its goal, but centres its interest on the respective rights of opposing claimants. The point of view of the surveyor differs from that of the engineer. A utility commission, unlike a court, must focus its attention on the particular needs and particular difficulties of the special situation and the special parties before it. It must seek a practical solution of one case rather than a rule for all cases; and this requires that its determinations, if the supremacy of law is to be maintained, must be subject ultimately to the check of an adjudicating body primarily interested in general rules of delimitation between opposing rights.

[81] Gegiow *v.* Uhl, 239 U. S. 3; Southern Pacific R. Co. *v.* Interstate Commerce Commission, 219 U. S. 433; Bowman's Case, [1898] 1 Q. B. 663; Waite *v.* Macy, 246 U. S. 606; People ex rel. New York R. Co. *v.* Pub. Serv. Com., 223 N. Y. 373 (1918).

CHAPTER VIII

COURT REVIEW OF DETERMINATIONS OF THE FEDERAL TRADE COMMISSION, AND THE DEVELOPMENT OF A LAW OF UNFAIR COMPETITION

ANOTHER body of new law is taking shape in the course of court review of orders of the Federal Trade Commission. This board has been but recently functioning, and the decisions now making, or to be made within the next few years, will have the importance of fundamental precedents defining the scope of the Commission's jurisdiction and the courts' area of control for the future.

I

The Commission is directed by the statute [1] to prevent "unfair methods of competition" in interstate commerce. The questions thus committed to it resemble those "unfair" discriminations and practices which the Interstate Commerce Commission oversees in the field of transportation. Questions of this kind differ from the reasonableness of a rate-schedule in so far as the latter, because of the constitutional issue involved, rests ultimately on a legal concept of "value." [2]

[1] Act approved Sept. 26, 1914, 38 U. S. Statutes at Large, 717, sec. 5. When the project of an administrative commission to regulate competition in interstate commerce was first under consideration, so distinguished a lawyer as W. B. Hornblower said in the course of an address before the American Bar Association: "These schemes for control by executive action . . . are, I submit, repugnant to our American traditions and principles. It has always been our boast that no one should be condemned except by the courts after an opportunity to be heard, and upon competent testimony. . . . It seems to me incredible that the American people should consent to have their acts approved or condemned and their property rights and their business rights licensed or outlawed by executive mandate. If this is to become a government by executive edict or by bureaucratic domination, the days of republican institutions are certainly numbered. I for one am not prepared to admit that we are reduced to this extremity," *Reports Amer. Bar Ass'n.* (1911), xxxvi, 304, at pp. 325–336

[2] See above, pp. 207–221.

The unfairness of practices, whether in transportation or commerce, can, on the other hand, be referred to no single conception, but requires the application of a standard to the facts and circumstances of each particular case. It was for this reason that in the transportation field what constituted improper discrimination was stamped by the courts as a "matter of fact" to be determined conclusively by the administrative body.[3] The result could hardly have been otherwise. Unfair practices in transportation exhibit a potentially unlimited variety of types in connection with switching, reshipping, use of terminal facilities, establishment of connections, and the like. The question is as broad as the whole field of transportation facts. On the other hand, unfair methods of competition in commerce have tended to run in certain familiar grooves, so that at least a number of definite varieties have become standardized, and can be identified and labelled;[4] although of course these particular practices cannot be regarded as exhausting or completing the list of all possible unfair methods.[5] The run of the decisions may, however, in time cause standardized competitive methods to be pronounced once and for all as either "fair" or "unfair," and that is no doubt what the Supreme Court had in mind when it said, in Federal Trade Commission *v.* Gratz:[6] "The words 'unfair method of competition' are not defined by the statute, and their exact meaning is in dispute. It is for the courts, not the Commission, ultimately to determine, as matter of law, what they include." In other words, the courts may from time to

[3] Interstate Commerce Commission *v.* Delaware, Lackawanna & Western R. Co., 220 U. S. 235; Interstate Commerce Commission *v.* Illinois Central R. Co., 215 U. S. 452; U. S. *v.* Louisville & Nashville R. Co., 235 U. S. 314; Pennsylvania Co. *v.* U. S., 236 U. S. 351; see above, pp. 159 ff.

[4] W. H. Stevens, *Unfair Competition* (Chicago, 1917), identifies at least twelve such methods.

[5] See *Report of Senate Committee on Interstate Commerce*, June 13, 1914, 63d Congress, 2d Session, No. 597, p. 13: "The Committee gave careful consideration to the question as to whether it would attempt to define the many and variable unfair practices which prevail in commerce, and to forbid their continuance, or whether it would by a general declaration condemning unfair practices, leave it to the Commission to determine what practices were unfair. It concluded that the latter course would be the better."

[6] 253 U. S. 421, at p. 427.

time establish as a rule of law that a particular competitive device is in all cases within or without the law, by reversing a determination of the Commission in a particular case, and laying down a general rule to govern for the future. The difficulty is that, even in the case of common and familiar practices, a method which is unfair when attended by certain surrounding circumstances may be fair enough under others. "Fighting ships" have been held to constitute an unfair method when employed by a concern having a dominant position in the business,[7] while not improper if employed between comparative equals.[8] The same thing is true of competitive price-cutting.[9] For this reason, the fairness or unfairness of a practice often depends on subsidiary facts, and the establishment of hard-and-fast categories is therefore unrealistic and ill-advised. More detailed rules may in time be developed to define the special set of subsidiary facts which will take a given competitive method out of a class otherwise legal; but where such rules are not yet at hand, the fairness or unfairness of the challenged method must remain a so-called "mixed question of law and fact" — that is, a conclusion to be drawn *en bloc* from the facts found by the Commission. What weight will be given to the Commission's own conclusion? There is, of course, no doubt about the power of the courts to lay down as a rule of law whether the method questioned can ever (or must always) be treated as unfair; or to examine whether the finding of the Commission on the question of fairness is within the bounds of reasonable inference from the evidence. The important issue is whether the courts themselves may draw from the evidence their own conclusion as to whether on the special facts of each case the practice in that particular case is or is not unfair. This is a recurrence of substantially the same question already considered in connection with the Ben Avon case.[10]

[7] Thomsen *v.* Cayser, 243 U. S. 66.

[8] Mogul Steamship Co. *v.* McGregor [1892], A. C. 25.

[9] See Stevens, *Unfair Competition*, ch. 1.

[10] 253 U. S. 287.

II

The statute provides that on court review of the Commission's orders, whether in a proceeding brought by the Commission to enforce an order, or by the party against whom the order was directed in an attempt to have it set aside, "the findings of the Commission as to the facts, if supported by testimony, shall be conclusive." [11] It also provides that in such review proceedings the court shall have power to affirm, modify, or set aside the order.[12]

The first case in which the Supreme Court was called on to review an order of the Commission was Federal Trade Commission *v.* Gratz *et al.*, 253 U. S. 421 (1920). The testimony before the Commission showed that the respondents were the Carnegie Steel Company's sole agents for selling and distributing the steel ties used in baling cotton. They were also sole agents of the American Manufacturing Company in a large area of the cotton-growing states for selling and distributing the jute bagging used in the baling process. The complaint before the Commission charged that the respondents refused to sell ties to persons who would not also buy from them their entire requirements of bagging, and the evidence showed many instances of such a practice. It also showed that the Carnegie Steel Company manufactured so large a proportion of the domestic output of steel ties that it dominated the cotton-tie situation, and was able to fix and control the price of ties throughout the country. It was proved that the American Manufacturing Company produced about 70 per cent of the better grade of cotton bagging. By virtue of their sole agency for the Carnegie Company, the respondents held a dominating position in the distribution of ties, which they were using as a lever to force the cotton growers to yield to a like monopoly of bagging in favor of the American Manufacturing Company.[13] On this evidence the

[11] 38 U. S. Statutes at Large, 717, sec. 5.

[12] *Ibid.*

[13] This practice is known as "full-line forcing." See Stevens, *op. cit.*, p. 71. It was enjoined in the decree entered March 14, 1913, in United States *v.* American Coal Products Co., U. S. Dist. Ct., So. Dist. N. Y., and in the decree in United States *v.* American Tobacco Co., 191 Fed. 371, at p. 429. In connec-

Commission found that the practice complained of was unfair, and made an order requiring its discontinuance. The respondents thereupon applied to the Circuit Court of Appeals, under the statutory procedure, for an injunction against enforcement of the order. This was granted on the ground that, while specific instances of the practice charged were shown by the evidence, it had not been proved to be their general or habitual practice.[14] On appeal, the Supreme Court affirmed the decision below,[15] but on the wholly different ground that the complaint on which the case had originally been heard before the Commission was fatally defective in not stating sufficient facts to support the charge of unfair competition. The Court pointed out that in the complaint "the amount [of ties and bagging] controlled by them [that is, the respondents] is not stated; nor is it alleged that they held a monopoly of either ties or bagging, or had ability, purpose, or intent to acquire one." [16] These facts were amply shown by the evidence, but the Court did not look at the evidence. In a dissenting opinion,[17] Mr. Justice Brandeis protested that it was an altogether novel and unheard-of requirement to hold that a complaint initiating administrative proceedings must set out with the completeness of a legal pleading the reasons why the practice complained of was objectionable, that no such requirement had ever been applied by the Court to the practice before the Interstate Commerce Commission, and no such practice was followed there. The pleading held defective was, furthermore, not a pleading in the case before the Court, but in the separate proceeding before the Commission, and the question of its defectiveness had never even been raised by counsel or the court below, but was taken *de novo* out of a clear sky by the Supreme Court.

It is questionable whether the decision can be made to stand on even the ground on which the Court put it. The

tion with the sale of patented articles it was disapproved by the Supreme Court in Motion Picture Patents Co. *v.* Universal Film Mfg. Co., 243 U. S. 502.

14 258 Fed. 314.

15 Opinion by McReynolds, J.

16 Opinion, at p. 428.

17 In which Mr. Justice Clarke concurred.

Court said the complaint was defective because it did not state that the respondents held a monopoly "or had ability, purpose, or intent to acquire one." But the complaint as recited in the opinion itself expressly charged that the practice complained of was pursued "with the *purpose, intent and effect* of discouraging and stifling competition in the sale of bagging." The case thus seems to come dangerously near to holding that as an absolute rule of law the practice of so-called "full-line forcing," even though pursued for the purpose and with the effect of establishing monopoly by the throttling of competition, does not constitute "unfair competition" in such a sense as ever to be illegal. If that is the holding, it indicates a signal failure to take account of the actual business methods by which monopoly is at present pursued. It is well enough to say abstractly, as the Court does, that "if real competition is to continue, the right of the individual to exercise reasonable discretion in respect of his own business methods must be preserved," but in announcing a rule of law the Court should be careful to scrutinize the economic facts which surround the pursuit of the methods called into question, and the consequences which those methods may be expected to generate in the light of current business experience.

Because of the ground on which the Gratz case went off, it sheds no light on the scope of judicial review of the Commission's orders other than to assert the obvious power of the courts to announce and enforce a rule of law. The same thing is true of the subsequent case of Federal Trade Commission *v.* Beechnut Packing Co.[18] Federal Trade Commission *v.* Sinclair Refining Co.,[19] on the other hand, represents a reversal for want of evidence reasonably sufficient to support the finding.

The latter case dealt with a practice followed by certain large oil companies of furnishing pumps gratuitously to retail distributors on condition that only products of the company supplying the pump should be handled therein. The Commission held that this constituted unfair competition. The distributors who received the pumps were not required to

[18] 257 U. S. 441.

[19] 261 U. S. 463.

enter into any agreement not to handle the goods of other producers. It was not alleged or shown that the respondents had any monopoly or control of the supply of pumps through patents or otherwise, and the cost of pumps was not so high as to place any obstacle in the way of competing producers' making a like offer to supply them to distributors. The Supreme Court therefore held that there was no sufficient ground on which to base a finding that the practice complained of was an unfair competitive method.

III

The Beechnut case is important as one of a line which illustrates the development of a rule of law from case to case by the courts. This particular series arises out of a common business practice whereby the producer or proprietor of "branded" goods sells them to retailers under some form of restrictive arrangement intended to bind the buyer to charge a fixed price on resale. The validity of even an express covenant to restrict resale prices was recognized in the earliest cases, and injunctive relief granted to prevent its breach.[20] But in Dr. Miles Medical Co. *v.* John D. Park & Sons Co., 220 U. S. 373, the Supreme Court held such an agreement illegal as a restraint of trade, on the ground that it foreclosed the possibility of competition between the different retailers, who were all bound to market the article at the uniform price set by the original vendor. Mr. Justice Holmes dissented in a searching opinion, and the decision provoked sharp criticism.[21] It must be kept in mind that there was no question of monopoly on the part of the original vendor, whose exclusive proprietary right to his product was unquestionable, nor was there any doubt that the vendor could lawfully have accomplished precisely the same business result as that pronounced illegal by selling, not through retailers, but through his own agents, and fixing the price at

[20] Grogan *v.* Chaffee, 156 Cal. 611; Garst *v.* Charles, 187 Mass. 144; see also Clark *v.* Frank, 17 Mo. App. 602; Elliman Sons *v.* Carrington [1901], 2 Ch. 75.

[21] See A. M. Kales, *Contracts and Combinations in Restraint of Trade*, pp. 31–40.

which these were to sell. If the economic significance of the practice, rather than its mere form, be looked to, it will be seen to be aimed against a very prevalent form of competition which is destructive to both the producer and small retailer. Producers of well-known "brands" in certain lines often find it advantageous to leave the final stage in the selling process to a number of widely scattered independent retailers. The producer advertises the goods and creates the demand, but does not undertake to establish a retail selling system of his own, utilizing instead existing drug or grocery stores.[22] In so far as this practice prevents the growth of great centralized selling organizations and favors the maintenance of small independent shops, it seems a helpful support for a régime of small-scale competition. In each local area these groceries or pharmacies compete with one another, and the small retailer in a single line has also to meet the competition of the large department store. If these rival retailers may compete in the price of the producer's branded goods, his market is likely to be so impaired as to drive him to a more autocratic form of direct distribution. If the goods are popular, experience shows that a large retailer, or more often a department store, will be apt to advertise them periodically at a cut rate, below cost, in order to attract customers to whom other goods can be sold at a compensatory profit. The retailers who cannot afford to meet the cut will cease to be interested in carrying the brand. The practice thus places the small retailer at an unfair advantage as compared with the department store,[23] and, unless it can be prevented, tends to drive the producer into a system of direct distribution, with a resulting combination of producing and selling functions. The fixing of a resale price by the producer is an effort to check this objectionable practice.[24] Of these facts the Supreme

[22] Cherington, *Elements of Marketing*, pp. 153 ff.

[23] In this respect price-cutting on a particular article is somewhat analogous to local price-cutting.

[24] For an economic argument *contra*, see W. H. Stevens, "Resale Price Maintenance," *Col. Law Rev.*, xix, 265 ff.; and C. T. Murchison, *Resale Price Maintenance* (*Columbia University Studies in History, Economics and Public Law*, vol. lxxxii), pp. 89–112, 120–141.

Court took no account in the Dr. Miles case, but looked solely to the formal restriction of price competition. The decision accordingly represents, in Professor Kales's language,[25] "a faithful adherence to the outward form of certain legal rules without, it is believed, any regard for their actual meaning." [26] It was approved and applied in the subsequent cases of Bobbs-Merrill Co. *v.* Straus [27] and Boston Store *v.* American Graphophone Co.[28]

The next step was taken in United States *v.* Colgate & Co.[29] There the respondents, proprietors of certain preparations widely marketed under their brand, were indicted under the Sherman Act for the alleged offence of fixing the price of their products on resale. The indictment, however, did not charge that there was any express contract or agreement between the respondents and the retailers whereby the latter directly bound themselves not to sell below the price fixed by the respondents, but merely set forth that the latter refused to sell to retailers who would not stipulate their adherence to the indicated prices. The Supreme Court, in a very brief opinion by Mr. Justice McReynolds, held that the indictment did not state facts sufficient to constitute an offense, saying that a trader may sell to whom he pleases, and may announce in advance the circumstances under which he will refuse to sell.

Ever since the Colgate case the Court has been busy explaining that that decision does not overrule or conflict with the Dr. Miles case.[30] It has sought to distinguish them on the

[25] *Op. cit., supra,* p. 28.

[26] A later exposition by Mr. Chief Justice White of the holding of this case is illuminating from the standpoint of Professor Kales's criticism: "In Dr. Miles Medical Co. *v.* John D. Park & Sons Co. it was decided that the owner of movables could not sell the movables and lawfully by contract fix a price at which the product should afterwards be sold because to do so would be at one and the same time to sell and retain, to project the will of the seller so as to cause it to control the movable parted with when it was not subject to his will because owned by another." From opinion in Boston Store *v.* American Graphophone Co., 245 U. S. 8, at p. 21.

[27] 243 U. S. 490.

[28] 245 U. S. 8.

[29] 250 U. S. 300.

[30] U. S. *v.* A. Schrader's Son, 252 U. S. 85, at p. 99; Frey & Son *v.* Cudahy Packing Co., 256 U. S. 208, at p. 210; Federal Trade Commission *v.* Beechnut Packing Co., 257 U. S. 441, at p. 452.

ground that in the latter there was a definite contract made by the retailers whereby they expressly obligated themselves not to sell below the price specified, while in the Colgate case there was a mere refusal to sell to retailers who failed to observe such a price. On the latter state of facts the Court has said that "the manufacturer but exercises his independent discretion concerning his customers, and there is no contract or combination which imposes any limitation on the purchaser. In the [former] the parties are combined through agreements designed to take away dealers' control of their own affairs and thereby destroy competition and restrain the free and natural flow of trade amongst the states." [31] Such a distinction seems spectral, and without basis either in the economic facts, or in the purposes of the law. But it may even be doubted whether on the facts of the two cases such a distinction can really be drawn. The indictment which was held in the Colgate case to be defective charged that the producer exacted from the retailer promises of future adherence to the resale prices specified, and that, following these promises, sales were made to the retailer. Under the elementary law of contracts it is hard to see why such a promise was not a part of the consideration for the sale. If so, there was as good a contract not to resell as in the Dr. Miles case, apart from a possible application of the parol-evidence rule. But all that the parol-evidence rule would do, even if applicable, would be to render the covenant unenforceable, and the point of the decision in the Dr. Miles case is that it would be unenforceable anyway. One would suppose that even a covenant unenforceable under the parol-evidence rule might be evidence of a conspiracy to restrain trade. The force of this consideration is emphasized by the fact that in Frey & Son *v.* Cudahy Packing Co.[32] the Court said that no express agreement was necessary, but that "the

[31] U. S. *v.* A. Schrader's Son, 252 U. S. 85, at p. 99. In this case, which was decided at the term following the Colgate case, the evidence showed an express written agreement by the retailer to observe the fixed resale price, and the case was accordingly decided on the authority of the Dr. Miles case.

[32] 256 U. S. 208, at p. 210; opinion by McReynolds, J.

essential agreement, combination, or conspiracy might be implied from a course of dealing or other circumstances."

These cases all arose under the Sherman "Anti-Trust" Act, but they are pertinent because the development which they represent was carried to its next stage in the Beechnut case,[33] in the course of review of an order of the Federal Trade Commission. A complaint was filed with the Commission against the respondents, who were proprietors of a variety of food products marketed under their brand, on the ground that they were engaged in unfair competition by fixing resale prices. The evidence showed that they entered into no definite agreements with their retailers not to sell below the prices fixed, but pursued an elaborate policy, known as the "Beechnut policy," which was designed to secure that result. In pursuit of this policy, the company issued circulars, price-lists, and letters showing "suggested" uniform resale prices, and let it be known generally to the trade that it would refuse to deal with retailers who failed to sell at the resale prices "suggested" by the company. A list of so-called "selected dealers" was kept, containing the names of retailers and jobbers of good credit who were willing to sell at such "suggested" prices. The salesmen of the company were instructed to watch the practice of dealers handling its products, and to report the names of all who sold at "cut" prices. To keep further watch over dealers, it employed a system of symbols stamped on the cases containing its goods, so that any such products sold at cut prices could be traced to the offending distributor. The names of these so-called "price-cutters" were enrolled on a list marked "undesirable," and they could be removed from that list, and restored to the list of "selected dealers," only by giving the company satisfactory assurances that they would discontinue selling at prices other than those "suggested." On these facts the Commission found that the respondents were guilty of unfair competition and ordered them to desist. This order was set aside by the Circuit Court of Appeals [34] on the authority of the Colgate case. The court thought that the only difference between the price-fixing policy condemned in

[33] 257 U. S. 441; opinion by Day, J. [34] 264 Fed. 885.

the Dr. Miles case and the Beechnut policy was that in the former there was an agreement in writing, while in the Beechnut case the plan depended on a tacit understanding; but the court, although confessing its difficulty in seeing any difference between a written agreement and a tacit understanding in their effect in restraining trade, regarded the Colgate case as establishing the rule that a mere tacit understanding constituted no illegal restraint. On appeal, this decision was reversed by the Supreme Court. The Court interpreted the Colgate case as holding that there is no restraint of trade, and therefore no unfair competition,[35] where a trader simply refuses to sell his goods to those who will not resell them at prices which he fixes. It held, however, that the so-called Beechnut policy was a "system going far beyond a simple refusal to sell to persons who will not resell at stated prices," and "constituted a scheme which restrains the natural flow of commerce and the freedom of competition in interstate trade." But the Court thought that the Commission in its order had gone too far, and directed that the order be limited to prohibition of the following practices: (1) the practice of reporting the names of dealers who did not observe "suggested" resale prices; (2) the practice of causing such dealers to be enrolled on a list of "undesirable" purchasers; (3) the practice of employing salesmen or agents to report dealers not observing such resale prices; (4) the practice of utilizing symbols marked on cases containing the company's products with a view to ascertaining the names of such dealers; (5) the use of any other "coöperative" means of maintaining the prices fixed by the company. The limitation of the order to these specific practices seems to be the clew to the holding of the case. The Court does not move from the position taken in the Colgate case that a "tacit understanding" that goods will not be sold to a dealer who fails to observe the price fixed for resale is lawful. But it holds that any "systematic" or "coöperative" scheme for observing the conduct of the

[35] It is interesting to note that the court in this case reasons from the analogy of a statute, the Sherman Act, to aid its interpretation of the Federal Trade Commission Act.

dealer, and ensuring that goods shall not be supplied to him if he violates the tacit understanding, is unlawful.[36] The logic of this position silences reason. In the words of Mr. Justice McReynolds's dissenting opinion: "Having the undoubted right to sell to whom it will, why should respondent be enjoined from writing down the names of dealers regarded as undesirable customers? Nor does there appear to be any wrong in maintaining special salesmen who honestly investigate and report to their principal the treatment accorded its products by dealers. Finally, as respondent may freely select customers, how can injury result from marks on packages which enable it to trace their movements? The privilege to sell or not to sell at will surely involves the right by open and honest means to ascertain what selected customers do with goods voluntarily sold to them."

The present status of the law as to the fixing of resale prices challenges comparison with the condition of the law of valuation for rate-making purposes. Issues of a broad political character are not so deeply involved in the one as in the other, but both situations are alike in calling for a searching analysis of economic facts if legal rules are not to be misapplied. Unless the courts are to develop and apply workable rules to the facts, the principal reason is removed for attempting to maintain the supremacy of law through court review of the determinations of administrative regulating agencies.

IV

In the recent case of Federal Trade Commission *v.* Curtis Publishing Co.,[37] the Supreme Court touched upon the power of the courts to control the Commission's conclusions on so-called questions of fact. The Commission had found that the Curtis Publishing Co., a concern publishing an ex-

[36] It is interesting to note that the indictment held insufficient in the Colgate case charged most of these "coöperative" methods which were held to make the Beechnut policy unlawful. Thus it charged the issuance of circulars and notices; investigation and reports on the conduct of dealers; the maintenance of "suspended" lists; restoration of offending dealers to good standing on receipt of satisfactory assurances, etc.

[37] 260 U. S. 568; opinion by McReynolds, J.

tensive line of magazines, required wholesale dealers handling its publications to enter into an agreement not to deal in other than its own periodicals; that many of these dealers before entering into this exclusive contract had handled the publications of a large number of other publishers; and that the effect of the contract was thus to limit competition by restricting the channels of distribution for such other publishers. An order was accordingly made, requiring the company to desist from enforcing the contracts in question and from making others of the same kind with dealers already engaged in the distribution of magazines and newspapers. The order was set aside by the Circuit Court of Appeals, and its decision was affirmed by the Supreme Court. Apparently the ground on which the decision ultimately went was that the contracts complained of were not contracts of sale, but of exclusive agency, and hence legally unobjectionable; but in feeling about for a basis of decision, the Court stumbled *obiter* into a discussion of its control of the Commission's findings of fact. The language of the statute was quoted, that "the findings of the Commission as to the facts, if supported by testimony, shall be conclusive"; and the Court then went on to say: "Manifestly the Court must inquire whether the Commission's findings of fact are supported by evidence. If so supported, they are conclusive. But as the statute grants jurisdiction to make and enter upon the pleadings, testimony and proceedings, a decree affirming, modifying, or setting aside an order, the Court must also have power to examine the whole record and ascertain for itself the issues presented, and whether there are material facts not reported by the commission. If there be substantial evidence relating to such facts from which different conclusions reasonably may be drawn, the matter may be, and ordinarily, we think, should be, remanded to the Commission, — the *primary*[38] fact-finding body, — with directions to make additional findings; but if, from all the circumstances, it clearly appears that, in the interest of justice, the controversy should be decided without further delay, the Court has full power under

[38] Italics mine.

the statute so to do. The language of the statute is broad and confers powers of review not found in the Interstate Commerce Act." This broad claim of power was doubted by Mr. Chief Justice Taft, who wrote, with the concurrence of Mr. Justice Brandeis: "Because the opinion may bear the construction that the Court has discretion to sum up the evidence *pro* and *con* on issues undecided by the Commission, and make itself the fact-finding body, I venture with deference to question its wisdom and correctness. I register this doubt because I think it of high importance that we should scrupulously comply with the evident intention of Congress that the Commission should be made the fact-finding body, and that the Court should not interject its views of the facts where there is any conflict in the evidence."

Exactly what power of review is claimed by the Court in the passage quoted from the opinion can hardly be ascertained until it is exercised in a concrete case; but meanwhile it seems an excessive deduction from the power to "modify" the Commission's orders. There is no reason why they might not be modified on the basis of the Commission's findings as well as on the independent conclusions of the Court. In view of the language of the statute, it would seem that the former practice was intended. Meanwhile, the Court's claim of power is an indication of the same tendency represented by the Ben Avon case.[39] In no field of the law is a measure of certainty more needed than in that which governs the business practices now under the jurisdiction of the Federal Trade Commission; the Commission was established to relieve business enterprise from the uncertainties with which court decisions had enveloped the Sherman Act [40]; and doctrines or practices which tend to multiply such uncertainty deserve special disapproval.

[39] 253 U. S. 287.

[40] These uncertainties have been increased by the conflicting pairs of decisions in The Hardwood and Linseed Oil cases (257 U. S. 377, 262 U. S. 371) on the one hand, and the Maple Flooring and Cement cases (268 U. S. 563, 268 U. S. 588) on the other. For discussion by I. L. Scharfman, G. C. Henderson, and M. W. Watkins, see *American Economic Review*, 1916 Supplement, pp. 211–238.

CHAPTER IX

COURT REVIEW OF ADMINISTRATIVE DETERMINATIONS IN THE FIELD OF GENERAL POLICE REGULATION

I

CASES involving administrative adjudications under the police power commonly affect in the first instance only the rights of isolated individuals, and do not, like utility cases or other cases of business regulation, bring large organized interests into the forum. The complexity of their issues is only the complexity inherent in the multiple small facts which go to make up the ordinary situations of daily life. It is the same sort of complexity, in short, which marks the usual type of tort cases. The questions which a building inspector, or a health board, or an industrial accident board have to determine are not essentially different from those which a jury has to face in deciding whether a nuisance has been committed, whether a sidewalk was safe, or whether a plaintiff was exercising due care. For such situations it is neither possible nor desirable to develop general rules of hard and fast law. They can be decided only by discretion, and if a strict measure of court review is insisted on, it must be for some other reason than the need for enforcing or developing rules of law.

It is to be noted at the outset that, much as the subject-matter of these determinations resembles that of ordinary tort cases, the form which the proceeding takes establishes a difference which cannot be ignored. It is the fundamental difference latent in the distinction between regulation by adjudication and regulation by governmental control. Under the common law, a proceeding of this character was left to be brought by some aggrieved party. There resulted a controversy between two private individuals, which was settled in a law court acting according to rules of law, or at least in the exercise of discretion controlled by law. The interests of the community at large could scarcely affect the dispute except as they were reflected in the lawful discretion of the jury or had come to be expressed in the legal rules at hand for application by the courts to its settlement. Under the administrative method, government acts directly as one of the parties to the proceeding, often on its own motion. The controversy thus comes to be one, not between private individuals, but between an individual on one side and government on the other. The defendant has the mobilized force of the organized community against him. For a person in this position our traditional law has always been peculiarly sedulous. The principle has always been that the individual is entitled to the protection of the law against possible governmental aggression. And, although it is true that this principle developed when government was not yet responsible to the community and that such responsibility has been subsequently established, it is needful to remember that even a popular government must operate through fallible human agents, whose action may be arbitrary or prejudiced. The danger is especially great in the case of the petty bureaucrats who wield minor administrative authority. These persons are immune from the light of publicity which beats on the occupants of high office, and are relieved by their sheer obscurity from effective responsiblity to public opinion.[1]

The dangers of oppression by small officeholders are enhanced by another feature of the machinery of administrative justice. Not merely does the citizen find himself opposed by officials with the whole weight of the public force behind them, but the very officials who are his adversaries are also the judges in the cause. The health board or building inspector, or whatever body or official it may be, that acts as the adjudicating agency, is generally also the complainant in the case. However honest may be the intention of officials under such circumstances, they are humanly actuated by a desire to justify their proceedings. They are not likely to

[1] See Presidential Address of Charles Evans Hughes, *Rep. New York State Bar Assoc.* (1919), xlii, 234 ff.

decide against themselves in a proceeding to which they are a party, or to go very deeply into the merits of a case to determine whether or not they should do so. There is an ever valid insight in Coke's dictum that the same persons ought not to be judges and parties in the same cause.

These considerations, taken by themselves, seem to point inexorably to the conclusion that when an individual feels himself aggrieved by the determination of an administrative tribunal in cases under the police power, he should in justice be entitled to a full retrial of the facts and merits of his case in a proceeding at law. But the considerations making in favor of the opposite conclusion are exigent. The system of administrative police regulation is supplanting the older method of regulation by the adjudication of private controversies precisely for the reason that there is need for more rapid, effective, and competent regulation of certain fields of human relations than can be administered through the courts. It has been applied only where there has seemed to be some special need for it. Buildings in rural areas are not subjected to the control of building inspectors,[2] and the haberdashery business is not placed under the regulation which applies to the trade in drugs and food. The whole policy of administrative regulation would be devitalized by subjecting its operations to the inevitable delays of legal proceedings, and by subordinating the judgment of experts to the opinion of a jury. That is the inevitable obverse of the shield.

II

These opposing considerations, however, hardly require that the law should be left in the fluctuating uncertainty which at present marks it. A number of distinctions can be taken which point to general principles to govern the relation between the administrative tribunals and the courts. It is possible to distinguish three situations: (1) those which require expert knowledge; (2) those which require summary action; (3) those which require neither. The cases show various combinations of these primary elements.

[2] Though they are, frequently, to that of sanitary inspectors.

First of all, there are cases which require expert knowledge but not summary action, as applications for a license to practise technical occupations, cases involving the condemnation of drugs and non-perishable foods, and those turning on the sufficiency of sanitary precautions. The questions arising in such cases are not matters for general rules but for discretion, and for scientific discretion of a sort which a court or jury is not qualified to apply; and in cases of this kind, accordingly, the courts should give to the conclusions of the administrative body at least the same weight that is given in a lawsuit to the verdict of a jury. The aggrieved individual will be sufficiently protected if the courts limit themselves to reversal on a showing of arbitrariness or absolute unreasonableness of the finding.[3] Where the latter charges are made

[3] This principle has been applied to determinations of the Secretary of Agriculture under the meat-inspection acts: Houston *v.* St. Louis Independent Packing Co., 249 U. S. 479, where it was said (at p. 584) that on questions of fact, "the conclusion of the executive will not be reviewed where it is fairly arrived at with substantial evidence to support it"; Brougham *v.* Blanton Mfg. Co., 249 U. S. 495: "the decision of the department, unless arbitrary, is conclusive"; and to determinations of the Board of Tea Appraisers, Waite *v.* Macy, 246 U. S. 606. The principle was also approved in the following cases of applications for licenses to practise a business or profession: Illinois State Board of Dental Examiners *v.* People, 20 Ill. App. 457, aff'd 123 Ill. 227 (dentistry); Illinois State Board of Health *v.* People, 102 Ill. App. 614 (medicine); Raaf *v.* State Board of Medical Examiners, 11 Idaho, 707 (medicine); Allopathic State Board of Medical Examiners *v.* Fowler, 50 La. Ann. 1358 (medicine); State ex rel. Johnston *v.* Lutz, 136 Mo. 633 (medicine); People *v.* Scott, 86 Hun. 174 (plumbing); State *v.* Briggs, 45 Or. 366 (barber); State ex rel. Coffee *v.* Chittenden, 112 Wis. 569 (dentistry). Under some statutes a direct "appeal" is allowed from the determination of the examining board to a court, and the court may hear the case *de novo*, and overrule the findings of the board: State *v.* District Court of 1st Judicial District, 19 Mont. 501 (medicine); State *v.* Estes, 34 Ore. 196 (medicine). On the other hand, it is elsewhere held that, because the action of the examining board is "judicial," its determinations are final, Van Vleck *v.* Board of Dental Examiners of California, 5 Cal. Unrep. 636. There is sometimes difficulty in getting at the exact holding of a case because of the nature of the remedy sought, *e.g.*, mandamus. In some states it is held that, where the action of the board in withholding a license is arbitrary and improper, the error may be corrected by mandamus: Illinois State Board of Dental Examiners *v.* People, *supra;* State Board *v.* White, 84 Ky. 626; State *v.* Adcock, 206 Mo. 550; State *v.* Prendergast, 8 Ohio Cir. Ct. Rep., 1st series, 401, dictum. But more frequently it is held that even where the action of the board is improper, nevertheless because the board must exercise discretion, or

out there seems no objection to granting injunctive relief in advance.[4]

In cases calling for summary action, on the other hand, like the isolation of persons suspected of having a contagious disease, or the destruction of diseased animals or disease-breeding articles or perishable food, injunctive relief should be denied. It is sometimes stated that subsequent compensation in the form of damages ought not to be allowed because of the possibly deterrent effect which would thereby be produced on officers whose action to be effective must be prompt.[5] The force of this objection against granting any relief at all to the injured individual is eliminated by the possibility of passing a statute whereby such damages would be paid out of the public treasury. The individual has been damaged without cause, and without corresponding benefit to the public; and if his injury is susceptible of direct proof, and does not lie within the twilight zone of differences of opinion among experts, he should be entitled to the verdict of a jury.[6] On the other hand, if the issues are of a technical character, the action of the administrative should be upheld

"act in a judicial capacity," mandamus will not lie: State *v.* State Board of Medical Examiners, 32 Minn. 324; State ex rel. Granville *v.* Gregory, 83 Mo. 123; Ewbank *v.* Turner, 134 N. C. 77. The logical remedy would appear to be certiorari, and this is sometimes allowed: Raaf *v.* State Board of Medical Examiners, *supra*, People *v.* Scott, *supra;* Henning's General Laws of California, ed. 1920, p. 2679 (license to act as real-estate broker; *cf.* Cal. Political Code, sec. 633a, license to act as insurance broker, where a court proceeding *de novo* is allowed with full power in the court to pass independently on the facts); but the scope of certiorari has in most jurisdictions been so restricted as to render that remedy unavailable, Hildreth *v.* Crawford, 65 Ia. 339. See *infra*, notes 13 and 17, this chapter.

4 Lung *v.* Jackson, 85 Fed. 502 (destruction by a customs official of tea claimed to be impure); State *v.* District Court of Cass County, 17 N. D. 285 (destruction by pure-food commissioner of manufactured food products); Nelson *v.* State Board of Health, 108 Ky. 769 (interference with complainant's practice of osteopathy); Weil *v.* Record, 24 N. J. Eq. 169 (order declaring a certain trade a nuisance).

5 On the other hand, a tort action is sometimes refused on the abstract ground that the action of the administrative body is "judicial" or "quasi-judicial." Raymond *v.* Fish, 51 Conn. 80; Forbes *v.* Board of Health, 28 Fla. 26; Seavy *v.* Preble, 64 Me. 120. See above, Chapter III, note 20, pp. 44 ff.

6 Miller *v.* Horton, 152 Mass. 540; Henry *v.* Chapin, 162 Mass. 176; Pearson *v.* Zehr, 138 Ill. 48.

unless there is a showing of arbitrariness or absolute unreasonableness.

We come finally to cases where administrative action requires neither summary execution nor expert knowledge. Examples are cases of refusals to grant a license because of the moral character of the applicant, and many cases of administrative orders for the abatement of nuisances. In the former class of cases the courts almost always refuse to review;[7] in the latter they have perhaps extended review too far.[8] The distinction appears to be one of policy. There is no real difference in the nature of the questions involved, and nothing in either type of case requiring special fitness or expert judgment for determination. On the other hand, cases of the former sort are of much more frequent occurrence than the latter. For the courts to take jurisdiction of them would involve practically taking over supervision of a large part of the petty operations of local government. Yet it is in cases of discretionary action by petty officers that there is the greatest danger of injustice to individuals from governmental oppression. If the consideration of policy could be overcome, it would seem on principle that there should be opportunity for review at law of the facts and merits of many cases of this description.[9] Perhaps the most feasible way to provide a sufficiently broad review without overburdening the existing courts would be the establishment of a special class of courts to review the action of minor administrative authorities enforcing the various non-technical branches of police regulation.

[7] People *v.* Grant, 126 N. Y. 473; People *v.* San Francisco, 20 Cal. 591. Harrison *v.* People, 121 Ill. App. 189; Florida *v.* Parker, 57 Fla. 170; State *v*; Holt County Court, 39 Mo. 521. See also People *v.* Mills, 91 Hun. (N. Y.) 142 (liquor license); Muller *v.* Buncombe, 89 N. C. 171 (liquor license); People *v.* Mayor, 7 How. Pr. (N. Y.) 81 (hackdriver's license). These cases are frequently put on the ground that the special terms of the statute vest the administrative agency with an absolute discretion, and that therefore the refusal of the license deprives the applicant of no legal right. But if the right to work is a property right (Coppage *v.* Kansas, 236 U. S. 1; Bogni *v.* Perotti, 224 Mass., 152, at p. 155) it would seem that this position is untenable, particularly in view of the increasing number of occupations which are being brought under license requirements.

[8] See above, pp. 54, 60.

[9] See Goodnow in *Rep. Amer. Bar Assoc.* (1916), xli, 414–419, 422, 423.

III

In any event, one defect of the practice currently prevalent, which should be corrected in the interest of the most elementary justice, is the too frequent denial of adequate review because of the absence of a technically applicable form of remedy. This is the situation where the administrative agency refuses improperly to issue a license and for technical reasons neither mandamus nor certiorari is available. In such a case the aggrieved party is practically without a remedy. There is a similar difficulty where review by certiorari is denied because the injured individual is held to have an action at law for damages against the offending officials.[10] Relief in the form of such a collateral tort action is always wasteful and circuitous, and resort to it should be required only where, because of the necessities of the case, the administrative action must be so summary as not to admit of waiting upon the outcome of a direct proceeding for review. Wherever possible, review by a direct proceeding should be available rather than by a collateral action for damages. Certiorari is the logical form for such review to take. The difficulty arises from the artificial limitations which have been hedged about this writ because of special theories as to what constitutes the so-called "judicial" action to which alone it is said to be applicable.[11] In some jurisdictions the courts have broken through the difficulty by extending the scope of mandamus;[12] but mandamus is not suited to secure the relief required in any but a restricted class of cases. By statute if necessary, certiorari [13] should be extended into a general "writ of re-

[10] People ex rel. Copcutt *v.* Board of Health, 140 N. Y. 1.

[11] See above, Chapter III, note 16. Indeed, there is hardly any part of the law which in complexity and technicality so much reminds one of the old rules governing the "forms of action" as the law of certiorari, mandamus, and actions for damages against public officials. *Cf.* People ex rel. Delaware and Hudson Canal Co., 117 N. Y. 86, with United States Trust Co. *v.* Mayor, 144 N. Y. 488.

[12] Illinois State Board of Dental Examiners *v.* People, 20 Ill. App. 457, affirmed in 123 Ill. 227; State Board *v.* White, 84 Ky. 626; State *v.* Adcock, 206 Mo. 550.

[13] In many states the effectiveness of certiorari is impaired by the fact that the scope of the writ has been shaped to the "jurisdictional" theory of review,

view" to cover all "quasi-judicial" action by administrative agencies acting under the police power, where summary action is not imperative.

The procedure which has been prescribed by statute, or grown up in the decisions, for review of determinations of in-

so that it brings up only the confusing question of whether the administrative determination was made "without jurisdiction," or "in excess of jurisdiction." This theory is natural and proper where the writ is used to review the proceedings of an inferior judicial court, which is vested with final jurisdiction over the subject-matter in question. In such cases it is properly held that irregularities or errors of law, where not jurisdictional, will not be reviewed on certiorari (Valentine *v.* Police Court, 141 Cal. 615; Wittam *v.* Police Court, 145 Cal. 474); nor will errors of "discretion" be reviewed (Buckley *v.* Fresno County Superior Court, 96 Cal. 119). In some states this rule has been broadened by statute or judicial decision (N. Y. Civil Practice Act, § 1304; Dinsmore *v.* Manchester, 76 N. H. 187); but where it persists, it is often extended to apply to review of the determinations of administrative tribunals with confusing effect (People ex rel. Whitney *v.* San Francisco Fire Dep't., 14 Cal. 479; Central Pacific R. R. Co. *v.* B'd of Equalization, 46 Cal. 667). To make the writ a satisfactory instrumentality for judicial review of administrative determinations, statutory modification of its scope is usually desirable in the direction followed by some workmen's compensation acts: *cf.*, e. g., Henning's General Laws of California, Act 2781, § 67, where a not altogether happy attempt is made to combine the "jurisdictional theory" of review with a proper doctrine as to the review of "facts." Perhaps the best statement of the law, warped to reach a sound result from this unsatisfactory standpoint, is in the opinion in State ex rel. Milwaukee Medical College *v.* Chittenden, 127 Wis. 468: "We must take note of a difference between jurisdictional error as to a court proceeding according to the course of the common law and such error as to a mere tribunal exercising quasi-judicial authority. In the former, jurisdiction of the party and subject-matter being established, the determination cannot be successfully challenged for such error, though the basic questions of fact rest upon insufficient evidence, or have no foundation whatever therein. The judgment in such circumstances may be erroneous, but not reversible upon writ of certiorari for jurisdictional defect. In the latter, a clear violation of law in reaching a result within the power of the tribunal to reach, proceeding properly, is jursidictional error. In the former, the evidence is not reviewable at all. In the latter, it may be reviewed, but only to the extent of determining whether there is evidence upon which the tribunal could reasonably and honestly have reached the conclusion which it did. The evidence cannot be weighed for the purpose of determining whether the same clearly preponderates against the decision. It may be looked into only to see whether there was competent evidence, sufficient in reason, to incline the mind efficiently to the conclusion reached. In the first, a conclusion without any credible evidence to support it, or any evidence at all, is mere judicial error. In the second, want of credible evidence which, in case of the verdict of a jury, would be sufficient upon appeal to require a reversal is jurisdictional error — error committed outside of jurisdiction, instead of in the exercise

dustrial accident boards under workmen's compensation acts illustrates the application of sounder principles of review. The statutes generally provide for review by certiorari or by a proceeding in the nature of an appeal,[14] upon which the courts decline to reëxamine the board's "findings of fact," except to determine whether there is evidence reasonably to support them.[15] The latter question is said to be one of law.[16]

of jurisdiction, where the writ takes hold, performing its function of returning the tribunal to its proper sphere of action." A more direct and sensible method of reaching the same result without any use of the doctrine of "jurisdictional facts" is followed in Jackson *v.* People, 9 Mich. 111; see above, Chapter III, note 79, p. 62. In Noble *v.* Union River Logging R. Co., 147 U.S. 165, a case involving review of a determination by public land officials of the Federal government, Mr. Justice Brown took an entirely different view of "jurisdictional facts." He drew no distinction whatever between "courts proceeding according to the course of the common law" and "special tribunals exercising quasi-judicial authority." On the contrary he divided "jurisdictional facts" in proceedings before both sorts of tribunals into two classes: (1) facts which are "strictly jurisdictional," such as whether in an action at law the defendant was served with process, or whether in proceedings before the Land Department the land patented by the officials was part of the public domain; (2) facts which are "quasi-jurisdictional," as the diversity of citizenship requisite to confer jurisdiction upon the federal courts, or the existence of the non-swamp character necessary to give jurisdiction over certain lands to the Land Department. As to this latter category of "quasi-jurisdictional" facts, Mr. Justice Brown asserted that while they "are necessary to be alleged and proved in order to set the machinery of the law in motion, yet, when established to the satisfaction of the court, they cannot be attacked collaterally. With respect to these facts, the finding of the court is as conclusively presumed to be correct as its finding with respect to any other matter in issue between the parties." The effect of this doctrine would be to withdraw from the courts the power even to examine whether "quasi-jurisdictional" facts were rationally supported by evidence, while on the other hand it would make it necessary for the court to reach its own independent conclusion from the evidence as to the existence of "strictly jurisdictional" facts; and meanwhile it would leave open the critical central question of what facts were "strictly," and what others "quasi," jurisdictional.

[14] *E. g.*, California Workmen's Compensation Act of 1917 (Henning, General Laws of California, ed. 1920, Act 2781), sec. 67; Mass. St. 1912, c. 571, §§ 12, 13. For statutory provisions governing judicial review of determinations of industrial accident boards in the different states, see *Workmen's Compensation Laws of the United States and Foreign Countries*, United States Dept. of Labor Bulletin 203.

[15] In re Burns, 218 Mass. 8; In re Nickerson, 218 Mass. 158; In re Mely, 219 Mass. 136; Kennerson *v.* Towboat Co., 89 Conn. 376.

[16] In re Buckley, 218 Mass. 354; California Workmen's Compensation Act of 1917, sec. 67.

This is a better way of expressing an obvious rule than the ambiguous distinction between so-called "jurisdictional" and other facts, and the statement that as to jurisdictional facts the courts will examine the evidence.[17] The danger latent in the latter form of expression is that it may tempt the Court to draw its own conclusion from the evidence as to the existence of such facts, instead of limiting itself to examining whether or not the board's conclusion was within the bounds of rational inference. The determinations of industrial accident boards are more obviously adjudications than those of almost any other administrative body, because they sit avowedly to determine contested rights between individuals. This is perhaps the reason for the application of a more intelligent doctrine of review, unobstructed by the limitations of precedents applying to older forms of purely executive action.

On the face of the decisions the really critical point in connection with court review of the determinations of administrative agencies acting under the police power is to guarantee to the individuals affected proper notice and hearing in the course of the administrative proceedings. This necessary protection is insufficiently safeguarded. Where the administrative action must necessarily be summary, as in the destruction of disease-breeding substances, preliminary notice

[17] Great Western Power Co. *v.* Pillsbury, 170 Cal. 180; Employers' Assurance Corporation *v.* Industrial Accident Commission, 170 Cal. 800. In the latter case the court said: "Award made by the commission is subject to review and annulment where the finding on any jurisdictional fact is without the support of substantial evidence, and this notwithstanding the provision of the act that the findings of the commission on questions of fact shall be conclusive and final." This language is due to the "jurisdictional" theory of review which governs the scope of the writ of review (*i. e.*, certiorari) in California. This requires the courts to determine the existence of the "jurisdictional" facts: "The industrial board has no jurisdiction to apply the act . . . to an accident not within the provisions of the act," Couter *v.* Simpson Construction Co., 264 Ill. 488, at p. 495. But in order to reach a sound result the courts, inconsistently with the theory, refuse to determine for themselves the existence of the "jurisdictional fact," but limit themselves to inquiring whether there was evidence upon which the commission could reasonably have found that it existed. The typical attitude of the courts is expressed in Milwaukee Coke Co. *v.* Industrial Commission, 160 Wis. 247: "There is evidence in the case

and hearing have no doubt to be dispensed with;[18] but where the question is as to such matters as the filling up of a pond or the stoppage of a discharge of sawdust into a pond, there seems no good reason why a hearing should not first be had, as the delay involved would be unimportant. Yet in both these situations it has been held that administrative orders could be made and enforced without giving the parties affected an opportunity to be heard.[19] President Goodnow attributes this result to a mere historical survival of old common-law methods for the abatement of a nuisance by private self-help,[20] "the sanitary officer possessing in theory the powers possessed by private individuals under the early English law. . . . The courts usually justify their decisions as to the remediless position of the individual by calling attention to the necessity of haste and the consequent impossibility of providing a hearing. The argument is valid with respect to cases of infectious disease, impure food and a series of similar matters. It is not valid, however, in cases such as reconstruction of buildings which when erected conformed to the law; but in such cases it is commonly the rule that no hearing is either provided by law or granted by the police authorities. Cases are too common where orders are issued by health or other police authorities, the compliance with which involves the expenditure of large sums of money, where the house-owner has never had the slightest opportunity to be heard and first learns of the proceedings through the service on him

which supports the findings of fact made by the Commission, hence it cannot be said that the board acted without or in excess of its powers, even though this court, if trying the fact, might reach a different conclusion. If there was substantial credible evidence supporting the findings of the Commission, the courts cannot interfere"; and again in Western Indemnity Co. *v.* Pillsbury, 170 Cal. 686: "The power of review extends to the inquiry whether a finding of a jurisdictional fact is wholly without the support of any substantial evidence. . . . The court may, under a writ of certiorari, inquire into the sufficiency of the evidence to sustain findings of the jurisdictional facts underlying the power of the commission to award compensation." In California this doctrine has been embodied in the statute.

18 North American Cold Storage Co. *v.* Chicago, 211 U. S. 306.

19 People ex rel. Copcutt *v.* Board of Health, 140 N. Y. 1; Commonwealth *v.* Sisson, 189 Mass. 247.

20 *Rep. Amer. Bar Assoc.* (1916), xlvi, 414.

of the order." [21] It should be held essential to due process that statutes authorizing administrative exercise of the police power in such instances should carry a requirement of proper notice and hearing. The clumsy resort to a subsequent damage suit against the officials, which almost never affords an adequate remedy, can then be dispensed with, and judicial review placed on a proper footing.

IV

A factor which should always be given due weight in the development of guiding principles as to the scope of court review is the relative prominence of the particular administrative agency to whose acts review is to be applied. This consideration has found tacit recognition in the rule which restricts the scope of the remedies available against certain high officers.[22] Where a governmental agency is sufficiently outstanding to be under the influence of public scrutiny and opinion, there is not the same necessity for judicial scrutiny of its discretion as to matters of fact and policy that there is in the case of minor officials whose obscurity offers a cloak to arbitrary action. Therefore, although the Interstate Commerce Commission often acts in the dual capacity of complainant and judge, the danger of its becoming an instrument of oppression is not sufficiently real to require or justify court review of its findings on the merits when balanced against the

[21] The situation criticised by President Goodnow is forcefully illustrated by the notorious English case of Local Government Board *v.* Arlidge, [1915] A. C. 120; [1914] 1 K. B. 160, where it was held in substance that an order of an administrative tribunal was not vitiated by the fact that the person against whom the order was directed was not permitted to have an oral hearing or access to evidence presented by the complainant. For criticism and discussion see note in *Harv. Law Rev.*, xxviii, 198; Pound, *Proceedings New Hampshire Bar Assoc.* (1917), p. 13; Dicey, *Law of the Constitution*, 8th ed., pp. xxxvii–xlvii.

[22] Judicial process will not issue to the Chief Executive, see People *v.* Bissell, 19 Ill. 229 (state governor); heads of executive departments of state are not liable in damages for their acts, Stokes *v.* Kendall, 12 Peters, 524; see also Spalding *v.* Vilas, 161 U. S. 483. But the state courts are in conflict on the question whether mandamus will issue to the governor to compel him to perform a "ministerial" act. Twelve states hold in the affirmative, seventeen in the negative. See H. F. Kumm in *Minnesota Law Review*, ix, 21; 6 L. R. A. (N. S.) 750; 32 L. R. A. (N. S.) 355; *Harv. Law Rev.*, xii, 208.

consideration of its special fitness to deal with the matters that come before it. In lesser degree the same consideration applies to utility commissions in the states.

On the other hand, the comparative obscurity of many so-called expert bodies in state and local administration may well counterbalance any argument that can be drawn from their supposed technical qualifications in favor of allowing them a wide freedom from court control. As matters stand, although these bodies are theoretically composed of experts, the facts are often otherwise. A recent enumeration mentions a commissioner of health in an American city who was a harness-maker; a commissioner of public utilities who was a barber; a commissioner of sanitation who was a house-mover; and another commissioner of health who was an undertaker.[23] The law must adapt itself to the society which it finds, and facts such as these cannot be minimized. The development of popular government since Coke has largely diminished the need for the courts to act as a protection for the individual against oppression by the great central organs of government; but popular government has brought its own evils, which are nowhere so evident as in the sedimentary levels of its administrative officialdom.

[23] Raymond B. Fosdick in *New Republic*, xxvi, 152. In this connection words written by Charles Francis Adams in 1878 *à propos* of the membership of state railroad commissions are still pertinent: "In America there are not many specialists, nor have the American people any great degree of faith in them. . . . Accordingly, in making up commissions to deal with the most complicated issues arising out of our modern social and industrial organization, those in authority are very apt to conclude that one man can do the work about as well as another. . . . The executives of the states in selecting the members [of the railroad commissions] seemed to regard any antecedent familiarity with the railroad system as a total disqualification. . . . Farmers, land surveyors, men of business and politicians were selected," *Railroads, Their Origin and Problems* (N. Y., 1878), pp. 132, 133.

CHAPTER X

COURT REVIEW OF DETERMINATIONS MADE IN THE ADMINISTRATION OF THE BUSINESS OF GOVERNMENT

Administrative determinations which touch private interests are made not only when government is interfering directly with conduct or property for purposes of economic regulation or police control, but also when it is providing for its own existence, managing its own business and disposing of its property. The two situations differ in that the interference involved in the former cases is the gist of the government's action, while in the latter it is relatively incidental and secondary. Recent developments, however, have introduced complications into any attempt to thus distinguish between the activities of government as an operating agency and its exercise of its function of regulation. For modern government responds to the demand for introducing order into a congested civilization not only by extending its supervision over ever more lines of human conduct, but also by undertaking itself to perform directly many services which formerly were left to private enterprise.[1] In its capacity of public-service corporation, determinations affecting individual interests are made in the course of managing the government's business, as, for example, in administering the post-office, which otherwise would belong to its regulatory function. And so, in discussing the application of law to administrative determinations made as part of carrying on the business of government, we must be alert to distinguish between a number of situations which call for the application of very different principles.

[1] *E. g.*, the post-office; Federal operation of railways; and the ownership and management of water and lighting systems by municipalities.

I

The basic type of cases in this field are those which concern the relations of governmental officers among themselves, involving the respective rights and duties of superior and inferior, the power of dismissal, and the rules of promotion. In such matters, whether or not closely governed by statutes, the courts interfere as little as possible. Public office is not private property and vested interests are not at stake.[2] Every consideration of operating efficiency, on the contrary, demands that free discretion should be allowed executives to mould the organization of their offices flexibly to the requirements of their policy, unhampered by strict rules of law, and undelayed by a resort to court proceedings.[3] Discipline must be maintained in a way that would not be possible if subordinates could appeal over the heads of their superiors to a law court. It has therefore been held that the power of appointment carries with it the power of removal or dismissal in the uncontrolled discretion of the appointing officer,[4] and statutes seeming to limit the power have been strictly construed so as to preserve it. The cases have gone far. In Parsons *v.* United States [5] a statute providing that United States district attorneys should be appointed for a term of four years, was construed to mean for a term of four years, unless cut short by prior removal. In Shurtleff *v.* United States [6] a statute creating the office of general appraiser provided that the officer might be removed at any time "for

[2] Butler *v.* Pennsylvania, 10 How. 402; Crenshaw *v.* United States, 134 U.S. 99; United States *v.* Fisher, 109 U.S. 143; People *v.* Devlin, 33 N. Y. 269.

[3] An injunction will not be granted to restrain an appointment or removal or reassignment of duties of a public employee, though in violation of law, White *v.* Berry, 171 U. S. 366. For an argument by a civil-service reformer in favor of leaving a wide discretionary power of removal to heads of departments to enable them to maintain discipline and efficiency, see W. D. Foulke's careful "Brief in Opposition to Exclusive Power over Removals by Civil-Service Commissions," printed as an appendix to his *Fighting the Spoilsmen*, pp. 326 ff.

[4] Ex parte Hennen, 13 Peters, 230, where the incumbent was removed merely to make room for a personal friend of the appointing officer; State *v.* Curtis, 180 Ind. 191; Town of Davis *v.* Filler, 47 W. Va. 413, 6.

[5] 167 U. S. 324.

[6] 189 U. S. 311.

inefficiency, neglect of duty or malfeasance in office." It was decided that the enumeration of specific grounds did not deprive the appointing power of the right to remove for other reasons, or for none at all. In Reagan *v.* United States,[7] where a statute provided for removal "for causes prescribed by law," and no causes were affirmatively specified by statute, the power of removal was held to be absolute.

The need for greater efficiency in the public service has sometimes been thought to require a more secure and less capricious tenure for civil officials. Civil-service laws passed with this public end in view would be of small avail had they not necessarily been construed to confer private rights on the holders of the protected positions.[8] But the degree of protection given by such laws depends in large measure on the attitude of the courts, which is not favorable to close scrutiny of the acts of the removing power. Thus, where a statute provides that an officer or employee may be removed only after charges have been preferred against him and an opportunity given him to defend himself, it has been decided that if these procedural requirements of notice and hearing have been met, the courts will not go behind a determination ordering his removal.[9] Again, where the statute provides that removals may be made only for specified causes, it is settled law that the power of removal cannot be exercised without due notice and after an opportunity to be heard;[10] but even here it has been held that the courts will not review the findings to see whether the statutory cause of removal has in fact been made out.[11] Nor does the protection of the

[7] 182 U. S. 419.

[8] People *v.* New York Civil Service Board, 5 App. Div. (N. Y.) 164; United States *v.* Wickersham, 201 U. S. 390.

[9] Dullam *v.* Willson, 53 Mich. 392; In re Guden, 171 N. Y. 529; People *v.* Brady, 166 N. Y. 44.

[10] In re Guden, 171 N. Y. 529, 64 N. E. 451; Ham *v.* Boston Police Board 142 Mass. 90; Benson *v.* People (Col. Ap.) 50 Pac. 212; Willard's Appeal, 4 R. I. 597; State *v.* Hawkins, 44 Ohio St. 98, at p. 115; Biggs *v.* McBride, 17 Ore. 640; Shurtleff *v.* United States, 189 U. S. 311.

[11] State *v.* Frazier, 48 Ga. 137; State *v.* Hay, 45 Neb. 321; State *v.* Wilson, 121 N. C. 425; State *v.* Hawkins, *supra; contra,* State *v.* Henry, 60 Fla. 246. The New York law is *contra.* See below.

civil-service laws prevent summary dismissals for "economy,"[12] unless economy is assigned as a reason under circumstances showing that it is palpably false.[13] The prevailing attitude of the courts was expressed in Keim *v.* United States:[14] "It has been repeatedly adjudged that the courts have no general supervising power over the proceedings and actions of the various administrative departments of the government. . . . The interference of the courts with the performance of the ordinary duties of the executive departments would be productive of nothing but mischief and we are quite satisfied that such a power was never intended to be given to them."

In New York, however, the power of removal from office for cause has been held to be a "judicial" power, so that a determination made in its exercise is reviewable on certiorari,[15] and on such review the courts may examine the facts and quash a determination without evidence reasonably to support it.[16] But this situation is exceptional, and even in New York the courts will not entertain certiorari except where the power of removal is restricted to a removal for cause.[17] Again, the New York courts have exercised a fairly broad review of determinations made by the state Civil Service Commission. Thus it has been held that, where the Commission is given power to determine whether or not it is practicable to select a particular class of employees by competitive examination, the question is one of law for the courts, and the determination of the Commission will be reviewed when the facts as to the nature and duties of the position have been

[12] Phillips *v.* Mayor, etc., 88 N. Y. 245; People *v.* Mayor, 149 N. Y. 215; People *v.* Dalton, 32 Misc. (N. Y.) 109; Stivers *v.* Jersey City, 70 N. J. Law, 606.

[13] United States *v.* Wickersham, 201 U. S. 390; Jones *v.* Willcox, 80 App. Div. (N. Y.) 167.

[14] 177 U. S. 290.

[15] People *v.* Nichols, 79 N. Y. 582.

[16] People ex rel. Masterson *v.* French, 110 N. Y. 494; People ex rel. Hogan *v.* French, 119 N. Y. 493; People *v.* Wright, 7 App. Div. (N. Y.) 185. In the two latter cases the court in effect decided on its own opinion as to the weight of the evidence.

[17] People *v.* Brady, 166 N. Y. 44.

ascertained;[18] but where the question is a fairly debatable one as to which men may reasonably differ, the courts will not substitute their conclusion for that of the Commission.[19] Where the name of an applicant should have been placed on the eligible list but was not, the courts will compel the Commission to place it there;[20] but they will not disturb a classification by the Commission which is not unreasonable.[21]

The arguments against judicial interference with the appointment and removal of public officials apply with greater force in the case of persons employed in the military and naval services;[22] and here the requirements of discipline are such that it is necessary to allow even the rights of life and liberty of persons in the service to be concluded by the judgment of courts martial.[23]

II

Next may be put cases where government comes into contact with private individuals in the exercise of a power essential to its own existence, as when it requires them to pay taxes, or drafts them to serve in the army or navy. Here from the point of view of the individual the need for protection against oppression is the same as that which sets limits to governmental exercise of the police power. On the other hand, the governmental functions concerned are fundamental to the existence of government itself, and so to the good order and welfare of society. There is accordingly a stronger argument against impairing executive efficiency by court review.

[18] Chittenden *v.* Wurster, 152 N. Y. 345.

[19] People *v.* McWilliams, 185 N. Y. 92.

[20] People *v.* Civil Service Commission, 13 App. Div. (N. Y.) 309. The Civil Service Commission may not alter its eligible list on the ground of fraud unless in the judgment of the court there was fraud in fact, People *v.* McBride, 226 N. Y. 252.

[21] Simons *v.* McGuire, 204 N. Y. 253, 97 N. E. 526.

[22] Crenshaw *v.* United States, 134 U. S. 99; Blake *v.* United States, 103 U. S. 227; Reaves *v.* Ainsworth, 219 U. S. 296; In re Giddings, 22 Pick. (Mass.) 406; Shattuck *v.* Gilson, 19 N. H. 296; In re Opinion of Justices, 4 R. I. 585; People *v.* Hill, 126 N. Y. 497.

[23] In re Reed, 100 U. S. 13; Smith *v.* Whitney, 116 U. S. 167; Johnson *v.* Sayre, 158 U. S. 109.

This argument seems to justify the courts in limiting their review to very narrow scope in the draft cases.[24]

In considering the tax cases a number of distinctions must be taken. Cases like Murray's Lessee *v.* Hoboken Land Co.,[25] are really disputes between the government and one of its own revenue officers, where the principles governing the relations of subordinate and superior apply, and the courts should so far as possible refuse to interfere. On the other hand, where the dispute is between the government and a private taxpayer, two of the same principles come into play as in administrative exercise of the police power. Where it is mainly expert knowledge and judgment which are required to settle the issues, the courts should treat as conclusive the determination of the proper officials. This is often true, for instance, in cases involving administration of the customs and internal-revenue laws. Whether or not this task is to be regarded as the interpretation of law, it is, in most instances, a technical matter, and only by leaving it to the determination of the administrative officials themselves can a helpful uniformity of decision, and ultimately a body of consistent administrative practice, be built up. This is not a field for the development of general rules of law but rather for the evolution of rules of technical practice. This seems the real justification for decisions like Cary *v.* Curtis,[26] Bartlett *v.* Kane,[27] and Hilton *v.* Merritt.[28] On the other hand, that the courts need to scrutinize the record for the purpose of developing rules of general law to meet situations which are important enough to demand such rules is fairly shown by the Stock Dividend case.[29] Sometimes only a general rule of law can

[24] See my *Building of an Army* (Century Co., New York, 1922), pp. 178–185; Angelus *v.* Sullivan, 246 Fed. 54; Boitano *v.* Dist. Board, 250 Fed. 812; ex parte Kitzerow, U. S. District Court for Eastern District of Wisconsin, reported in Department of Justice, *Interpretation of War Statutes Bulletin,* No. 98. But it was said that the decisions of the draft boards would be sustained only where there was "evidence to support the finding," ex parte Blazekovic, 248 Fed. 347, Pascher *v.* Kinkead, 250 Fed. 692, ex parte Romano, 251 Fed. 762; and would be reviewed by the courts upon a question of law going to the board's jurisdiction, Matter of MacDonald, 253 Fed. 99.

[25] 18 How. 272. [26] 3 How. 236. [27] 16 How. 263.

[28] 110 U. S. 105. [29] Eisner *v.* McComber, 252 U. S. 89.

give the needed certainty for an important and doubtful situation of frequent occurrence; and a rule of this nature, as we have seen, can properly come only from a law court.

Another factor which should move the discretion of the courts in determining whether or not to review in tax cases is one which was also suggested in considering police regulation — namely, the prominence and tenure of the officers whose acts or determinations are questioned. There is a sound principle in cases like Field *v.* Clark.[30] From acts of aggression and arbitrary oppressiveness the citizen ought to be protected against great officers as against small; but where the question is not one of arbitrary action but merely of the reasonable or unreasonable exercise of discretion, the protection of the courts is not so vital where the competency of the officer is subject to public scrutiny and correction. As a general rule, then, for cases involving the exercise of the taxing power, we may say that the courts ought to review the merits of the exercise of discretion only in cases of action by petty officials in matters calling for no expert or technical judgments of fact.

This protection, however, is not accorded to the taxpayer in as full measure as it might be. President Goodnow has thus described the existing situation: "The individual is by the American law of taxation quite commonly subjected to the arbitrary discretion of the tax authorities, so far as concerns questions of assessment and valuation; and because of the inadequacy of the judicial remedies available finds it difficult, — if not impossible, — in many cases, to secure a judicial review even of questions of law. This is particularly true of the smaller taxpayers." [31]

It has been held by the Supreme Court that the "due process" clause of the Constitution does not require that there should be an opportunity to review judicially assessments made by tax officials.[32] It has also been said that "due process" as applied to the assessment and collection of taxes

[30] 143 U. S. 646. See also Louisiana *v.* McAdoo, 234 U. S. 627.

[31] *Rep. Amer. Bar Assoc.* (1916), xli, 408, at p. 414.

[32] McMillen *v.* Anderson, 95 U. S. 37.

does not imply the right to such notice and hearing as are considered to be essential to the validity of the proceedings of judicial tribunals.[33] It has been held, for instance, that notice by statute need be the only notice given, and the Court has said: "Nor is there any hardship in this matter. The Board [of Equalization] has its time of sitting, fixed by law. Its sessions are not secret. No obstructions exist to the appearance of anyone before it to assert a right or redress a wrong, and in the business of assessing taxes this is all that can reasonably be asked. As all valuation of property is more or less a matter of opinion, we see no reason why the opinion of the court should be better or should be substituted for that of the Board whose opinion the law has declared to be the one to govern the matter." [34] The doctrine of Murray's Lessee *v.* Hoboken Land Co.[35] has in fact been extended from disputes between the government and its tax collectors to the relation between government and taxpayer.[36] But the Court, in cases where it has expressed these views, has generally said or implied that the taxpayer would be entitled to injunctive relief against a tax absolutely illegal, or at least might bring an action at law to recover the amount of such a tax paid under protest.[37] In short, the effect of the decisions is that there need be no judicial review of the determinations of tax officials on questions of assessment or valuation, although such review is constitutionally necessary as to the legal question of liability to the tax.

Accordingly, it is the prevailing rule that the valuation of property for taxation by the administrative authorities is final and conclusive upon the courts in any action brought by the taxpayer to contest the tax.[38] Some courts, however, have held, even in the absence of statute, that where the tax

[33] Kentucky Railroad Tax cases, 115 U. S. 321, at p. 331. See also the Bimetallic case, 239 U. S. 441.

[34] State Railroad Tax cases, 92 U. S. 575, at p. 610.

[35] 18 How. 272.

[36] Davidson *v.* New Orleans, 96 U. S. 97, at p. 107.

[37] McMillen *v.* Anderson, 95 U. S. 37, at p. 42; Davidson *v.* New Orleans, 96 U. S. 97, at p. 105.

[38] San José Gas Co. *v.* January, 57 Cal. 614; Bank *v.* San Francisco, 142 Cal. 272, at p. 288; Birch *v.* County of Orange, 59 Cal. App. 133.

officials have proceeded arbitrarily and in wilful disregard of the law so as to impose unequal burdens upon certain taxpayers, or where there has been "a grossly inequitable and palpably excessive over-valuation," the assessment will be treated as "constructively fraudulent," and the taxpayer may recover the excess taxes paid.[39] Elsewhere statutes impose upon the courts the duty of amending assessments when satisfied that the assessed valuation is too great.[40]

In general, however, the protection accorded the taxpayer against arbitrary assessment is sporadic and uncertain. The tendency of the courts is against granting relief. Their attitude has been expressed by the Supreme Court: "It is upon taxation that the several states chiefly rely to obtain means to carry on their respective governments and it is of the utmost importance to them that the modes adopted to enforce the taxes levied should be interfered with as little as possible. Any delay in the proceedings of the officers upon whom the duty has devolved of collecting the taxes may derange the operations of government and thereby cause serious detriment to the public."[41]

No fault can properly be found with this refusal of the courts to revise the findings of administrative officials on questions of valuation where not beyond the bounds of reasonableness. The real basis of criticism of the judicial review available in tax cases is the almost insuperable difficulty experienced by the aggrieved taxpayer in securing judicial relief against unfair and discriminatory assessments and even against the collection of palpably illegal taxes. Much of this difficulty is due to procedural obstacles which effectively block up all channels of substantial relief. Thus it has been held in New York that an assessment for taxes is in the nature of a judgment, which cannot be attacked collaterally, and that therefore no suit can be brought to recover taxes

[39] Birch *v.* County of Orange, 186 Cal. 736; Gold Mines *v.* Stevens County, 91 Wash. 437; Southern Oregon Co. *v.* Coos County, 39 Ore. 185; Danforth *v.* Livingston, 23 Mont. 558; Keokuk Bridge Co. *v.* People, 161 Ill. 514; People's Gas Light Co. *v.* Stuckart, 286 Ill. 164.

[40] Royal Mfg. Co. *v.* Rahway, 75 N. J. Law, 416.

[41] Dows *v.* Chicago, 11 Wall. 108, at p. 110.

paid under protest, because such a suit is a collateral attack.[42] Again it has been held that where a tax is invalid, an injunction against its enforcement will not be granted, on the theory that to grant such an injunction would be to recognize a nullity.[43] One of the outstanding defects long noticed by economists in the so-called general property tax which supplies so large a part of the revenue of our state and local governments is the gross inequality of assessment which almost always characterizes its administration.[44] The helplessness of the taxpayer is illustrated by the case of Mercantile National Bank *v.* The Mayor.[45] There personal property in the city of New York was assessed for taxation at its full value. The taxpayer claimed that, inasmuch as real estate in the same city was assessed at not more than sixty per cent of its value, personal property should be assessed accordingly. He therefore tendered to the tax collector sixty-five per cent of the tax demanded, and, when the collector refused to accept anything less than the full tax, brought suit to restrain the collection of the excess over the amount tendered. A demurrer to the complaint was sustained and the decision was affirmed on appeal. The Court of Appeals recognized that the substance of the complaint was that real property was assessed at a different rate from personal property, but said that this inequality did not constitute a legal grievance, inasmuch as different classes of property might be taxed at different rates. The court admitted that the assessor disregarded a general statutory rule, but said that this "was in the exercise presumably of an honest and reasonable judgment. . . . Real property bears a greater proportion of taxes for the reason that, unlike personal property, it cannot be concealed. It is a fact of common knowledge that a disproportionate share of

[42] United States Trust Co. *v.* Mayor, 144 N. Y. 488. In an earlier case, Weaver *v.* Devendorf (1846), 3 Denio 117, it was held that no action for damages would lie against assessors for overvaluing the plaintiff's property, because their action is "judicial," and entitles them to judicial immunity.

[43] Stewart *v.* Palmer, 74 N. Y. 183. See cases in Ames, *Cases in Equity*, ii, 72, note.

[44] Seligman, *Essays in Taxation*, 8th ed., p. 20.

[45] 27 N. Y. Misc. 32; affirmed 50 App. Div. (N. Y.) 628; affirmed 172 N. Y. 35.

the public burdens is thrown on certain kinds of property because they are visible and tangible, while others are of a nature to elude vigilance. Such considerations may well influence a board of assessors to assess real estate upon a different basis of valuation in order to equalize the burdens of taxation."

The effect of this decision is, in the language of a critic, to declare "that the assessors may lawfully disobey the law; that in their discretion they may use a standard of valuation which the people of the state through the legislature have expressly declared that they may not use." [46] Its significance is that it emphasizes in an extreme form the predisposition of the courts to sustain the action of tax officials in every case.

Decisions connected with the collection of customs duties on imports by the Federal Government show a number of interesting peculiarities. While it was held in cases like Bartlett *v.* Kane and Hilton *v.* Merritt (*supra*) that valuations fixed by the customs officials were absolutely conclusive, and could not be re-examined in an action against the collector to recover back duties paid under protest, it was long possible in such an action to try the question whether the officials had classified the imported goods under the proper schedule of the tariff statutes, on the theory that if the classification was erroneous, the duty based upon it was illegal and so could be recovered. The reports are accordingly full of actions to determine such questions as whether almonds were dried fruits,[47] whether "Scotch bonnets" were hats or caps,[48] whether dried beans were seeds or vegetables,[49] and whether

[46] Abbot, *Justice and the Modern Law*, p. 221; but *cf.* Johnson *v.* Wells Fargo & Co., 239 U. S. 234, where the Supreme Court sustained a decree granting an injunction against the collection of a state tax on express companies, on the ground that the method used by the state administrative officials in assessing the value of the property of such companies on the basis of their gross income was a violation of a provision of the state constitution that taxes on the property of corporations should be assessed as nearly as possible in the same manner as taxes on the property of individuals. This decision was reached in spite of repeated refusals by the Supreme Court to restrain by injunction the collection of state taxes alleged to be illegal and void. See Singer Sewing Machine Co. *v.* Benedict, 229 U. S. 481.

[47] Holmes *v.* Collector, 1 Wall. 486.

[48] Toplitz *v.* Hedden, 146 U. S. 252.

[49] Sonn *v.* Magone, 159 U. S. 417.

anchovy and bloater paste was a "sauce." [50] Sometimes the task of interpretation was assumed by the court as a "matter of law," resulting in a directed verdict; sometimes, as in the case of the bloater paste, it was held that it should be left to the jury as depending upon "commercial designation," and so an issue of fact. The outcome was, that instead of a body of uniform technical interpretation being built up, the details of the tariff acts were in part filled in by the courts in the midst of their other duties, and in part left at the mercy of the fluctuating discretion of separate juries. By the act of 1890 [51] a new procedure was instituted which abolished the right of action against collectors to recover illegal duties, and provided that protests against decisions of the lower customs officials were to be heard first by an administrative board of general appraisers, and might then be appealed to a United States Circuit Court. It was at once held that administrative determinations of value were as conclusive under the new procedure as under the old, and could not be reëxamined by the courts in the appeal proceedings; [52] but the courts continued to decide questions of classification. The jury was eliminated, but such questions as whether loose pearls were jewelry,[53] and whether skins of less than ten pounds weight were hides,[54] were ultimately determined by the courts, which, however, professed to apply the rule that "findings of fact" by the general appraisers would not be disturbed if based upon conflicting testimony, nor unless without evidence reasonably to support them.[55] But within a period of four days one judge held "commercial similitude" to be first a "question of law,"[56] and afterward a "question of fact." [57] Furthermore, following earlier practice,[58] even

[50] Bogle *v.* Magone, 152 U. S. 623.

[51] Act of June 10, 1890, c. 407, U. S. Stat. at L., vol 26, p. 141.

[52] Passavant *v.* United States, 148 U. S. 214.

[53] Tiffany *v.* United States, 112 Fed. 672.

[54] Helmath *v.* United States, 135 Fed. 913.

[55] In re Van Blankensteyn, 56 Fed. 474.

[56] Dana *v.* United States, 91 Fed. 522, per Wheeler, J.

[57] United States *v.* Hahn, 91 Fed. 755, per Wheeler, J.

[58] Oberteuffer *v.* Robertson, 116 U. S. 499; Oelberman *v.* Merritt, 123 U. S. 356.

questions of valuation were reëxamined when it was claimed that the officials had "acted on a wrong principle or contrary to law," as by including items not legally forming a part of the dutiable value,[59] or by following a wrong method in converting foreign money into American,[60] or by failing to examine the goods as required by the statute.[61] And when the claim was made that the goods were not legally imports at all, and so not within the jurisdiction of the customs officials, it was held that the prohibition of the act of 1890 against suits to recover back the duty paid did not apply, but that such suits could be brought and sustained.[62] This control of customs administration by the regular courts was practically eliminated by the act of 1909 [63] creating the court of Customs Appeals, and transferring to it the appellate jurisdiction previously exercised by the regular Federal courts over the board of general appraisers. This tribunal, while a court, like the Court of Claims, in respect to its procedure, is in another sense practically an administrative body, in so far as its business is exclusively confined to cases arising under the administration of the tariff laws. Its decisions were at first made absolutely final, and remain so except for the fact that by a later statute [64] it has been made possible for the Supreme Court in its discretion to call up by certiorari decisions which it regards as of sufficient importance to review. I have found no instance where this power has yet been used. There has thus at last been created a mechanism whereby the details of tariff administration have been put beyond the reach of the ordinary courts and entrusted to a specialized body competent to build up a consistent body of technical practice, with full opportunity reserved for the protection of ultimate substantive rights by the Supreme Court of the United States.[65] Development in the administration

[59] United States *v.* Passavant, 169 U. S. 16.

[60] United States *v.* Klingenberg, 153 U. S. 93.

[61] United States *v.* Loeb, 107 Fed. 692.

[62] In re Fassett, 142 U. S. 479; De Lima *v.* Bidwell, 182 U. S. 1.

[63] Act of Aug. 5, 1909, c. 6, U. S. Stat. at L., vol. 36, p. 100.

[64] Act of Aug. 22, 1914, c. 267, U. S. Stat. at L., vol. 38, p. 708.

[65] For an interesting non-technical account of customs administration, see Benjamin Arthur Levett, *Through the Customs Maze* (17 State St., N. Y., 1923);

of the internal revenue and income tax laws seems to be moving slowly in the same direction.[66]

III

In disposing of public lands to private individuals, the government is in effect dispensing a bounty, and, while the distribution must of course be made in accordance with statutory requirements, the would-be beneficiary has no standing to object to a fairly wide latitude of discretion on the part of the land officials.

To the review of determinations of the United States Land Office,[67] there is, as in the tax cases, the obstacle of technical limitations on the procedure available for relief. The scope of review, as might be expected, is narrowest of all in the mandamus cases.[68] The courts have practically refused to correct by mandamus even constructions of a statute made by the land officials. The Supreme Court has said in the leading case:[69] "Congress has constituted the Land Department a special tribunal with judicial functions. . . . Neither an injunction nor mandamus will lie against an officer of the Land Department to control him in discharging an official duty which requires the exercise of his judgment and discretion. . . . The head of an executive department in the administration of the various concerns of his office is continually required to exercise judgment and discretion. He must exercise his judgment in expounding the laws under which he is from time to time required to act. Whether he decided right or wrong is not the question. Having jurisdic-

see also for the earlier period, J. D. Goss, *History of Tariff Administration* in *Columbia University Studies in History, Economics, and Public Law*, vol. i (1891).

[66] See Charles D. Hamel, "The United States Board of Tax Appeals," in *Bulletin of the National Tax Association* (Nov. 1924), vol. x, pp. 44–51.

[67] For the quasi-judicial function of the land officials, see C. R. Pierce, "The Land Department as an Administrative Tribunal," in *Amer. Pol. Sci. Rev.*, x, 271 ff., and Edward C. Finney, "The Board of Appeals, Department of the Interior," *ibid.*, pp. 290 ff.

[68] See above, Chapter III, p. 63.

[69] United States ex rel. Riverside Oil Co. *v.* Hitchcock, 190 U. S. 316. The rule is the same as to injunctions. Santa Fé Pacific R. R. Co. *v.* Lane, 244 U. S. 492.

tion to decide at all, he necessarily had jurisdiction, and it was his duty, to decide as he thought the law was, and the courts have no power whatever under those circumstances to review his determination by mandamus or injunction." [70]

Of course a patent may be attacked directly by the government in a proceeding in equity to set it aside because procured by fraud [71] or mistake.[72] The courts will then examine whether or not fraud was practised on the land officers or essential facts misrepresented, and their finding of fact represented by the issue of the patent will not conclude the government from showing the fraud;[73] but the Supreme Court has said that this jurisdiction should be exercised with extreme caution and the relief refused unless the fraud is proved not merely by a preponderance of the evidence but beyond a reasonable doubt.[74]

[70] Accord, United States ex rel. Ness *v.* Fisher, 223 U. S. 683; United States ex rel. Hall *v.* Payne, 254 U. S. 343. In United States ex rel. McBride *v.* Schurz, 102 U. S. 378, where a patent had already been duly signed by the President, sealed with the seal of the United States, recorded in the proper book of the general Land Office and countersigned by the recorder, and thereafter the Secretary refused to deliver it to the patentee, the writ was allowed on the ground that the administrative officials no longer had any rightful control over it, but were under a legal obligation to perform the purely ministerial act of delivery. See also In re Emblen, 161 U. S. 52. In Santa Fé Pacific R. R. Co. *v.* Fall, 259 U. S. 197, an injunction was granted restraining the Secretary of the Interior from cancelling selections of lieu lands by a railroad company. The Court held that the Secretary had no authority under the statute to take into consideration facts as to the value of the land which did not appear at the date the selection was made. For further discussion of the decision see below, p. 286.

[71] Williams *v.* United States, 138 U. S. 514; Maxwell Land Grant Case, 121 U. S. 325; Linn Timber Co. *v.* United States, 236 U. S. 574. But the land officials themselves may not, on the theory that their predecessors have been imposed upon, revoke a patent which has been duly issued, Noble *v.* Union River Logging R. Co., 147 U. S. 165.

[72] Germania Iron Co. *v.* United States, 165 U. S. 379. In such a case the cancellation of the patent simply restores to the Land Department its jurisdiction to issue a patent or not to the defendant, as it may finally determine.

[73] Washington Securities Co. *v.* United States, 234 U. S. 76.

[74] "The deliberate action of the tribunal [*i. e.*, the Land Department] to which the law confides the determination of all preliminary questions . . . demands that to annul such instruments and destroy the title claimed under it, the facts on which the action is asked must be clearly established by evidence satisfactory to the court. . . . The testimony must be unequivocal and convinc-

Determinations of the land officials come most frequently into question in collateral proceedings at law or in equity between contending claimants for the land covered by a patent. The grounds which the courts have assigned for their consent or refusal to review the administrative determination in such cases are by no means consistent, but the principles followed are fairly clear. On the one hand it is said that the Land Office is a "special tribunal" created by Congress, which, in hearing testimony and reaching a decision between opposing claimants, acts judicially. Therefore "their judgment as to matters of fact properly determinable by them is conclusive when brought to notice in a collateral proceeding. Their judgment in such cases is like that of other special tribunals upon matters within their exclusive jurisdiction, unassailable except by a direct proceeding for its correction or annulment."[75] On the other hand, it is said that the courts "cannot exercise any direct appellate jurisdiction over the rulings[76] of the land officials, because such a function is not judicial; it is administrative, executive and political in nature. The right to interfere in such cases would break down the distinction, so important and well defined in our system, between the several separate and independent branches of our government." [77] In so far as this distinction between "executive" and "judicial" action has any importance, the view that the land officials act in an executive capacity rather than judicially seems more in line with the decisions: for while it has been held that, as in collateral attacks upon the judgments of a court, no question can be raised of perjured testimony or forged documents offered in the proceedings before the Land Department, but only of such fraud practised upon the Department as prevented the

ing and it cannot be done upon a bare preponderance of the evidence. If the proposition as thus laid down is sound in regard to the cancellation of ordinary contracts of private individuals, how much more should it be so where the attempt is to annul a solemn evidence of title emanating from the government of the United States under its official seal." Miller, J., in the Maxwell Land Grant Case, 121 U. S. 325, at pp. 380, 381.

[75] St. Louis Smelting & Refining Co. *v.* Kemp, 104 U. S. 636.

[76] Quinby *v.* Conlan, 104 U. S. 426.

[77] Matthews, J., in Craig *v.* Leitensdorfer, 123 U. S. 189.

unsuccessful party from getting a fair hearing,[78] it is also settled law that in such collateral attacks on land determinations, the courts will relieve not merely against mistake and fraud, but also against patenting to one claimant land which rightly should have been patented to another.[79] The subject was fully discussed in the leading case of Johnson *v.* Towsley[80] where Lyman Trumbull argued for the appellant that on collateral attack the decision of the land officials had been made "final" by statute. The Court said, per Miller, J.: "In the use of the word 'final' we think nothing more was intended than that with the single exception of an appeal to the Secretary of the Interior the decision of the Commissioner of the General Land Office should exclude further inquiry within that department . . . but while we find no support to the proposition of counsel in the special provision of the statute relied on, it is not to be denied that the argument is much stronger when founded on the general doctrine that when the law has confided to a special tribunal the authority to hear and determine certain matters arising in the course of its duties, the decision of that tribunal within the scope of its authority is conclusive. . . . It is fully conceded that when those officers decide controverted questions of fact in the absence of fraud or imposition or mistake, their decision of those questions is final except as they may be reversed on appeal in that department; but we are not prepared to concede that when in the application of the facts as found by them, they by misconstruction of the laws take from a party that to which he has acquired a legal right under the sanction of those laws, the courts are without power to grant relief."

Thus it is clear that where, in issuing a patent, the land officials acted wholly without authority, as where the land patented was not public land of the United States at all, the courts will disregard the patent at the suit of an injured party.[81] They have refused, for example, to recognize the

[78] Vance *v.* Burbank, 101 U. S. 514; Steel *v.* St. Louis Smelting & Refining Co., 106 U. S. 447.

[79] Marquez *v.* Frisbie, 101 U. S. 473.

[80] 13 Wall. 72.

[81] "When we speak of conclusive presumptions attending a patent for lands, we assume that it was issued in a case where the department had jurisdiction

title of persons claiming under a patent from the Land Department where it was established that the tract in controversy was embraced in a Spanish or Mexican grant, it being held as a matter of law that such land was never public land of the United States and therefore never within the jurisdiction of the Department.[82] So the courts will take jurisdiction of the question whether the land in controversy has been reserved by law from sale, and, if so, will not enforce or protect a title founded upon a patent; [83] or if the Land Department has erroneously regarded the land as so reserved, will protect the rights of an applicant whose patent has been wrongfully refused.[84] Similarly when land has already been lawfully patented to one, and later by mistake is patented to another, the courts will treat the second patent as void.[85]

The difficult cases are the ones where these questions as to whether the land was public land, or land reserved from sale by law, depend on a "jurisdictional" question of "fact" as to the correctness of a survey, or the mineral or swamp character of the land. It has been said that on "mixed questions of law and fact" the decision of the administrative officials is conclusive.[86] And so in Knight *v.* United Land Association,[87] where the plaintiff contested a government patent on the ground that the land was below high-water mark and had therefore never passed to the United States, but a survey

to act and execute it; that is to say, in a case where the lands belonged to the United States, and provision had been made by law for their sale. If they never were public property or had been previously disposed of, or if Congress had made no provision for their sale or had reserved them, the Department would have no jurisdiction to transfer them, and its attempted conveyance of them would be inoperative and void, no matter with what seeming regularity the forms of law may have been observed." St. Louis Smelting & Refining Co. *v.* Kemp, 104 U. S. 636.

[82] Newhall *v.* Sanger, 92 U. S. 761; Doolan *v.* Carr, 125 U. S. 618.

[83] Wilcox *v.* Jackson, 13 Pet. 498; Wisconsin, etc. R. Co. *v.* Forsythe, 159 U. S. 46; Burfenning *v.* Chicago, St. Paul, Minneapolis, & Omaha R. Co., 163 U. S. 321.

[84] Lake Superior Ship Canal Co. *v.* Cunningham, 155 U. S. 354; Sjoli *v.* Dreschel, 199 U. S. 564; Osborne *v.* Froyseth, 216 U. S. 571; Svor *v.* Morris, 227 U. S. 524.

[85] Lytle *v.* State of Arkansas, 9 How. 314.

[86] Quinby *v.* Conlan, 104 U. S. 420; Ross *v.* Day, 232 U. S. 110, at p. 116.

[87] 142 U. S. 161.

approved by the Land Department showed it as above high-water mark, the survey was held conclusive; and this is the general rule as to surveys.[88] On the other hand, in the earlier case of Morton *v.* Nebraska [89] where the Department had issued a patent to the plaintiff, and it was pleaded in defence that the lands were saline, and as such had previously been granted to the state, the defendant was allowed to prove the saline character of the lands in the action; [90] and in Wright *v.* Roseberry [91] a similar result was reached where it was claimed that the land had passed to the state of California as swamp land. The latter case has, however, been practically overruled; [92] and it has been said that "it is the duty of the Land Department to determine whether land patented to a settler is of the class subject to settlement" and its judgment as to this fact is not open to contest.[93] In the later case of Duluth & Iron Range Railway Co. *v.* Roy,[94] however, where the plaintiff applied to the Land Office for a patent and while his application was pending the land was "through mistake and inadvertence" patented to the state as swamp land, he was allowed to recover in an action to quiet title against the state's grantee on showing that the lands were not in fact swamp lands. "We cannot presume," said the Supreme

[88] Cragin *v.* Powell, 128 U. S. 691, and cases there cited. Where a previous survey has never been finally approved by the Department, a new survey will not be enjoined, New Orleans *v.* Paine, 147 U. S. 261. As to the conclusiveness of harbor lines established by the Secretary of War, see Philadelphia Co. *v.* Stimson, 223 U. S. 605.

[89] 21 Wall. 660, relied on in Burfenning *v.* Chicago, etc. R. Co., 163 U. S. 321, at p. 323.

[90] The lands were noted as saline on the field books of the government survey, but by some mistake these notes were not transferred to the register's general plats.

[91] 121 U. S. 428. Hannibal & St. Joseph R. Co. *v.* Smith, 9 Wall. 95, where the same result was reached, has been subsequently distinguished on the ground that there it did not appear that the Department had ever made any determination as to the character of the lands in controversy. French *v.* Fyan, 93 U. S. 169.

[92] McCormick *v.* Hayes, 159 U. S. 331.

[93] Ehrhardt *v.* Hogaboom, 115 U. S. 67, cited with approval in McCormick *v.* Hayes, 159 U. S. 331, where the other swamp-land cases are reviewed. In Heath *v.* Wallace, 138 U. S. 573, it was said that the decision of the Land Department on the question of whether lands were swamp and overflowed within the meaning of the Swamp Land Act, was the decision of a "question of fact."

[94] 173 U. S. 587.

Court, "that the Land Department will decide against the fact which the state courts have found, that the lands are not, nor were they ever, swamp lands" within the Swamp Land Act. The decision may have been affected by the fact that the plaintiff was an ignorant foreigner, and seems to have been unfairly imposed upon by subordinate officials of the local Land Office.

When the question is a technical one as to the mineral or non-mineral character of the lands in controversy, the decisions are clearer. It is held that on that question the determination of the Land Department is final.[95] In Barden *v.* Northern Pacific Railway Co.[96] the Court said: "If the Land Department must decide what land shall not be patented because reserved, sold, granted, etc., it must also decide whether lands are excepted because they are mineral lands. . . . The officers will be governed by the knowledge of the lands obtained at the time as to their real character. The determination of the fact by those officers that they are one or the other will be considered as conclusive."[97] But in Iron & Silver Mining Co. *v.* Campbell,[98] where a placer patent was issued by the Land Department to one applicant and later the Department issued a lode patent to another, it was held that the priority of right between the two patentees was a question for judicial cognizance, and that the holder of the lode patent was entitled to a trial at law of the question whether the existence of a lode under the land was known to the placer patentee at the date of his patent, it being ruled as a matter of law that in such event the placer patent would be void.[99]

Where there is no question as to the public character of the land covered by the patent or its reservation from sale, *i. e.*, where the authority of the Department to deal with the land is not drawn into question, the decision of the officials on such matters as the qualifications of the applicant, the

[95] Steel *v.* St. Louis Smelting & Refining Co., 106 U. S. 447, at p. 450.

[96] 154 U. S. 28.

[97] *Accord,* Burke *v.* Southern Pacific Railroad Co., 234 U. S. 669.

[98] 135 U. S. 286; see also Cameron *v.* United States, 252 U. S. 450.

[99] *Accord,* Iron & Silver Mining Co. *v.* Mike & Starr Mining Co., 143 U. S. 394.

character of settlement, the intention with which settlement was made, whether requisite improvements have been duly made and whether or not there has been an abandonment, is treated by the courts as conclusive.[100] Furthermore, even on questions of law, where these do not go to the Department's authority to deal with the land but involve only the manner or details of exercising that authority, the courts have frequently treated the departmental construction of the law as conclusive where two or more constructions are possible and that of the Department was not palpably unreasonable. Thus, where a certain railroad land-grant adjustment act provided for the protection of *bona fide* purchasers but without specifying whether subsequent *bona fide* purchasers were included, and the Land Department had ruled that they were, this construction was held binding,[101] and similarly where the Department had ruled as to the sufficiency of an affidavit required of one claiming under a soldiers' bounty act.[102] The

[100] Lee *v.* Johnson, 116 U. S. 48; Ross *v.* Day, 232 U. S. 110; Burke *v.* Southern Pacific R. Co., 234 U. S. 669. But in Moore *v.* Robbins, 96 U. S. 530, the Court apparently looked at the testimony given in the departmental proceedings, to see whether the patentee had properly established a preëmption right and overruled the departmental decision that he had. It may be said, however, that this holding was not essential to the decision in the case. It is settled law that the evidence in the Land-Office proceedings may not be reexamined in court, St. Louis Smelting & Refining Co. *v.* Kemp, 104 U. S. 636. It is to be noted that in the land cases the courts do not speak of any requirement that the administrative determination, to be conclusive, must rest upon evidence rationally sufficient to support it, nor do they seem to examine the record in the administrative proceedings to determine whether such evidence was present. Apparently their practice is either not to review at all, — *i .e.*, to accept the decision of the land officials as absolutely conclusive, — or else to reëxamine the whole question anew. This practice may be due to the procedural fact that the review occurs in a collateral action. It was theorized by Mr. Justice Brown in the opinion in Noble *v.* Union River Logging R. Co., 147 U. S. 165, where he divides "jurisdictional facts" into those "strictly jurisdictional" and those "quasi-jurisdictional." As to the former, the whole question will be decided anew in the review proceeding — *e. g.*, whether the land patented was in fact a part of the public domain. As to the latter, the determination of the officials is absolutely conclusive — *e. g.*, whether the land was swamp and overflowed (citing French *v.* Fyan, *supra*).

[101] Logan *v.* Davis, 233 U. S. 613.

[102] Hastings & Dakota R. Co. *v.* Whitney, 132 U. S. 357. *Cf.* also U. S. *v.* Burlington & Missouri River R. Co., 98 U. S. 336, at p. 341; Svor *v.* Morris, 227

Supreme Court has said: "It is a settled rule that the practical interpretation of an ambiguous or uncertain statute by the executive department charged with its administration is entitled to the highest respect, and if acted upon for a number of years may not be disturbed except for very cogent reasons";[103] and in even stronger language, "Where patents have been issued, bonds given, mortgages executed and legislation had upon this construction, this uniform action is as potential and as conclusive of the soundness of the construction as if it had been declared by judicial decision."[104]

In Heath *v.* Wallace[105] the Supreme Court followed a departmental construction where this went directly to the jurisdiction or authority of the department. The question was whether land marked on the official plat as "subject to periodical overflow" was to be interpreted as "swamp and overflowed" within the meaning of the Swamp Land Act. If so, title would have passed directly to the state government at the date of the act, and the jurisdiction of the Land Office would have been ousted. The Land Office, however, had ruled that such land was not within the terms of the act, and the Supreme Court sustained this ruling, saying: (1) that the administrative construction of a statute ought not to be overruled except upon the most cogent reasons; (2) that the

U. S. 524; Santa Fé Pacific R. R. Co. *v.* Lane, 244 U. S. 492, where the administrative construction of a statute was followed. This power of construction is substantially identical with the well-recognized power of the Department to fill out the details of a statute by appropriate regulations. See, *e.g.*, Houghton *v.* Knight, 219 U. S. 537; United States *v.* Midwest Oil Co., 236 U. S. 459, and *cf.* United States *v.* AntiKamnia Co., 231 U. S. 654.

103 Logan *v.* Davis, 233 U. S. 613. See also Louisiana *v.* Garfield, 211 U. S. 70. This is a well-established principle which has been frequently applied in cases concerning the disbursement of public moneys and compensation due to government employees. See Hahn *v.* United States, 107 U. S. 405; United States *v.* Graham, 110 U. S. 219; United States *v.* Philbrick, 120 U. S. 59; United States *v.* Healy, 160 U. S. 145; United States *v.* Finnell, 185 U. S. 236.

104 United States *v.* Burlington & Missouri River R. Co., 98 U. S. 336, at p. 341. Weyerhaeuser *v.* Hoyt, 219 U. S. 380 is sometimes cited as "virtually recognizing the rulings of the Land Office in refusing to follow a former decision of the Supreme Court"; but the opinion of the majority went on the ground that there was no inconsistency between the earlier court decision and the administrative construction which was being attacked.

105 138 U. S. 573.

question was "one of the definition of words or terms rather than of the interpretation of the statute"; and (3) that such a question was one of fact. The reasons are at least ample, however incompatible they may seem to the mere lawyer.

A fortiori, the administrative interpretation of a statute, where within the bounds of a possible construction, will not be disturbed in mandamus or injunction proceedings.[106] Thus, in United States ex rel. Ness *v.* Fisher,[107] the Supreme Court refused to reverse administrative action taken upon a construction of the law which had been held erroneous by the courts, saying that the different construction adopted by the courts, "instead of indicating that the Secretary's decision was arbitrary and capricious, illustrates that there was room for different opinions as to the true construction of the law"; and the writ was likewise refused in United States ex rel. Hall *v.* Payne [108] because "the construction for which the relator contends was not so obviously and certainly right as to make it plainly the duty of the Secretary to give effect to it." This seems the view currently taken by the Supreme Court, instead of the absolute refusal to examine the Secretary's construction of law which was announced in the Riverside Oil case;[109] and in Santa Fé Pacific R. R. Co. *v.* Fall [110] an injunction was granted to restrain action by the Secretary taken on the basis of a construction of the law which the Court held wholly untenable.

The effect of the decisions is thus, if one employs the language customarily used in the opinions, that in land cases the courts will follow substantially the same practice with regard to so-called "questions of law" which in the review of other administrative determinations they follow with regard to so-called "questions of fact," *i. e.*, they will reverse for error of law only where they feel that the error is so gross as to be beyond the bounds of reason. In other words, they will not substitute their own opinion of the law for the legal opinion of the Land Department except where they regard the latter's

[106] United States ex rel. Riverside Oil Co. *v.* Hitchcock, 190 U. S. 316.

[107] 223 U. S. 683.

[108] 254 U. S. 343.

[109] *Supra*, pp. 277–278.

[110] 259 U. S. 197.

opinion as a rational impossibility. This result, when so expressed, appears as a paradox furnishing added proof of the inadequacy of the ordinary formula for expressing the boundaries of court review. The paradox vanishes if we say that what the courts really do is to refuse to treat as matters for the application of legal rules, or to lay down such rules to govern, many of the details of procedure and even of classification and interpretation which they properly prefer to regard as the subject-matter for a body of technical administrative practice. Such an explanation does away with the inconsistency of having to say that the courts will refuse to review for error of law, by emphasizing once more the fact that what are questions of law is properly a matter of policy for the courts to determine, depending on the desirability or feasibility of establishing fixed rules of permanent and universal application.[111] Where the issue is as to such a matter as the distribution of government land to individuals on terms favorable to the latter, the policy in favor of a strict development of legal rules is weak.

The same thing is true of the distribution of pensions; and in fact the attitude which the courts have pursued in the land cases as to questions of "law" originated in the pension case of Decatur *v.* Paulding.[112] There Congress had passed a general act providing pensions for the widows of naval officers who had died in the service. A special resolution was also passed at the same time granting a pension to the widow of Commodore Stephen Decatur. The Secretary of the Navy ruled that she might make her election to receive either pension, but was not entitled to both. Mrs. Decatur applied for a writ of mandamus to compel the Secretary to make payments to her under both the act and the resolution. The case obviously turned on the interpretation of the resolution granting the special pension, and whether or not it was intended to increase the amount of the pension payable under the general act. But the Supreme Court refused to take juris-

[111] See language in National Life Insurance Co. *v.* National Life Insurance Co., 209 U. S. 317, at p. 325.

[112] 14 Peters, 497.

diction of this question, saying by Mr. Chief Justice Taney: "The duty required by the resolution was to be performed by the Secretary of the Navy as the head of one of the executive departments of the government in the ordinary discharge of his official duties. The head of an executive department in the administration of the various important concerns of his office must exercise his judgment in expounding the laws and resolutions of Congress under which he is from time to time required to act. If he doubts, he has a right to call on the Attorney-General to assist him with his counsel and it would be difficult to imagine why a legal adviser was provided by law for the heads of departments unless their duties were regarded as executive in which judgment and discretion were to be exercised. If a suit should come before this court which involved the construction of any of these laws, the court certainly would not be bound to adopt the construction given by a head of a department and if they supposed his decision to be wrong they would of course so pronounce their judgment. But their judgment upon the construction of a law must be given in a case in which it is their duty to interpret the act of Congress in order to ascertain the rights of the parties in the cause before them. The court could not entertain an appeal from the decision of one of the secretaries nor revise his judgment in any case where the law authorized him to exercise discretion and judgment." The position taken by the Court in the language just quoted appears to reflect the view given weight and currency at the time by President Jackson, that the executive and judicial departments have concurrent and independent power to interpret the law in the regular course of their separate duties.[113] This is indicated in the concurring opinion of Catron, J., in the

[113] This view goes back to Thomas Jefferson, Letter to Jarvis, September 28, 1820 (*Complete Works*, ed. H. A. Washington, vii, 178): "The constitution . . . has wisely made all the departments co-equal and co-sovereign within themselves. . . . The judges . . . can issue their mandamus or distringas to no executive or legislative officer to enforce the fulfilment of their official duties any more than the president or legislature may issue orders to the judges." The classic expression of Jackson's view is in his Bank veto message of July 10, 1832, *Messages and Papers of the Presidents*, ed. Richardson, ii, 582.

same case, who said that an open contest for power between the courts and the administration was involved. "Stripped of the slight disguise of legal forms, the conflict between the executive and judiciary departments could not well be more direct nor more dangerous. The idea that they are distinct and their duties separate is confounded if the judgment of the court below is sustained, placing the executive power at its mercy. I maintain that the executive power of this nation, headed by the President and divided into departments, in its administration of the finances acts independently of the courts of justice in paying the public creditors, and that the decision of the Secretary of the Navy in this case was final on the laws as they stood."

The doctrine thus established prevailed with practical unanimity in mandamus and injunction cases until the recent opinions in United States *v.* Payne and Santa Fé Pacific R. R. Co. *v.* Fall have disclosed the new ground on which such cases are coming to be rested, requiring that the courts shall no longer refuse altogether to control administrative constructions of law where these cannot possibly be sustained in reason. In short, the same attitude toward review of administrative constructions of law is properly coming to be taken in mandamus proceedings as in the other cases where the question comes before the Court, although in the pension[114] as in the land cases such a construction will not be disturbed where it is held to be within the bounds of reason.[115]

[114] United States ex rel. Dunlap *v.* Black, 128 U. S. 102; Burnett *v.* United States, 116 U. S. 158. Following the land cases it has been held that the United States cannot recover moneys paid out as a pension because procured by fraud, where the fraud is shown merely by a preponderance of the evidence and not proved beyond a reasonable doubt, Lalone *v.* United States, 164 U. S. 255.

[115] NOTE ON THE CONCLUSIVENESS OF DETERMINATIONS OF THE PATENT OFFICE. The courts exercise a much broader review over such determinations than might be expected. In the first place there is a direct statutory "appeal" from the decision of the Commissioner of Patents to the Court of Appeals of the District of Columbia: U. S. Revised Statutes [1878], section 4911; Act of Feb. 9, 1893, 27 Stat., at L, 436; Butterworth *v.* Hoe 112 U. S. 50. It has been held that such an appeal is constitutional, since the action of the Commissioner which is appealed from is "judicial" in nature, United States *v.* Duell, 172 U. S. 576, at p. 586. But even where the District Court of Appeals affirms the action of the Commissioner, the defeated party may file a bill in

IV

The immigration statutes which exclude certain descriptions of aliens from the country, or authorize the deportation of aliens who have already entered, necessarily entrust to administrative officers in the first instance the identification of the aliens falling within the excluded classes. By various statutes since 1891 it has been provided that "in every case where an alien is excluded from admission into the United States under any law or treaty now existing or hereafter made, the decision of the appropriate immigration officers if adverse to the admission of such alien shall be final unless

equity and retry the question: U. S. Revised Statutes [1878], section 4915; McKnight *v.* Metal Volatilization Co., 128 Fed. 51. The proceeding is original in its nature and not appellate, and new evidence may be presented. In such collateral proceedings the decision of the Commissioner of Patents in the allowance and issue of a patent creates only a *prima facie* right and is subject to examination by the courts, Reckendorfer *v.* Faber, 92 U. S. 347. It is not final upon the question of the novelty and utility of the patentee's device, nor upon that of his priority of invention. The Supreme Court seems to have reached this result on the ground that the Commissioner's action is not expressly vested with finality by statute, Reckendorfer *v.* Faber, *supra.* Nor does the action of the Commissioner in granting a patent conclude the question whether there has been an abandonment, Woodbury Patent Planing Co. *v.* Keith, 101 U. S. 479; but as to certain matters, conclusive effect is given to the administrative determination, *e. g.*, the issue of a patent is conclusive evidence that the statutory requirements as to the application and procedure in the Patent Office have been complied with, Philadelphia etc. R. Co. *v.* Stimpson, 14 Peters, 448. A patent obtained by fraud must be respected and enforced until annulled in a direct proceeding, and cannot be attacked collaterally, Crompton *v.* Belknap Mills, 30 Fed. Cases 18, 285. But even where the determination of the patent officials is not conclusive, it establishes a *prima facie* case which throws the burden of proof upon the contestant and is entitled to the highest respect: Smith *v.* Goodyear Co., 93 U. S. 486; Lehnbeuter *v.* Holthaus, 105 U. S. 94; Cantrell *v.* Wallick, 117 U. S. 689; and the Supreme Court has said in Morgan *v.* Daniels, 153 U. S. 120, at p. 124: "This is something more than a mere appeal. It is an application to the court to set aside the action of one of the executive departments of the government. The one charged with the administration of the patent system had finished its investigations and made its determination with respect to the question of priority of invention. That determination gave to the defendant the exclusive rights of a patentee. A new proceeding is instituted in the courts — a proceeding to set aside the conclusions reached by the administrative department, and to give to the plaintiff the rights there awarded to the defendant. It is something in the nature of a suit to set aside a judgment, and as such is not to be sustained by a mere preponderance of evidence. Butter

reversed on appeal" to the head of the department.[116] In construing the degree of finality so attached to these determinations, the courts have assimilated the control of immigration, which might otherwise be regarded as a measure of police regulation, to those matters like taxation and military defence which go directly to the existence or safety of government, and have accordingly tended to confine very narrowly the scope of their review. This is, no doubt, because the power to exclude aliens has been based by the courts either on the right of a nation "to preserve its independence against foreign aggression and encroachment,[117] which brings the exercise of that power within the field of so-called "matter of state," or else on the power to regulate commerce with foreign nations, which assimilates it to control over the entrance and clearance of ships and the importation of goods, or, in other words,

v. Shaw, 21 Fed. 321, 327. It is a controversy between two individuals over a question of fact which has once been settled by a special tribunal, entrusted with full power in the premises. As such it might be well argued, were it not for the terms of this statute, that the decision of the Patent Office was a finality upon every matter of fact. In Johnson *v.* Towsley, 13 Wall. 72, a case involving a contest between two claimants for land patented by the United States to one of them, it was said: 'It is fully conceded that when those officers (the local land officers) decide controverted questions of fact, in the absence of fraud, or impositions or mistake, their decision on those questions is final, except as they may be reversed on appeal in that department.' Upon principle and authority, therefore, it must be laid down as a rule that where the question decided in the Patent Office is one between the contesting parties as to priority of invention, the decision there made must be accepted as controlling upon that question of fact in any subsequent suit between the same parties, unless the contrary is established by testimony which in character and amount carries thorough conviction. Tested by that rule the solution of this controversy is not difficult. Indeed, the variety of opinion expressed by the different officers who have examined this testimony is persuasive that the question of priority is doubtful, and if doubtful the decision of the Patent Office must control." Finally in a suit for infringement the question of the validity of a patent is open for reëxamination by the courts.

116 Review is practically always sought by means of a petition for a writ of habeas corpus brought by the excluded applicant.

117 Chinese Exclusion Case, 130 U. S. 581. "It is an accepted maxim of international law that every sovereign nation has the power as inherent in sovereignty and essential to self-preservation to forbid the entrance of foreigners within its dominions or to admit them only in such cases and upon such conditions as it may see fit to prescribe," Ekiu *v.* United States, 142 U. S. 651, at p. 659.

to customs regulation.[118] Accordingly, the doctrine of Murray's Lessee *v.* Hoboken Land Co.[119] and Hilton *v.* Merritt,[120] restricting judicial review to the narrowest point, has been applied to the immigration cases.

It has been held that where the officials have determined that an immigrant belongs to a class not entitled to enter, the statutory provision that their determination shall be final makes them the sole and exclusive judge of the existence of the facts upon which their determination rests, "and no other tribunal is at liberty to reëxamine or controvert the sufficiency of the evidence on which they acted." [121] In the Ju Toy case [122] this doctrine was extended even to the "jurisdictional," fact of citizenship. Ju Toy, who had been excluded by the officials, claimed that they had no authority over him because he was not an alien but a citizen of the United States, in which event the exclusion act would of course not apply to him. His citizenship, however, depended on the fact of his birthplace, and the Supreme Court held that he had no right to have the administrative finding on that fact reëxamined in a law court. Three justices concurred in a vigorous dissent which characterized the decision

[118] Ekiu *v.* United States, 142 U. S. 651, at p. 569; United States ex rel. Turner *v.* Williams, 194 U. S. 279.

[119] 18 How. 272.

[120] 110 U. S. 97.

[121] Ekiu *v.* United States, 142 U. S. 651; Lem Moon Sing *v.* United States, 158 U. S. 538.

[122] 198 U. S. 253. Some of the mischievous implications of the Ju Toy decision are pointed out in Chafee, *Freedom of Speech*, pp. 252 ff. The Supreme Court has subsequently expressly refused to apply the doctrine of the Ju Toy case to deportation, as distinguished from exclusion, cases, Ng Fung Ho *v.* White, 259 U. S. 276, saying per Brandeis, J. (at p. 284): "Jurisdiction in the executive to order deportation exists only if the person arrested is an alien. The claim of citizenship is thus a denial of the essential jurisdictional fact. . . . If the jurisdiction of the Department of Labor may not be tested in the courts by means of the writ of habeas corpus where the prisoner claims citizenship, and makes a showing that his claim is not frivolous, then, obviously, deportation of a resident may follow upon a purely executive order, whatever his race or place of birth. . . . To deport one who so claims to be a citizen obviously deprives him of liberty. . . . Against the danger of such deprivation without the sanction afforded by judicial proceedings, the 5th Amendment affords protection in its guaranty of due process of law."

as "appalling," and contended that whenever a claim of citizenship was made the applicant was entitled to a judicial trial of the fact, since any other doctrine might result in allowing administrative officials to impose what amounted to a sentence of banishment. The point raised in the Ju Toy case goes not so much to the question of judicial control of an administrative finding as to the right to a retrial of the facts by a trial court and jury. No doubt the determining motive behind the opinion of the majority was that an opposite holding would bring practically every Chinese exclusion case into the Federal district courts, since there would be nothing to prevent a claim of citizenship, however unfounded, from being set up in order to secure a jury trial with at least the benefits of procedural delay.

On the matter of judicial review, the statement of the courts that they are without power to "reëxamine or controvert the sufficiency of the evidence on which the administrative officer acted" is of greater significance. This doctrine, if consistently applied, would obviously open a dangerous door to executive oppression; [123] and in fact it does not seem to have been strictly applied in the more recent cases. On the contrary, the courts have implied that they will regard themselves as concluded by the administrative finding only where the evidence on which the officials acted was reasonably adequate to support it.[124]

On so-called "questions of law" the courts will review. Thus in Gonzales *v.* Williams [125] a determination of the immi-

[123] The only case in which the doctrine seems to have been applied is Lem Moon Sing *v.* United States, 158 U. S. 538, where the evidence as set forth in the statement of facts certainly does not seem sufficient to support the administrative finding, but the point was not raised by petitioner's counsel.

[124] United States ex rel. Turner *v.* Williams, 194 U. S. 279. This was an exclusion case under the act prohibiting the entry of alien anarchists. The rule has seemingly never been laid down in an exclusion case under the Chinese Exclusion Acts; but that it would be applied in such a case has been intimated in the opinion in Ng Fung Ho *v.* White, 259 U. S. 276, at p. 284, a deportation case. The rule has been squarely laid down for the deportation cases in Zakonaite *v.* Wolf, 226 U. S. 272; Lewis *v.* Frick, 233 U. S. 291; Healy *v.* Backus, 221 Fed. 358.

[125] 192 U. S. 1; United States *v.* Wong Kim Ark, 169 U. S. 649.

gration officials was reversed on the ground that the petitioner, who was admitted to have been a native inhabitant of Porto Rico at the date of its cession to the United States, was legally not an alien immigrant. In Gegiow *v.* Uhl [126] the officials undertook to exclude at the port of New York certain Russians bound for Portland, Oregon, under the clause of the statute excluding immigrants "likely to become public charges." They based their decision on the ground that reports showed the labor market at Portland to be overstocked. The Supreme Court took jurisdiction of the question "whether an alien can be declared likely to become a public charge on the ground that the labor market in the city of his immediate destination is overstocked," and held that they might be "excluded under the clause only on the ground of permanent personal objections accompanying them, irrespective of local conditions."

On the analogy of revenue cases, the courts have not been scrupulous to insist on the procedural rights of the alien applicant before the immigration officials. They have required only the loosest kind of notice and hearing. It has been held that the immigration officer in reaching his decision need not take any testimony, and may decide on his own inspection and examination the question of the right of the immigrant to land.[127] In Yamataya *v.* Fisher [128] the petitioner alleged that she was ignorant of the English language and at the time of the investigation did not know that it had reference to her being deported. The Court held that if her situation "put her at some disadvantage, that was her misfortune," and went on to say that the notice given her, although informal, was sufficient. However, the Court said: "We must not be understood as holding that administrative officers when executing the provisions of a statute involving the liberty of persons may disregard the fundamental principles that inhere in due process of law. One of those principles is that no person shall be deprived of his liberty without opportunity at some time to be heard before such officers in respect

[126] 239 U. S. 3.

[127] Ekiu *v.* United States, 142 U. S. 651.

[128] 189 U. S. 86.

of the matters upon which that liberty depends — not necessarily an opportunity upon a regular set occasion and according to the forms of judicial procedure, but one that will secure the prompt and vigorous action contemplated by Congress, and at the same time be appropriate to the nature of the case upon which such officers are required to act." [129]

The later amendments to the statutes have done something to broaden the immigrant's rights. Under the earlier acts the decision was left with a single official. For this procedure there have been substituted special boards of inquiry consisting of three members, and required to keep a record of their proceedings.[130] At the same time, in the more recent cases a trend seems observable toward greater insistence on procedural safeguards. Thus in Chin Yow *v.* United States [131] a writ of habeas corpus was ordered to issue on the ground that the immigration officials had prevented the petitioner from offering relevant testimony of certain named witnesses in his behalf, and the Court said: "As between the substantive right of citizens to enter and of persons alleging themselves to be citizens to have a chance to prove their allegation, on the one side, and the conclusiveness of the commissioner's fiat, on the other, when one or the other must give way, the latter must yield." In the more recent case of Kwock Jan Fat *v.* White [132] the Court went even further. The testimony of important

[129] In Hagar *v.* Reclamation District, 111 U. S. 701, the Court said: "Undoubtedly where life and liberty are involved due process requires that there be a regular course of judicial proceedings which imply that the party to be affected shall have notice and an opportunity to be heard, so also where title or possession of property is involved; but where the taking of property is in the enforcement of a tax the proceeding is necessarily less formal and whether notice is at all necessary may depend upon the character of the tax and the manner in which the amount is determined. The necessity of revenue for the support of the government does not admit of the delays attendant upon proceedings in a court of justice and they are not required for the enforcement of taxes or assessments." This distinction between tax cases and other cases has not been uniformly observed by the Court. Thus no case is more frequently relied upon in the immigration cases than Murray's Lessee *v.* Hoboken Land Co., 18 How. 272, a revenue case.

[130] Acts of 1907, ch. 1134, sec. 25; 34 Stat. at L., 906. These safeguards were incorporated in sec. 17 of the Act of 1917, 39 U. S. Stat. at L., pp. 874 ff.

[131] 208 U. S. 8.

[132] 253 U. S. 454.

witnesses favorable to the applicant was omitted or suppressed from the report made to the Commissioner of Immigration, on the basis of which he affirmed a decision denying the petitioner's right to enter. Accordingly, the Supreme Court directed a writ of habeas corpus to issue, saying: "The acts of Congress give great power to the Secretary of Labor over Chinese immigrants and persons of Chinese descent. It is a power to be administered not arbitrarily and secretly, but fairly and openly under the restraints of the traditions and principles of free government applicable where the fundamental rights of men are involved, regardless of their origin or race. It is the province of the courts in proceedings for review to prevent abuse of this extraordinary power, and this is possible only when a full record is preserved of the essentials on which the executive officers proceed to judgment. For failure to preserve such a record for the information not less of the Commissioner of Immigration and of the Secretary of Labor than for the courts, the judgment in this case must be reversed. It is better that many Chinese immigrants should be improperly admitted than that one natural-born citizen of the United States should be permanently excluded from his country." [133] If the necessity of a fair hearing is thus insisted on by the courts and the practice is adhered to of disregarding administrative determinations unsupported by evidence, no more can be asked. There is no room for building up a body of substantive law. On the question of citizenship as it arose in the Ju Toy case, it would perhaps be desirable to provide by statute for a jury trial, where the applicant can make a *prima facie* case by affidavits of two or more domiciled citizens of other than his own race.[134]

[133] From the opinion by Clarke, J. See also Tang Tun *v.* Edsell, 223 U. S. 673; Wah Suey *v.* Backus, 225 U. S. 460, where claims that a fair hearing had been denied were made and overruled.

[134] In deportation as well as exclusion cases the courts have attempted to guarantee to the alien the benefits of fair administrative procedure. See Whitfield *v.* Hanges, 222 Fed. 745 where an administrative order of deportation was reversed because the aliens had not been allowed to see the warrant on which they were arrested, or to consult with counsel before their hearing; and also because in the opinion of the court the finding was contrary to the "indisputable character of the evidence." For a discussion of the power of immi-

V

A fifth class of cases consists of those where government undertakes to sell some service to the public, the typical instance in our Federal government being postal service. The courts have assimilated the postal cases to the land cases, as they have assimilated the immigration cases to customs and revenue cases. Review is most frequently sought of postal determinations which involve the right to the service, as affected by so-called "fraud orders," or the rate to be charged under the so-called "second-class" privilege. It is provided by statute that "the Postmaster-General may upon evidence satisfactory to him that any person or company is conducting a scheme for obtaining money through the mails by means of fraudulent representations" deny to such person the right to receive letters through the mails. In the case of fraud orders, therefore, a power of determination is directly conferred by law on the Postmaster-General. No such power is given in the case of mail matter entitled to second-class privileges, but the statute itself undertakes to define what matter shall be so entitled. The power, however, follows from the duty of the Postmaster-General in the course of administering the system to identify the matter falling within the statutory definition.

These administrative determinations affecting the right to mail service and the rates to be charged are of substantially the same character, at least with respect to the interests affected, as determinations of public-service commissions or of the Interstate Commerce Commission made in the course of regulating public utilities. The courts have not, however, proceeded on this analogy, but have dealt with postal service as a privilege offered by the government which it is under no obligation to supply, and to which it can therefore attach whatever conditions and limitations it sees fit. It has been said: "The postal service is by no means an indispensable

gration officials under statutes authorizing the deportation of alien radicals, see Chafee, *Freedom of Speech*, chapter v. For valuable material illustrative of the administration of the immigration laws, see Edith Abbott, *Immigration, Select Documents and Case Records* (University of Chicago Press, 1924).

adjunct to a civil government. . . . It is not a necessary part of civil government in the same sense in which the protection of life, liberty and property, the defense of the government against insurrection and foreign invasion and the administration of public justice are. . . . The legislative body in establishing a postal service may annex such conditions to it as it chooses."[135] Accordingly, the courts have restricted very narrowly their review of determinations made by the officials. They have emphasized in dealing with them, not the private rights affected, but, as in the land cases, the necessities and convenience of carrying on the public business. Thus the Supreme Court said, in one postal case: "If the ordinary daily transactions of the departments which involve interference with private rights were required to be submitted to the courts before action was finally taken, the result would entail practically a suspension of some of the most important functions of government."[136] Accordingly, on the authority of the land cases the courts have accepted the action of the Post-Office Department as final even when involving questions of law, unless clearly erroneous.[137] Thus, they have allowed a very free hand to the Department in determining whether or not a serial publication is a "periodical" within the meaning of the statutory grant of second-class privileges to "periodicals," even going so far as to refuse to interfere when the Department reversed its own interpretation of many years' standing so as to deny the privilege to a whole class of publications which had hitherto enjoyed it.[138] In the case of fraud orders they will uphold the decision of the Postmaster-General "where it is fairly arrived at and has substantial evidence to support it so that it cannot be justly said to be palpably wrong and therefore arbitrary."[139] But in American

[135] Public Clearing House *v.* Coyne, 194 U. S. 497, at p. 506.

[136] *Ibid.*, at p. 509.

[137] Houghton *v.* Payne, 194 U. S. 88; Bates & Guild Co. *v.* Payne, 194 U. S. 106; Smith *v.* Hitchcock, 226 U. S. 53.

[138] Houghton *v.* Payne, 194 U. S. 88.

[139] Leach *v.* Carlile, 258 U. S. 138. In Bates & Guild Co. *v.* Payne, 194 U. S. 106, it was said: "Where the decision of questions of fact is committed by Congress to the judgment and discretion of the head of a department, his de-

School of Magnetic Healing *v.* McAnnulty,[140] where on the record nothing further was shown against the complainant than that he was engaged in the business of practising so-called "mental healing," the Supreme Court reversed a decree which had denied an injunction against the issue of a fraud order, saying that whether or not mental healing was *per se* fraudulent was not a question for the Postmaster-General, and that to sustain such an order it was not sufficient to show opinions which *might* be false, but that a case of "actual fraud in fact" must be made out. The distinction is illustrated by Leach *v.* Carlile,[141] where a fraud order which had been issued against the vendor of a medicine was sustained by the Court, not on the ground that the substance was in fact worthless as a medicine, but that it obviously fell fraudulently short of the extravagant representations made by the vendor as to its virtues.[142]

On the whole, no criticism can fairly be directed against the decisions in these cases. What is open to criticism as mak-

cision thereon is conclusive; and even upon mixed questions of law and fact, or of law alone, his action will carry with it a strong presumption of its correctness, and the courts will not ordinarily review it, although they may have the power and will occasionally exercise the right of so doing."

[140] 187 U. S. 94.

[141] 258 U. S. 138.

[142] A weakness of the statute authorizing the issuance of fraud orders is that there is no requirement of a hearing; but apparently a hearing is usually granted. One obstacle to review of postal determinations, as elsewhere, is encountered in technicalities as to the form of review procedure available. It has been held that certiorari will not lie because the administrative action sought to be reviewed is not "judicial" in character (Degge *v.* Hitchcock, 229 U. S. 162), with the result that review must be sought in injunction proceedings. At various times proposals have been made and bills introduced in Congress to provide for a wider judicial review of the Postmaster General's determinations in fraud order cases. They have been opposed by the Department on the ground that "the value of the law depends upon the promptness with which schemes to defraud may be denied the use of the mails to further the swindle. If action is delayed any considerable time, — as would necessarily be the case in a judicial proceeding, — the scheme will consummate its fraud before the interference occurs." Another proposal has been for the creation of an administrative "Commission of Postal Appeals," like the Board of Tax Appeals in the Treasury Department, to review the issuance of fraud orders. See Lindsay Rogers, *The Postal Power of Congress* (*Johns Hopkins University Studies in Historical and Political Science*, Series xxxiv, no. 2), pp. 58–60.

ing for possible error in the future is the attitude and language of the courts. It is not sufficient to see in the postal system merely a service performed by government, which it is under no duty to perform and to which it can therefore attach arbitrary conditions; or to regard disputed issues simply from the standpoint of the necessities and convenience of carrying on the service. That view is open to the objections pointed out by Mr. Justice Holmes in his dissenting opinion in Leach *v.*Carlile *(supra)*. How well founded those objections are can be seen from a decision like that in Masses Publishing Co. *v.* Patten.[143] There the so-called Espionage Act[144] had made certain kinds of language and the expression of certain opinions criminal, and provided that "every newspaper . . . or other publication, matter, or thing in violation of any of the provisions of this act is hereby declared to be non-mailable." The Postmaster-General, claiming to act under this statute, denied to a certain publication the privilege of the mails. The publishers applied for a temporary injunction, which was granted by the District Court, but the order allowing the injunction was reversed by the Circuit Court of Appeals. The court interpreted the statute as vesting the Postmaster-General with authority to determine whether any given publication fell within the classes declared to be non-mailable, and, on the authority of earlier postal cases like Public Clearing House *v.* Coyne, and land cases like Burfenning *v.* Chicago etc. R. Co., said that, as such a determination required the exercise of judgment and discretion, the administrative decision "must be regarded by the courts as conclusive unless clearly wrong. . . . The burden is upon the plaintiff to overcome the presumption that the Postmaster-General's decision is right, or that he has exceeded his power, or exercised it wantonly or maliciously. . . . This the complainant should do by a preponderance of the evidence." The concurring judge[145] thought that the administrative determination which had been made rested upon "a conclusion of fact to

[143] 246 Fed. 24, per Rogers, Circuit Judge.

[144] Act of June 15, 1917, c. 30, tit. xii, 40 U. S. Stat. at Large, 230.

[145] Ward, J.

be drawn from the text of the excluded publication . . . and the conclusion of the Postmaster-General in matters of fact, whether we agree with him or not, is final." The power here surrendered to postal officials is obviously a vastly wider one than the mere application of a common-sense standard of fraud, as in Leach *v.* Carlile, or of a technical standard of reasonableness, as in cases of rate-fiixng orders. While it is probably no greater than the power which would be exercised by a jury in a criminal prosecution under the same statute, the aggrieved party would at least have, in a criminal prosecution, the benefit of the rule as to reasonable doubt; and, furthermore, the issues involved in the determination, unlike those in any other type of administrative adjudication, touch so closely the self-interest of the government in perpetuating its own supremacy, that the power is a dangerous one to commit conclusively to administrative hands. In effect it puts the channels of public opinion at the mercy of the very agency which in theory should be subject to public opinion. On an earlier hearing of the same case [146] the Court used language of even broader import, saying: "In respect of the mails, the United States is certainly not a common carrier; it is pursuing a high governmental duty, and it is at least arguable whether any constitutional government can be judicially compelled to assist in the dissemination and distribution of something which proclaims itself revolutionary."

VI

The difficulty with the view that in the performance of postal service the government is acting in a political capacity is that such service is but the entering wedge of a very important development which seems to be in progress. Government agencies are more and more assuming the task of supplying service to the public in a variety of fields which up to the present have been normally filled by private enterprise; so that some persons, like M. Duguit, are coming to regard the supply of public service as one of the main, if not the main, function of government in the future. When the public

[146] 245 Fed. 103.

supply of service in a given field becomes so thoroughly established that private enterprise is completely banished, the citizen is at the mercy of government with respect to some of the most important and necessary facilities of modern life; for it is chiefly the field of necessaries like transportation, light, water, power and the services of communication that becomes monopolized by government. To say that when these fields are taken over by government they become removed from the operations of law, and that thenceforward their administration is to be left to the free discretion of executive officials, and that conditions may be attached to the service at the arbitrary choice of the government, would be to expose the individual in some of his most important social and business relations to a wilful and intolerable tyranny. It would amount to banishing the rule of law entirely from that field of public utilities which it is now felt should, more than any other business activity, be subjected to law.

This result, however much it might seem to be foreshadowed by the language of the Federal courts in the postal cases, is, as a matter of fact, not in line with the large number of decisions affecting the supply of water and other public services by municipalities. In this field a fairly complete body of law has already been built up on the central proposition that "a municipal corporation which supplies its inhabitants with gas or water does so in its capacity of a private corporation and not in the exercise of its powers of local sovereignty";[147] and that, just as "it is a rule of common law that parties carrying on a business which is public in its nature or which is impressed with a public interest must serve all who apply on equal terms and at reasonable rates, so in the case of water works there is no reason why a different rule should apply when the works are owned and operated by the city from those which prevail where the business is carried on by a private corporation."[148] Accordingly, it is held that the

[147] Jolly *v.* Monaca, 216 Pa. St., 345.

[148] Wagner *v.* City of Rock Island, 146 Ill. 139. In Borough of Collingswood *v.* State Water Supply Commission, 84 N. J. Law, 104; 85 N. J. Law, 673, it was held that municipal water works were subject to the control of the State Water

rates charged by municipal water works must be reasonable,[149] allowing, however, to the municipality a fair surplus over and above actual operating expenses; and with the reservation, of course, that "some reasonable discretion must abide in the officers whose duty it is to make such rates and unless the court can say from all the circumstances that the rate fixed is an excessive one the judgment of the officers fixing the rate must stand." [150] Or, in even stronger language: "Every presumption must be made in favor of the validity of the action of such a body."[151] Rates or practices, however, which are alleged to be discriminatory will be closely scrutinized by the courts, and if the discrimination is proved, corrected. Thus in Gordon *v.* Doran [152] water commissioners adopted a rule that if charges for water furnished on metered rates should exceed the sum due from the same consumer for service which could not be metered, there should be remitted to him the charges due for the unmetered service; while, on the other hand, if the charges for the unmetered service exceeded the sum due for water furnished under the metered rate, credit should be given for the latter. The court said that the rule was as unfair as if the post-office should undertake to deduct the postage on one class of mail matter from the postage on another, or if a railway company allowed a rebate of freight rates to the amount of passenger tickets bought. Accordingly, an injunction was granted against enforcement of the rule. Similarly a city may not insist on the collective use of a single meter by a number of consumers,[153] nor deny a consumer using water through various meters the

Supply Commission in the same manner as privately owned water works, and that where the Commission had refused a permit to the borough to construct its own water works, the Court of Errors and Appeals would not disturb its determination where on certiorari the lower court had found that the Commission's determination was not unreasonable on the evidence before it.

[149] Edgerly *v.* City of Ottumwa, 174 Ia. 205; Feil *v.* City of Coeur d'Alene, 23 Idaho, 32; Ladd *v.* Boston, 170 Mass. 332; Twitchell *v.* City of Spokane, 55 Wash. 86.

[150] Twitchell *v.* City of Spokane, 55 Wash. 86.

[151] Woodruff *v.* Mayor of East Orange, 71 New Jersey Eq. 419.

[152] 100 Minn. 343.

[153] City of Montgomery *v.* Greene (Ala., 1913), 60 So. 900.

benefit of the lower rate to which the aggregate amount of water used through all the meters would entitle him, nor require patrons of the service to sign an agreement absolving the city from its legal liability for negligence on pain of having to pay a double rate.[154] Municipal water officials may not require a consumer to install a meter who does not fall within the statutory class as to which they have such power,[155] and the correctness of a meter reading and the charge based thereon are not conclusive but may be disputed in an action.[156]

Perhaps, however, through influence of the tax cases, this field is not wholly free from the embarrassing procedural obstacles which so frequently stand in the way of effective review of administrative determinations. Thus in a dispute between a consumer and the water officials there is some question as to whether the former may have an injunction against the turning off of his water supply pending the determination of the dispute. There is a line of cases which grant such relief absolutely.[157] Other cases require the giving of a bond.[158] In still others an injunction will not be granted until after the controversy has been judicially determined in the consumer's favor.[159] Again, where certiorari is available to review the determination of water officials it has been held that on application for an injunction to restrain the turning off of the applicant's water the courts will not consider the reasonableness of the rate complained of, on the ground that this question should be raised by certiorari.[160]

That the supply of a public service should be controlled by law even where it is the government which supplies the service, has been recognized by the Federal courts in the

[154] Dittmar *v.* New Braunfels, 20 Tex. Civ. Ap. 293.

[155] Foster *v.* Monroe, 40 N. Y. Misc. 449.

[156] Healy *v.* City of New York, 9 App. Div. (N. Y.) 170; City of Mansfield *v.* Humphreys Mfg. Co., 82 Ohio St. 216.

[157] Wood *v.* City of Auburn, 87 Maine, 287; Crumley *v.* Watauga Water Co., 99 Tenn. 420.

[158] Van Ness Land Co. *v.* New York, 7 App. Div. (N. Y.) 295; City of Mansfield *v.* Humphreys Mfg. Co., 82 Ohio St. 216.

[159] McGregor *v.* Case, 80 Minn. 214.

[160] Woodruff *v.* Mayor of East Orange, 71 N. J. Eq. 419.

important instance of the operation of the railroads by the government during the War. Even in the absence of a statute, the Supreme Court held that, after the taking over of the roads by the government, an action for personal injury resulting in the course of their operation not merely could be, but must be, brought against the Director-General of Railroads rather than against the railroad company.[161] This decision is to be contrasted with the opposite tendency of the British case of Bainbridge *v.* Postmaster-General.[162]

VI

No cases could really be more dissimilar in principle than those, on the one hand, which involve the supply of an indispensable public service of which the government has a monopoly, and, on the other, land cases or pension cases arising out of the distribution of a public bounty. The former are preëminently cases for the application and development of law in the same degree as is found feasible in the course of administrative regulation of privately owned utilities. The latter involve privileges rather than fundamental interests, and in the absence of arbitrary or fraudulent favoritism there is no good reason why the details of administration should be interfered with by the courts.

At the opposite pole of importance from the pension and land cases stand cases of another class where court control of executive action is neither practicable nor wise. Just as it is not advantageous to build into a body of strict law the administrative distribution of pensions and land grants because the value of the result would not match its difficulty and disadvantages, so for the opposite reason it is not practicable for the courts to attempt to deal as a matter of law with those important political determinations of the executive which are called "matters of state," such as the recognition of foreign

161 Missouri Pacific R. R. Co. *v.* Ault, 256 U. S. 554, at p. 561. In delivering the opinion of the Court, Mr. Justice Brandeis said: "As a matter of law the government or its agency for operation could be sued, for under the existing law the legal person in control of the carrier was responsible for its acts." See also Dahn *v.* Davis, 258 U. S. 421.

162 [1906] 1 K. B. 178.

governments, the calling out of the militia, or the declaration of a state of war. Apart from the obstacles which such interference would throw in the path of political action, these matters are not properly cognizable by a judicial tribunal because each case is so essentially unique, and the critical factors never repeat themselves so as to give any place or opportunity for the application or development of general rules to govern them. The questions involved are questions of pure policy; and whether or not it will ultimately become possible to win over a portion of this field of policy for the rule of law will depend on a much deeper canalization of international contacts by international courts and arbitrations than has ever yet been effected.

It is on the middle ground of police regulation and the regulation of business affected with a public interest that the question of court control of administrative determinations is of the greatest and most urgent importance.

CHAPTER XI

REVIEW OF ADMINISTRATIVE DETERMINATIONS OF "FACT"

I

THE law of court review of administrative determinations has been infected with a hidden confusion by the transformation which has quietly shifted the emphasis of so much executive action to the function of adjudication. The earlier law of review, which was shaped before adjudication had become a prominent executive function, took its starting-point from the principle of *ultra vires;* so that review became focused on the issue of jurisdiction or extent of authority, instead of appearing openly in the guise of a proceeding in error to correct an adjudication by an inferior tribunal. The older theory persists, with the result that, even in reviewing the orders of a body like the Interstate Commerce Commission, the courts seem never quite sure whether they are dealing with a question of the Commission's area of "jurisdiction," or with a question of the law applied by it in the order under review. A form of expression has been invented and frequently employed which combines and conceals both theories in a single formula, running to the effect that if the Commission acts in disregard of a principle of law or without evidence to support its order, it acts without jurisdiction.[1] No fault need be found with this formula if it is applied to reach sound results; its danger lies in the misunderstanding which it is likely to generate as to the proper nature and limits of the reviewing function, particularly in connection with review of so-called findings of fact.

The *ultra vires* theory of review coöperated with American

[1] Interstate Commerce Commission *v.* Louisville & Nashville R. Co., 227 U. S. 88.

constitutional doctrine [2] to present the review proceeding as a proceeding essentially collateral in character. The typical form of such collateral review is the traditional tort action for damages against an officer who has exceeded his authority. Since there was no question of an old-fashioned officer like a sheriff or bailiff having held a hearing or made a formal finding of fact preliminary to taking the action complained of, the facts were of necessity tried by a jury in the collateral tort action — that is, in the review proceeding itself. Where review was sought by injunction, the facts again had to be tried in the equity proceeding, and were found by the court rather than by a jury only because of the peculiarity of the equity procedure. In short, so long as the usual type of executive action brought under review was not "quasi-judicial," it was not only natural but inevitable that the fact-finding process should be a part of the review proceeding, and not of the administrative process itself.[3] But, with the entrusting to administrative officers of functions which are of a substantially judicial nature, the formal duty of fact-finding was expressly imposed on the administrative agency [4] in those technical fields requiring special expert knowledge which are precisely the fields most commonly committed to administrative regulation. The question at once emerged as to whether in such cases the expert finding should be subject to reëxamination of the facts in the review proceeding. In cases

[2] The doctrine that, because of the separation of powers, the courts may not hear appeals from executive agencies.

[3] People ex rel. Copcutt *v.* Board of Health, 140 N. Y. 1. As a matter of fact, the older doctrine was that if the administrative action was "judicial" in character, the officials were protected by the principle of judicial immunity and so were not liable to suit at all. See above, Chapter III, note 20, p. 44, and cases there discussed. On this theory, the only kind of action which could be reviewed in a damage suit was action where there had been no administrative "findings," and where in consequence the "findings" had to be made in the review proceeding. This is really the only field in which review by damage suit is properly applicable.

[4] Considerable difficulty has arisen because certain statutes have permitted administrative authorities to make their finding on the basis of their own investigation and without according the party to be affected by their action a hearing. These are the cases especially where the courts have felt that there should be a reëxamination of the facts in a proceeding at law; and this seems the real explanation for the holding in Miller *v.* Horton, *infra.*

where review was sought by a tort action, the difficulty could not be evaded; hence such decisions as Miller *v.* Horton [5] and Pearson *v.* Zehr,[6] and the strained attempt to escape from it in Fath *v.* Koeppel.[7] It happens, however, that an action for damages is a form of relief not well adapted to many of the newer kinds of administrative regulation, and seldom resorted to in connection with them; with the result that the extent to which administrative findings should be subject to the verdict of a jury is to-day of comparatively limited importance. On the other hand, review by injunction proceedings or certiorari is among the commonest of all the modes of testing administrative determinations; and here, as under the other usual modes of review, the doctrine that the review proceeding is in essence, as in form, collateral, although seldom directly expressed, has left its mark deeply on the cases. One troublesome incident of the tradition is the doctrine of so-called "jurisdictional facts."

II

The doctrine of "jurisdictional facts" is the second important legacy to the modern cases from the older theory of review. If the right of review is rested on the theory of *ultra vires*, and an administrative officer is given authority, for instance, to destroy infected articles or diseased animals, it is possible to argue that he is "without jurisdiction" or authority over articles not actually infected or over animals not really diseased.[8] Consequently, in order to determine the question

[5] 152 Mass. 540. [6] 138 Ill. 48.

[7] 72 Wis. 289. For the three cases mentioned in the text, see *supra*, p. 44.

[8] See the valuable discussion in Vanfleet on *Collateral Attack*, § 63, with references to cases in other branches of the law where the same point emerged. Sir Matthew Hale seems chargeable with the authorship of the doctrine of "jurisdictional fact." See Terry *v.* Huntingdon, Hardres, 480. Of course there is no reason why it could not be argued that the officer was given jurisdiction over "animals," for the purpose of determining whether or not they were diseased. This would admit, however, a judicial element in the nature of his duties, and under the older theory, if the administrative action was "judicial," the official was protected from suit by judicial immunity. The theory of jurisdictional fact seems to have been seized upon as an entering wedge to make room for some judicial review in cases where the doctrine of judicial immunity excluded such review altogether save for improper motives. Its development

of his "jurisdiction," it becomes necessary to determine in the review proceedings these "jurisdictional facts." It may be, and usually is, the case, however, that the very essence of the administrative proceeding has been the determination by expert specialists of precisely these facts after due notice and hearing. On the doctrine of "jurisdictional facts," the determination must be made over again, and independently, by the court or jury, in order to determine whether the administrative agency exceeded its competence. Such a doctrine logically applied would eviscerate the whole administrative process, and it is not applied logically; but enough of it is left to confuse very badly the utterances of the courts on the question of review of facts. Even the United States Supreme Court has slipped into the statement that the Interstate Commerce Commission is "without jurisdiction" over reasonable rates; [9] and while the implications of the words have never been followed, it has been held occasionally in land cases that a determination of the Land Office as to the saline or swamp character of lands was a determination of a "jurisdictional fact" which might be reëxamined at law.[10] But the great weight of authority is now the other way; the old doctrine lingers on only enough to infect the cases with the irritating uncertainty of an equivocal phrase. Sometimes the phrase is employed to conceal and confuse an altogether different ground of review, as in Great Western Power Co. *v.* Pillsbury,[11] where it was apparently used to mean only that it was within the power of the courts to give a legal definition to the term "wilful misconduct" as used in a statutory provision depriving employees guilty of "wilful misconduct" of the benefits of a workmen's compensation act. This is an instance of the dangerously easy transition between "fact" in the sense of proved circumstances, and "fact" in the sense

was aided by the fact that certiorari has also come to be limited, like a tort action, to the question of jurisdiction. See *supra*, Chapter III, note 20, pp. 44 ff., and note 79, pp. 62 ff. For another discussion of the doctrine of "jurisdictional facts" see *supra*, Chapter IX, notes 13 and 17, pp. 257 and 260.

[9] Interstate Commerce Commission *v.* Louisville & Nashville R. Co., 227 U. S. 88.

[10] Morton *v.* Nebraska, 21 Wall. 660.

[11] 170 Cal. 180.

of the meaning of the word or term into which those circumstances are summed up for the purpose of attaching legal consequences to them. The United States Supreme Court steered a true line, even if with a harsh result, between the Ju Toy case [12] on one side and Gonzalez *v.* Williams [13] on the other.

The Pillsbury case was one in which the doctrine of jurisdictional fact was invoked in a review proceeding brought by certiorari. Such a proceeding is not even formally collateral like a tort action or a bill for an injunction. It is in the nature of direct review for error,[14] and recognizes of itself the essentially judicial nature of the action sought to be reviewed. For such a proceeding the doctrine of *ultra vires* no longer provides an adequate basis. The reviewing court sits as a court of error from an inferior tribunal, and not to hear an independent complaint. There is therefore no such need as in a collateral proceeding for an independent retrial of the facts. On the contrary, ordinary principles of direct review are clearly applicable, with the presumption which they carry in favor of the correctness of the finding of fact made by the inferior tribunal. The way is opened for allowing to expert administrative findings that conclusiveness on matters other than precepts of law which is essential to the effective functioning of administrative regulation.

We have seen that the tendency of the courts and the weight of authority is in the direction of allowing such con-

[12] 198 U. S. 253.

[13] 192 U. S. 1.

[14] Certiorari is not "collateral" but "direct" attack, Great Western Power Co. *v.* Pillsbury, 170 Cal. 185; Vanfleet on *Collateral Attack*, § 2. Thus a writ of error was originally only a species of certiorari, 2 Williams' Saunders' Reports, 101a. "And a distinction is taken by Lord Holt, that whenever a new jurisdiction is created by act of parliament, and the court or judge that exercises this jurisdiction, acts as a court or judge of record according to the course of the common law, a writ of error lies on their judgments; but where they act in a summary method, or in a new course different from the common law, a writ of error does not lie, but a certiorari. 1 Salk. 263," *ibid.* The case referred to by Serjeant Williams is Groenvelt *v.* Burwell, also reported in 1 Lord Raymond 454, see especially p. 469; s. c., 12 Mod. 386. The opinion of Lord Holt in this case, as given in Lord Raymond's report, contains an elaborate statement of the law as it then existed relating to the review of administrative adjudications by actions against officials and by certiorari.

clusiveness in many instances. This tendency marks the recognition of an essentially new basis of review, and a departure from the earlier conception of administrative adjudication as on all fours with the executive act of an old-fashioned officer like a sheriff. The courts have come to speak frequently of administrative adjudicating agencies in frank terms as "special tribunals" or "tribunals of limited jurisdiction," [15] and to define the scope of court review in language at once broader in some respects, and narrower in others, than that appropriate to *ultra vires*. Other analogies have been sought, and the forms of expression most frequently employed are those which are borrowed from review by a court of error of the verdict of a jury. Thus it is said that "the court will not consider whether on like testimony it would have made a similar ruling"; [16] "the courts are not entitled to substitute their judgment for that of the commission"; [17] "the finding of the administrative body will not be disturbed unless unsupported by evidence"; [18] and sometimes the analogy of a jury has been frankly drawn.[19]

In what has already been said concerning the power of the courts to review on points of law, emphasis has been laid on the impossibility of hoping to establish a clear line between so-called "questions of law" and "questions of fact" by any substantive test of definition. All that can be said is, that any factual state or relation which the courts conclude to regard as sufficiently important to be made decisive for all subsequent cases of similar character becomes thereby a matter of law for formulation by the court. The difficulties which arise on review of administrative orders are for the most part of the same nature as those applying to the review of verdicts. The danger is greater, however, that in the administrative cases there will be undue interference by the

[15] United States *v.* Commissioner, 5 Wall. 563; Johnson *v.* Towsley, 13 Wall. 72.

[16] Interstate Commerce Commission *v.* Union Pacific R. Co., 222 U. S. 541.

[17] People ex rel. New York Gas Co. *v.* McCall, 245 U. S. 345.

[18] Manufacturers' R. Co. *v.* United States, 246 U. S. 457.

[19] Papinaw *v.* Grand Trunk R. Co., 189 Mich. 441, at p. 445; People ex rel. Edison Co. *v.* Willcox, 151 Ap. Div. (N. Y.) 823, at p. 842.

court with the conclusions of the fact-finding body. This danger arises both from a misunderstanding of the nature of the distinction between questions of law and questions of fact, and also from the exercise by the courts of their power to say whether or not a finding was unsupported by evidence.

III

One of the most frequent sources of confusion between law and fact is suggested by the Pillsbury case. Certain facts are established by the fact-finding body, having a bearing on the question of whether or not the conduct of an employee was "wilful misconduct." From these facts, the fact-finding body draws the conclusion of the presence or absence of such misconduct. This is no doubt a legal conclusion — that is, a conclusion having significance for the legal result of the case. Is it therefore a conclusion to be drawn by the court rather than by the fact-finding body? There are two possible methods of approaching this question. In the first place, it may be said that whether or not the special facts found sum up into the legal conclusion of wilful misconduct depends on the definition given to the latter term. If it is desired to give a fixed and explicit definition of wilful misconduct, the construction of such a definition is obviously a matter of law for the court. It is not sound, however, to argue that this means that the question of whether the special facts proved in any particular case amount to wilful misconduct is therefore a question of law for the court. If that were so, the question of whether the facts in a tort case amount to negligence would likewise have to be for the court to determine. But it is elementary that such a question is for the jury. The confusion arises from failure to distinguish between the task of establishing a definition, and that of saying whether or not particular facts correspond with it.[20] The former is the question for

[20] "It is important and difficult to distinguish properly between the *interpretation* and *application* of language. . . . The process by which, having a term given, we discover its meaning, or the facts which *may* be subsumed under it, is interpretation; the process by which, starting with certain facts, we ascertain the legal category under which they *must* be placed . . . is that of the application of the law. These two terms, therefore, taken in their full extent, are each

the court, the latter is for the fact-finding body. The court may examine the facts to see whether by any rational possibility of inference they can be summed up into the established definition, or to single out from among them as a step forward in the development of a rule of law some new fact to be hence-

the converse of the other: one denoting the process by which we descend from the general to the particular; the other that by which we rise from the particular to the general," Professor W. G. Hammond, in his edition (3d) of Lieber's *Hermeneutics*, pp. 246, 247. Professor Hammond also quotes Trendelenburg: "The application of every law may be presented in the form of a syllogism in which the legal provision constitutes the major premise; and after this has been determined, the question is upon the subsumption of facts in the minor," *Naturrecht auf dem Grunde der Ethik*, § 78. *Cf.* also Alexander Hamilton: "Every specific case is a matter of fact, for the law gives the definition. . . . The crime is matter of law as far as definition is concerned; fact as far as we are to determine its existence" (*Works*, ed. Lodge, viii, 397). This distinction between "interpretation" and "application," between "definition" and "subsumption," traces the line marked out in our law between the provinces of the court and jury: "definition" is for the court, "subsumption" for the jury. Thus a typical statement is the following: "For the court to say to the jury that certain facts *per se* constitute negligence is improper. Negligence is a question of fact to be proved like any other fact in issue. But of course this does not mean that the definition of negligence is a question of fact. . . . Negligence does not become a question of law alone unless the acts constituting it are of such a character that all reasonable men would concur in pronouncing it so. . . . It is for the jury to determine whether the facts proved do or do not constitute negligence. . . . But where the act or conduct of the party charged with negligence is so clearly and palpably negligent that all reasonable minds would pronounce it so without hesitation or dissent, then the court may state to the jury by instruction that such acts constitute negligence. Also, when the admitted facts are such that no other conclusion could be reached than that of negligence, it then becomes a question of law," Hughes, *Instructions to Juries*, § 183. I submit that a failure to distinguish properly between "interpretation" or "definition" of law on the one hand, and its application on the other, is responsible for much of the confusion as to whether such questions as "reasonable time," "reasonable cause," "necessaries," and "negligence" are questions of "law" for the court, or of "fact" for the jury. It is clear that the court is, and must always be, at liberty to narrow or broaden the scope of these terms by exacter definition —*i. e.*, to continue to develop general rules of law to govern their meaning. But this does not mean that where the court is unable or has no desire to lay down such specific rules of general application, it yet remains at liberty to say in each case whether the evidence satisfies the existing definition. The latter power is by no means essential to the existence of the former. Yet it seems to be some latent idea that it is thus essential, and that one power cannot exist without the other, which underlies the view of Mr. Justice Holmes discussed in the next note, *infra*, and leads to the doctrine that reasonableness of time — *e. g.*, for giving notice of the dishonor of a bill of exchange — is a "question of

forth incorporated in the definition; but it may not pronounce in gross upon whether the facts meet the definition, if it cannot show the rational impossibility of their doing so.

There is a second way of approaching the question and reaching the same result by a simpler and more tangible line of reasoning. We start from the obvious proposition that a term like "wilful misconduct," or "due care," or "negligence," or "adequate service" cannot be defined with mechanical completeness. It must apply to so many different types of situations that it can be filled out in any given case only by the application of a standard — an undefined sense or intuition of what is proper under the circumstances. There is, in other words, always a gap to be bridged between the special subsidiary facts of such a case and the ultimate conclusion of "reasonableness" or "adequacy" or "wilfulness." The application of the standard is what bridges this gap. But such an application of a standard is precisely the function of the so-called "fact-finding" body, whether jury or administrative tribunal. Indeed, "standard-applying" body would seem a better designation.[21] The normal function of

law" for the court. All that the courts seem to have been reaching for by the statement that the latter question was one of law was the idea that they must be at liberty to develop rules, if they should so choose, to give greater definiteness and certainty to the content of reasonableness. Thus in a leading case Chief Justice Abbott said: "It is of the greatest importance to commerce that some plain and precise rule should be laid down to guide persons in all cases as to the time within which notice of the dishonor of bills must be given," and he proceeded to lay down such a rule, Williams *v.* Smith, 2 B. & Ald. 496. But when the courts then proceed to say that such a question is one of "law" for the court rather than of "fact" for the jury (Commercial National Bank *v.* Zimmerman, 185 N. Y. 210 — reasonableness of time for presentment for payment), they often understand themselves as reserving the power to say in each case, without laying down any rule, whether the legal conclusion is made out by, and is to be inferred from, the evidence. This is a very different power from the power to lay down a rule; yet it is the power which has established itself in the case of "reasonable cause" in actions for malicious prosecution, in the case of material loss by varying the risk of a surety, which was long on the point of establishing itself as to what constitutes necessaries for an infant, and which has been repudiated, except by Mr. Justice Holmes, as to negligence. See above, Chapter III, note 47, p. 53, and note 48, p. 53; Chapter V, note 72, p. 147.

21 With reference to the jury, this view has been challenged by Mr. Justice Holmes: "I do not believe that the jury have any historic or *a priori* right to

juries is to render general rather than special verdicts, and the application of a standard like "due care" is universally recognized as no part of the duties of the court. They may,

decide any standard of conduct. I think that the logic of the contrary view would be . . . that all the law properly is in their breasts," *Collected Legal Papers*, pp. 236, 237. And elsewhere: "It has often been said that negligence is pure matter of fact, or that, after the court has declared the evidence to be such that negligence *may* be inferred from it, the jury are always to decide whether the inference shall be drawn. But it is believed that the courts, when they lay down this broad proposition, are thinking of cases where . . . the main or only question is what the conduct [which is to be passed upon] was, not what standard shall be applied to it after it is established," *Common Law*, p. 124. For a case in which Mr. Justice Holmes applied his theory on the bench, see Lorenzo *v.* Wirth, 170 Mass. 596. Mr. Thayer, on the other hand, supported the view that the application of a standard was not merely for the jury, but raised only a question of fact — *i. e.*, an issue which was bound to differ in every specific case from every other, *Prelim. Treat. on Evidence*, p. 250. Professor Bohlen seems to be looking for middle ground ("Mixed Questions of Law and Fact," *Univ. of Pa. Law Rev.*, lxxii, 111 ff.). Starting from different premises, all three writers converge on strikingly similar and sound enough conclusions; but the premises are important because in less trusty hands they can diverge as well as converge in their results. Mr. Justice Holmes's view seems to be dictated fundamentally by a desire to harden standards into rules. "The tendency of the law must always be to narrow the field of uncertainty," *Common Law*, p. 127. "It ought to be possible to formulate these standards. . . . The featureless generality that the defendant was bound to use such care as a prudent man would do under the circumstances ought to be continually giving place to the specific one that he was bound to use this or that precaution under these or those circumstances," *ibid.*, p. 111. On the other hand, Judge Cooley writes: "The question [is] whether in the infinite variety of human transactions the law can say that as to certain of them the party was negligent. . . . Manifestly this is impossible. There is no clear line by which the infinite diversity of cases where injury has resulted may be classified. Seldom indeed is one case in its facts exactly like one which has preceded it. . . . Rules of law must be certain so as to constitute guides; but the rule in one case can never constitute a guide in the next if the facts and conclusions flowing from them are of that indeterminate character that the question whether the one runs parallel to the other is one upon which different minds . . . would be likely to disagree." *Treatise on the Law of Torts*, 2d ed., p. 801. But whether or not rules are desirable, it is of course always within the power of the courts in their control of the standard-applying body to lay them down — that is a different question from the one with which we are at present concerned; for when the rule comes, the standard goes; and what we are now interested in has reference to the period when a standard is still being applied on the theory that a rule is as yet impossible or is undesirable; our question is, shall the standard, while it still remains a standard, be applied by the court, or by the jury? Mr. Justice Holmes argues that it should be done by the court because the standard ought always to be

indeed, if they choose, narrow the room for the operation of the standard by inserting the wedge of a rigid rule like the so-called "stop, look, and listen" rule; but they exceed their

the same: "Any legal standard must in theory be one which would apply to all men under the same circumstances. . . . The standard must be fixed. . . . The ideal average prudent man . . . whose culpability or innocence is the supposed test, is a constant," *Common Law*, p. 111. "When we rule on evidence of negligence, we are ruling on a standard of conduct, a standard which we hold the parties bound to know beforehand, and which in theory is always the same upon the same facts and not a matter dependent upon the whim of the particular jury or the eloquence of the particular advocate," *Collected Legal Papers*, p. 235. But where the facts from case to case are sufficiently uniform to admit of an identical standard, what difference is there between such a standard, consistently applied, and a rule? And if they are not sufficiently uniform to admit of, or to justify, a rule, how can an identical standard be applied to them? Mr. Justice Holmes appears to fall into a type of reasoning he has done much to eliminate when he says, "It is obvious that a standard of conduct does not cease to be law because the facts to which that standard applies are not likely often to be repeated," *ibid.*, p. 236. Admitting that it is possible to use the term "law" in such a sense that there will be a "law" for every case, "a wilderness of single instances," there is danger that such "law," if laid down by judges, will be taken as of general application and applied to other cases as well,—that what was meant for a party will be bestowed on mankind. See some examples in Thayer, *op. cit.*, pp. 242 ff. "Precedents which have turned upon some question of fact, or some limited and incidental principle of evidence or common sense, have come to stand as settling the main doctrine of substantive law involved in the case," *ibid.*, p. 244. Mr. Justice Holmes is aware of this difficulty, and answers that "these considerations only lead to the conclusion that precedents should be overruled when they become inconsistent with present conditions," *Common Law*, p. 126. But if the precedent is established only to be in constant danger of being overruled, what becomes of the "fixity" of standard which Mr. Justice Holmes is seeking? And if the precedents are in continual need of being overruled, how can we say that there is sufficient uniformity to require or even to support a "fixed" standard? There are two great dangers to guard against: (1) the establishment of an excessive number of minute rules, or, what amounts to the same thing, "fixed" standards, which are no sooner established than an effort must be made to get rid of them; (2) the confusion between a general rule and a conclusion not meant to extend beyond the case in hand. It is submitted that both these dangers are enhanced by committing to the same hands the function of pronouncing rules and applying standards. The difference between the general and the particular ought so far as possible not to be blurred. Where no two cases ought to be treated as if exactly alike, it is misleading to seek for a common standard. Room must be made for that "administrative" element of free discretion which Professor Bohlen says is left to the jury because of "the public's desire to have its conduct judged by laymen, by the man in the street," *op. cit.*, p. 116. For a confused statement by Coke which has been the cause of some subsequent uncertainty, see Priddle and Napper's case, 11 Coke Rep. 8b, at 10b.

province if they undertake to apply the standard themselves directly to the facts. This is well understood in the law as to review of verdicts. It does not seem so well understood with regard to the determinations of administrative tribunals. And yet in the latter cases, where the standard is often a technical one, requiring scientific knowledge and insight for its application, there is all the greater need for unhampered action by the standard-applying body except where the courts desire to interfere for the purpose of applying or establishing some clearly formulated general rule of law.

The well-worn language about questions of law and questions of fact serves largely to conceal these considerations. It is easy to borrow from the law of pleading the phrase that a term like negligence is a "conclusion of law," and, as the next step, to slip into the specious inference that a matter which is a conclusion of law is one which must necessarily be determined by the court. This tendency is successfully avoided for the most part in the review of verdicts; on review of administrative determinations it is still a delusive snare.[22] Familiar formulae lend it attractiveness, like the oft-repeated one that "the legal effect of evidence is a question of law." [23] This can easily be taken to mean that the question of whether or not the subsidiary facts proved in the case sum up into the legally pertinent conclusion of reasonableness or adequacy, for example, is a question for the court;[24] which would be in effect to remove from the administrative body and impose on the court the function of applying the appropriate standard. In truth, the formula when rightly used is only a misleading ellipsis for a perfectly correct proposition connected with the power of the courts to reverse a verdict or adminis-

[22] The Supreme Court perhaps fell into it in Federal Trade Commission *v.* Gratz, 253 U. S. 421, where it said that it was ultimately for the courts to determine what was unfair competition.

[23] Interstate Commerce Commission *v.* Louisville & Nashville R. Co., 227 U. S. 88. For the same proposition announced in reviewing a jury's verdict, see Indiana R. Co. *v.* Watson, 114 Ind. 20.

[24] This was the view taken by eighteenth-century English courts in the seditious libel prosecutions, see above, Chapter V, note 79; and it seems to be Mr. Justice Holmes's view; see above, Chapter III, note 55; this chapter, note 20; and Lorenzo *v.* Wirth, 170 Mass. 596.

trative finding which is arbitrary because beyond the bounds of rational inference from the evidence. It is but an ambiguous shorthand way of saying that "when it is contended that an order was made without any evidence whatever to support it, the consideration of such a question involves not an issue of fact but one of law." [25]

This disposes of another erroneous doctrine latent in the conventional formula for stating the grounds of review — the doctrine, namely, that, where the evidence before the fact-finding body is undisputed, the reviewing court is free to draw its own conclusions from it, independently of the conclusions reached by the former. This is the doctrine which was applied by the Commerce Court and rejected by the Supreme Court in United States *v.* Louisville & Nashville R. Co., 235 U. S. 314. It is a natural corollary of the deceptive formula that "the legal effect of evidence is a question of law." [26] Whether evidence *can* rationally have the legal effect attributed to it is one question, and is the question for the court; whether evidence *shall* have a legal effect of which it is rationally susceptible is another question, and is for the body to which the application of the standard is entrusted.[27]

[25] Florida East Coast R. Co. *v.* United States, 234 U. S. 167.

[26] For the same doctrine erroneously applied to jury verdicts, see discussion in Wigmore on Evidence, 2d ed., v, 559. For the correct doctrine see Bowen L. J., in Davey *v.* London & Southwestern R. Co., 12 Q. B. D. 70: "It is not because facts are admitted that it is therefore for the judge to say what the decision upon them should be. If the facts which are admitted are capable of two equally possible views which reasonable people may take, and one of them is more consistent with the case for one party than for the other, it is the duty of the judge to let the jury decide between such conflicting views." And *cf.* Mr. Justice Buller in Company of Carpenters *v.* Hayward, Douglas 373, at p. 375: "Whether there be any evidence is a question for the judge. Whether sufficient evidence is for the jury."

[27] "From any given state of facts the judge must say whether negligence can legitimately be inferred, and the jury whether it ought to be inferred," Lord Cairns in Metropolitan Ry. Co. *v.* Jackson, 3 A. C. (1877), 193, at p. 200. "To ask, 'Should we have found the same verdict' is surely not the same thing as to ask whether there is room for a reasonable difference of opinion," Brett, M. R. in Belt *v.* Lawes, London *Times*, March 18, 1884, quoted in Thayer, *Cases on Evidence*, 2d ed., p. 163.

IV

The door through which a way is properly opened for judicial interference with administrative application of standards is the well-established doctrine that a determination will be set aside which is without evidence to support it; [28] or, differently expressed, which could not rationally have been reached by fair-minded men from the evidence.[29] This is a rule obviously borrowed from the law governing court control of the verdicts of juries. It is familiar law that, where the existence of negligence or some similar matter is at issue, "the correctness of the finding of the jury thereon will not be reviewed except to determine if there is evidence on which a reasonable man might reach the conclusion arrived at." [30] But on review of administrative orders the statement of the rule is often colored by vestiges of the old *ultra vires* theory of review. Thus it is said that "to make an essential finding without supporting evidence is arbitrary action"; [31] and accordingly "arbitrariness" is generally the ground expressly assigned for reversal. It has not been observed, however, that this slight difference in phrasing the rule has produced any important difference in the manner of applying it from that which prevails on review of verdicts.

A case of the latter kind affords the simplest illustration of the rule. In Union Pacific R. Co. *v.* Milliken [32] it was as a matter of law essential to plaintiff's recovery to show the defendant's knowledge of the incompetence of the engineer whose conduct had caused the injury complained of. No evidence was offered on this point. A verdict in favor of the plaintiff was accordingly set aside. There was, in other words, no ground upon which rational men could have inferred a fact legally essential to recovery. In Rowland *v.* Boyle, 244 U. S. 106, a proceeding to review a rate order of a state railroad commission, the carrier had in the proceedings before

[28] Interstate Commerce Commission *v.* Union Pacific R. Co., 222 U.S. 320.

[29] San Diego Land and Town Co. *v.* Jasper, 189 U.S. 439.

[30] Ricker *v.* Hall, 69 N. H. 592.

[31] Chicago Junction case, 264 U. S. 258, at p. 265.

[32] 8 Kans. 647, opinion per Brewer, J.

the commission presented the results of traffic studies, showing that the proposed rates would produce income below a fair return on the agreed value of the property. No attempt was apparently made by the advocates of the new rates to present rebutting figures, or any figures at all. An order establishing the rate was accordingly set aside. These are cases of the complete absence of evidence on an essential point.[33]

The strongest cases are those like the one last cited, where an order is made wholly on the basis of evidence which points in an opposite direction. Such was Dube's case, 226 Mass. 591. This was review of an order of an industrial accident board awarding compensation under a workmen's compensation act. The uncontradicted evidence showed that the decedent had met death by attempting to clean some machinery while in motion. The cleaning of machinery was apparently not within the scope of his employment. The board made a finding that he had been caught in the machinery while on his way to the toilet or for some other unknown purpose incidental to his employment, and awarded compensation. To reach this result the board had to disbelieve the testimony of every eye-witness and base its conclusion solely on the fact that the machinery which caused the accident was located on the way between decedent's work-bench and the toilet. The court held that the board's conclusion was not a rationally possible inference from the evidence before them.[34]

[33] See also Foster's case (review of workmen's compensation award), 242 Mass. 386; Voelz *v.* Industrial Accident Commission, 161 Wis. 240.

[34] In Carroll *v.* Knickerbocker Ice Co. (N. Y., App. Div., 1915), 155 N. Y. Supp. 1; (N. Y. Ct. of Appeals, 1916) 218 N. Y. 435, the decedent, the driver of an ice-wagon, after returning home from work, developed delirium tremens, of which he died. Before death, he told his wife and physician that his illness was due to his having been struck during the day by a 300-pound cake of ice in the course of his employment. His body showed no marks or bruises, and there was affirmative evidence that no cake of ice had struck him, but that at the time when the accident was supposed to have occurred, he was drinking in a saloon. Because the statute permitted hearsay evidence, the compensation commission felt bound to believe the decedent's statement that he had been struck, and awarded compensation to his widow. The award was sustained by the Appellate Division of the Supreme Court, and reversed by the Court of Appeals. The Court of Appeals said: "The act . . . gives the workmen's com-

A third type of case is where the inference of the fact-finding body involves an obvious logical error. Such a case was Florida East Coast R. Co. *v.* United States et al., 234 U. S. 167. There the Interstate Commerce Commission had considered in the same proceeding the question of reducing rates on three railroads running through the state of Florida, of which the East Coast was one. The evidence showed reduced costs on the other two lines, but negatived the inference of a reduction in costs on the East Coast. Nevertheless, the Commission included all three roads in its order putting the reduced rates into effect. The order was set aside by the Supreme Court, so far as it affected the East Coast.[35]

Again, a conclusion of a fact-finding body will be set aside where it rests upon an inference at variance with the known principles of physics or mechanics.[36] Thus in Nugent *v.* Milling Co., 131 Mo. 241, the court thought that it was physically impossible to reconcile the testimony as to how the accident occurred with the facts necessary to support a recovery. In setting aside the verdict, the court said: "How a scoop held by the right hand of plaintiff resting upon the frame of the crushing rollers could be struck by a descending object so as to cause the left hand, that was independent and working above it, to be knocked downward into the crushing roller involves a principle of mechanics that is incomprehen-

pensation commission free rein in making its investigations and in conducting its hearings, and authorizes it to receive and consider, not only hearsay testimony, but any kind of evidence that may throw light on a claim pending before it. . . . This is all true, but, as I read it, section 68, as applied to this case, does not make the hearsay testimony offered by the claimant sufficient ground to uphold the award which the commission made. The section does not declare the probative force of any evidence. . . . The only substantial evidence before the commission was to the effect that no cake of ice slipped and struck the decedent, and there were no bruises or marks upon his body which indicated that he had been so injured. The findings to the contrary rest solely on the decedent's statement made at a time when he was confessedly in a highly nervous state, which ended in his death from delirium tremens. Such hearsay testimony is no evidence."

[35] For a similar case, see Northern Pacific R. Co. *v.* Department of Public Works, 268 U. S. 39. *Cf.* Louisville and Nashville R. Co. *v.* United States, 238 U. S. 1.

[36] See Quigley *v.* Naughton, 100 Appeal Div. (N. Y.) 476.

sible. The occurrence or non-occurrence of a given thing as a fact, that contravenes laws of mechanics that are so general that the courts cannot ignore them, cannot be said to be matters of fact that must go to the jury." Whatever we may think of the application of the principle to the facts of the case, it is clearly sound.[37] A verdict based on an inference that an injury had been caused by witchcraft or the "evil eye" would doubtless have to be set aside.[38]

V

The difficult cases are those which occur when the doubt arises not from the logical or physical impossibility of the inference, nor from the total absence of evidence, but from its meager and unsatisfactory character. If there is a reversal on such a ground, must it be said that the reviewing court is interfering improperly with the function of the body responsible for applying the standard? The difficulty is illustrated by a number of cases reviewing orders of state railway commissions which required the stopping of trains at certain stations on the ground of the inadequacy of other service.[39] One of the earliest cases was Mississippi Railroad Commission *v.* Illinois Central R. R. Co., 203 U. S. 335. There the Supreme Court, without analyzing the evidence, flatly announced that in its opinion the towns affected already enjoyed adequate service. "The question is before us on uncontradicted evidence as to whether there were or were not proper facilities, and we hold that there were." This seems clearly wrong. It looks like an application, in the erroneous sense, of the dictum that "the legal effect of evidence is a question of law." [40] It was a direct assumption by the Court

[37] See also Spiro *v.* St. Louis Traction Co., 102 Mo. Ap. 250, and Scanlon *v.* Railroad Co. (Cal., 1898), 55 Pac. 694, holding that the courts must take judicial notice of the "laws of nature," and the principles of mathematics.

[38] Query whether this result can be said to incorporate into the law all the currently accepted principles of natural science as legal propositions?

[39] Cases should be distinguished where the question was as to the constitutionality of stop-orders made by direct legislative enactment — *i. e.*, not as a result of quasi-judicial procedure. See the discussion of these cases in note 39, Chapter VI, p. 183, above.

[40] Above, p. 318.

of the function of applying the standard of adequate facilities. The next case, that of Atlantic Coast Line *v.* Wharton, 207 U. S. 328, shows the proper method of approach.[41] The issue was the same. This time, however, the Court in its opinion made a careful analysis of the evidence. The trains which were ordered to stop were fast through trains running between New York and Florida. Latta, the town where the stop was to be made, had a population of about four hundred people. The back country was sparsely settled. The evidence presented by those who had petitioned for the stop-order was to the effect that only four or five persons a week desired to use the trains. They were already making a regular stop at a point a few miles distant. The Court pointed out that on such a showing there were inevitably a large number of other towns which had as good a claim as Latta to have the trains stop. "To stop these trains at Latta and other stations like it which could bring equally strong reasons for the stoppage of the trains at their stations, would wholly change the character of the trains," and convert them from fast through trains into locals. The order was accordingly set aside. This is certainly an interference with the application of a standard, but the Court presents, so to speak, a bill of the particulars wherein the attempted application had exceeded the bounds of reason. In effect, the order of the state commission either involved the logical inconsistency of giving Latta a fast train by converting it into a slow train, or violated the legal principle that towns similarly conditioned are entitled to the same service.

A later case of substantially similar character was Mississippi Railroad Commission *v.* Mobile and Ohio R. R., 244 U. S. 388. Here the question was whether the discontinuance of certain trains deprived the communities affected of adequate service. The state railroad commission ruled that it did, and ordered the trains restored. Again the Supreme Court in its opinion carefully analyzed the evidence. It was admitted that the trains could be run only at a heavy loss.

[41] Opinion by Mr. Justice Peckham, who also wrote the opinion in the preceding case.

The company's passenger business was not paying its way, and the operation of the road as a whole showed an increasing deficit each month. The company was cutting down expenditures at all points, had decreased the salaries of its officers, and had stopped making needed repairs to rolling-stock. It was shown that the trains in question had originally been put on as an experiment, with the idea of developing local business which had not materialized. After their removal, the through trains, which had not stopped before, took over all their local stops, though at less convenient hours. Affidavits from a large number of prominent business men in the territory served declared that because of the slow-down in business the removal of the trains would not materially injure the communities affected. On the other hand, "the evidence on which the railroad commission acted is impressively meager in extent and inadequate in character. It consists of the testimony of two men, wholly without qualifying training or experience, as to the cost of operating such trains, and of a number of men as to the inconvenience which would be caused by the taking off of the trains, chiefly to commercial travellers living in Meridian and desiring to visit the small villages and hamlets on the line. . . . We [think] that the order, at the time and under the circumstances when it was issued, was arbitrary and unreasonable." This is at least not the mere setting of the opinion of the Court against the opinion of the commission; the misapplication of the standard is corrected under an obvious sense of full responsibility to point out the errors committed, and to avoid even the appearance of an arbitrary substitution of the Court's independent judgment for that of the commission.[42]

[42] *Cf.* Washington ex rel. Oregon R. R. & Navigation Co. *v.* Fairchild, 224 U. S. 510, where an order of a state commission requiring the establishment of certain connections was set aside as unreasonable. The Court said: "The question presented is whether as a matter of law the facts proved show such a public necessity as authorizes the taking of property. . . . The testimony introduced as to the character of traffic movement is not very satisfactory. A careful examination of the record fails to show what business would be routed over these connections or what saving would come to the public if they were constructed. There is nothing by which to compare the advantages to the public with the expense to the defendant."

VI

Cases like Philadelphia and Reading R. Co. *v.* United States, 240 U. S. 334,[43] illustrate the way in which a supposed review of the sufficiency of evidence to support a finding often turns on a concealed or unconsciously apprehended rule of law. Another such instance is the recent case of United States *v.* New York Central R. Co., 263 U. S. 603. There Congress had passed an act directing the Interstate Commerce Commission to require interstate railroads to issue interchangeable mileage coupons at just and reasonable rates in such denominations as the Commission might prescribe. The Commission construed the act to require the issue of such tickets at lower than the regular rate of passenger fares, and made an order accordingly. The order was set aside by the Supreme Court on the ground that there was no evidence to show that the reduced rate was "just and reasonable" as required by the act. The Court examined the Commission's findings, and said: "The Commission in its report pointed out that the net railway operating income was below the return fixed as reasonable, discarded the supposed analogy between the carload rate and the mileage ticket, intimated that the supposed benefit that the carrier might get from the advance use of money would be more than offset by the increased expenses, and said that the question whether the scrip ticket would stimulate travel was a matter of speculation. After thus excluding the grounds upon which the order could be justified, the Commission held that the obvious spirit and apparent purpose of the law required that the experiment should be tried, and on these premises declared that the reduced rates would be 'just and reasonable' for this class of travel." It seems clear that the case really turned on the question of the proper interpretation of the act of Congress. There was no evidence to support the finding because the Court chose to hold that the words 'just and reasonable' as used in the statute had no other meaning than when applied to rates in general. On the interpretation adopted by

[43] See Chapter VI, p. 173 *supra.*

the Commission, the question of the sufficiency of the evidence would not have arisen in the same form.

Sometimes it is not so easy to disentangle the point of law which causes the defect of evidence. One of the most serious grounds of confusion in the cases is the frequent failure in the opinions to indicate whether the holding rests on some new legal rule which the Court chooses to adopt in carrying forward the development of the law, or on the correction of what is held to be a mere error of inference in the application of a standard. This confusion is suggested by comparing United States *v.* Baltimore and Ohio R. Co., 231 U. S. 274, with Manufacturers' R. Co. *v.* United States, 246 U. S. 457. In the former case a large shipper, the Arbuckle Sugar Refining Company, owned and maintained a dock in Brooklyn, and operated a ferry from the dock to the rail-ends of the trunk-lines in Jersey City. About one third of the freight handled by the dock and ferry consisted of the products of the Arbuckle Company, while the rest was received from the public generally. The railroads were in the habit of providing at their own expense receiving docks and ferry service for freight offered in Brooklyn and Manhattan. They therefore entered into an agreement with the Arbuckle Company to pay to the latter for its service an allowance out of the freight rate on all goods which it delivered to the rail-ends. This had the effect of making a slight reduction in the freight rate on the Arbuckle Company's own products. A competing refinery, which likewise delivered its products to the rail-ends but did not offer ferry service to the public generally, demanded a similar allowance and was refused. It filed a complaint with the Interstate Commerce Commission, which ordered that the allowance be either extended to the competitor or discontinued as to the Arbuckle Company. This order the Supreme Court set aside. The result seems correct on a principle of law analogous to that later announced in the Tap-line cases, 234 U. S. 1, without any need of considering inferences of fact. It is interesting to compare this result, however, with that later reached in the Manufacturers' Railway case, 246 U. S. 457. There different parts of the city of St. Louis were served by two terminal railroads. One of these, the so-called Terminal Railway, was owned by the trunk-lines. The other, the Manufacturers' Railway, was owned by the Anheuser-Busch brewing interests, from which a considerable portion of its freight was derived. The trunk-lines refused to absorb the Manufacturers' Railway's charges and thereby extend their flat St. Louis rate to the territory served by it, while doing so with respect to the territory served by the Terminal Railway. On complaint to the Interstate Commerce Commission, the Commission refused to do more than order the trunk-lines to establish a joint rate with the Manufacturers' Railway which should be higher than the St. Louis flat rate by an amount equal to the Manufacturers' Railway's division of the joint rate. This, of course, did not remove the alleged discrimination against the territory served by the latter, and the case was taken to the Supreme Court. The Court refused to interfere with the order, saying: "Whether a preference or advantage of discrimination is undue or unreasonable is one of those questions of fact that have been confided by Congress to the judgment and discretion of the Commission. . . . In the present case, the negative finding of the Commission upon the question of undue discrimination was based upon a consideration of the different conditions of location, ownership, and operation as between the Manufacturers' Railway and the Terminal Railway. The conclusions were reached after full hearing, are not without support in the evidence, and we are unable to say that they show abuse of discretion." This language clearly does not mean, in view of the result reached in cases like the Baltimore and Ohio case, that the broad ultimate conclusion of discrimination is one on which the opinion of the Commission will be taken immediately as final; for in reaching that conclusion the Commission body may run against rules of law laid down by the Court, which annul the effect of subsidiary facts that might otherwise be regarded as amounting to discrimination. Thus it seems to be established by the Baltimore and Ohio case that it cannot be held to be illegal discrimination merely to grant a division of rates to a public carrier which is owned by, and mainly serves, a single shipper. The Tap-line cases [44] went still further and, reversing another order of the Commission, held that the Commission must affirmatively require trunk-lines to grant a division of rates to such a carrier. This, however, the Court refused to compel in the Manufacturers' Railway case, except in a way which still subjected the territory served to the disadvantage of relative inequality of rates as compared with the territory served by a competitor. The latter result may be contrasted with that reached in the more recent Knoxo case, United States *v.* Illinois Central R. Co., 263 U. S. 515. There the Commission made an order compelling the establishment of a joint rate with a tap-line to Knoxo at the flat rate which prevailed for competing points. This was substantially the relief sought in the Manufacturers' Railway case and there denied. The Supreme Court sustained the order on the ground that it was within the discretionary power of the Commission and was not without evidence to support it. In other words, in the Manufacturers' Railway case and in the Knoxo case the Supreme Court sustained two orders of the Commission which reached opposite results on facts which in main outline were similar. The Court, in short, did not choose to lay down a rule of law either way. It did not decide to single out any of the subsidiary facts and make a matter of law of it. It did say, however, in the Manufacturers' Railway case that ownership of the short-line was one of the facts which it was within the discretion of the Commission to consider in determining whether a division of rates would amount to illegal discrimination. This seems hard to square with the result reached in the Baltimore and Ohio case. Can it be that the latter decision was reached, after all, not as the result of the application of a rule of law, but as a result of the Court's drawing its own inference from all the facts? [45] The important

[44] 234 U. S. 1.

[45] The alternative form of the Commission's order in the Baltimore and Ohio case no doubt had much to do with bringing upon it the disapproval of

point for our purpose is that there is nothing in the language of the opinion to give the basis for a conclusion on this question.

These cases where the decision of the fact-finding body is set aside by the Court as beyond the bounds of rational inference, without indicating whether the impossibility of inference is or is not due to the operation of some principle which the Court chooses to regard as a principle of law, are often the very cases which in the course of time lead to the emergence of new legal rules and principles.[46] By a comparison of the facts of case after case of such a character, it becomes possible in time to draw distinctions and recognize conformities which amount to a rule of law even before it has been formulated in express language by the courts.[47] This process may be thought essential to a law like ours, which advances from case to case. The facts and the decision are, after all, the thing, and not the judicial expression of opinion.[48] But such a process, exclusively applied, would ignore the important part which attempted formulation plays in legal growth, and would in effect deny to law articulate expression. It is

the Court. It is interesting that this case has never been subsequently cited by the Court. Another case as to which it has proved difficult to determine whether it was meant to lay down a rule of law, and if so what rule, is Sjoli *v.* Dreschel, 199 U. S. 564: see the conflicting views in the majority and dissenting opinions in Weyerhaeuser *v.* Hoyt, 219 U. S. 380.

[46] "When a judge rules that there is no evidence of negligence, he does something more than is embraced in an ordinary ruling that there is no evidence of a fact. He rules that the acts or omissions proved or in question do not constitute a ground of legal liability, and in this way the law is gradually enriching itself." Holmes, *Common Law*, pp. 120, 121.

[47] See Jeremiah Smith, *Harv. Law Rev.*, xxv, 306, 307.

[48] "The force of a precedent does not lie in the language of the judge deciding it. It is a commonplace of the bench that the authority of a case lies in the point decided, and not in the language of the judge; that it is the reason and spirit of the cases which form the law; that the law consists in the principles recognized by the cases, and not in the terms employed. No judge hesitates, even while following a precedent, to criticise the language in which it is stated, or to restate, in a form he deems more exact, the principle upon which the former decision rested." Professor William G. Hammond, in Appendix N to his edition (3d) of Lieber's *Hermeneutics*, p. 324.

inconsistent with the time-honored practice of accompanying decisions with reasoned opinions.[49] It is perhaps less detrimental to the growth of law in the long run than it is to the immediate decision of the actual case, which should be reached by a court that has a clear idea of what it is doing. No court should make a decision without understanding whether it is applying a legal principle or merely differing from the fact-finding body as to an inference peculiar to the case. Without such understanding, the one will inevitably invade the province of the other; and the process of administrative application of standards should not be interfered

[49] See Wambaugh, *The Study of Cases*, 2d ed., secs. 13–19, especially at p. 24: "If this reasoning be carried out to its logical conclusions, the result must be that the proposition involved in a case can be written by examining the questions presented in the record, and by then examining the result shown by the judgment, wholly ignoring the opinion on which the judgment was based. In other words, the proposition would be one and the same whether there was or was not an opinion. Yet this is not true." *Cf.* also Sylvester Douglas, in preface to his Reports, at p. v: "The immediate province of the courts of justice is to administer law in particular cases. But it is equally a branch of their duty, and one of still greater importance to the community, to expound the law they administer upon such principles of argument and construction as may furnish rules which shall govern in all similar or analogous cases." *Cf.* also Beck, J., in Dubuque *v.* Illinois Central Railroad Co., 39 Iowa, 56, at p. 80: "A case is to be regarded as a precedent when it furnishes rules that may be applied in settling the rights of parties. These rules are to be discovered in the opinions of the judges, and constitute the reasons for the decision." The United States Supreme Court held in Murdock *v.* Memphis, 20 Wallace, 614, that on writ of error from a state court it would look at the opinion of the court below as well as at the record, to determine what questions were actually decided. In the National Prohibition Cases, 253 U. S. 350, the Supreme Court handed down its decision sustaining the validity of the Eighteenth Amendment and the constitutionality of the Volstead Act, accompanied merely by a brief list of "conclusions" instead of a reasoned opinion. Chief Justice White wrote a separate concurring opinion in which he gave his reasons for supporting the decision and expressed his regret that in a case of such magnitude the Court "deemed it proper to state only ultimate conclusions without an exposition of the reasoning by which they have been reached." This case gave rise to a note on "Decisions without Opinions," in *Harv. Law Rev.*, xxxiv, 314, wherein it is said: "Certain cases . . . mould or modify the law. Such sources must contain the principles and the ratiocination which guided the court. Without reasons a decision is authority only for the special set of facts to which it is addressed. And if this were the only species of decision, the evolution of the law must proceed by some course other than the judicial."

with except for the conscious purpose of developing or enforcing precepts of law.[50]

[50] In cases within the field of administrative regulation, particularly regulation of public utilities and business practices, it is much harder than in tort or commercial cases to let the facts and the decision speak for themselves without the aid of an opinion; for the facts are ordinarily so numerous and complicated that it is practically impossible to infer, without articulate expression by the court, precisely the ones which dictated the decision. This is the difficulty about applying in this field the doctrine that successive decisions will gradually "prick out a line" by approaching it from point to point on opposing sides. Too often the "points" lie nowhere in the neighborhood of one another, so that the result has few of the characteristics of a line.

CHAPTER XII

THE SUPREMACY OF LAW AND THE PROBLEM OF LEGAL EDUCATION

THE tendency to restrict judicial review of administrative determinations to narrow limits appears to have its source in two widely divergent considerations. On the one hand, in the case of ordinary police regulation by minor officials, it springs mainly from the need for summary administrative interference, and the inconvenience of having the courts clogged with a mass of petty cases which involve duplicating the work of local government agencies. In this field the courts themselves are a party to the movement. *Boni judicis est ampliare jurisdictionem* is a maxim which seems to have gone prevailingly out of fashion since judges ceased to be interested in the emoluments of litigation. But the consideration here touched on is impressive, and the problem of overcrowded dockets cannot be evaded. The solution suggests itself of establishing special courts with no other function than to review administrative action of this character in the first instance. Whether they should be "administrative courts" in the continental sense, which is the form the suggestion often takes, is a different matter altogether. If by administrative courts is meant anything more than courts dealing exclusively with review of administrative acts, the conclusions reached in preceding chapters would seem to require that they should not be. Certainly they should be courts of law and not of state, as, indeed, we are informed the French administrative tribunals themselves are coming more and more to be.[1] This phase of judicial review is therefore largely a mere matter of improving the machinery of review and, al-

[1] See H. J. Laski, "Responsibility of the State," in *Foundations of Sovereignty*, p. 133; Duguit *Law in the Modern State*, tr., Laski, pp. 184–196; G. Jèze, *Das Verwaltungsrecht der Französischen Republik* (Tübingen, 1913), pp. 394–396.

though of the utmost importance, does not touch directly the problem of the relation of law to discretion.

The second ground of opposition to a broad scope of review applies to the more outstanding fields of administrative control, such as the regulation of utilities and of business competition, where the opposition comes from progressive thinkers, who see in the courts an agency for thwarting social progress and who regard law as necessarily a Procrustes' bed of narrow precedent. I have already sought to show that the action of government requires in some degree to be brought to the touchstone of judicial decision if progress is to be orderly and consistent. At the same time it was found necessary to recognize that the application of law in practice often results in unsound decisions, which harden into inappropriate rules because of the failure of judges to carry forward legal development with due regard for its underlying principles. While the direct effect of such specific miscarriages of justice is generally overcome in time, the cumulative result is unfortunate in that it tends to strengthen opposition to the application of law at all in fields of social change. Nothing is more important for the attainment of the advantages of a régime of law than that it should more and more show a record of wholesome application and growth. It must demonstrate increasing usefulness in order to retain the opportunity to be useful at all. And this need for a proper rather than an improper application of law exists, as we saw, not more strongly in the new fields of social controversy than along the beaten paths of the law as well. There is about as much opportunity for a mechanical application of legal rules and concepts to work unjust results in the law of torts or contracts or trusts as in the field of utility regulation. The supremacy of law is throughout inextricably linked to its application and development along lines true to the changing facts and needs of the society to which it is sought to be applied.

I

Everything depends, then, on bench and bar acquiring and maintaining a sound insight into the nature and processes of the law.[2] The basic problem is as to the way in which lawyers and judges regard and understand the law, and this problem leads back to one of legal education.[3] The ordinary mind is not mobile, and the practitioner more or less carries through life the ideal of legal method which his law studies dictated, however much his practice may admittedly diverge from that ideal. If he later comes to the bench, the ideal is likely to resume its ascendency with force proportioned to atone for past infidelities. This is the more easy in that the "practical" attitude of many practitioners is after all not so far removed

[2] See address by Felix Frankfurter on "The Law and Law-Schools," in *Rep. Amer. Bar Assoc.* (1915), xxxix, 365. *Cf.* also the following: "The law is a public profession by which, more than by any other profession, the economic life and the government of the country are moulded. The proportion of lawyers in legislative bodies greatly exceeds the proportion of lawyers in the whole population. In executive office they are more numerous than are the followers of any other profession or occupation. Of course all men in judicial office are lawyers. And last, but of great importance, is the influence of lawyers as practicing attorneys in helping to shape the course of judicial decisions and to draft statutory and constitutional provisions which vitally affect the law," "Report of the Special Committee on Legal Education and Admissions to the Bar of the American Bar Assoc.," *Rep. Amer. Bar Assoc.* (1921), xlvi, 684. *Cf.* also Judge Baldwin: "There is no country in which it is as important that lawyers should be as well educated for their profession, as it is in the United States. Here they hold a political position. They are a recognized part of the machinery of government. All are officers of courts that have the acknowledged power of interpreting constitutions and statutes, which may be invoked as grounds of action or defence in pending litigation, and of holding statutes inconsistent with a constitution so interpreted to be void. . . . In the last resort, questions of constitutional law and statutory construction will be decided in a court, manned exclusively by those who have been trained for the bar, after hearing argument from lawyers who have been educated in the same manner," *Amer. Pol. Sci. Rev.*, ix, 437.

[3] "I have spoken little to my purpose if I have not made clear the necessity for broadening much the qualification of the general body of our judiciary to meet the important and responsible requirements that the present crisis in our community has thrust upon them. Their coming duties call for a basic knowledge of general and sociological jurisprudence, an intimate familiarity with the law as a science, and with its history, an ability to distinguish in it the fundamental from the casual, and constructive talent to enable them to reconcile the practical aspirations of social reformers with the priceless lessons of experience from the history of government and of law in practical operation. How can this be brought about? Only by broadening the knowledge and studies of the members of the legal profession. It is they who make the judges, who contribute to their education, and who help them to just, broad, and safe conclusions." W. H. Taft, *Popular Government*, pp. 235, 236.

as might at first appear from the most rigid ideal of law as a fixed system of geometrical abstractions. Both attitudes have in common that they are apt to regard any attempt to investigate the meaning and purpose of legal rules by reference to what lies outside of technical law as visionary and improper. An early training in law as a sort of geometry, followed by years of shrewd effort to circumvent its rules in the interest of clients, tends to produce in the end a judge or advocate incapable of recognizing distinctions which rest on solid differences from those which do not, and analogies which are substantial from those which are only formal.[4] In order to counteract the consequences of practice, a strong bent seems necessary at the beginning toward a conception of law as something other than a logical game where counters are manipulated to achieve formal symmetry or a forensic victory. If law is to play its part in social order, the lawyer should start with his eyes open as to the nature of legal premises and the valid method of drawing conclusions from them.

The matter of premises comes first. Too often a chain of legal reasoning goes forward apparently without conscious recognition that there is a premise at the bottom of it at all. Perhaps even more unhappy are cases where a premise is taken to be fundamental which validly is only secondary. For legal premises, like all others, rank themselves in an open hierarchy or series leading back from the more specific to the more general. Convenience demands that one lying somewhere along the line shall be taken as the abrupt starting-point for any given chain of reasoning. But no such starting point must ever be mistaken for absolute, and none should be taken at all without at least some tentative probing into what lies behind it. It may well be that a premise which

[4] "Under present conditions judges . . . are almost always chosen from the bar, and members of the bar usually represent private rather than public interests. It is only after service on the bench has begun that prejudice and bias in favor of private interests cease. The longer the judicial service, the more easy it is for considerations of public interest to secure an influence on the judicial attitude of mind." President Goodnow, *Social Reform and the Constitution*, p. 331.

under one set of conditions does well enough as a working hypothesis will under others prove inadequate, with the result that search must be made still further back, for one more remote and broader. The Trans-Missouri Freight Association case affords an illustration.[5] There the Supreme Court in its opinion seems to have adopted the premise that the law, in making restraints of trade illegal, had made everything illegal which lessened competition. At certain stages of economic development such a premise would perhaps have been well-enough justified as a working hypothesis. But the Court seems to have taken it as fundamental and did not inquire whether it was perhaps only a phase of a more ultimate and larger principle—for example, the principle that those acts are illegal which clog the channels of exchange and distribution so as to sap the economic vitality of a community. It may be that under certain economic conditions, all acts lessening competition fall automatically under this category; but there may well be other times when certain kinds of competition themselves come under it. When conditions change, a reexamination of principles more fundamental than those on which we have been acting becomes necessary in order to see whether our currently accepted working hypotheses or secondary premises still square with the purposes which the law embodies. If not, we must go back to some deeper premise, and from it fashion a new working hypothesis for use thereafter. Nor is this, as it might superficially seem, to throw overboard the doctrine of precedent. That doctrine depends on a wide choice of resemblances between cases, because the circumstances in which cases differ must always be vastly more numerous than those in which they concur. Two cases may be alike in a given circumstance and yet no necessity will follow of deciding both in the same way. Because in one case acts which lessened competition were held illegal, it does not follow that the same acts must always be illegal in other cases. Everything depends on whether legal importance is to be attached to the elements of difference. This depends in turn on the narrowness or broadness of the premise on which

[5] 166 U. S. 290.

the original decision rested. Did it go on the narrow ground that acts lessening competition are illegal *per se* and always, or on the ground that some broader class of acts is illegal, and that in the case under consideration the particular acts that lessened competition happened to fall within that broader class because of the presence or absence of special attendant circumstances?

Such a question cannot be intelligently faced nor such a choice made without some thought about the goals and purposes of the law. For it is the purposes which the law is regarded as furthering that dictate the premises of legal reasoning, and through them the extent and limits of legal rules and concepts as applied. Whether or not a difference in fact shall be heightened and dignified into a legal distinction depends on the view taken of the law's ends; and the taking of a legal distinction always means falling back on some broader premise than the rule of the case distinguished. Hence it is only an adequate view of the law's purposes which will prevent limited and secondary premises from being mistaken for fundamental.[6] The illustration already used will again show what is meant. The purpose of the law of restraints of trade may be thought to be the preservation of a particular economic system under which no intentional limits are placed on the operation of free competition, be the business results what they may. If this view is correct, it is sound to hold that any act which lessens the operation of competition is by virtue of that fact alone illegal. But on the other hand, the law's purpose may be regarded as not so clean-cut and inelastic. It may be that the law aims to protect no special system of economic methods, but to preserve productive economic action against whatever threatens from generation to generation to stunt or cramp it. If so, acts lessening competition may be illegal against a certain background of facts or at a certain stage of economic development, and legal

[6] Professor Nathan Isaacs, in "The Law and the Facts," *Columbia Law Rev.*, Jan., 1922, p. 11, points this out in connection with a non-controversial doctrine of private law. See also Judge Cardozo's discussion of Oppenheim *v.* Kridel, 236 N. Y. 156, in his *Growth of the Law*, pp. 105 ff.

otherwise. This is not to say, of course, that these facts and conditions should be left to the arbitrary determination of particular judges from case to case, but that they should be recognized and classified in the decisions with accumulating experience.

Lawyers are always subject to the temptation of viewing the law's purposes in too narrow and specific a way. They naturally tend to regard it as existing to protect the particular pattern of social arrangements which they find about them and which is only the transitory attempt to express more basic and permanent interests under conditions for the time existing.[7] The real purpose of the law is not so much to pro-

[7] For an illustration of this point of view see E. Parmalee Prentice, *The Federal Control over Carriers and Corporations*, New York, 1907, especially Chapters 1, 2. Commenting on this attitude as applied to constitutional construction, Mr. Justice Holmes has said that if it prevailed, "a constitution, instead of embodying only relatively fundamental rules of right, as generally understood by all English-speaking communities, would become the partisan of a particular set of ethical and economic opinions, which by no means are held *semper ubique et ab omnibus*," Otis *v.* Parker, 187 U. S. 606, 609. The actual danger of such a method of constitutional construction is envisaged by Judge Anderson as imminent: "Signs are not wanting, — ominous signs, — that under the guise of enforcing the 'due-process-of-law' provision in the fourteenth amendment, some judges are willing, even desirous, of putting their own economic theories as law paramount to the enactments of any legislature," *Debates in the Massachusetts Constitutional Convention of 1917–18*, i, 522. The tendency of judges to erect their economic presuppositions into a system and regard them as vested with the authority of law is no doubt due to the traditional lawyer's habit of identifying the common law with "reason," and of regarding it as therefore necessarily embodying not merely the principles of logic and mechanics, but also of such "economic and political science" as the judge may have been taught to believe orthodox. This is the logical result of the "natural-law" attitude. If law is law not because it is enacted, but because it is reasonable (and this is, after all, the common-law theory), the whole circuit of what the judge has learned to think reasonable and for which he can find some justification in the precedents, tends to be regarded by him, when it seems pertinent to the decision of a case, as law. If we must accept this attitude as inevitable, as perhaps we must, it is at least unfortunate that the "economic and political science" which forms the stock in trade of the average lawyer is so obsolete. Not many years ago a leading practitioner cited Montesquieu and Burlamaqui as current authorities on the "origins of civil society," and the resulting limitations upon political control. (*Report of the United States Industrial Commission*, i, 1141.) This practitioner was in fact in advance of many of his brethren; most lawyers, indeed, appear to think that "political science" "stopped short at the cultivated court of Queen Anne," with the death of John Locke. This is no doubt in part a consequence of the doctrine of

tect any special scheme of social arrangements as to further the ends for which the scheme itself exists; and when by virtue of altered circumstances the scheme becomes obsolete, it is not for the law to neglect the substance by perpetuating the form. It has been a sound judicial instinct which has built up a different fencing law in the western grazing states from that which prevailed in older and more thickly settled jurisdictions.[8] It was a sound instinct in the Middle Ages which caused the judges to recognize new interests in land and to create a law of simple contracts. But the concrete situations with which the lawyer has to deal in his daily practice and the special expedients which he adopts to meet them are for the most part so enclosed within the framework of the larger social arrangements of the time that, if he lacks imagination, he often comes to look on these as fundamental to the law itself. Hence the stubborn opposition with which the lawyers of the generation of Eldon and Parke met all attempts to bring the law into accord with the new face of an altered society. Hence the tendency of so many lawyers of the past generation to regard Mr. Herbert Spencer's "Social Statics" as the groundwork of the common law.[9] The lawyer's eyesight from the nature of his task must be so contracted to the range of particulars that he develops a sort of political myopia which leads him to find his horizon of fundamentals within a much narrower circumference than is advantageous to the proper growth of the law. In the darkness beyond his short vision he sees the terrifying spectres of many "isms,"—paternalism, socialism, communism, bolshe-

precedent. The earlier writers by being taken up into the earlier opinions have won for themselves a position of permanent authority which excludes their successors at all points where the latter show inconsistencies with the former — *i. e.*, at all points where the "science" has made progress. American constitutional law has petrified Locke into an immortality of infallibility.

[8] Little Rock R. Co. *v.* Finley, 37 Ark. 562; Wagner *v.* Bissell, 3 Iowa, 396; Delaney *v.* Erickson, 11 Neb. 533. So also with the law of the western states as to water rights; see Cardozo, *The Growth of the Law*, pp. 118 ff.

[9] See dissenting opinion of Field, J., in Munn *v.* Illinois, 94 U. S. 113. So also Judge Dillon: "The right to pursue what is *in fact* a lawful business ought not to be dependent upon the epithets with which a legislative majority may see fit to characterize it," *Laws and Jurisprudence of England and America*, p. 204.

vism;[10] and he raises to combat them a spectral army of opposed abstractions — individualism, nationalism, or constitutionalism. What he really needs to see, beyond the range of the particulars with which he has to deal, are not such phantom abstractions but rather a wealth of other particular facts, equally concrete,[11] — historical facts, economic facts, social facts, psychological facts, — stretching away to the boundaries of knowledge before the realm of ultimates begins ever to be reached.[12] Only so can decisions like those in the Ives and Lochner cases be avoided.

The tendency inherent in the nature of the lawyer's task needs to be counteracted by a habit of viewing law always in connection with its history and purposes. Nothing is so fatal to the idea that law embodies some particular scheme or system of social arrangements as a study of the growth and

[10] See the language of Field, J., quoted above in Chapter VII, note 66, p. 229. In holding unconstitutional a state statute authorizing declaratory judgments, the Supreme Court of Michigan seems to have been influenced by a fear of "bolshevism." The court said in its opinion: "Under our government, the State does not till our farms, manufacture our automobiles, conduct our department stores, or do our law business for us. The unfortunate people of one country are at present trying such experiment in government. We are still a government of laws," Anway *v.* Grand Rapids R. Co., 211 Mich. 592 (1920), at p. 597.

[11] See W.F. Willcox, "The Need of Social Statistics as an Aid to the Courts," in *Quarterly Publications of the American Statistical Association* (New Series), xiii, 329–340. *Cf.* also Mr. Justice Brandeis in his dissenting opinion in Burns Baking Co. *v.* Bryan, 264 U. S. 504, at p. 520: "Knowledge is essential to understanding; and understanding should precede judging." This opinion is a model of skilful judicial use of the fruits of technical research.

[12] "The element of most enduring effect in legal development is professional and judicial ideals of the social and legal order. . . . We must learn how to make [this ideal picture] the best, the most critical, and the most complete that is compatible with social progress. We must learn where such pictures are to be resorted to and where not, and how to use them with intelligence and assurance," Dean Pound, in *Harv. Law Rev.*, xxxvi, 661, 662. *Cf.* also Francis Bacon: "For the laws, I think good to note one deficiency. . . . For the lawyers, they write according to the states where they live, what is received law, and not what ought to be law; for the wisdom of a law-maker is one, and of a lawyer is another. . . . The wisdom of a law-maker consisteth not only in a platform of justice, but in the application thereof; taking into consideration what influence laws touching private right of meum and tuum have into the public state, and how they may be made apt and agreeable . . . and how they are to be pruned and reformed from time to time," *Advancement of Learning*, Book II.

development of law. Rather does such a study show how the path of the law has been a struggle toward certain ever-expanding purposes through a variety of transformations adapted to the changing social, economic, and political medium through which the law has passed. At times, it has worked through the strictest form of so-called paternalism and again through the freest of *laissez-faire;* and rules and doctrines which at one period have produced results of one character have at other times and places worked effects exactly contrary. Individualism has been in one generation the creed of Tom Paine and in another of Judge Gary; Alexander Hamilton and the Non-Partisan League have both been accused of paternalism.

II

A full appreciation of matters which go so vitally to a correct understanding of the law requires more than a mere knowledge of the history of case-law and legal institutions; it requires an understanding of social history and development as well. Mr. Elihu Root went to the heart of this necessity in an address before the section on Legal Education of the American Bar Association, in which he said:

"To-day there must be systematic education. To perform the duty of the Bar to the public there must be labor, there must be effort. It can no longer be a matter of first impression and superficial quickness of wits. The finding of the guiding line of principles that are to steer the lawyer through this wilderness of the law to-day requires a knowledge of the history and background of the law.

"The background of the law, it should be understood, consists not merely of the adjudicated cases, not merely in finding out how this judge decided on this state of affairs, and another judge decided on another similar state of affairs, or the same state of affairs; but it requires the competent lawyer, competent to exercise his authority and to vindicate his privilege, to steep his mind in the background of the law and the background of the literature which explains its growth, the true character and scope of its principles, the true method and spirit of its application, which is to be found in the history of America and England. It is to be found in the literature and the life and the social development out of which the common law has grown.

"The background of the law is found in Chitty and Coke and Blackstone, and Marshall and Kent and Story; but it is also found in Milton and Shakespeare and Chaucer, and Spenser and Hawthorne and Emerson and Bancroft and Parkman and all the great array of Americans who made their country's literature and who have been for the last century gradually building up the noble structure of recorded American history." [13]

Nor are history and literature enough. If law is in fact mainly a matter of purposes, then to the proper application of it an understanding and analysis of human purposes and the meaning and significance of human life and effort is fundamental. This is the field of ethics, or, in a broader sense, of philosophy, which is the study of value and meanings; and no one can long have studied either dogmatic law or the history of legal institutions without realizing how he meets these questions of value and meaning in almost every knotty point. The task is not to discover some philosophical system which will automatically unlock every difficulty with the easy key of a catch-word drawn out of Locke or Spencer or Mill; but rather to come to a realization of the challenges which human life has thrown down to nature in every age and under all types of institutions, and to be alive to the alternatives of choice and what they severally imply. No less important is an appreciation of the limitations of human thinking in its search after certainties; a study of Kant and James and Dewey would prove a potent inoculation against that mistaking of abstractions for realities with which some "practical" lawyers and judges seem so chronically infected. Speaking of the superiority for even practical purposes of a study of the ultimate branches of knowledge over a mere intensive development of technical learning, a great lawyer said long ago: "If you will have a tree bear more fruit than it hath

[13] *Rep. Amer. Bar Assoc.* (1920), xlvi, 660.

used to do, it is not anything you can do to the boughs, but it is the stirring of the earth and putting new mould about the roots that must work it." [14]

So far we have been speaking of studies which go only to the formation of a proper attitude toward the nature and methods of legal reasoning; they indicate a method which only leads on to other and further studies of a different kind. A correct approach to legal problems is distinguished by a sense of the need for acquaintance with the economic and social and psychological facts within which the law operates as its environment. Such a knowledge is essential to an application of analogies and distinctions which shall be free from confusion between substance and form. What the history of law and the study of social and ethical theory mainly teach is the importance of understanding the factual circumstances and origins of the claims which call for the formulation and application of legal rules. If law is no frozen world of arbitrary *a priori* abstractions existing in a vacuum and held together only by a formal logical consistency, it must be studied as a way of bringing into order a mass of human relations which get most of their significance from the facts and circumstances which must guide the formulation and application of the legal principles that are to govern them. Fencing law must be based largely on the dominant occupation of the community, and the manner and purposes for which land is utilized. The law of carriers must take account of the mechanical technique of transportation, its financial organization, and its relation to the needs and business of society. Tort law must regard the contemporary physical conditions and environment of human life and labor, and what men are thereby led to demand of each other's conduct. Land law must note the systems and objectives of land ownership, and whether it aims to satisfy the ambition to found a family, or to promote agricultural or industrial production, or to create a body of small independent husbandmen. Commercial law will depend on the dominant type of industrial organization and the prevailing forms and objectives of enterprise. There

[14] Francis Bacon, Dedication to Book II of the *Advancement of Learning*.

is no hazard in a statement as broad as that the competent lawyer must understand in a full sense the society in which he practises — its motives, methods, and ideals.[15] To start him on the road to such an understanding is an essential function of legal education. It is not many years since a competent critic said that the Supreme Court of the United States in a notable case [16] had shown itself absolutely unable to understand current economic conditions.[17]

III

An awakened interest in legal education has recently been shown by the American Bar. In 1913 the Committee of the American Bar Association on Legal Education and Admissions to the Bar requested the Carnegie Foundation to investigate the present state of legal education in the United States.[18] The task was undertaken and the investigation carried out exhaustively, resulting in an elaborate report by Mr. Alfred Z. Reed published in 1921.[19] The report raises the fundamental question of the continued possibility of a so-called "unitary bar." Given the elaborately broad training which has become necessary for the fully equipped lawyer, and the length of time which it requires, together with the very limited period which many students can afford to devote to their professional education, it has become next to impossible for a large number of lawyers to acquire adequate preparation. The suggestion is therefore put forward by Mr. Reed that the field of the law might be classified and specialized into departments. Students with but little time at their disposal might seek preparation for limited practice in one or more of these departments — for example, conveyancing,

[15] In states where real-estate speculation is an important business there is a noticeable tendency on the part of the courts to treat real-estate contracts as less binding than is the case elsewhere.

[16] The Tobacco Trust case.

[17] Louis D. Brandeis in hearings before the Committee on Interstate Commerce of the United States Senate, 62d Cong. (Sen. Res. 98), i, 1192 (1911).

[18] See letter printed in *Rep. Amer. Bar Assoc.* (1921), xlvi, 657.

[19] *Training for the Public Profession of the Law,* by Alfred Zanzinger Reed, Carnegie Foundation for the Advancement of Teaching, N. Y., 1921.

probate practice, or criminal law.[20] To meet the needs of this type of students, specialized law schools frankly offering a limited training might be developed, leaving the practice of the more general departments of the law which call for wider preparation to those who have the time and opportunity to equip themselves for it.

From this suggestion the Committee of the Bar Association dissented in their report.[21] "It has been suggested," said the report, "that there should be different kinds of training to produce different kinds of lawyers. With this position we do not agree. In spite of the diversity of human relations with respect to which the work of lawyers is done, the intellectual requisites are in all cases substantially the same. From the first interview with his client to the last step in litigation the lawyer must be trained to apprehend the pertinent facts in logical sequence, to perceive clearly the questions of law presented, and to extract from statutes and decisions the principles of law applicable. And in every case, whatever its nature, he must be able to apply the fundamental principles of the common law. If an admiralty lawyer's work were fundamentally different in kind from a probate lawyer's work, a different training would be required for each and a consequent classification of the bar would follow as a matter of course. In our opinion, however, there is no such difference between kinds of legal work. All require substantially the same intellectual preparation."

Theoretically the position taken in the report of the Committee appears to be sound for the reasons there set forth. And furthermore, if it be said that the suggestion of a classified bar is addressed to a condition and not a theory, it fails because it raises practical difficulties of its own which appear insurmountable. Opposed as it is to all the currents of our tradition and habits, legal and political, it seems to have no chance of adoption and therefore holds out no hope of solution for the very pressing practical problem which, at the expense of sound principle, it seeks to meet.

[20] *Training for the Public Profession of the Law*, p. 419.

[21] *Rep. Amer. Bar Assoc.* (1921), xlvi, 681.

The path of progress seems to lie along other lines. The direction and methods of legal education have come more and more in the past generation to be dictated by the example of a number of leading law schools, which adequately or inadequately, and for good or ill, have been imitated by the smaller schools that train the mass of the bar. Whatever improvements in legal education are to come in the visible future will come, it is natural to suppose, in the same way, being first introduced by the leading schools and finding their way afterwards into the others by a process of imitation. Any effort to improve or elevate the level of legal education can probably be made most effectively by the pioneer effort of a small number of schools, leaving the others to be brought into line with the passage of time.

The attempt deserves urgently to be made.[22] The practical question for the consideration of those who are interested in better legal education is how the special demands which the present tasks of the law make upon such education can be met by the schools which through the length of their course are equipped to meet them.

IV

What is needed is not merely the development of an attitude toward law which is the result of a certain type of study, but in addition, a familiarity with certain fields of fact within which the law is to be applied. It is not possible, nor would it be desirable, for the student to acquire both these elements of training during his years of professional study at a law school. It is not possible because the study of strictly technical law leaves insufficient time, and it would not be

[22] "The last fifty years have brought a great change in professional life. Industrial development and the consequent growth of cities have led to a high degree of specialization — specialization not only in the nature and class of questions dealt with, but also specialization in the character of clientage. . . . We are powerless to restore the general practitioner. . . . Intense specialization must continue. But we can correct its distorting effects by broader education — by study undertaken preparatory to practice — and continued by lawyer and judge throughout life: study of economics and sociology and politics which embody the facts and present the problems of to-day." Louis D. Brandeis, in *Ill. Law Rev.*, x, 461, at p. 469.

desirable because if the student would make the most of his professional studies he should bring to them at the outstart an attitude and outlook based on other studies of a fairly definite character already pursued elsewhere.

There has not been wanting among persons interested in legal education an interest in the pre-professional training which students should have before taking up the study of technical law; but too generally this has assumed the form of more or less vague discussion of so-called "general education" or "culture." That is distinctly not the question in point; and while it is no doubt desirable that as many lawyers as possible should be broadly grounded in what are called the liberal arts and sciences, there is no such professional necessity for this cultural training as there is that they should approach their legal studies with the special kind of preliminary equipment which will arm them with a proper attitude toward the law. Indeed, a loose and random cultural education may prove positively disadvantageous to a proper study of law. The college education which precedes a course at one of the leading law schools should include definite training in certain specific subjects if the student is subsequently to pursue his law studies in the most fruitful and advantageous way. And this is the more true for an additional reason. The case method has come to be regarded as the most satisfactory vehicle of legal instruction in full-time American law schools. But the case method is simply a very excellent educational medium and, because it is that, it is colorless and can be worked toward the most diverse ends. Its results are only an index of the content of the minds which apply it. No system makes more depend on the attitude and knowledge which are brought to it. For this reason it can be used to develop a narrow technique of pettifogging or to construct an abstract structure of mechanically logical law as effectively as to emphasize the relation of law to the facts of life and the ends of human action. Indeed, in the hands of an instructor with a propensity toward logic and of students without much background of thought or information, it almost inevitably works in the former direction. The wide prevalence of the case method almost more than anything else demands that the student be equipped with such previous training as will enable him to use the method to the best advantage and resist the meretricious allurements of dichotomy and syllogism.[23]

The leading law schools at present require either a college degree or some amount of collegiate work as a condition of entrance. It would appear desirable that they should do more, and in a direction where the more progressive schools of medicine have pointed the way. This is to require not merely a collegiate degree, or a stated quantity of college work, but definite college courses in certain subjects. Just what these courses should be leaves room for valid differences of opinion, which would have to be worked out by careful and mature discussion. Some of the courses, however, which

[23] An added difficulty connected with the case method of instruction is the presupposition which it tends to foster in the mind of the student that somewhere behind the apparent inconsistency of decisions there must lie a mysterious higher rule which, could it but be discovered, would bring them into complete logical harmony, and by this means alone vindicate its claim to inherent authority. The quest for such an undisclosed higher rule whose only title to validity is its ability to harmonize inconsistent decisions often diverts the search for a rule of law from the fruitful test of justice and social expediency, and cultivates on the part of the student an attitude which demands and will rest content with a rule which meets only the test of reconciling judicial inconsistencies often more or less accidental, wholly irrespective of the fitness or unfitness of such a rule to satisfy the actual demands of the situation to which it is to be applied. The mental attitude thus promoted is unrealistic in the extreme and tends to foster the general idea that law need conform to no more concrete or exacting test than that of a purely abstract and verbal logic. To be sure, this attitude is to some extent inevitable and even necessary on the part of lawyers under a legal system which rests on the doctrine of precedent; but a sound application of that doctrine demands that in the last analysis not all precedents should be treated as of mathematically equal authority. This requires that a precedent should frequently be subjected to the test of some external criterion not apparent on the face of the case itself: *e. g.*, circumstances such as the prevailing state of public opinion at the time of the decision, or the bias of a particular court, or, again, such a fact as that the case was inadequately argued or considered, or that one or more of the counsel arguing the case enjoyed an exaggerated prestige. These considerations are usually not obvious on the face of the report, to which the case system as commonly applied strictly confines itself, and, if they are to be given weight, require the cultivation and practice of a habit of seeking and using material which lies not merely outside the case-book, but outside reports themselves.

fall in line with the considerations here advanced, may be tentatively suggested:

1. A survey course in English literature from the time of Chaucer, centering upon such authors as Shakespeare, Milton, Defoe, Fielding, Wordsworth, Shelley, Dickens, Carlyle and Ruskin, and conducted to present a history of the development of English social institutions and ideals.

2. A course in English and American constitutional history, treated as an outline of political development keeping step with social and economic changes.

3. A course presenting a comparative view of modern governmental systems, the relation of central to local government, the federal principle, the adaptation of governmental machinery to the tasks imposed upon it, and the fundamental conceptions of what is called "political science."

4. A course in analytical and historical politics, based upon such books as Willoughby's "Nature of the State," Dunning's "History of Political Theories," Maine's "Ancient Law," and Jenks's "Law and Politics in the Middle Ages."

5. A course in economics, preferably taught historically rather than dogmatically, and culminating in some such general survey of the current economic situation as Alfred Marshall's "Industry and Trade."[24]

6. A course in the history of philosophy, followed by an analytical study of the chief contemporary philosophical attitudes, with particular attention to newer conceptions of logic.[25]

It is not believed that a proposal to require some such list of college courses as a preliminary to law-school work is open to any such objections as David Hoffman's plan for a law-school curriculum of an impossibly encyclopaedic character.[26]

[24] Compare also such books as L. C. Marshall's *Readings in Industrial Society* (Univ. of Chicago Press, 1918), and W. H. Hamilton's *Current Economic Problems* (Univ. of Chicago Press, rev. ed., 1919).

[25] See F. C. S. Schiller, *Formal Logic.*

[26] *A Course of Legal Study, Addressed to Students and the Profession Generally*, by David Hoffman, 2d ed., 2 vols., Balto., 1836; see *Training for the Public Profession of the Law,* Carnegie Foundation (1921), p. 124. "Every law school should require those who are to be admitted to its halls to have a gen-

The idea is merely that, as certain law schools already require an amount of preliminary collegiate training, a further step should be taken which would require that from the offerings available in most colleges the student should choose what promises to be of greatest assistance to a subsequent fruitful study of the law. There can be little advantage to a law student in having had a college course mainly devoted to fine arts, romance languages, or the modern drama, or even to biology or physics. The proposal is not to overload the law-school course itself, but to pave the way toward it along the lines indicated by Mr. Root.

For the prospective student of law, a college course should be something more than an end in itself — it should link concretely into his legal training and prepare him to go forward, not in a vacuum, but properly oriented within the special field of general information which will afford an appropriate framework for what technical legal learning he may then proceed to acquire. The object of preliminary training is to equip him with an attitude of mind, a conception of problems, and a set of questions to put to the cases as he approaches the concrete situations of technical law. The point of view which this training, if it does its work, should develop is one which will, above all else, demand an understanding of the practical and non-legal aspects of legal situations — which will seek to grasp their economic and human bearings as a necessary preliminary to the search for the proper legal rule or principle to be applied. This attitude is one which needs to be ingrained during the period of actual instruction in legal rules, and not left to be acquired or missed, as the case may be, in subsequent years of practice. The law needs to be taught always in its setting and against its background

eral education furnishing a sufficiently broad foundation upon which to base a thorough legal education. That general education ought to include a study of economics and a study of sociology, and the curriculum of every law school should include a close study of the science of general and sociological jurisprudence as a basis for the study of the various branches of our law; and this raising of law school standards should meet a sympathetic response from Supreme Courts in requirements for admission to the Bar," W. H. Taft, *Popular Government*, pp. 237, 238.

of non-legal facts if it is not to be impressed on the student's mind as an abstract system of geometrical deductions. For such teaching the case method offers unusual opportunities, provided that along with analysis of the cases from a purely legal standpoint goes a process which brings the student into contact with the pertinent economic and social facts which will enable him to put the proper questions to the cases. Why was it that the so called mercantile theory of negotiability came to be applied to documents of title? And why was it later in being applied to them than to bills of exchange and notes? The answer to these questions summarizes the revolution in transportation which has enabled the fluidity of goods to catch up with the fluidity of money and has made credit based on goods a fundamental exchange-medium of the modern world. Why was a case like See *v.* Heppenheimer [27] decided as it was? No understanding is adequate which fails to bridge the gap between Drew's operations in Erie [28] and the capitalization of the United States Steel Corporation.[29] Why did equity develop the rule that a partnership creditor must proceed first against partnership assets before reaching out for the assets of individual partners? Why was the doctrine of moral consideration for a contract abandoned? Why does the rule as to mortgages of after-acquired property tend to be different in the case of corporate mortgages from what it is in the case of mortgages made by individuals?

Such questions are significant for any true understanding of legal rules and doctrines; and they not only cannot be answered, they cannot even be put, except in the light of information which lies outside the immediate province of legal learning. Such information may be brought in, and, to a certain extent, must be brought in, as a part of the ordinary law courses where it is pertinent to the cases; but it interrupts the sequence of topics and doctrines, and consumes time which is needed for other purposes, with the result that

[27] 69 New Jersey Eq. 36.

[28] *Chapters of Eric and Other Essays*, by Charles Francis Adams and Henry Adams, New York, 1886.

[29] *Report of the Commissioner of Corporations on the Steel Industry*, Pt. I, Washington, Gov't. Printing Office, 1911, pp. 98–252.

it is apt to be glossed over or tacitly taken for granted. And it is hard to see how any other result is possible, for in technical law courses the function of such information is to be used rather than to be acquired; it must be acquired elsewhere, if at all, and the problem is to supply some means whereby it can be acquired alongside of, and at the same time with, knowledge of the legal rules which it serves to explain and illustrate. Again certain tentative suggestions may be advanced of a possible way of supplying the need.

The typical law-school course consists of twelve hours of class-room work weekly through three years. The work is intensive and if properly pursued can be made to occupy the student's entire working time. Materially to increase the number of class-room hours would raise serious and proper objections from students and teachers alike. But it might well be found that a slight increase in the number of class-room hours, if given up to a sort of work which students otherwise would be left to pursue on their own initiative, would save time in the long run for those students who would otherwise work without a guide, and would give to the remaining students something practically indispensable which they cannot be trusted to obtain for themselves. This seems to be the case with the collateral subjects mentioned in the last paragraph. If an additional course of two hours weekly, planned along the lines about to be suggested, were added to the law-school curriculum in each year, an actual saving of time might be effected in the technical courses touching on related subjects.

The suggestion, then, is that during the second year of law-school work, which generally covers the subjects of bills and notes, sales, trusts, and carriers, an additional course should be introduced, divided into two parts, of which the first should deal with the instrumentalities of commerce and finance, banking operations, credit instruments, financing companies, export houses, and the like, and the second half-year with transportation. A like additional course might be included in the third year, dealing in the first term with corporate promotions and reorganizations, to accompany and illustrate the course in corporation law, and during the second term with labor problems and police regulation, to supplement the courses in constitutional law and equitable relief against torts. The additional work of the first year is left for treatment at a later point.

It would be easy to conduct courses such as those suggested in a manner which would render them of no advantage whatever to the law student. This would be the case, doubtless, if they were given from the generalized and more or less systematic standpoint which is almost inevitable in college courses on economic subjects. The result of such a course is apt to be a residuum of impressions and generalities which, whatever it is worth, would not justify the time that it would consume in the midst of intensive law-school work. What is necessary is something of more direct and tangible value. It is believed, however, that a type of course could be devised which would satisfy this requirement. The method of these courses, dealing as they would with material covered in the technical legal courses, should be to present the obverse side, and turn the law course, as it were, inside out. In a course on the law of carriers the facts and history of transportation occur as incidental. In a course on transportation, legal doctrines and rules should be made to appear as they do to the practising lawyer — as elements in a great mass of business, technical, and social facts. The method which most readily suggests itself would be to take a limited number of important and complex situations which have actually arisen, and study and analyze them in detail, the legal details being presented as they occurred in the midst of all the other details. In this way the Rice case, the Traffic Association case, the Cincinnati Freight Bureau case, the Shreveport case, the Inter-Mountain rate case and the Reading cases might be studied. Such a method would have the advantage of permitting the use of the case system and enabling the student to apply that system to documents other than law reports. It would make it possible to acquire a grasp of transportation principles in a firmer and fuller way than from the slippery surface of a textbook, however good. The same method would apply equally to the suggested courses on corporate promotions and reorganizations and on labor problems. A limited number of typical instances should be selected and followed through in detail with the help of governmental reports and published volumes of hearings. The course on finance which is suggested for the first term of the second year would probably have to be conducted with greater generality, but here also descriptive material is available to illustrate the operations of particular types of financial houses, and their relations with producers and shippers.

After all, what is suggested is nothing more than an amplification and extension of the case system. The difficulty with the standardized form of that system is that it does not leave sufficient time for study and analysis of those elements of a case which are non-legal in character. But somewhere in the law school it should be insisted that the student cut deeper into the facts before him and uncover not merely legal doctrines but the difficulties, needs, desires, motives, and conflicts in which those doctrines move and have their being and which are the reason for their existence.

It remains to suggest a course of a slightly different character during the first year of law-school work. It is at this stage in his technical studies that the student in courses on torts, contracts, and procedure is brought into contact with the "forms of action" and the whole obsolete machinery of the old common-law pleading and practice. It is usually felt, and rightly, that, obsolete as these topics are, they are essential to a proper understanding of the growth and development of some very fundamental principles of modern substantive law. They are therefore brought in, more or less incidentally, in connection with the teaching of those principles. It is questionable whether this method secures adequately the results aimed at. It amounts to an effort to teach a difficult and remote subject piecemeal in the interstices of more or less systematic practical courses. The connection of the old procedure with current doctrines of substantive law needs of course to be pointed out constantly during the courses devoted to the latter; but it is questionable whether this would not be better done, not by undertaking to present in the process the detailed facts of the old procedure, but by relegating the latter frankly to a separate course where they could for the time being form the centre of interest and attention. Under the present method the student is distracted by having his attention perpetually diverted from current issues by casual references to a body of remote and difficult learning with which he is as yet entirely unacquainted, which is more difficult and foreign to him than anything else that he is asked to understand, and which he gets no opportunity to observe as a connected whole. The meaning and significance of seven centuries of procedural change cannot be properly grasped merely from the fragments of it which are necessary to an understanding of Weaver *v.* Ward [30] or Slade's case; [31] and the fragments so presented are apt to be misleading or misunderstood apart from the whole process of which they formed a part. The suggestion seems therefore warranted that during the first year of law-school work a special course of a half-year's length should be devoted to the history of English law, with particular reference to procedure and the forms of action — the nature of an "appeal," and of a "writ of right," the relation of the "appeal" to criminal prosecutions and tort actions, the appearance of trespass, the evolution of the register of original writs, and the development of the action on the case. This last development, coupled with a survey of the origin and growth of trial by jury, might well occupy the major part of the course, and it seems likely that much time could thereby be saved in the regular systematic courses on torts, contracts, procedure, and evidence. At the very time when he most needs it, that is, at the beginning of his course, the student would thus get a taste of the sources and basic materials of English law, which, however obsolete they may have become for directly practical purposes, "rule us from their graves" in countless subtle ways, which the practising lawyer is none the worse for being aware of. During the second half-year another course, which seems to be

[30] Hobart, 134. [31] 4 Coke Rep. 92b.

almost called for by the first, might well be devoted to a study of the legal reforms of the last century conducted from the standpoint of such a book as Dicey's "Law and Opinion in England in the Nineteenth Century," [32] accompanied by appropriate statutes and cases. Such a course seems necessary to supplement and correct the impressions apt to be produced by the course on origins; and would at the same time cover as fully as is desirable some topics of the law, like that of persons, and statutory construction, which are otherwise likely to remain *terra incognita* to the law student. The course would further serve as a connecting link between the constitutional history of the student's college days and his courses in constitutional law and police regulation in the third year of the law school.

It could hardly be argued with success that the additions to the law-school course which have just been suggested would increase the practical efficiency of graduates in the sense of making them more useful law-clerks immediately upon graduation, or of enabling them to win more cases for clients in the courts. But it is now generally recognized that the law is a public profession and not merely a private business. The lawyer in every aspect of his practice affects by his conduct and example not merely his personal fortunes and those of his clients, but the growth and tendencies of the law. He is under a responsibility of considering not merely personal success but his duty to the profession and to the public as well. This is at least the fundamental assumption on which the American Bar Association has been proceeding in its whole treatment of the matter of legal education. The considerations which bear on the problem are not only those relating to the equipment of individuals to earn a livelihood, but the greater ones of how best to promote and maintain a régime of justice according to law.

The burden of this essay from the beginning has been to insist upon the practical advantages to a people of a system of government based upon the supremacy of law. That su-

[32] See also *A Century of Law Reform; Twelve Lectures delivered at the request of the Council of Legal Education* (London, 1901), by various scholars.

premacy is threatened by recent developments — by the emergence of new problems, and by the resort to new devices for meeting them. The supremacy of law with its attendant advantages can be maintained only by a proper application, development, and adaptation of law; and such development and adaptation require a bench and bar whose leaders have had a legal education which enables them to recognize and face the new needs of a new day.

"He that thinks a state can be exactly steered by the same laws in every kind as it was two or three hundred years ago, may as well imagine that the clothes that fitted him when a child should serve him when he was grown a man. The matter changeth, the custom, the contracts, the commerce, the dispositions, educations, and tempers of men and societies, change in a long tract of time, and so must their laws in some measure be changed, or they will not be useful for their state and condition; and besides all this, time is the wisest thing under heaven. These very laws, which at first seemed the wisest constitution under heaven, have some flaws and defects discovered in them by time. As manufactures, mercantile arts, architecture and building, and philosophy itself, secure new advantages and discoveries by time and experiences, so much more do laws which concern the manners and customs of men." [33]

[33] Sir Matthew Hale, "Considerations touching the Amendment of the Law," Hargrave's *Law Tracts* (Dublin, 1787), i, 269. See also Jefferson, letter to Samuel Kercheval, July 12, 1816, *Complete Works*, ed. Washington, vii, 9, at p. 15.

TABLE OF CASES

TABLE OF CASES

(Cited or referred to in the text and notes.)

INDEX

INDEX

Of matters contained in the text and notes

www.ingramcontent.com/pod-product-compliance
Lightning Source LLC
LaVergne TN
LVHW101455200926
848483LV00001B/132